Praise for
The Real History Behind the Da Vinci Code:

"If, like Sam Cooke sang, you 'don't know much about history,' Newman's encyclopedic, A-to-Z look at topics ranging from 'Apocrypha' to 'Wren, Christopher' provides perspective and insight." —*Pittsburgh Tribune-Review*

"Witty and charming, but nonetheless rational in explanation and complete in background research, *The Real History Behind the Da Vinci Code* seeks not so much to refute the novel, but to elucidate on the truth, and not so much to disparage the mistakes of Mr. Brown but to make readers realize that the history is bigger than any one person, popular novelists included."
—*Business World*

"The book . . . gives the truth about topics used in Brown's fiction. . . . Well-written and precise, it is the work of a woman who writes what she knows." —*Statesman Journal* (Oregon)

"For fans of Dan Brown's popular *The Da Vinci Code*, Sharan Newman's *The Real History Behind the Da Vinci Code* is a must-have companion."
—*The Sunday Oregonian*

"Newman has arranged her discussion of the people, places, and events in *The Da Vinci Code* in an encyclopedic format, creating a book that is both accessible and fun to read. Recommended for all libraries."
—*Library Journal*

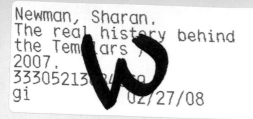

The Real History Behind the
TEMPLARS

SHARAN NEWMAN

BERKLEY BOOKS, NEW YORK

THE BERKLEY PUBLISHING GROUP
Published by the Penguin Group
Penguin Group (USA) Inc.
375 Hudson Street, New York, New York 10014, USA
Penguin Group (Canada), 90 Eglinton Avenue East, Suite 700, Toronto, Ontario M4P 2Y3, Canada
(a division of Pearson Penguin Canada Inc.)
Penguin Books Ltd., 80 Strand, London WC2R 0RL, England
Penguin Group Ireland, 25 St. Stephen's Green, Dublin 2, Ireland (a division of Penguin Books Ltd.)
Penguin Group (Australia), 250 Camberwell Road, Camberwell, Victoria 3124, Australia
(a division of Pearson Australia Group Pty. Ltd.)
Penguin Books India Pvt. Ltd., 11 Community Centre, Panchsheel Park, New Delhi—110 017, India
Penguin Group (NZ), 67 Apollo Drive, Rosedale, North Shore, 0745, Auckland, New Zealand
(a division of Pearson New Zealand Ltd.)
Penguin Books (South Africa) (Pty.) Ltd., 24 Sturdee Avenue, Rosebank, Johannesburg 2196,
South Africa

Penguin Books Ltd., Registered Offices: 80 Strand, London WC2R 0RL, England

THE REAL HISTORY BEHIND THE TEMPLARS

Copyright © 2007 by Sharan Newman
Cover design by Richard Hasselberger
Cover illustration of Knight Templar by Bridgeman Art Library
Book design by Tiffany Estreicher

PRINTING HISTORY
Berkley trade paperback edition / September 2007

Berkley trade paperback ISBN: 978-0-425-21533-3

An application to register this book for cataloging has been submitted to the Library of Congress.

PRINTED IN THE UNITED STATES OF AMERICA

10 9 8 7 6 5 4 3 2 1

Acknowledgments

Professor Malcolm Barber, for his generosity now and over the years in sharing his profound knowledge of the Templars and for enduring my many e-mail questions and ventings.

Professor Paul Crawford, California University of Pennsylvania, for his help on the Templars, Philip the Fair, and the University of Paris.

Dr. Rozanne Elder, Cistercian Institute, for giving me instant information on Bernard of Clairvaux.

Professor Norman Hinton, University of Illinois, Springfield, emeritus, for Middle English references to the Templars.

Professor Janus Moeller Jensen, University of Southern Denmark, for giving me literary background on Templar ideals in Danish sagas.

Professor Kurt Villads Jensen, University of Southern Denmark, for advice on the likelihood of Templars in Denmark.

Courtney de Mayo, Rice University, for spending a tedious day copying all of the Marquis D'Albon for me.

Professor Brian Patrick McGuire, Roskilde University, for checking my section on Denmark and the Cistercians.

Professor Helen Nicholson, Cardiff University, for advice on Templars and Hospitallers and for referring me to other excellent sources.

Professor Jeffrey Russell, UC Santa Barbara, emeritus, (but not with me) for checking my Latin translations and giving advice on medieval theology.

Mme. Alessandra Tchernik for checking my Italian translations.

Kyle Wolfley, Ball State University, for copying several books I couldn't find in my own library.

And all the members of the Mediev-L list, who debated just what "interdict" consisted of when I couldn't find a solid answer.

All of these people kindly helped me in my research. Any errors in this book are totally my own. They did their best.

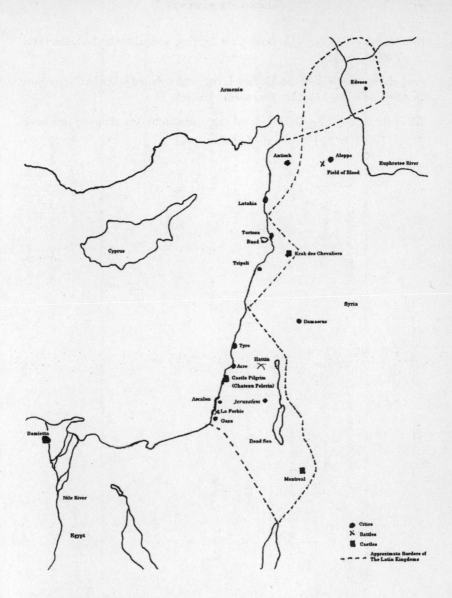

Map drawn by Marcia Noland

Rulers of the Kingdom of Jerusalem

BALDWIN II m. MORFIA
1118–1131

- MELISANDE m. FULK of ANJOU
  1131–1161
  - BALDWIN III
    1141–1163
  - ALMARIC m. 1 Agnes de Courtenay .... m. 2. Maria Commena
    - BALDWIN IV
      1174–1185
    - SYBILLA m. 1 William of Monferrat m. 2. Guy of Lusignan
      1186–1190
      - BALDWIN V
        1185–1186
    - ISABEL I m. 1. Humphrey of Toron
      1190–1205 m. 2. Conrad of Monferrat
      - 2 daughters d. 1190
      - MARIA m. John of Brienne
        1205–1212
        - ISABEL II m. FREDERICK II, Holy Roman Emperor
          1225–1228
          - CONRAD of Sicily and Jerusalem
            1243–1254
          - CONRADIN 1254–1268
- ALICE m. BOHEMOND of ANTIOCH
  - Constance m. 1. Raymond of Poitiers
- HODIERNA m. RAYMOND of TRIPOLI
  - Raymond III m. Eschiva
- YVETA
  (Abbess)

ISABEL I. (continued)
m. 3. Henry, count of Champagne 1192–1197
- Alice m. 1. Hugh Lusignan of Cyprus

m. 4 Amaury of Lusignan, king of Cyprus
- Melisande m. Bohemond IV of Antioch
  - Maria of Antioch d. 1307

Contents

PART TWO

The Glory Years

PART THREE

The End of the Order
of the Poor Knights

PART FOUR

The Beginning of the Legends

Introduction

Last year I was in France to speak about Dan Brown's book *The Da Vinci Code*, explaining the places where the fiction diverged from history. At one stop a teenaged boy from the Netherlands asked me (in excellent English) about the Templars. I went into my standard lecture about their literary connection to the Grail and the myths surrounding their dissolution in 1312. He listened politely for a while and then interrupted to ask, "Yes, but what were the Templars? Did they really exist?"

I came to a full stop. That young man had accepted that the novel was fiction. Therefore, he had assumed that the Templars were also fiction.

When I started to think about it, it made perfect sense. When I read science fiction, I can't judge what's based on cutting-edge science and what the author made up. Why should I expect readers of historical fiction to know which characters in a book really existed?

The story of the Templars is definitely the stuff of epic romance. From the time of the creation of the order, legends began to swirl around them. Some of these legends the Templars created themselves. Others appeared in popular chronicles of the late twelfth and early thirteenth century. Over the years the Templars were admired and reviled, adored and loathed. They were considered by some to be the closest that a fighting man could come to salvation and by others nothing more than materialistic money-grubbers. Their mass arrest on October 13, 1307, shocked the Western world. Some defended them; others believed they were heretics. Many who thought they were probably innocent of the charges still felt the Templars had gotten a comeuppance that they richly deserved.

Since the Order of the Knights Templar was dissolved, the stories about them have grown and mutated until they are hardly recognizable. For three hundred years after the end of the order, the Templars were largely forgotten. If anything, they were seen as an anachronism that had ended well after it had ceased to be of any use. The other military orders survived by changing and adapting to the new world.

Then there were two great spurts of interest in the Templars. The first was at the end of the eighteenth century when they were rediscovered by Protestant Europe. They became a symbol of resistance to papal tyranny and, in France, the tyranny of the monarchy. Catholics responded by remembering the Templars as the last defense against the enemies of Christ.

At the end of the eighteenth century, the creation of Templar myths took a huge leap. The new society known as the Freemasons was spreading across Europe. Through the enthusiastic efforts of a German baron, Karl von Hund, who published under a pen name, the story of the Templars was grafted on to Masonic ritual and lore. This opened the door for a wealth of imaginative theories regarding the Templars, all of which had more to do with the political situation in Europe at that time than the history of the Templars.

The second great development in the Templar myth came in the twentieth century. Late Victorian writers, such as Jessie Weston, had woven the Templars into European folklore. But it was not until the latter part of the century that the general public became intrigued by theories linking the Templars to everything from the Holy **Grail**, to **Cathar** Heresy, to modern secret societies. Currently, there are so many beliefs about the Templars that I find it impossible to keep up with them. They seem to have been involved with everything except the Kennedy assassination, and that might be next.

This book is an attempt to give the known facts about the Knights Templar, from their beginnings in 1119 or 1120 to the dissolution in 1312 and beyond. It is my hope that this will make it easier for people who are reading the latest Templar book, either fiction or history, to separate fact from fiction and give them a base from which to evaluate the ideas presented. I have arranged the book chronologically, with some chapters being an overview of events and others focusing on individual people or subjects. When there are words in **bold type**, that means there is a section devoted to that one topic. Some sections overlap in subject matter, giving a different view of people and events.

I have often heard that readers are put off by footnotes. Please don't be. You don't have to read them. They are there to let you know that I've done my best to find the most accurate information available. They are also there so that if you wish, you can go to these sources and check them for yourselves. Then you can decide if I'm right or not. But if you're willing to trust me, then just ignore them. I'll be very flattered. Studying history means that one has to be part scientist, part detective, and part psychologist. The evidence is not always complete and that's why, when historians come to conclusions, they always let people know what sources those conclusions are based upon.

So don't worry about my citations. I'll be very happy if you simply enjoy the book.

PART ONE

The Poor Knights of Christ

CHAPTER ONE

The Beginning of the Order

How does a legend begin?

In the case of the Knights of the Temple of Solomon at Jerusalem, it began in obscurity. No contemporary chronicler mentions their existence. We only know they existed by 1125 because there is a charter from that year witnessed by **Hugh de Payns** in which he is called the "Master of the Temple."[1]

Later generations would tell the story of the first Templars, each one a little differently:

> At the beginning of the reign of Baldwin II, a Frenchman came from Rome to Jerusalem to pray. He had made a vow not to return to his own country, but to become a monk after helping the king in the war for three years; he and the thirty knights who accompanied him would end their lives in Jerusalem. When the king and his barons saw that they had achieved remarkable things in the war . . . they advised the man to serve in the army with his thirty knights and defend the place against brigands rather than to become a monk in the hope of saving his own soul.[2]

That is the explanation for the beginning of the Templars given by Michael, the Syrian patriarch of Antioch, in about 1190. At about the same time, an Englishman, Walter Map, gave a somewhat different account:

> A knight called Payns, from a district of Burgundy of the same name, came as a pilgrim to Jerusalem. When he heard that the Christians who watered their horses at a cistern not far outside the gates of Jerusalem were constantly attacked by the pagans, and that many of the believers were slain in these ambuscades, he pitied them, and . . . he tried to protect them as far as he could. He frequently sprang to their aid from well-chosen hiding places and slew many of the enemy.[3]

Walter views the founder of the order as a sort of Lone Ranger who eventually enlisted other knights to join him in his work. This would make a good movie plot, but it is unlikely that a man doing this would live long enough to establish an order of knights.

Yet another story of the first Templars is from a later writer, Bernard, a monk at Corbie. He wrote in 1232, over a hundred years after the order began, but he was drawing on a now lost version by a nobleman named Ernoul living in Jerusalem about the same time as the other writers. Bernard wrote:

> When the Christians had conquered Jerusalem, they installed themselves at the Temple of the Sepulcher and many more came there from everywhere. And they obeyed the prior of the sepulcher. The good knights there took counsel among themselves and said, "We have abandoned our lands and our friends and have come here to elevate and glorify the rule of God. If we stay here, drinking, eating and hanging around, without doing work, then we carry our weapons for nothing. This land has need of them. . . . Let us get together and make one of us the master of us all . . . to lead us in battle when it occurs."[4]

So Bernard believed that the men had originally been pilgrims, perhaps staying at the church of the Sepulcher under the supervision of a priest, and it was only through boredom that they decided to form a fighting unit.

Finally we have the account of William, Archbishop of Tyre. He is the one most often quoted and it is his version that has most often been accepted. Since he was born in Jerusalem and educated in Europe, he had both access to the records and the polished style necessary to present the history.

In that same year [1119] some noblemen of knightly rank, devoted to God, pious and God fearing, placed themselves in the hands of the lord patriarch for the service of Christ, professing the wish to live perpetually in the manner of regular canons in chastity, and obedience, without personal belongings. The leading and most eminent of these men were the venerable Hugh of Payns and Godfrey of St. Omer. As they had neither church nor fixed abode, the king gave them a temporary home in his palace which was on the south side of the Temple of the Lord, . . . Their main duty, imposed on them by the patriarch and the other bishops for the remission of their sins, was that they should maintain the safety of the roads and the highways to the best of their ability, for the benefit of pilgrims in particular, against attacks of bandits and marauders.[5]

These explanations have a few things in common. They all imply that **Hugh de Payns** was the first of the Templars and that **King Baldwin II** of Jerusalem was the one to recognize them, either as knights committed to the protection of pilgrims or as a group of religious men who wished to devote their military skill to the defense of the Christian settlements. They also agree that at first the Templars lived at the site the crusaders believed to be the temple of the Holy Sepulcher, the place where Jesus had been buried. It was only after they became a military order that the men moved to the king's palace, in what was believed to be the Temple of Solomon. They may have shared quarters at the beginning with the **Hospitallers**, who had been established in the Holy Land since 1070.

The chronicles are unclear on whose idea it was to have an order of men who lived like monks and fought like soldiers. After all, fighting monks? That didn't make sense. Men who fought had to shed blood; shedding blood was a sin. Monks prayed for the souls of warriors while deploring their violence. The idea was that fighting men were a necessary evil to protect society from the lawless. Some of them would find religion, give up their aggressive ways, and join a monastery, but who ever heard of a religious order whose mission was to go into battle?

It was an idea born of desperation. With the success of the first wave of crusaders, Jerusalem and the sites of the Bible were once again open to Christian pilgrims. And the pilgrims came in droves from all the corners of Christendom.

But, while the cities of Jerusalem, Tripoli, Antioch, and Acre had been taken, the roads that connected them were still, for the most part, in the hands of the Moslems. And there were a number of towns that had not been conquered. The pilgrims were fair game for raiding parties. At Easter in 1119 a party of some seven hundred was attacked while going from Jerusalem to the Jordan River. Three hundred of them were killed and another sixty captured and sold into slavery.[6]

Walter Map's story of Hugh de Payns single-handedly guarding a watering hole may have come not from the Templars but from the experiences of a Russian, the abbot Daniel. In about 1107, he told of a place between Jaffa and Jerusalem where the pilgrims could get water. They would stay there for the night "in great fear" for it was near the Moslem town of Ascalon from "whence the Saracens would issue and massacre the pilgrims."[7]

Despite the dangers, people were still determined to make the journey. The initial conquest of the Holy Land had been meant to re-open Jerusalem to pilgrims. Something had to be done to protect them. But King Baldwin and the other crusader lords didn't have the men or the resources to patrol all the routes to the sites of the Bible that the pilgrims were determined to see. Whoever had the idea for the Templars, it was greeted with enthusiasm by local lords. In the end it was decided that Hugh and his friends could serve God best by keeping His pilgrims safe.

The Templars were at first a local group with no connection to the papacy. They received the approval of the patriarch of Jerusalem, Garmund,* and may have been presented at a church council held at the town of Nablus on January 23, 1120.

The council was not convened to establish the Knights of the Temple but to discuss problems that had developed in the twenty years since the founding of the Latin kingdoms. The main worry was that grasshoppers had been destroying the crops for the four years past. The general feeling was that this was a divine punishment because morals had slackened since the conquest of Jerusalem. So most of the twenty-five pronouncements that the council passed addressed the sins of the flesh.[8]

It is interesting that even though this was a religious council, there were as many lay lords as bishops participating. This shows that the concerns were widespread and needed to be solved by all those in power.

This council interests me because several historians of the Templars mention it as if it were important to the formation of the Templars, but, when I went to the official records, nothing was said about them.[9] Instead, the canons (laws) that were enacted at Nablus dwell on which sins the lords and clerics of Jerusalem thought were the worst. Seven of them forbid adultery or bigamy and four concern sodomy. Five more deal with sexual and other relations between Christians and Saracens, which were not allowed unless the Saracen had been baptized. The general implication seems to have been that if people stopped doing these things, the next harvest would be better.

There is no official report as to whether the decrees of the council were followed or if the next year's crops were unmolested. From other sources, it appears that sins of the flesh were committed as usual.

The only canon that might relate to the Templars, a group still in its infancy, is number twenty: "If a cleric takes up arms in the cause of

---

*Also spelled Warmund and other variations. I'm not sure what his mother called him.

defense, he is not held to be guilty."[10] It does not mention knights becoming military clerics.

All the same, this was a radical departure. Despite the loosening of the command against general warfare in the case of those who fought for God, priests and monks had always been absolutely forbidden to fight.

However, at Antioch, the year before the council, Count Roger and most of his army had been killed outside the walls of the city in a battle still known as the "Field of Blood." In order to save Antioch, the Frankish patriarch, Bernard, issued arms to anyone who could carry them, including monks and priests. Luckily, the clerics didn't have to fight, but the precedent had been set.[11]

This was the atmosphere in which the Order of the Temple was formed.

ONE of the myths that the Templars told about their own beginning was that for the first nine years there were only nine knights. This is first mentioned in William of Tyre but was often repeated by later chroniclers who learned it from the Templars of their own time.[12]

Were there only nine members? Probably not. While the Order of the Temple didn't seem to have grown very much in the first few years, it wouldn't have lasted at all with so few men. The number nine might have been chosen because it went with the nine years from the founding until the **Council of Troyes**, where the order was given formal recognition.

Some scholars think the Templars may have been influenced by medieval number symbolism. Nine is a "circular number": no matter how much it is multiplied, the digits always add up to nine or a multiple of it, "and therefore could be seen as incorruptible."[13] Many years after the founding, the poet Dante surmised that the number nine was chosen because "nine is the holy cipher of the order of angels, three times the holy cipher three of the Trinity."[14]

I don't think that the first knights were well enough educated to come up with something that esoteric. However, William of Tyre was, and it is in his chronicle that we first find this idea. It's very possible that the number was William's invention and that it was taken up by the Templars of his time and added to their own version of their legend. There's no way to tell, but the number nine did become part of Templar lore and was used in the artwork in some Templar chapels.[15] From there it came to be considered a fact simply because the legend had been repeated so often.

So we know very little about the first years of the Knights Templar. There are a few charters from Jerusalem and Antioch that are witnessed by the early members. But these are not gifts to the Templars, merely evidence that these men existed and were in the Holy Land. There are no surviving records of donations to the order before 1124.[16]

It is human nature to want to fill in the gaps, the blank spaces on the maps, the parts of the story that don't seem enough. This is what happened to the story of the first Templars. At the time, they weren't considered important enough for the chroniclers to mention. But sixty-odd years later, when they were an important part of society, people wanted to know how it all began.

And so the legends were born and started to grow. They are growing still.

---

1 Charters of the Holy Sepulcher no. 105, in Thierry Leroy, *Huges de Payns* (Troyes, 2001) p. 194.

2 Michael the Syrian, in Malcom Barber and Keith Bate, *The Templars: Selected Sources Translated and Annotated* (Manchester University Press, 2002) p. 27. Taken from the *Chronique de Michel le Syrien, Patriarche Jacobite d'Antioch (1166–90)*, ed. and tr. J. B. Chabot (Paris: Ernest Lerous, 1905) p. 201.

3 Walter Map, *De nugis curialium/Courtiers' Trifles*, tr. Frederick Tupper and Marbury Bladen Ogle (London, 1924) p. 33.

4 Text in Anthony Luttrell, "The Earliest Templars," in *Autour de la première croisade. Acts du Colloque de la Society for the Study of the Crusades and the Latin East* (Clerment-Ferrend, 22–25 juin 1995) ed. M. Balard (Paris: Publications do la Sorbonne, 1996) p. 196. "Quant li Chrestiien orent conquis Jherusalem, si se rendirent asses de chevaliers au temple del Sepucre; et mout s'en rendirent pius de toutes tieres. Es estoient obeissant au prieux dou Sepucre. Il i ot de boins chevaliers rendus; si prisent consel entr'ias et disent: "Nous avoumes guerpies noz tieres et nos amis, et sommes chi venu pour la loy Dieu i lever et essauchier. Si sommes chi arreste pour boire et pour mengier at por despendre, sans oevre faire; ne noient ne faisons d'armes, et besoinge en est en le tiere: . . . Prendons consel et faisons mestre d'un de nos, . . . ke nous conduie en bataille quant lius en sera." (my translation)

5 William of Tyre in Barber and Bate, pp. 25–26. Text in Guillaume de Tyr, *Chronique*, ed. R. B. C. Huygens, 2 vols. Corpus Christianorum Continuatio Mediavales 63 and 63A (Turnholt, 1986) 12.7 pp. 553–54 "Eodem anno quidam nobiles viri de equstri ordine, deo devotei religiosi et timentes deum, in monu domini patriarche Christi servicio se mancipantes, more canonicorum regularium in castitate et obedientia et sine proprio velle pertpetuo vivere professi sunt. Inter quos primi et precipui fuerenut viri vernerabiles Hugo de Pagainis et Gaufridus de Sancto Aldemaro. Quibus quoniam neque ecclesia erat neque certum habebant domicilium rex in palatio suo, quod secus Templum Domini as australem habet partem, eis ad tempus concessit habitaculum, . . . Prima autem eorum professio, quodque eis a domino patriarcha et reliquis episcopis in remissionem peccatorum iniunctum est, ut vias et itinera maxime ad salutem peregrinorum contra latronum et incursantium insidias pro viribus conservarent."

6 Malcolm Barber, *The New Knighthood* (Cambridge University Press, 1994) p. 9.

7 Quoted in Edward Burman, *The Templars, Knights of God* (Rochester, VT: Destiny Books, 1986) p. 16.

8 Charles-Joseph Hefele and H. Leclerq, *Histoires de Conciles d'apres les documents Originaux*, t. Va (Paris: Letouzey et Ané, 1912) p. 592.

9 Benjamin Z. Kader, "On the Origins of the Earliest Laws of Frankish Jerusalem: The Canons of the Copuncil of Nablus, 1120," *Speculum* April 1999 (Latin Canons reproduced from Bibiloteca Apostolica Vaticana, MS Vat. Lat. 1345 Fols. 1r–3r) pp. 331–34.

10 Ibid. p. 334. "Si clericus causa defenssionis [sic] arma detulerit, culpa non teneantur." (my translation)

11 Ibid. p. 332 and in article. See also Steven Runciman, *A History of the Crusades* Vol. II (Cambridge University Press, 1952) pp. 150–52.

12 William of Tyre, p. 554. "Cumque iam annis noven in eo fuissent proposito, non nisi novem errant."

13 Barber and Bate, p. 3.

14 Quoted in Marie Luise Buist-Thiele, "The Influence of St. Bernard of Clairvaux on the Formation of the Order of the Knights Templar," ed. Michael Gervers *The Second Crusade and the Cistercians* (New York: St. Martin's Press, 1992) p. 58.

15 Ibid.

16 Marquis d'Albon, *Cartularie Général de l'Ordre du Temple 1119?–1150* (Paris, 1913) p. 1. It was a donation made in Marseille and there are several uncertainties about it.

CHAPTER TWO

Hugh de Payns

Amid all the different theories about the beginning of the Templars there is one constant. The founder of the order was a certain Hugh de Payns, knight.

Some say he and a few comrades first approached the patriarch of Jerusalem, asking to live a monastic life in the city. Others report the men went to **Baldwin II**, king of Jerusalem. Still others suggest that it was Baldwin who asked Hugh and his friends to act as protectors to the many pilgrims coming from the West to Jerusalem.

In all of these, the main constant is Hugh.

But who was Hugh? Where is Payns? What was his background and who were his family? What could have led him to devote his life to fighting for God?

Despite his importance, even in his own day, a contemporary biography of Hugh has never been found. Nor has any medieval writer even mentioned reading one. I find this interesting because it indicates to me the uneasiness people felt about the idea of warrior monks. Other men who founded orders, like Francis of Assisi or Robert of Arbrissel, had biographies written about them immediately after their deaths. The main purpose of this was to have an eyewitness account of their saintliness in case they were suggested for canonization. Of the little that was written about Hugh, nothing was negative, but there

Hugh de Payns and Godfrey of St. Omer before King Baldwin II. *(Bibliotheque Nationale)*

does not seem to have been any sense that he was in line for sainthood.

So how do we find out more about this man who started it all?

The first clue we have is from the chronicler William of Tyre. He says that Hugh came from the town of Payns, near Troyes in the county of Champagne.[1] William also mentions Hugh's companion, Godfrey of St. Omer, in Picardy, now Flanders. These two men seem, in William's eyes, to be cofounders of the Templars, but it was Hugh who became the first Grand Master. This may have been through natural leadership, but it also may have been because Hugh had the right connections.

Payns is a small town in France, near Troyes, the seat of the counts of Champagne. It is situated in a fertile farmland that even then had a reputation for its wine. It's not known when Hugh was born, or who his parents were. The first mention of him in the records is from about 1085–1090, when a "Hugo de Pedano, Montiniaci dominus," or Hugh of Payns, lord of Montigny, witnessed a charter in which **Hugh, count of Champagne**, donated land to the abbey of

Molesme.[2] In order to be a witness, our Hugh had to have been at least sixteen. So he was probably born around 1070.

Over the next few years, four more charters of the count are witnessed by a "Hugo de Peanz" or "Hugo de Pedans." Actually, the place name is spelled slightly differently each time it appears.[3] It is also spelled "Hughes." Spelling was much more of a creative art back then. However, it's fairly certain that these are all the same man. These show that Hugh was part of the court of the count of Champagne, perhaps even related to him.

The last of these charters in Champagne is from 1113. The next time we find the name Hugh de Payns, it is in 1120 in Jerusalem. This is highly suggestive, as Hugh is witness to a charter confirming the property of the Order of St. John (the **Hospitallers**).[4] So now we have confirmation of the story that Hugh was in Jerusalem in 1119–1120 to found the Templars outside of later histories. However, it is not until five years later that Hugh witnesses a charter in which he lists himself as "Master of the Knights Templar."[5] In between, he is witness to a donation made in 1123 by Garamond, patriarch of Jerusalem, to the abbey of Santa Maria de Josaphat. Here Hugh is listed only by the name "Hugonis de Peans." There is no mention of the Templars and Hugh is near the end of the list of witnesses, showing that he was not one of the most important people present.[6]

How did Hugh get to Jerusalem? What happened in those five years between witnessing a charter as a layman and becoming Master of the Templars? We can guess, but unless more information appears, we can't know for certain.

The most likely reason for Hugh to have gone to the Holy Land was in the company of Count Hugh. The count made a pilgrimage to Jerusalem, his second, in 1114.[7] There is no list of his companions, but it would fit that Hugh de Payns would have been in his company. Hugh was already among those at court often enough to be a witness to the count's donations and therefore one of his liege men. But he must have been released from his obligation to his lord for, when Count Hugh returned home, Hugh de Payns remained in Jerusalem. Why?

Again, Hugh hasn't left anything to tell us. Was it as penance for his sins? Most pilgrimages were intended as a quest for divine forgiveness. Many people have insisted that knights only went to the Holy Land for wealth, either in land or goods looted from those they conquered. But in Hugh's case, once he decided to remain in Jerusalem he resolved to live the life of a monk, owning nothing.

It is even more surprising because Hugh apparently left a wife and at least one young child behind. His wife was named Elizabeth. She was probably from the family of the lords of Chappes, land quite close to Payns.[8] Their son, Thibaud, became abbot of the monastery of La Colombe.[9] Hugh may have had two other children, Guibuin and Isabelle, but I don't find the evidence for them completely convincing.[10]

In principle, any married person wishing to join a religious order had to have the permission of his or her spouse and that spouse was also to join a convent or monastery. In practice, however, this didn't happen that often, especially among the nobility. When Sybilla of Anjou, countess of Flanders, remained in Jerusalem to join the nuns at the convent of Bethany in 1151, her husband, Thierry, returned to Flanders and continued his life.[11] Sometimes, the spouse remarried. It is not known what happened to Elizabeth. Perhaps she died before Hugh left Champagne.

Hugh did not abandon the place of his birth. When he returned to Europe to drum up support for the Knights of the Temple, he received his greatest support in Champagne. It was at the **Council of Troyes**, only a few miles south of Payns, that the order received official papal approval.

There were also several Templar commanderies near Payns. One of them, at least, was founded by Hugh. Donations continued to the Templars of Payns until the early fourteenth century, just before the arrest of the Templars.[12] Many of the "donations" are clearly sales under another name, as when in 1213, a knight named Henri of Saint-Mesmin gave two fields near the preceptory to the Templars of Payns. In return, the Templars gave Henri fourteen livres. In another case, Odo of Troyes "gave" the Templars some mills. Odo was about to leave on Crusade and so the Templars gave him forty livres with the promise of twenty more when (or if) Odo returned.

However, after founding the commandery, it appears that Hugh donated nothing more to it. He returned to Jerusalem, probably around 1130, and died in 1136. May 24 is the traditional date.

The records we have from the early twelfth century give no more information on Hugh de Payns. Of course, much has been lost over the years. Some of the Templar records in Europe were destroyed after the dissolution of the order at the **Council of Vienne**. This doesn't seem to have been because the information was secret or heretical, simply that it was no longer needed and the parchment could be scraped and reused.

The main Templar archives, which might have had more information on Hugh, were not in Europe, however, but in Jerusalem. They were moved to Acre and then Cyprus, where they were in 1312. War and conquest ensured that anything left was scattered or destroyed.

Perhaps there was once a biography of sorts of Hugh de Payns. It seems to me that someone would have wanted to tell the world more about him. What we can deduce from his actions is that he must have been a strong-willed man, very devout and with the ability to convince others to see and follow his vision. He does not seem to have been particularly well educated. Nothing in his life or background would indicate that he was involved in anything of a mystical nature, nor that he founded the Templars to protect some newly discovered treasure or secret, as modern myths state.

Hugh de Payns was most likely a deeply devout layman who wanted to serve God by protecting His pilgrims and His land. Hugh used his wealth, such as it was, and his family and social connections to make this possible. Nothing more.

---

1 William of Tyre, ed. R. B. V. Huygens, CCCM 63 12.7.6 (Brepols, Turnholt 1986) "Inter quos primus et precipui fuerunt viri venerabiles Hugo de Paganis et Gaufridus de Sancto Aldemaro."
2 Thierry Leroy, *Hughes de Payns, Chevalier Champenois, Fondateur de L'Ordre des Templiers* (Troyes: La Maison du Boulanger, 2001) p. 194. Cartulaire de Molesme, n. 230 p. 214.
3 Leroy, p. 194. Charters listed are for abbeys all in the area of Troyes.
4 Henri-François Delaborde, *Chartres de Terre-Sainte Provenant de l'Abbaye de N.-D. de Josaphat*. B.E.F.A.R. 29. (Paris: Ernst Thorin, 1880) no. 101.

5 Leroy, p. 194. Cartulaire de Saint Sépulcre no. 105, "magister militium Templi."
6 *Chartres de Terre-Sainte Provenant de l'Abbaye de N.-D. de Josaphat*, ed. H-Francois Delaborde, (Paris, 1880) p. 38. Charter no. 12.
7 Michael Bur, *La formation du comté de Champagne* (Université de Lille III, 1977) p. 275.
8 Leroy, p. 98. Despite several popular modern books of fiction and some that say they are non-fiction, there is no truth to the tale that Hugh's wife was named Catherine St. Clair.
9 Thibaud was elected abbot in 1139. "Thibaud de Pahens, filius Hugonis primi magistri temple Jerosolymitani." Quoted in Leroy, p. 95.
10 Leroy, pp. 95–114. Neither of the children is listed as son or daughter of Hugh. They might be from another branch of the family who took over Payns after Thibaud entered the monastery.
11 Karen Nicholas, "Countesses as Rulers in Flanders," in *Aristocratic Women in Medieval France*, ed. Theodore Evergates (Philadelphia: University of Pennsylvania Press, 1999) p. 123.
12 Leroy, p. 120.

CHAPTER THREE

Baldwin II, King of Jerusalem

Baldwin of Le Bourq accomplished the dream of many of the knights of the First Crusade. He went from being a shirttail relative of Godfrey of Bouillon and his brother, Baldwin I, the heroes of the crusade, to becoming king in his own right, marrying a princess and ruling a realm that had been conquered for the glory of God.

He also was the man who first gave the Temple of Solomon to **Hugh de Payns** and his knights, thus starting both the reality and the legend of the Templars.

Baldwin was the son of Hugh, count of Rethel, and a cousin of the Lotharingian brothers Eustace, Godfrey, and Baldwin. He went with them on the First Crusade and remained. When Eustace returned home to become count of Boulogne, Godfrey, "the Protector of the Holy Sepulcher," died and Baldwin became the first king of Jerusalem; their cousin was given the county of Edessa to rule.

When the crusaders arrived, Edessa had only been under Moslem control a short time, and three-quarters of its population was Christian.[1] Most of them were Armenian Monophysites, who were considered heretics by the Greek Orthodox Byzantines.[2] Thoros, the Orthodox previous ruler of the county, had been deposed by his people shortly after the arrival of the crusaders.[3] The Armenians were willing to be ruled by the Western crusaders as long as they could practice their form of Christianity.

Unlike many of the early settlers, Baldwin seems to have adapted to the customs of his new land. He accepted the Armenian patriarch with "all the honors due to his high ecclesiastical dignity, gave him villages, loaded him down with gifts and showed him great friendship."[4] The different Christian sects of the county were allowed to continue their forms of worship, not forced to conform to the Roman rites.

In his desire to assimilate with his new subjects, Baldwin also took an Armenian bride. Her name was Morfia and she was the daughter of Khoril, prince of Melitene. Although it was a politically sound move and she came with an excellent dowry, there also seems to have been genuine affection between Baldwin and Morfia. The rest of the marriages among the noble families of the Latin kingdoms make the steamiest soap operas look tame, but in their years together Baldwin and Morfia provoked no scandal and no talk of divorce. When only daughters were born to them, Baldwin saw no reason why the eldest one shouldn't inherit Edessa.

When in 1118, Baldwin I, king of Jerusalem, died without an heir, he left no provision for the succession to the throne.[5] The patriarch of Jerusalem, Arnulf, called the lords together to decide what to do. Some felt that the king's last remaining brother, Eustace, should be summoned from Boulogne to take up the kingship. Others felt that it was unsafe to wait for Eustace. The time it would take to send a messenger to Europe and back would leave the kingdom open to anarchy and attack.[6]

Jocelyn of Courtenay, another early crusader, put in a vote for Baldwin of Le Bourq. Baldwin was of the same family as the late king, he had done a good job ruling Edessa, and, even if his children were all girls, he had proved he could produce children. There was still hope for a boy.[7]

Just by chance (or perhaps not), Baldwin of Le Bourq was visiting Jerusalem at the time. He accepted the nomination and was crowned without delay.

It turned out that Eustace wasn't thrilled with the idea of taking over the governance of Jerusalem. He had started out for the Holy Land when he heard of his brother's death, but had only reached Italy when he learned of Baldwin's coronation. He was apparently quite content to go back to his home in Boulogne.[8]

Eustace may have realized that the Kingdom of Jerusalem was a prize that would need constant defending. Or he may have remembered what the summer sun in the Near East does to fair northern skin. So Baldwin became the second king of Jerusalem without a serious struggle. He gave Edessa to his supporter Jocelyn of Courtenay.[9]

The new king faced a mountain of problems, both military and economic. The capital city of Jerusalem had been cleared of all non-Christians by the first crusaders and there hadn't been much interest among the Franks to repopulate it. The city was a place for pilgrims to visit, see the sights, buy some souvenirs, and go home. Baldwin gave concessions to anyone "Latin" who would set up shops and homes. He also gave Syrians, Greeks, and Armenians—everyone except **Saracens** and Jews—the right of free trade, especially in foodstuffs.[10] It worked to some extent, but Jerusalem was important more for its historical and religious connections rather than as a major center of trade. It was the port cities that maintained the crusaders' hold on the land and most of the Westerners lived along the coast.

Outside of the cities, there was little control over the area. The pilgrims, who brought cash in, were being waylaid on the road by robbers. It was impossible to patrol the whole area between Jerusalem and the port cities. Also, many of the pilgrims couldn't seem to understand that they couldn't just trot off to spend a day in Bethlehem or go for a dip in the Jordan without guards. Baldwin had neither the men nor the resources to protect them. And yet, without the pilgrims, Jerusalem could not survive.

It's not certain whether it was Baldwin or **Hugh de Payns** who first suggested that a group of knights take on the job of pilgrim herding.[11] In either case, Baldwin was undoubtedly thrilled to turn the problem over to the new Order of knights. The **Hospitallers** had long been established within Jerusalem to provide shelter and care to the pilgrims, many of whom came with the intention of dying in the Holy Land. But in 1119, when the Templars were founded, the hospital had no military duties. So there was a definite niche for the knights to fill.

King Baldwin gave them the use of a section of the royal palace, thought to be on the site of the **Temple of Solomon**, and left them to settle in as best they could.

The next few years for Baldwin were spent outside of Jerusalem. He had to mop up after Roger of Antioch decided to ride out and fight the Ortoqid Turk Ilghazi without waiting for reinforcements. The place where Roger realized that he'd made his last mistake was ever after known as the "Field of Blood."[12]

Baldwin took over the governance of Antioch until Roger's heir, Bohemond, could reach adulthood and arrive from his home in Apulia. He also kept an eye on Edessa and when, in 1123, Count Jocelyn was captured by Ilghazi's nephew Balak, Baldwin rushed north to maintain order in the city. Unfortunately, Baldwin fell into the same trap as Jocelyn had and became Balak's prisoner in April 1123.

The barons of Jerusalem chose a regent, Eustace de Garnier, lord of Sidon and Caesarea. He held things together quite well until Baldwin was released in 1124, after paying a heavy ransom and giving Balak his five-year-old daughter, Yveta, as a hostage.

During his captivity the city of Tyre was captured from the Turks by the Franks and the Venetians. The unimportance of the Templars at this time is clear from the fact that the treaty was signed by the patriarch of Jerusalem, the archbishop of Caesarea, three other bishops, the abbot of Santa Maria of Josaphat, and the priors of the Holy Sepulcher, the Temple of the Lord, and Mout Sion. The master of the Temple isn't even among the witnesses.[13]

As soon as he was free, Baldwin needed to reassert his authority. He immediately gathered his troops to fight the Turks in northern Syria. He then attempted to take Damascus, but, like all the crusaders after him, failed.[14]

In between battles, Baldwin was busy marrying off his daughter, Alice, to the count of Antioch, Bohemond II, now old enough to take charge. His third daughter, Hodierna, was then married to the count of Tripoli. For his eldest daughter, **Melisande**, Baldwin sent a delegation back to Europe to ask for the hand of the widowed count of Anjou, **Fulk**. Although there isn't much mention of the Templars in Jerusalem up to this point, Hugh de Payns and Godfrey of St. Omer, the two first knights of the order, were in the party.[15]

This mission back to Europe was the turning point for the Templars. Hugh and Godfrey returned with men, money, and papal approval. This last allowed them to collect donations and set up branch houses to manage property. The houses, called preceptories or commanderies, provided horses, fodder and food as well as cash for the constant needs of the front line Templar knights.

The trip was also good public relations for Baldwin and the Kingdom of Jerusalem. Hugh and Godfrey reminded people of the purpose of the crusades. The Templar knights were not looking for individual wealth or land or political power. The order itself wound up having all three but no one could have foreseen that in 1125, when the men set out. What people in Europe saw were men of good birth who had abandoned their lands and families in order to defend the places where Christ had lived and died for all people. The example of the Templars was a shaming reminder to those who had stayed behind.

When Baldwin II died in August 1131, the Kingdom of Jerusalem was firmly established. His daughter and son-in-law had given him a grandson, the future Baldwin III, who would carry on his line. Construction on the new Church of the Holy Sepulcher had begun. He must have felt that he had given his people a good base to continue expanding the territory.

He may not have considered the Templars one of his major accomplishments but they would outlast the Latin city of Jerusalem by more than a hundred years and their legend would survive long after the mighty castles of the crusaders had become only crumbling piles of stone.

1 René Grousset, *Histoire des Croisades et du Royanme Franc de Jérusalem* (Paris, 1934) p. 388.
2 Monophysites: This is a Christian sect that stresses the divine nature of Jesus over the human one. The Armenian Monophysites began in the fifth century and still exist.
3 Hans Eberhard Mayer, *The Crusades* (Oxford University Press, 1988) p. 49.
4 Grousset, p. 259 (quoting Matthew of Edessa).
5 He had been married twice, once to an Armenian princess whom he had refused to accept because she had been captured for a short time by Moslems and he said she had been raped by them. The second time was to Adelaide of Sicily, whom he repudiated. Mayer says that "to all appearances, the king was homosexual" (p. 71) but he doesn't say what those appearances were. Baldwin was buried next to his brother, Godfrey.
6 William of Tyre, *Chronique* ed. R. B. C. Huygens, CCCM 63 (Turnholt, 1986) 12, 3 p. 549.
7 Ibid., p. 549 (I added the part about his daughters). William listed the other reasons.
8 Ibid., p. 550.
9 Grousset, p. 537.
10 William of Tyre, p. 565. "Dedit etiam Surianis, Grecis, Armenis et harum cuiuslibet nationum hominibus, Sarracenis etiam nichilominus, liberam potestaem sine exactione aliqua inferendi in sanctam civitatem triticum, ordeum et quodlibet genus qequminus."
11 Please see chapter 1, **The Beginning of the Order**.
12 Mayer, p. 73.
13 William of Tyre, 12, 28, p. 581.
14 Mayer, pp. 79–80.
15 Please see chapter 2, **Hugh de Payns**.

❊

CHAPTER FOUR

Hugh,
Count of Champagne

One of the earliest members of the Templars was also one of the few members of the high nobility to join. Hugh of Champagne remains one of the more mysterious of the first Templars.

As with so much of the politics in the eleventh and twelfth centuries, the story of Hugh, first count of Champagne, is that of family. When he was born, the county of Champagne didn't exist. For most of his life he called himself the count of Troyes, which was the main holding of his ancestors.

Hugh was the youngest son of Thibaud I, who was count of Blois, Meaux, and Troyes, and of Adele of Bar-sur-Aube. Thibaud had gained some of his property by taking over lands belonging to a nephew.[1] Therefore, he had something to give to Hugh, his last-born son. Hugh's older brother, Stephen-Henry, got the best property, that of Blois and Meaux. Hugh inherited Troyes and other bits from his mother and the property of his middle brother, Odo, who died young.[2]

Hugh did not go on the First Crusade in 1096, although Stephen-Henry did. He may not have been interested or he may have been too busy subduing all his far-flung properties. One of these properties was the town of Payns not far from Troyes. A son of the lord of the town,

Hugh de Payns, became one of Hugh's supporters and a member of his court.[3]

Hugh scored a coup in 1094 by his marriage to Constance, daughter of Philip I, king of France. She brought with her the dowry of Attigny, just north of Hugh's lands.

As the twelfth century dawned, Hugh seemed to be an up-and-coming young nobleman, with an expanding amount of land and royal connections.

In 1102, Stephen-Henry died in battle in Palestine. He left several young sons and a formidable wife, Adele, the daughter of King Henry I of England. This was Stephen's second trip to the Holy Land. It was said that Adele wasn't pleased with her husband's military exploits on the first trip. He had deserted the crusader army before reaching Antioch. Adele insisted he return and fight more bravely before showing his face at home again.[4] Stephen-Henry's death in battle apparently satisfied her.

At about the same time, 1103, Hugh had a very strange encounter. One day while he was traveling in the valley of Suippe, a man named Alexander, a pilgrim from the Holy Land, came to see him. A charter from the convent of Avenay tells what happened next. "Hugh . . . used to ransom captives and aid the destitute. Among these was a certain Alexander, an impoverished man from overseas whom the count took into his own household. The most noble count and his family treated this man so well that he even ate and often slept in the count's personal quarters."[5]

Hugh's confidence in Alexander was misplaced for, one night, "judging the time and place appropriate, [he] tried to slit the throat of the sleeping count."[6]

The records don't give a reason for the attack, nor do they say anything more about the pilgrim. This is one of the frustrations of historical records.

Hugh only survived the attack because his men took him directly to the nearby convent of Avenay, where he spent several months recovering. In return he gave a large donation to the nuns, whose care and prayers he felt had saved his life when doctors couldn't.

It may have been the combination of his brother's death and his own near miss that convinced Hugh to make a pilgrimage to the Holy Land. He left in 1104 and returned around 1107.[7] It's not clear whether he and his retinue aided in the ongoing fight to keep the land won by the first crusaders or simply visited the pilgrim sites.

While Hugh was off on his journey his wife, Constance, decided she'd had enough. She and Hugh had been married eleven years and had no children. Fortunately, most of the nobility of France were related in one way or another and so she was able to have the marriage dissolved on the grounds that they were cousins. This was the medieval way around the prohibition of divorce and it was used all the time. Constance later married Bohemond I, ruler of Antioch, and ended her days there.[8] Her descendants, especially the women, played important roles in the history of the Latin kingdoms.

So upon his return to Champagne in 1107, Hugh found himself single. He soon married again, this time to Elizabeth of Varais, daughter of Stephen the Hardy of Burgundy. Elizabeth was related to a number of strong, powerful women of the time. She was the niece of Clemence, countess of Flanders, and also Matilda, duchess of Burgundy. Her first cousin was Adelaide, the wife of Louis VI, king of France.

In October 1115, Count Hugh was attending Pope Calixtus II at the Council of Reims, where he and his men provided an escort to the bishop of Mainz.[9] The pope was, by the way, Elizabeth's uncle. Life was going well again for the count of Champagne.

Therefore, it was strange that when Elizabeth presented Hugh with a son, he refused to believe it was his and said so publicly. The dating of the blessed event is uncertain, around 1117. Hugh had gone on his second pilgrimage to Jerusalem in 1116 and it could have been that his wife tried to convince him that she had had a fourteen-month pregnancy. But the reason Hugh gave was that his doctors had all told him that he was sterile, so he may have thought that it was chronologically possible for him to be the father.[10] In any event, the child, Eudes, and his mother were repudiated.

Apparently, there was enough doubt among others of the family as to the legitimacy of the baby that no great storm of protest hit Hugh. While Eudes had friends who took his side over the years, he was never able to attract enough support to be a threat to the next count of Champagne, Hugh's nephew, Thibaud. Eudes was given a small fief and allowed to live out his life in peace.

Hugh did not try another marriage. In 1125 he abdicated as count and returned to Jerusalem, where he joined the newly formed Templars.[11] He died there sometime after 1130.

The story of Hugh, count of Troyes and Champagne, is one of the real mysteries of the Templar saga. According to legend, the order was formed in 1119, after Hugh de Payns decided to remain in Jerusalem while Count Hugh returned to Troyes. Did the count have any influence on the decision of the future founder of the order to stay behind? As Hugh's overlord, Count Hugh would have had to give his permission for Hugh to leave his service. Was the count part of this initial decision to form a monastic military order?

We don't know. None of the chroniclers mention him, except to note that he ended his life as a Templar. Is it because they were embarrassed to say that the count of Champagne chose to become subservient to a man who had once been one of his vassals? Count Hugh seems to have been a consummate warrior. He spent most of his life fighting or on pilgrimage. He seems a much more likely candidate for being the founder of the Templars than Hugh de Payns.

But he wasn't. He died as a member of the order, nothing more. Champagne went to Thibaud, the great-grandson of William the Conqueror and the son of Count Stephen-Henry, who had died as a soldier of God. And Hugh faded into a footnote to Templar history.

---

1 Michel Bur, *La formation du comté de Champagne* (Universite de Lille III, 1977) p. 259.

2 Bur, p. 267.

3 Thierry Leroy, *Hughes de Payns, Chevalier Champenois, Fondateur de l'Ordre des Templiers* (Troyes: La Maison du Boulanger, 2001).

4 Bur, 473–74, quoting the anonymous historian of the First Crusade.

5 Theodore Evergates, tr., *Feudal Society in Medieval France: Documents from the County of Champagne* (University of Pennsylvania Press, 1991) p. 124. Translation of text found in Lalore, *Cartularie de l'abbale de Saint-Loup de Troyes* (Paris: E. Thorin, 1875) 14–16 no. 4.

6 Ibid.
7 Bur, p. 274.
8 Ibid. Constance's life story is really much more interesting than Hugh's in my opinion.
9 Oderic Vitalis, *The Ecclesiastical History of Orderic Vitalis* Vol. VI, p. 252.
10 Bur, p. 275.
11 Ibid.

❋

CHAPTER FIVE

Bernard of Clairvaux

He called himself the chimera of his age. He was a mass of contradictions. Bernard, abbot of Clairvaux, was a monk who spent most of his time out of the cloister, a spiritual man who seemed always embroiled in politics and a man of peace who convinced thousands to fight and die for their faith. There are many who believe that it was his championship of the Templars that made their survival possible.

Bernard enters history in 1113 when he appears at the gates of the monastery of Citeaux demanding to become a monk. This is a common theme in stories of medieval saints. But Bernard's story is slightly different. Instead of fleeing the world, he seems to have brought it along. Bernard had convinced thirty of his friends and relatives to enter the monastery with him.[1]

Bernard was born in 1090, the third son of Tecelin de Trois Fontaines and his wife, Aleth de Montbard. They were of the lower nobility of the area around Dijon. Bernard's brothers were all trained warriors who fought for their lords, usually the duke of Burgundy.[2] His childhood seems to have been happy. He was devoted to both parents, particularly his mother, who died when he was in his teens.[3]

It was common in the early twelfth century for at least one child in a large family to enter the Church. Bernard was the one appointed for this. And yet, when he arrived at Citeaux, his brothers Guy, Gerard,

Bartholomew, Andrew, and Nivard and his uncle Gaudry also became monks. Guy was already married and had small daughters and yet Bernard had convinced him to leave his family and join him. Not only that, he also convinced Guy's wife to agree to this and enter a convent.[4]

Such enthusiasm couldn't be contained in one place. Within three years, Bernard had left Citeaux to found a Cistercian abbey of his own at Clairvaux, just north of Dijon.

It's clear that from an early age, Bernard had incredible powers of persuasion.

But how did this devout monk become involved with the Templars? At first glance, it seems an unlikely pairing.

However, when we look a bit closer, the distance between Bernard of Clairvaux and the Knights of the Temple isn't so far. The founder of the Templars, **Hugh de Payns**, came from an area near that of Bernard's family. They may even have known each other before Bernard left for Citeaux. Bernard certainly knew Count **Hugh of Champagne**, who had abandoned his lordship to join the Templars in Jerusalem.[5] In a letter to Hugh, written about 1125, Bernard laments that the count has decided to travel so far away to devote himself to God, and, even though he is certain that it is the will of the Most High, he still will miss the count, who has been so generous to the Cistercian order.[6]

The strongest connection is that the first Templars came from the same world that Bernard was born into. They were generally from the lower nobility, men trained for war in the service of greater lords. They were not well educated, perhaps learning to read French but not Latin. Yet many of them felt uneasy about the role they were asked to play in society. They received mixed signals from the Church, which forbade the killing of other Christians, but honored knights as protectors of the weak and the literature of the time, which praised valiant and successful warriors. The knights knew that success in battle was the key to advancing their position.

That was all very well for this life, but what about the next?

Even though Bernard would have preferred that every man become a monk, he knew that wasn't likely to happen. An order of knights who fought for Christ was the next best thing. Perhaps it was Count Hugh who suggested to **Baldwin II**, king of Jerusalem, that the Templars ask Bernard to use his influence to convince the pope, Innocent II, and the great lords of Europe, to support the new order.[7]

As one might guess, Bernard never did anything halfway. He was present at the **Council of Troyes** in 1129 to see the official recognition of the Templars. Even before that, he may have written his passionate defense of the order, *On the New Knighthood*.

On the New Knighthood was written in the form of a letter to Hugh de Payns, in response to his request for a "sermon of exhortation" to the brothers of the Temple. Scholars have puzzled over this open letter for centuries. In it, Bernard writes like a Roman general sending the centurions off to battle the barbarians.

He begins by comparing the Knights of the Temple to secular knights. The secular knight fights and kills for his own benefit and glory. He also dresses like a dandy, with long hair, dragging sleeves, pointed shoes, and his body bedecked with gold and jewels. Bernard contrasts this with the simple and practical gear of the Templars. Both the Latin and French **Rules** of the order reflect this concern with extravagant clothing and may show Bernard's influence.

But Bernard is just warming up. He soon goes beyond even the crusading idea that it is meritorious to fight for God. He states several times that killing the enemy of God is a good thing and dying while doing so means instant admission to heaven. "For death for Christ is no sin, whether one kills or is killed, but merits great glory."[8] Again he says, "If he kills an evildoer, it is not homicide but, if I might put it so, evilcide."[9]

This is not only a classic case of making the enemy something inhuman, it also implies that dying while doing so means a straight shot to heaven. "If those who die in the Lord are blessed, how much greater are those who die for the Lord?"[10] Even those who have committed terrible crimes can find redemption—"impious wretches, sacrilegious plunderers and rapists, murderers, perjurers and adulterers." He adds that it's a win-win deal. Europe is glad to be rid of these men and the defenders of the Holy Land glad to receive them.[11]

Of course, that doesn't say much for the pool the Templars have to recruit from.

After praising the lifestyle and mission of the knights, Bernard then takes the reader on a tour of the main pilgrimage sites: the Temple of Solomon, Bethlehem, Nazareth, the Mount of Olives and the Valley of Josaphat, the Jordan River, Calvary, the Holy Sepulcher, Bethpage, and Bethany.

What is going on here? Why is this monk telling these men that it's not only all right to kill non-Christians, it's actually a good thing? Bernard does rein in a bit at one point, saying that the infidels shouldn't be destroyed if there is some other way to keep them from attacking the pilgrims, but better infidels die than us.[12]

Certainly, the "letter" to the Templars fits in with the crusading tradition. Three hundred years before the First Crusade, Charlemagne invaded and conquered the Saxons several times, under the excuse of "converting" them. But Bernard doesn't mention persuasion when dealing with the **Saracens**. He seems determined to glorify slaughtering them.

Was this letter really written to stiffen the backbones of the Templars? Did they doubt the righteousness of their cause? Or was this for the rest of Christendom, including those who were uneasy about these knight-monks? Bernard says that he wrote the letter at the insistence of Hugh de Payns. But who was the real intended audience?

It seems clear that this was Bernard's attempt to make sure that the Order of the Templars would be accepted in Europe. It's possible that he even wrote his exhortation before the official recognition of the order at the **Council of Troyes**.[13] Everything about it sounds like a recruiting speech. First Bernard points out how much more noble the Knights Templar are than the fops hanging around castles at home and causing trouble. Then he tells the listener that the Order of the Temple could make even the worst criminal shape up—and do it far, far away. Finally, he winds up with a tour of the pilgrim sites, places he had never seen but the Templars knew well. This was likely meant as a reminder of why the Templars were so much needed. Did Christendom want the sites of the Bible to remain in the hands of unbelievers?

Finally, why was it so important that this abbot get the word out? Why not a letter by the pope or at least an archbishop?

One answer is that from about 1120 through 1147, Bernard, abbot of Clairvaux, was probably the most influential man in Christendom. The same intense passion that convinced most of his friends and family to give up a worldly life for a strict monastic one had been let loose upon the rest of Europe. Bernard was a tireless writer and he never minced words. He gave advice to most of the rulers of the day, chided other abbots for laxity, and lured the rowdy students of Paris away from the brothel and into the cloister.

I have been trying to get a handle on Bernard for more than thirty years now and he still slips away. The man was obviously immensely charismatic. He had a way with words that no translation can completely evoke. It's worth learning Latin just to watch Bernard play with the language. His personal life seems to have been above reproach.

On the other hand, he was a terrible nag. Some of his letters are so critical that people must have cringed when they saw his seal on them. He also tended to go overboard for causes he believed in. The exhortation to the Templars is one example. Another thing that I haven't quite forgiven him for is his determination to see that the work of the teacher and philosopher Peter Abelard was condemned.

His enthusiasm finally backfired on him with the failure of the **Second Crusade**, in 1149, which he had preached. The first sign that things were unraveling was when he learned that a monk named Radulf was encouraging the crusaders to massacre the Jews in the Rhineland. Bernard was horrified and he immediately raced there to stop the murders, with much success. Ephraim, a Jew from Bonn, who was a child at the time, later wrote, "The Lord heard our outcry, and He turned to us and had mercy upon us . . . He sent a decent priest, one honored and respected by all the clergy in France, named Abbé Bernard of Clairvaux, to deal with this evil person. Bernard . . . said to them: 'It is good that you go against the Ishmaelites. But whosoever touches a Jew to take his life, is like one who harms Jesus himself.'"[14]

What are we to make of this man? In his own life, he was considered a saint by some and an opinionated busybody by others. He was canonized shortly after his death and, even before he died, at least one of his friends started writing his biography with an eye to sainthood.

There were those who also vilified him for his preaching of the crusades and for his intolerance of Peter Abelard and other scholars. One of the most vicious of Bernard's detractors was the English writer Walter Map. Map was only about thirteen years old when Bernard died in 1153, but his later association with Cistercian monks and his admiration for Abelard seems to have soured him on the abbot. He calls Bernard a Lucifer, shining brighter than the other stars of night, and tells stories of how he failed to perform miracles, including how Bernard could not raise a boy from the dead. "Master Bernard bade the body be carried into a private room, and, 'shutting every one out he lay upon the boy, and after a prayer arose; but the boy did not arise, for he lay there dead.' Thereupon I [Map] remarked, 'He was surely the most unlucky of monks; for never have I heard of a monk lying down upon a boy without the boy arising immediately after the monk.'"[15]

Walter Map also despised Templars, Hospitallers, Jews, and heretics but he saved his most acid comments for the Cistercians and their revered abbot. His greatest complaint about Bernard and, by extension, the Templars, was not that they were depraved or sacrilegious but that they were proud and greedy. This view of the Templars was to continue throughout their existence.

It may be that Bernard's fame did go to his head, although his pride was mostly in his absolute conviction that he knew best. The Cistercians who came after him may well have done their best to get and keep all the property they could, but in that they were no different from most other monastic orders.

Whatever opinion one has of Bernard, he is far too complex a person to label simply. His influence over society in the first half of the twelfth century was incredible and, to me, still hasn't been satisfactorily explained, although many have tried. This is a pity because, in order to understand the early years and astonishing growth of the Templars, the role of Bernard of Clairvaux must be taken into account.

1 William of St. Thierry, *Vita Prima Bernardi*, Books IV–VIII.

2 Robert Fossier, "La Fondation de Clairvaux et la Famille de Saint Bernard, in *Mélanges Saint Bernard* (Dijon, 1953) pp. 19–27.

3 Brian Patrick McGuire, *The Difficult Saint.*

4 William of St. Thierry, Book V, *Sancti Bernardi Abbatis Clarae-Vallensis, Opera Omnia* Vol. I (Paris: Mabillion, 1839). Guy could not become a monk without his wife's permission. The convent of Jully was founded for other female family members and wives of men wishing to become Cistercians.

5 Thierry LeRoy, *Hugues de Payns* (Troyes: Maison du Boulanger, 1999) p. 71.

6 Bernard of Clairvaux, "Epistola XXXI," *Sancti Bernardi Abbatis Clarae-Vallensis, Opera Omnia* Vol. I (Paris: Mabillion, 1839) p. 175.

7 Marquis d'Albon, *Cartularie Général du l'Ordre du Temple 1119?–1150* (Paris, 1913) p. 1.

8 Bernard of Clairvaux, "Exhortatio ad Milites Templi," ibid. Caput III 4, cols. 1256–57. "Quandoquidem mors pro Christo vel ferenda, vel inferenda, et nihil habeat criminis, et pluimum gloriae mereatur."

9 Ibid. "Sane cum occidit malefactorum, non homicida sed, ut ita dixerum, malicida."

10 Ibid., Caput I 1, col. 1255. "Nam si beati qui in Domine moriuntur, num multo magis qui pro Domino moriuntur?"

11 Ibid., Caput V 10, col. 1262.

12 Ibid., Caput II 4, col. 1257. "Non quidem vel Pagani necandi esset, si quo modo aliter possent a nimia infestione seu oppressione fidelium cohiberi. Nunc autem melius est ut occidantur, quam carte reliquatur viga extendant justi ad iniquitatem maunus suas." Mine is a loose translation, but that's the gist of it.

13 The work is not dated and could have been written anytime between about 1125 and 1130.

14 Ephraim of Bonn, *Sefer Zekira*, tr. Scholmo Eidelman in *The Jews and the Crusaders* (University of Wisconsin Press, 1977) p. 122.

15 Walter Map, *De Nugis Curialium* tr. Frederick Tupper and Marbury Bladen Ogle (London: Chatto & Windus, 1924) p. 49.

CHAPTER SIX

Hugh de Payns Takes the Templars on the Road

By 1127, the Knights of the Temple were established in the Holy Land. Even in their early state, they had so impressed **Fulk of Anjou** that, in 1124, he had given them thirty thousand livres from the rents of his lands.[1] Other lords had also donated property, especially in Hugh de Payns' home county of Champagne.

But the number of men who had decided to devote their lives to the order was still far too few. So it was decided that Hugh, along with fellow knights Godfrey of St. Omer, Payns of Montdidier, and Robert of Craon, would undertake a journey of recruitment.[2] It is interesting that the men chosen were from various parts of France. Godfrey was from Picardy in the north and Robert was a Burgundian.

The group probably made a stop at Rome, although there is no record of it or of a meeting with the pope, Honorius II. They then went on to Troyes, the seat of the counts of Champagne. Although **Hugh of Champagne** was still alive, he did not accompany the party. His nephew, Thibaud, was now count. Thibaud welcomed the knights and here Hugh may have seen his family for the first time in over ten years and made further arrangements for the disposal his own land.

Next, in early 1128, the men went to Anjou, where their old friend Fulk renewed his donation to the order. He also made a new donation that was split among the Templars, the bishop of Chartres, the abbey of the Trinity at Vendome, and the abbey of Fontevrault.[3] At this point, Fulk probably received the offer from King Baldwin to marry his eldest daughter, **Melisande**. On Ascension Day (May 28) of 1128 Fulk decided to take the cross (and the kingdom). Hugh was present for this ceremony, as was Gautier de Bure, the constable of Jerusalem, who had been sent expressly to bring the marriage proposal.[4]

The party went on to the county of Poitou, northwest of Anjou, where various lords gave generously to the new order. It would be nice to think that at this time Hugh may have seen the young Eleanor of Aquitaine, who would one day make the pilgrimage to the Holy Land, on the **Second Crusade**, as the wife of Louis VII of France. But there is no evidence that she or her father, the count of Poitou, met with the Templars.

Hugh then visited King Henry I of England at his court in Normandy, before going on to England and Scotland. Henry apparently gave the Templars "gold and silver" and annually added "many subsidies in arms and other equipment."[5]

The chronicles of Waverley Abbey in England tell of Hugh's trip "with two knights of the Temple and two clerics." The knights went all over England and as far north as Scotland, "and many took the cross that year and those following and took the route for the Holy places."[6]

At the next stop, Hugh felt confident of a good reception. Thierry, count of Flanders, was well disposed to the Templars. He also encouraged his barons to be generous. On September 13, 1128, Thierry held a solemn assembly before the bishop of Thérouanne at which he confirmed the donations made to the Templars by his predecessor, William Clito. Present to witness it were Hugh, Godfrey of St. Omer, Payns of Montdidier, "and many other brothers."[7] It's never made clear, but I believe that these "other brothers" were some of the new recruits that the Templars so desperately needed. A public gathering such as this would be a perfect place for a rousing speech. A young man carried away by the moment would find it hard to renounce a vow taken before so many people.

Finally the party returned to Troyes sometime around January 1129. There they received a house, a grange, land and fields near the suburb of Preize from a Raoul Crassus (the fat) and his wife, Hélène. This donation almost certainly became the commandery of Troyes.[8] Witnessing it were Hugh, Godfrey, and Payns along with Templars named Ralph and John. It seems that the trip had been worth it.

Only one thing more was needed to make sure the Order of the Knights of the Temple of Solomon was securely established. And Hugh was about to get it.

---

1 Orderic Vitalis, *The Eccesiastical History of Oderic Vitalis* vol. VI, ed. and tr. Margery Chibnall (Oxford: Oxford University Press, 1978) pp. 310–11.
2 Thierry LeRoy, *Hugues de Payns.* (Troyes: Maison du Boulanger, 1999) pp. 72–76.
3 Ibid., p. 195.
4 Ibid., p. 76.
5 Robert of Torigni, *Gesta Normannorum Ducam* Vol. II, Book VII, pp. 32–34, ed. and tr. Elisabeth M. C. Van Houts (Oxford: Oxford Medieval Texts; 1995) p. 257. I say apparently because there isn't any record of Henry's generosity, except Robert's account.
6 Quoted in LeRoy, p. 76.
7 Marquis d'Albon, Charter no. 16.
8 Ibid., Charter no. 22.

❖

CHAPTER SEVEN

The Council of Troyes

A t the end of 1128, **Hugh de Payns** made his way back from the tour of northern France, England, and Flanders to his birthplace in Champagne. Here he would at last receive official recognition of the Templars as a monastic order.

A church council convened at the town of Troyes on January 13, 1129.[1] The pope, Honorius II, did not attend. Instead he sent his legate, Matthew, cardinal-bishop of Albano, who had been a priest in Paris. There were two archbishops, Renaud of Reims and Henry of Sens. There were also a number of abbots, four from the Cistercian order, among them **Bernard of Clairvaux**.[2] There were also ten bishops and two "masters," that is, scholars, Alberic of Reims and Fulger.[3]

Abbot Bernard supported the Templars but he doesn't seem to have been eager to attend the council. He asked to be excused on the grounds of ill health.[4] But there was no way he could get out of it. Even in 1128, Bernard had a reputation for wisdom and piety. His support was all important. And after the council, that support would coutinue.

The council heard Hugh tell the story of how he began the order and its mission. He asked the clerics for an official habit to mark the Templars as knight-monks and also a Rule to live by like that of other monks. The clerics deliberated and gave the Templars permission to wear a white habit, as the Cistercians did. They also provided a monastic Rule in Latin, based on that of other monastic orders.[5]

However, the clerics were not really prepared to make a monastic Rule for men whose main function was not to pray but to fight. Wisely, they asked the advice of men who understood the active life. Along with the clerics, Thibaud, count of Champagne and nephew and heir of **Hugh of Champagne**, and William, count of Nevers, were present. The secretary of the council, Matthew, explains the presence of these "illiterates" by saying that they were lovers of the Truth who carefully went over the Templar Rule and threw out anything that didn't seem reasonable. "It was for this that they were at the council."[6]

The Latin Rule made provisions for the needs of the knights. Unlike other monks, who ate fish and eggs, Templars were allowed red meat three times a week.[7] If they were too tired, they needn't get up in the middle of the night for prayers.[8] The Rule also allowed the knights to have horses and servants to maintain them.

The clerics did take the opportunity to come out strongly against current fashion. They forbade the knights to wear immoderately long hair and beards, shoes with long curling points, lacy frills, or excessively long tunics.[9] Obviously the average knight on the road was a bit of a dandy.

The noble pursuits of hunting and hawking were also forbidden, with the exception of lion hunting, "because he [the lion] is always searching for someone to devour and his strength is against all so all strength is against him."[10] This shows that not all the danger in a pilgrimage was from human attackers. However, the council may have been thinking of a biblical analogy here, of the lion falling upon the flock of faithful pilgrims.

Other sections of the Rule concern behavior at meals, caring for brothers who become ill, and other common customs of monastic life; for instance, all property was kept in common and prayers were said seven times a day. Since the knights were not expected to understand Latin, they were told to simply repeat the Lord's Prayer at the correct times.

One subject that the council was extremely firm about concerned association with women. Knowing the reputation of knights for sexual conquests, two sections of the Rule make it clear that they were not even to kiss their own mothers or sisters. "We believe it dangerous for any man of religion to pay too much attention to the faces of women; therefore no brother may take the liberty of kissing a widow, nor a virgin nor his mother, nor his sister, nor his friend, nor any other woman."[11] This was taken for granted in most monastic houses, where the monks spent most of their time well out of sight of any female temptation. But it's clear that the council worried that after a hard day of fighting **Saracens**, it might be difficult for a Knight of the Temple to remember that, while he could still pillage, rape was no longer an option.

While the Latin Rule soon proved to need a lot of editing and additions, for the present Hugh de Payns was satisfied with the results of the council. He returned to Jerusalem by 1131, with fresh recruits, donations, and a formal Rule for the Knights Templar to live by. They were now an accepted part of the religious life in the West as well as the East.

---

1 Older accounts give this date as 1128 but this was caused by confusion surrounding the fact that many people in the twelfth century started the New Year in spring, not the middle of winter.

2 Charles-Joseph Hefele and Dom H. Leclercq, *Histoire de Conciles d'après les Documents Originaux* Vol. V (Paris: Letouzey et Ané, 1912) p. 670.

3 Laurent Dailliez, *Règle et Status de l'Ordre du Temple*, 2nd ed (Paris: Éditions Dervy, 1972). Reprint of the Latin Rule from 1721, pp. 325–26. The bishops were from Chartres, Soissons, Paris, Troyes, Orleans, Chalons, Laon, and Beauvais, all roughly from the north and east of France. William of Nevers's son, Raynald, died a prisoner of the Turks during the Second Crusade. William ended his days as a Carthusian monk.

4 Bernard of Clairvaux, *Opera Omnia* Vol. 1 (Paris, 1839) letter 21, col. 164–65. "Savientis siquidem acutae febris exusta ardoribus, et exhausta sudoribus." That is, he had a fever that wore him out.

5 Dailliez, pp. 327–59.

6 Ibid., p. 326.

7 Ibid., p. 332, capitula 10.

8 Ibid., pp. 335–36, capitula 18.

9 Ibid., p. 340, capitula 29. "De rostris & laqueis manifestum est & Gentiles: & cum abominabile, hoc omnibus agnoscatur, prohibimus . . . capillorum superflitaten & vestium immoderatan longitudinem barbere non permittimus."

10 Ibid., p. 348. "Quia ipse circuit, quaerens quem devoret, & manus ejus contra omnes, omniumque manus contra eum."

11 Ibid., p. 359, capitula 72. "Periculosum esse credimus omni Religioni vultum mulierum nimis attendere, & ideo nec vicuam, nec virginem, nec matrem, nec sororum, nec amitam, nec ullam aliam foeminam aliquis Frater osculi praesumet."

※

CHAPTER EIGHT

Go Forth and Multiply

One can trace the recruiting journey of Hugh and his companions by records of the gifts donated to them. Both great lords and minor ones lined up to make donations to the Templars. This was not only because they believed in the cause but, as is still true, the support of important people brought in gifts from the rank and file, who wished to associate themselves in charity with their local rulers.[1]

After the **Council of Troyes**, Hugh de Payns returned to Jerusalem, but other Templars continued to crisscross Europe seeking support for the new order.

In the south, Hugh Rigaud, another Templar, was busy canvassing for the order. As early as 1128, he was in Toulouse, where Peter Bernard and his wife, Borella, gave themselves and everything they owned to the Templars, with the provision that, if they had children who wanted to join the order, they would be allowed to.[2] Rigaud spent the next several years getting donations for the Temple, ranging from lands, tithes, and vineyards to "a shirt and pants" from a townswoman "and, after her death, her best cloak."[3] Hugh Rigaud can be found accepting donation charters in southern France and northern Spain through the 1130s.

However, unlike other monastic groups, the Templars had no system in place for receiving and maintaining the donations.[4] Remember, these mostly didn't come in the form of money, but goods. It's all very well to receive grants of fields, houses, vines, horses, old clothes, and even serfs, but these weren't things that could be put in an online auction for quick cash. Many of the gifts couldn't be used until the donor had died. Others consisted of a certain part of a harvest each year or so many cheeses.

The nature of the gifts to the order meant that the Templars needed to establish way stations of some sort to receive goods and transfer them from Europe to the Crusader States. Great monastic houses like Cluny and Citeaux would establish priories, which were dependent houses, staffed with only a few monks. But the Templars were desperate for more men of fighting age to join in the battle, so new recruits were encouraged to leave for Jerusalem as soon as possible. That didn't leave anyone to direct the collection and processing of supplies.

The fact that the earliest Templars weren't all that well organized is evident by the various titles that Hugh Rigaud is given in the charters. Sometimes he is a brother of the society,[5] sometimes he is mentioned only by name, and sometimes by the title "procurator,"[6] which seems a good description of his work, although it's not listed in the Rule as an administrative position.

The Templars may have eventually established houses on the model of those already run by the **Hospitallers**, who had been receiving gifts in the West since just after the First Crusade (around 1100), particularly in Spain and the south of France as well as Italy.[7]

Eventually, the order organized itself in territories that were grouped according to the languages of the brothers. These were mostly French, Spanish, and English, with some Italians and Germans. The Templars never established themselves in Scandinavia but there were some commanderies in Hungary and Croatia.

OCCITANIA

For the purpose of this book, I'm defining Occitania as the southern part of France from the Atlantic Ocean on the west, along the Pyrenees Mountains in the south, roughly to Marseille in the east. I'm not interested in precision; the people who lived there in the twelfth and thirteenth century were used to flowing borders. The region was divided among various counties and lordships in the west and a loose attachment to the Holy Roman Empire in the east. The language, called Occitan or Provençal, was closer to that of northern Spain than to France.

The earliest recorded gift to the Templars is from Marseille. There is no indication of how the donor, William of Marseille, even knew about the order, but he gave them a church on the Côte d'Azur in the early 1120s. It shows how strongly the Templars believed in not living the soft life on the beach that they gave it back in 1124.[8] Actually, it's likely that the gift was more expensive to maintain than it was worth.

It wasn't until after **Hugh de Payns** had secured papal approval for the order that the donations in Occitania started rolling in. This was due in large part to the promotional activity of Templar brothers Hugh Rigaud and Raymond Bernard. After the **Council of Troyes** they spent several years traveling through the region drumming up support. While Hugh worked north of the Pyrenees, Raymond concentrated on Spain and Portugal.[9]

Between about 1130 and 1136 Hugh Rigaud seemed to be everywhere in the south. Either on his own or with other brothers of the Temple, he received donations, bought land, and established commanderies.[10] The amount of organization this implies makes me think that Hugh must have been a court official in his previous life.

Hugh Rigaud was present in 1132 when one of the most powerful families in the region, the Trencavels, gave the Templars the services of a person, Pons the Gascon, along with his family.[11] Pons had a house and other property near the town of Carcassonne, which the Trencavels promised never to harass.[12]

Members of this family were strong supporters of the Templars in those early years and their prestige in the area meant that others were encouraged to donate, as well. In 1133, the families of Bernard de Canet and Aymeric of Barbaira gave the Templars the castle of Douzens, which was to become a major commandery in Occitania.[13] More importantly, Aymeric and his brother William Xabert gave themselves to the Templars. They did not agree to serve right away but at some future date, and if they weren't able to, the Templars would get one hundred sous.[14]

These families continued to give land to the Templars for at least twenty years and perhaps longer.[15]

Hugh de Rigaud vanishes from the records in 1136, presumably because he died. His successor was Arnold of Bedocio. Arnold came from Catalonia and so there was no problem with language when he came to Occitania. Arnold lived at the commandery at Douzens but continued the work of acquiring more property in the area. He received the donation of Hugh de Bourbouton that would become the other great commandery in Occitania, Richerendes.[16]

As in other regions, most of the Templars living at the commanderies came from the region. Young men were sent east as soon as they could be ready and older or infirm recruits stayed behind to provide the fighting men with provisions.

CROATIA AND HUNGARY

Templar commanderies first began appearing in Croatia a few years after the **Second Crusade** (1148–1150). At the same time, the first Hospitallers were also established there.[17] It's not at all clear what prompted this, although it's possible that the master of the Templars in France, Everard de Barres, who accompanied the army of Louis VII, saw the need to protect pilgrims taking the route through Croatia on their way to the Holy Land and the lords there agreed.[18]

By 1169, the pope had given the Templars the old Benedictine monastery of Vrana. The only catch to this gift was that the Templars had to house any papal legates who happened to be passing through along with their sometimes large entourages. The bishop of Zagreb, Prodanus, also gave the Templars property in and around Zagreb which had no strings attached since the bishop already had a place to sleep there.[19]

In 1173, Bela III became king of Hungary and Croatia. Instead of allying himself totally with the Byzantine Empire, as earlier kings had done, Bela looked to the West. He was a strong supporter of the Third Crusade (1189–1192) and took an oath to go on crusade himself, although he never did.[20] In 1185, Bela sent ambassadors to Philip II, the king of France, asking for the hand of the king's sister, Margaret. Bela had been "lured by the honor of an alliance with the ancient house of the kings of France and by the good reputation for religion and wisdom of this princess."[21] Margaret was the widow of Henry Plantagenet, "the Young King" whose death had made **Richard the Lionheart** heir to the throne of England. She and Philip agreed to the marriage and she returned with the ambassadors to Hungary.

Bela III died in 1192 and was succeeded by Emeric, his son from a previous marriage.[22] Margaret, widowed again, with no children of her own, sold her dower. Then "she took the cross and, bringing a fine company of knights, came with the Germans to Syria and arrived at Tyre."[23] She died shortly after, presumably not in battle. The chronicler doesn't mention any Templars in her company but it would have been strange if there hadn't been any.

The highest responsibility ever accorded to a Templar was in Croatia when, in 1217, King Andrew II went on crusade and, instead of taking the Templars with him, left them in charge of the kingdom. Pontius de Cruce, Grand Master of Hungary and Croatia, governed the countries from the commandery in Vrana.[24]

It is intriguing that, while there must have been native Templars and Hospitallers, most of the commanders in Croatia were French or Italian.[25] Croatian Templars also served in other countries, bringing to mind the lines from the ceremony of reception into the order warning that Templars went where they were posted.[26]

THE BRITISH ISLES

While King Henry I is reported to have given gifts to the Templars, it was his successor, Stephen, who donated the first land in England. Stephen was Henry's nephew and the son of Stephen-Henry, the count of Champagne who had died while on his second crusade.[27] Stephen's wife, Matilda, was the niece of the heroes of the First Crusade, Godfrey of Bouillon and Baldwin I. The king and queen were already predisposed to give what they could to aid in the defense of the Holy Land. Matilda gave the first donation in 1135, in honor of her father, Eustace, count of Boulogne, who had almost become king of Jerusalem when his brother Baldwin had died.[28] Stephen confirmed the donations of his vassals and then gave property himself.

Although the Templars were in existence in England from at least 1135 and certainly before, the first master of the Templars in England we know of is Hugh of Argenten in 1140.[29]

In 1185, the Templars took a census of their properties in England. This document has survived and shows that the Templars' property was much like that of other religious houses. They had fields and flocks of sheep, tithes from churches and rents from land and houses. They were as much a part of the community as the monks and nuns of traditional monastic orders. In the town of Bristol, the weavers' guild even had their chapel in the Templar church.[30]

In Ireland the Templars held most of their property in the east after the land was conquered by King Henry II of England. Henry gave the first gift of land in 1185. The Anglo-Norman settlers in Ireland followed his lead and by 1308 "the Irish lands were the third most valuable of all the Templar holdings and worth over L400 a year."[31]

The master of the Templars in Ireland was one of the financial overseers of the Irish exchequer. Although the native Irish probably saw the Templars as part of the English invasion, the master seems to have acted as a mediator between the Irish and the English from time to time.[32]

Apart from collecting the usual tithes and rents in Ireland, the Templars also used their land to breed and raise horses for the knights.[33]

At the time of the first Templar foundations, Scotland was an independent nation, although the royal family was tied to that of England through intermarriage. King David I (1124–1153) gave the Temple the tithes of the church in Renfrewshire.[34] He must have given them other property but most of the charters have been lost. There doesn't seem to have been a master for Scotland at the beginning, all administration coming from England.

The most important commandery in Scotland was Balantrodoch, just south of Edinburgh. It was not a wealthy community; most of the income was from sheep and a water mill the Templars operated. In the partial list of preceptors of the commandery, all the names are Norman.[35]

Evelyn Lord comments that "We know less about the Templars in Scotland than elsewhere in the British Isles. . . . Perhaps because of this a panoply of myth has developed around them that has obscured reality and cloaked them in mystery."[36]

We shall look at the myths and mysteries later in this book.

SPAIN AND PORTUGAL

Many of the earliest and largest donations to the Templars came from the Iberian Peninsula. This is not surprising. The rulers of Aragon, Navarre, Castile, and what would soon be Portugal had been slowly retaking territory from the Moslems for over four hundred years. The crusading fervor focused on Jerusalem had increased interest in the struggle nearer to home. One of the earliest Iberian gifts to the Templars is from Queen Teresa of Portugal, daughter of Alfonso of Castile. She gave them the castle of Saur with all the surrounding lands.[37] Presumably, she intended them to maintain it personally and supply warriors in her battles against the Moors.

In 1122, when few, if any, had heard of the Order of the Temple, Alfonso I, king of Aragon, had founded a military confraternity at Belchite.[38] It wasn't as structured as the Templars and other military orders would be and it was under the control of the king, not a bishop. Members could join for a limited time and could participate in the spiritual benefits without fighting.

"The *cofradía* of Belchite is clearly a military religious institution, composed of brothers who defended Christendom against its Muslim enemies. Anyone rendering this meritorious service or any other assistance in the form of pilgrimages, donations of alms, bequests of horses and weapons, and bequests to houses of captives, received indulgences. In addition, the members of the confraternity could retain any lands they had captured from the Muslims."[39]

It's unlikely that Alfonso had heard about the Templars when he founded the order. This is an indication that the crusading ideal of fighting for God was leading to the formation of military orders not just in Jerusalem. The Templars might have become so popular and so widely imitated because they filled a long felt need.

Unlike the gifts from other parts of Europe, which were intended to produce funds and supplies for the support of the Templars in the Latin kingdoms, the donations in Spain and Portugal were often fortified castles. Often these were either on the borders of Moslem Moorish territory or even inside it. The Iberian rulers expected the Templars to fight the Saracens on their own doorstep, not on the other side of the sea.

In 1130, the count of Barcelona gave the Templars the castle of Grañena. This was "in my frontier opposite the Saracens."[40] It's clear that the count expected the Templars to defend the castle and participate in the reconquest of Spain. This was many years before the Templars were assigned the defense of border castles in the Latin kingdoms.[41]

The Templars don't seem to have been eager to take on a war on two fronts. They were pulled into the defense of Spain eventually, partly through the will of King Alfonso of Aragon, who left his entire kingdom to the Hospitallers, the Church of the Holy Sepulcher, and the Templars, to share. All three of the heirs eventually settled for large donations rather than control of Aragon.

The Templars were the last to do so. As part of the settlement with the new ruler, Raymond Berengar, count of Barcelona and "lord of Aragon," they acquired several castles in Spain, a tenth of all the royal income from taxes and judicial fees, and a thousand *solidos* a year. Count Raymond also promised them one-fifth of all land conquered from the Moors, if they took part in the expeditions. Raymond Berengar encouraged the Templars to build new castles and promised not to make a treaty with the Moors without their approval.[42]

The Order of the Temple was now firmly committed to the Spanish cause.

---

1 The best study of this is Stephen D. White, *Custom, Kinship and Gifts to Saints* (University of North Carolina Press, 1988). For a more specific study, Barbara H. Rosenwein, *To Be the Neighbor of St. Peter: The Social Meaning of Cluny's Property, 909–1049* (Cornell University Press, 1989).

2 Marquis d'Albon, *Cartulaire Général de l'Ordre du Temple 1119?–1150* (Paris, 1913) p. 12, no. 18.

3 Ibid., p. 14, "camisiam et bracas et, ad obitum suum meliorem mantellum."

4 I am grateful to Professor Malcolm Barber for pointing this out to me. Private correspondence, July 18, 2006.

5 "Fratris societatis Templi Salomonis," Albon, p. 25, no. 33.

6 Ibid., p. 45, no. 62. "Procurator" is actually a cross between a lawyer and a business manager.

7 Helen Nicholson, *The Knights Hospitaller* (Woodbridge, Eng.: Boydell and Brewer, 2001) p. 9.

8 D'Albon, pp. 1–2, charter 1.

9 Ibid., pp. 7–8, charters 10 and 11. See below, "Spain and Portugal."

10 *Cartulaires des Templiers de Douzens* ed. Pierre Gérard et Élisabeth Magnou (Paris, 1965) charters A 1, 21, 36, 38, 40, 115, 171, 185, 186, C 1, 4, 5, 6, 7, 8, 9, 10, 11.

11 Douzens, charter A 171, p. 158.

12 I think there is more to this story, but the charter is all we have.

13 Douzens, charter A 1, p. 3

14 Ibid., charter A 1, p. 5.

15 I'm not sure if the William Sigari de Canet, who witnessed a charter in 1170, is a relative or just from the same place. Douzens, B 71, p. 246.

16 Dominic Sellwood, *Knights of the Cloister: Templars and Hospitallers in Central-Southern Occitania c. 1100–1300* (Woodbridge, Eng.: Boydell and Brewer, 1999) p. 67.

17 Leija Dobronic, "The Military Orders in Croatia," in Vladimir P. Goss, ed., *The Meeting of Two Worlds: Cultural Exchange between East and West during the Period of the Crusades* (Kalamazoo, MI: Medieval Institute, 1986) p. 432.

18 For Everard de Barres, please see chapter 15, **Grand Masters 1136–1191.**

19 Dobronic, p. 433. (The bishop may have dropped by for dinner now and then, though.)

20 Ibid., p. 432.

21 Eudes Rigord, *Vie de Philippe Auguste* ed. and tr. M. Guizot (Paris, 1825).

22 Some sources say his brother.

23 The Continuator of William of Tyre, in *The Conquest of Jerusalem and the Third Crusade* tr. Peter W. Edbury (Ashgate, Aldershot 1998) p. 143.

24 Thomas of Spalato, *ExThomae Historia Pontificum Salonitanorum et Spalatinorum, Monumenta Germania Historia Scriptores*, ed. G. H. Pertz, Vol. 29, p. 578. "Sed accersito quodam Pocio, cui erat magister milicie domus Templi per regnum Hungarie, comsisit ad manus eius custodiam et tutelam ispius castri."

25 Dobronic, p. 435. I found no more information on this but would like to know if anyone has done more research.—

26 Ibid., p. 437.

27 See chapter 4, **Hugh, Count of Champagne**.
28 D'Albon, p. 86, charter no. 123.
29 Evelyn Lord, *The Knights Templar in Britain* (London: Longman, 2002) p. 16.
30 Lord, p. 119.
31 Ibid., p. 138.
32 Ibid., p. 140.
33 Ibid., p.141.
34 *The Charters of David I*, ed. G. W. S. Barrow (Woodbridge, Eng.: Boydell Press, 1999) p. 164.
35 Lord, p. 145.
36 Ibid., p. 143.
37 Ibid., p. 7, no. 10.
38 Alan Forey, *The Templars in the Corona of Aragon* (London, 1973) p. 15.
39 Theresa M. Vann, "A New Look at the Foundation of the Order of Calatrava," in *Crusaders, Condottieri, and Cannon: Medieval Warfare in Societies around the Mediterranean*, ed. Donald J. Kagay and L. J. Andrew Villalon (Leiden, Netherlands: Brill, 2003) p. 110.
40 Marquis d'Albon, p. 25, charter no. 33, "in mea marchia contra Sarracenos."
41 Forey, p. 16.
42 D'Albon, pp. 204–5, document 314, November 27, 1143.

CHAPTER NINE

The Life of a Templar, According to the Rule

I n the first days of the order, while their numbers were still few, the Templars seem to have lived by the same Rule as the canons at the Church of the Holy Sepulcher, where they first found shelter. But at the **Council of Troyes**, along with recognition as a quasi-monastic order, the Templars also received a list of seventy-nine rules detailing how they should conduct their lives. The collection of these rules is known as the Rule.

This first Rule was written in Latin, but most of the monks couldn't read Latin. Actually, only a few of them could read at all. So, shortly after the council, the Rule was translated into French. Very soon after the first translation, new problems arose that weren't covered in the original list and the Rule was expanded until, by the middle of the thirteenth century, the Templars had almost seven hundred separate directives covering every aspect of their lives![1]

No one could keep track of all of these and the knights weren't expected to. The commanders of each geographical region had a copy of the list. Most of the knights, sergeants, and servants only knew as much as they needed to in order to do their work and follow the regulations for daily living.[2]

Many parts of the Templar Rule were the same as those for all monks. They were to attend the reciting of the monastic hours—matins, prime, terce, nones, vespers, and compline—although it was understood that they needn't learn the Latin; instead they were to recite a number of Our Fathers. They ate together in silence, listening to a devotional reading. They met once a week in Chapter, where assignments were given out and discipline administered. Monks were encouraged to confess their lapses, beg forgiveness, and take their punishment. If a monk was accused by others of infractions of the Rule and denied his guilt, then a mini trial would take place. The faults could range from tearing one's habit on purpose or hitting another Templar to patronizing a brothel or converting to Islam. The penalties ranged from extra fasts to having to eat on the floor in the infirmary to outright expulsion from the order.

Templars were not allowed to own anything individually and to carry money only for immediate needs while traveling or doing business for the order. If a Templar died and was found to have a hidden cache of gold or silver, "he will not be placed in the cemetery, but thrown out for the dogs."[3] If his hoarding was discovered while he was alive, he was immediately thrown out of the order.

Every article of clothing and equipment for the monks was specified, including the material. Only the "true" knights, those who were of noble birth and also had signed on for life, were allowed to wear the white cloak.[4] Sergeants, servants, and men who only signed up for a certain period wore either black or brown cloaks. Because of the heat in the eastern Mediterranean lands, Templars were permitted to wear linen shirts from Easter to All Saints' Day (November 1). Unlike other monks, they were permitted meat three times a week but not on Friday, when they ate "Lenten meat"—that is, fish or eggs.

Particular attention was paid to the military equipment of the Templars. Each knight was to have three horses and one squire to take care of them. And if the squire was serving without pay for the sake of charity, the knight could not beat him, no matter what he did wrong.[5] The knights were expected to oversee the care of their horses and equipment, checking on them at least twice a day.

Of course, all of this happened when the knights were residents in

Two Templars on one horse with the Beausant, the Templar standard.
(Matthew Paris © The British Library)

the Temple house, the commandery or preceptory. But it was understood that they would spend much of their time in the field. Among
the crimes that would merit immediate expulsion from the order were
running away from the battle or letting the standard fall. Here the
rules were different for the sergeants and the knights. If a sergeant or
servant lost his weapons, he was allowed to retreat without dishonor.
A knight, however, "whether he is armed or not, must not let the standard fall, but stay by it no matter what, even if he is wounded, unless
given leave."⁶

The Templars lived up to this. They were the first into battle and
the last to retreat. Of all the negative things said about them over the
years, no one ever questioned their bravery. The number of Templar
knights killed in battle was enormous.

This was probably the reason for two changes in the Rule. The Latin
form of the Rule forbid men who had been excommunicated by the
Church to become Templars. Often the reasons for excommunication

were those that **Bernard of Clairvaux** had given in his exhortation to the Templars: murder, rape, and theft. This was modified in the French to state that if the crime had been minor so that the man had only been forbidden to hear Mass, one might make an exception, if the commander of the house allowed it.

Of course, becoming a Templar might well be part of one's penance for murder. It was rather like a medieval Foreign Legion in that respect.

Another way in which the Templars differed from most monastic houses was that they had a very short probationary period for new recruits. The time between applying to become a Templar and acceptance into the order was originally left to the discretion of the commander or the Master and the other brothers.[7] But at some point any trial period seems to have vanished. This may be due to the desperate need for more fighting men in the East. There wasn't time to test the men either for understanding or for ability to cope with the lifestyle.[8]

This meant that, for many of the Templars, the only instruction they received was a list of rules recited to them on the day of their admission. This was made much of at the various **trials of the Templars** in the early fourteenth century, where it was shown that each man seemed to have had a slightly different introduction to the Temple.[9] However, all new recruits seem to have understood that there was a Rule and, in many commanderies, it was one of the books read aloud during meals, so they eventually learned what was expected of them.

Even if individual Templars or even remote Templar houses didn't follow or even know all of the rules, they existed, and in many copies. They weren't secret. Brothers who could read were given copies to study.[10] So if they were asked by one of the commanders to do something contrary to religion or decency, they would have known it wasn't official. Two of the faults that would earn a Templar immediate expulsion from the order were heresy and sodomy, and yet these were the most serious of the charges made against them in 1307.

This will be discussed more elsewhere in this book, but it's important to know that these were offenses forbidden by the Rule, along with killing a horse or letting the standard fall. Is it likely that the entire order broke those fundamental rules? Is it possible that such a thing could have been going on for years, with Templars traveling all over Europe, with no one finding out that they were secret heretics? The activities of the knights were known to the sergeants and the servants, many of whom were not members of the order but hired help.

These people lived in a society where one had to go into the desert and become a hermit to get a little privacy (and even that didn't always work). If the Rule of the Templars was being so flagrantly broken, someone would have found out and spread the word around long before **Philip the Fair** decided to accuse them.

---

1 There are a number of editions of the Rule of the Templars. The earliest I know of is Maillard de Chambure, *Règle et status secrets des Templiers* (Burgundy, 1840), then Henri de Curzon (see note 2 below). Laurent Dailliez did an edition in both Old and Modern French (Paris: Edition Dervy, 1972). A Modern French translation along with an introduction giving the social background of the Crusades is Alain Degris, *Organisation & Vie des Templiers: Sociologie Féodale d'Orient & d'Occident* (Paris: Guy Trédaniel, 1996). There is also an English translation, J. M. Upton-Ward *Rule of the Templars: The French Text of the Rule of the Order of Knights Templar* (Woodbridge, Eng.: Boydell and Brewer, 1992).

2 Henri de Curzon, *La Règle du Temple* (Paris: Librairie Renouard, 1886) p. xxvii.

3 Regle no. 225, "Il ne seroit mie mis en simittire, mais seroit jetes hors a chiens."

4 Regle no. 9, "Et a trestoz les freres chevaliers en yver et en este se ester puet, avoir blans mantiaus, et a nul nest otrie davoir blanc mantel."

5 Regle no. 33, "Et si celui escuier sert de son bon gré a la charité, le frere ne le doit batre por nule colpe que il face."

6 Regle no. 419, "Mais I frere chevaluers ne le porroit pas faire en tel aniere, ou fust armé de fer ou non: quar cil de doit laissier le gonfanon pour nule chose sons congié, ni par bleceure n p or autre chose."

7 Regle no. 7, "Ét de ci en navant soit mis en esprove seloc la provoiance du mestre et des freres."

8 A. J. Forey, "Novitiate in the Military Orders," *Speculum* Vol. 61, No. 1, Jan. 1986, p. 5.

9 Ibid., pp.10–17.

10 Forey, p. 13.

✳

CHAPTER TEN

Melisande,
Queen of Jerusalem

The second king of Jerusalem, **Baldwin II**, had the wisdom to marry not a bride imported from Europe, but an Armenian princess, Morfia, whom he met while he was ruler of the Armenian city of Edessa. The marriage seems to have been successful in all respects but one. Baldwin and Morfia had only daughters—four of them. As a matter of fact, many of the crusader states were inherited by women. Fortunately, they all seem to have been smart and strong. And the men around them, for the most part, were smart enough to let them rule.

Baldwin's eldest, Melisande, was the first of the new generation of rulers who had been born in the Latin kingdoms. Jerusalem was the only home she ever knew. On her mother's side, she had a rich heritage of an Eastern Christian culture. From her father she inherited a family network that covered the Crusader kingdoms and reached back to the royal families of Europe.

In a world where family loyalty was only exceeded by family betrayals, it's a pleasure to report that Melisande and her three sisters seem to have been devoted to each other. It was good that they had each other, for all four of them led tumultuous lives.

The second daughter, Alice (or Alix), married Bohemond II, the son of Bohemond, prince of Antioch, and Constance, sister of Louis VI of France.* Bohemond was about eighteen at the time of the marriage, tall, blond, and good looking.[1] Alice seemed destined for a happily ever after, when Bohemond was killed in battle, leaving Alice with a young daughter, named Constance for her grandmother. While it isn't part of the story of the Templars, it should be noted that Alice had no intention of letting anyone rule for her child. Over the years she tried several times to regain control of Antioch, even after young Constance was married to Raymond of Poitiers.[2]

The third sister, Hodierna, married Raymond, count of Tripoli, in about 1133. She had a daughter, Melisande, and a son, Raymond. The marriage went well for a time but the count apparently was extremely jealous and drove Hodierna crazy with his suspicions. In 1152, Melisande went to Tripoli to help her sister work out a reconciliation with her husband and then bring her back to Jerusalem for a visit. Shortly after, Raymond of Tripoli became the first known Christian victim of an **Assassin**. Hodierna became regent for her son, who was twelve at the time.[3] She governed Tripoli on her own for many years.

Yveta, the youngest, had the most traumatic childhood. At the age of five she was sent to be a hostage in exchange for her father, who had been captured by the Ortoqid Turk Balak. She was kept by the Turks until Baldwin could raise the ransom money. It may have been that experience, or the knowledge of her sisters' chaotic marriages and family entanglements, that made Yveta opt for the monastic life. That didn't mean she retired completely from the world. Her big sister Melisande built the convent of Bethany for her, at the supposed site where Jesus raised Lazarus from the dead. Abbess Yveta became powerful in the church and also at the court of Jerusalem.[4]

Baldwin was content to have his younger daughters marry locally to increase the ties between the Crusader states, but his eldest,

---

*You may remember Constance. She dumped her first husband, **Hugh of Champagne**, while he was on pilgrimage. He became a Templar in 1125. So they both wound up in the Holy Land.

Melisande, was heiress to his kingdom, Jerusalem, and for her he needed someone who was not only a proven battle leader, but also outside the constant family squabbles among those same states. He settled on **Fulk of Anjou**.

Baldwin had met Fulk when the count made a pilgrimage to Jerusalem in 1120 and had been impressed with him. By 1127, when Melisande was old enough to marry, Fulk was a widower with children of her age. Baldwin sent his constable, Gautier de Bures, to Anjou with an offer of marriage and a kingdom. This was the same party that included **Hugh de Payns** on his journey to recruit more men for the Templars.

Fulk liked the idea and returned with Gautier, to the great joy of the populace.[5] At the time, Fulk was still on the sunny side of forty, Melisande about eighteen. He was stocky and redheaded, not exactly a princess's dream man. It seems that Melisande wasn't thrilled with the match, especially after seeing the young, good-looking husband her sister Alice had snagged. However, she made the best of it.

King Baldwin died two years later, on August 21, 1131. When he knew he was dying, he had himself taken to the home of the patriarch at the church of the Holy Sepulcher, so that he could die as near as possible to the place where Christ was buried. At that time he formally called Melisande and Fulk with their year-old son and entrusted the kingdom to them.[6]

Unlike England a few years later, there was no protest against Melisande's right to rule. This is amazing because she was both a woman and quite young. Also, the crown of Jerusalem had up until then been decided by an election among the barons and the bishops. The choice had always been a relative of the conqueror of the city, Godfrey of Bouillon, but not the closest one. Baldwin II had been chosen over Godfrey's last surviving brother, Eustace of Boulogne.[7] So the fact that Melisande was accepted so easily was likely due to Fulk's military ability.

That doesn't mean that Melisande ever let her husband take over the kingdom. While he certainly took care of the defense of the realm, Melisande held court, in the original sense of hearing disputes and dispensing justice. She would have heard arguments over land rights among the nobility and the church and also cases of rape, murder, and treason.[8]

Melisande and Fulk were crowned on September 14, 1131.[9] Shortly afterward, the newly widowed Alice decided that her brother-in-law might rule Jerusalem, but he had no say in the regency of her daughter, Constance. She revolted against Fulk, putting Melisande in the position of having to favor her sister or her husband. She seems to have put the stability of the kingdom over sisterly love. Alice was defeated and retired to the town of Latakiya, although she would be heard from again.

However, Melisande didn't let Fulk have his way in everything. William of Tyre relates with great relish a story of how the queen was having an affair with her cousin, Hugh of Le Puiset.[10] The tale says that, one day at dinner, one of Hugh's stepsons accused him of being Melisande's lover and plotting to kill the king. The young man challenged Hugh to prove his innocence in combat. When the day came, Hugh was nowhere to be found. He was judged guilty and his lands forfeit.

Now, William of Tyre was three years old when all this took place so it's likely he learned all of this through local gossip long after everyone concerned was safely dead. It is certain that Hugh lost his lands and wound up in Sicily. What is intriguing is Melisande's role in all this.

If the story of the accusation is true then Melisande seems to have survived without any stain on her character. She either convinced everyone that poor Cousin Hugh was imagining the relationship or else Fulk and the rest of the court suddenly remembered that it was Melisande who was the legitimate heir and so it didn't really matter who fathered her children.

Without more evidence, we'll never know. It is certain that after the incident, Fulk deferred to his wife a great deal more. Melisande and her friends may have taken this opportunity to let him know that they were in charge.

Fulk died in a hunting accident in 1143, leaving two sons, Baldwin III, age thirteen, and Almaric, age nine.[11]

Instead of remarrying, Melisande retained control of the government. She made it clear that she wasn't a regent but queen in her own right, ruling alongside her son. William of Tyre, who was generally nasty about women who exercised power, was very positive toward her ability as queen. He said that she maintained the government and ruled competently, by right of law.[12]

Melisande ruled for herself and her son with no complaints until Baldwin was in his early twenties. He was tired of being a king in name only and mounted a rebellion against his mother. They agreed to divide the Kingdom of Jerusalem in half but after a few weeks Baldwin decided to take it all. He besieged his mother in Jerusalem until she gave in and retired to her property in the region of Nablus.[13]

She was soon back, but more subdued. Mother and son eventually reconciled and she regained some power, issuing charters of donations to various religious institutions.

Melisande also intervened to return land that the Frankish invaders had taken from native Christian owners. Her Armenian heritage made her sympathetic to the rights of the Monophysite Christians, whose ancestors had never left the Holy Land.[14] She made donations to the Greek/Syrian hospice of St. Sabas in Jerusalem.[15]

In 1161 Melisande suffered what seems to have been a stroke, which left her unable to participate in government. She lingered for several months, dying on September 11. Her sisters Hodierna and Yveta cared for her in her last days.[16]

So, what does Queen Melisande have to do with the Templars?

When most people think of the Templars and the Crusader States, a very masculine society comes to mind. It's true that the Latin kingdoms were constantly either at war or anticipating one. But it was not a world of men. For some reason, more female than male babies survived in that place and time. And, of course, the number of young men killed in battle was much higher than the average for western Europe. So, by default, for much of the two centuries of the kingdoms, women were the inheritors.

Most of these women married men who could wield a sword and

lead an army. But they were often widowed young with underage children. Once they left the battlefield, the Templars found themselves in a world run by women. In order to understand the order, it's necessary to know more than just the highlights of their military exploits but also the society that they were a part of.

A specific example of this is Philip, lord of Nablus. Philip was the son of Guy of Milly and, like Melisande, had been born in the East. He first appears in the documents in 1138. For most of his life he was a soldier and an important part of the defense of the country. He was also one of the few people who stood by Melisande throughout her struggle with her son. He married and had three children. Then, in 1166, he decided to join the Templars. He gave them a large part of his land, which was now near the Egyptian border. In August 1169, he became Grand Master.[17]

But even as Grand Master of the Templars, Philip of Nablus was clearly more devoted to the land of his birth than to an international order. In 1171, he resigned as master so that he could go to Constantinople on a mission for King Almaric. He died there on April 3, 1171.

When the Templars are studied as an independent group with only military or financial ties to the countries they lived in, it results in an incomplete picture. Philip of Nablus lived a full life as a military leader and royal adviser before he joined the order. He was very much a part of the political life of the Kingdom of Jerusalem. His story shows that becoming a Templar was a natural progression for a man in later years, perhaps growing fearful for the state of his soul but unwilling to turn his back on a society in which he was still needed.

Without knowing what that society was, we can't understand the Templars.

ONE of the rare treasures left from Melisande's reign is her psalter, or prayer book. It was created by the monks of the Church of the Holy Sepulcher, probably around 1140.[18] It is beautifully illustrated and it not only gives images from Jerusalem at the time, but also a portrait of

"The Harrowing of Hell," the Melisande Psalter. Fulk and Melisande are on the right.

(The British Library)

Melisande and Fulk, clearly showing the difference in their ages. It is interesting to note that the king and queen are dressed in the Byzantine style, rather than that of European royalty.

---

1 Regine Pernoud, *Les femmes au temps des Croisades* (Paris: Stock/Laurence Penoud, 1990) p. 76.

2 William of Tyre, *Chronique*, ed. R. B. C. Huygens, 2 vols. Corpus Christianorum Continuatio Mediavales 63 (Turnholt, 1986) pp. 623–24 (13, 27). William calls Alix an "insane woman." For the life of Alix see Thomas Asbridge, "Alice of Antioch: A case study of female power in the twelfth century," in Peter Edbury and Jonathan Phillips, eds., *The Experience of Crusading, Volume Two: Defining the Crusader Kingdom* (Cambridge University Press, 2003) pp. 29–47.

3 Ibid., vol. 63A, pp. 786–87 (17, 19).

4 Pernoud, pp. 87–88.

5 William of Tyre, p. 593 (14, 24).

6 Ibid., vol. 63A, p. 625 (13, 28).

7 Joshua Prawer, *The Crusaders' Kingdom: European Colonialism in the Middle Ages* (London: Phoenix Press, 1972) p. 96.

8 Ibid., p. 120.

9 William of Tyre, pp. 633–34 (14, 2).

10 Ibid., pp. 641

11 Ibid., p. 711 (15–27).

12 Ibid., "reseditque rengi potestas penes dominam Milissendem deo amibilem reginam, cui iure hereditario competebat."

13 Ibid., pp. 777–81 (17, 13–14).

14 Prawer, p. 222.

15 Ibid., p. 224.

16 Bernard Hamilton, "Queens of Jerusalem," in Derek Baker, ed., *Medieval Women* (London: Blackwell, 1978) p. 156. My sisters might take note of this example of family devotion, just in case.

17 Malcolm Barber, "The career of Philip of Nablus in the kingdom of Jerusalem," in Peter Edbury and Jonathan Phillips, eds., *The Experience of Crusading, Volume Two: Defining the Crusader Kingdom* (Cambridge University Press, 2003) pp. 60–75, for the full story of Philip's life. Barber suggests that Philip was elected after the king, Almaric (Melisande's younger son) put pressure on the Templars. If so, it would indicate that the Templars were not as autonomous as they have been seen.

18 Hamilton, op. cit.

❈

CHAPTER ELEVEN

Fulk of Anjou, the Queen's Husband

Fulk, count of Anjou, came from a family that was both militant and eccentric. His father, Fulk Rechin, was count of Anjou and Touraine. Fulk's mother, Bertrada, was the scandal of Christendom. When her children were still quite young, she ran off with Philip I, king of France, who dumped his first wife for her. No amount of threats, not even excommunication, could separate the couple. They had three children together, including a daughter, Cecilia, who married Tancred, count of Tripoli, and would have many encounters with her half brother when he became king of Jerusalem.[1]

Unlike his parents, Fulk had a fairly quiet and apparently happy first marriage to Eremberga, the heiress to the county of Maine. They had four children: Geoffrey, Hélie, Sybilla, and Matilda. Before Fulk left for Jerusalem, he saw to it that Geoffrey married the daughter of Henry I of England. Sybilla had already married Thierry, count of Flanders. Matilda, who had briefly been married to Henry, crown prince of England, was widowed when he drowned in the disaster of the White Ship. She entered the convent of Fontevraud.[2] Hélie seems to have died young. These family connections were to be important to the Latin kingdoms for the next three generations.

In his mid thirties, after the death of his wife, Fulk went on a pilgrimage to Jerusalem, where he first encountered the Templars. He was very impressed with them.

> Fulk, count of Anjou . . . became very anxious to seek reconcilia-
> tion with God and procure his salvation. He devoted himself to
> penance for the crimes he had committed and . . . , he set out for
> Jerusalem, where he remained for some time, attached to the
> Knights of the Temple. When he returned home, with their con-
> sent, he voluntarily became their tributary, and paid out to them
> thirty livres a year in the money of Anjou. So by divine inspiration
> the noble lord provided an annual revenue for the admirable
> knights who devote their lives to the bodily and spiritual services
> of God, and rejecting all the things of this world, face martyrdom
> daily.[3]

Fulk was in his late thirties when the embassy came from **Baldwin II** asking him to leave his home and children for the crown of Jerusalem and the hand of its eighteen-year-old heiress.

It is not recorded how long it took Fulk to decide.

He left the county in the hands of his son, Geoffrey, a year younger than his new fiancée. Geoffrey's wife, Matilda, was eight years older than her new husband and had already been an empress. The young count may have been envious of his father's luck.

One of the men who brought the invitation to the count was **Hugh de Payns**, whom Fulk must have known well from his stay with the Templars in Jerusalem. Hugh was at the beginning of his tour of England, Flanders, and France in a search for support for the new order. The knowledge that the soon-to-be king of Jerusalem was already in favor of the Templars could only have encouraged Hugh.

Fulk confirmed his donation to the order before he went to Jerusalem to marry **Melisande**.[4]

Melisande was probably aware of who Fulk was, even though she had been about ten when he had lived in Jerusalem. Whatever her private feelings were, she seems not to have protested the match. William of Tyre writes, "Fulk was a redhead . . . faithful, gentle, and unlike most of that coloring, affable, kind and merciful."[5] Perhaps kindness won out over looks. The two were married as soon as Fulk arrived. As a wedding present, Baldwin gave them the towns of Tyre and Acre. They repaid him by producing a son almost immediately.[6]

Fulk was apparently content to hold the title of count until the death of Baldwin on August 21, 1131. Three weeks later he and Melisande were crowned king and queen of Jerusalem in the Church of the Holy Sepulcher.[7]

One of the first tasks before Fulk was to deal with his sister-in-law Alice, who was determined to rule Antioch for her young daughter. One of her supporters was the count of Tripoli, Pons, who just happened to be married to Cecilia, Fulk's half sister by his mother and King Philip of France. So his first battle was not fought against Saracens but family.[8]

Fulk won the battle and also managed to patch up a peace with the count and settle affairs in Antioch under a constable, although Alice was not a woman to stay down for long.

In 1133, Fulk heard that the Turks had invaded from Persia and were attacking Antioch. He was on his way to help them when he was met by Cecilia. She had come to beg him to come to the aid of her husband, who was being besieged in his castle of Montferrand by Zengi, the atabeg of Aleppo. Fulk apparently had no grudge against his sister for the attack two years before and detoured to help Pons. Now, William of Tyre says that Zengi learned that Fulk and his army were approaching and abandoned the siege.[9] However, Ibn al-Qalanisi reports that Zengi marched out to meet Fulk's army and nearly beat them, but they retreated.[10] At any rate, Pons and his men were rescued. The Templars are said to have been in the army at that time although they are not singled out for any important roles.

Fulk spent a lot of his time over the next year or so fending off attacks on the city of Antioch. His wife seemed to be keeping things running well enough in Jerusalem, but the nobles of Antioch really wanted their own ruler. The rightful heir, Constance, was still only nine years old, but desperate times call for desperate measures.

After many secret meetings between the king and the nobles, as well as the patriarch of Antioch, it was decided to send for Raymond, the brother of William, duke of Aquitaine. Raymond was about twenty and not yet attached. So a Hospitaller named Jeberrus was sent with letters asking Raymond how he felt about marrying a little girl and becoming lord of Antioch.[11]

Raymond thought it would be fine. According to law, the marriage couldn't be consummated before Constance was twelve but he must have thought the title was worth the inconvenience. Just to be sure that Constance's mother, Alice, didn't find out about these plans, the patriarch apparently convinced her that Raymond was coming to marry *her*.[12] You can imagine her feelings when Raymond arrived and was very hastily married to little Constance.

Fulk, however, was pleased to turn the military protection of Antioch over to someone else. He was learning that the politics of the Holy Land were not very different from those of Europe. He was also learning that the Moslem states were not alike, nor were they unified. In 1129, he was able to acquire the town of Banyas from the **Assassins**. They preferred paying tribute to the Franks to being at the mercy of Zengi.[13] He also established a treaty with Damascus to fight off the same Zengi who had come from Mosul to rule Aleppo and was rapidly carving out territory for himself from both the lands of the Franks and those of sects of Islam that did not agree with his.[14]

Fulk spent most of his time as king in warfare of one kind or another, against Moslems, Greeks, and relatives. He certainly must have used the Templars to help him, but there is almost no mention of them in surviving records. We are not even sure how Hugh de Payns died, although we know that it was in May 1135 or 1136.

Hugh's successor, Robert of Craon, had been a member of Fulk's entourage in Anjou. He witnessed a charter of Fulk's in 1127, in the Touraine,[15] but he seems to have been one of those who stayed in Europe to help with the establishment of local commanderies, for he was in France in 1133, where he is listed as seneschal of the order.[16] He must have been in France when he was elected Grand Master, for he was still accepting donations there in 1136.[17] He was in the East by 1139. He was also at the council of war held near Acre in 1148, long after Fulk's death.[18]

It may be that in the 1140s the number of Templars still wasn't very great. Even though membership had grown considerably since the **Council of Troyes** there still weren't enough men willing to become fighting monks. But it's more likely that there once was more information on the Templars during Fulk's reign that might have told us about the activities of the Templars. Time and war have destroyed many of the documents that the Templars in the Latin kingdoms undoubtedly preserved, as well as the royal records.

One indication that the Templars were earning respect in their chosen profession comes from an account of a siege in 1139. Robert, master of the Temple, fought under Bernard Vacher, one of the king's knights. They were chasing some Turks who had attacked a village. Thinking they had the enemy on the run, the soldiers "wandered off in all directions, shamelessly hunting out spoils of war instead of pursuing the enemy."[19]

The Turks took advantage of this and returned to the attack. Some of the knights hastily tried to organize a defense but the lines broke. The Christians were chased through rocky and harsh terrain outside of Hebron. Among the dead was "the most excellent man, a brother of the knights of the Temple, Odo of Montfaucon. His death brought tears and sorrow to all."[20]

While this defeat doesn't speak well for the crusaders, it is clear that the Templars were not in charge of the knights and they are not mentioned as being among those out looking for booty. The fact that Odo was considered an example of a brave and worthy knight is a sign that the Templars were becoming known.

So we can only assume that King Fulk trusted his former follower, Robert, as Grand Master of the Temple. He needed all the help he could get to maintain a semblance of order in his chaotic realm.

Fulk did not die in battle, as might have been expected. He was out riding with Melisande near Acre one fine autumn day when someone spotted a rabbit running across the fields. In a spurt of boyish zeal, the king joined in the chase. His horse threw him and he was then hit in the head by the saddle. He lay in a coma for four days before dying.[21]

Fulk's legacy to Jerusalem was a sound defense, supported by the Templars. He also left two children who would carry on his line and add to the incredibly complex web of family ties that caused conflicts even the Templars could not avoid.

---

1 *Les Grandes Chroniques de France* Vol.V, ed. Jules Viard (Paris, 1928) pp. 82–84.

2 Alfred Richard, *Histoire des Comptes de Poitou* t. IV 1086–1137 (Pau: Princi Negue, 2004) p. 163.

3 Orderic Vitalis, *The Ecclesiastical History of Orderic Vitalis* Vol. VI, ed. and tr. Marjorie Chibnall (Oxford: Medieval Texts, Oxford University Press, 1978) Book XII 29 (pp. 308–311). "Fulco Andegavorun comes postquam pacem cum Regis Anglorum pepigit, . . . desalute sollicius Deo nichilominus reconciliari peroptauit. Scelrum ergo fecerat penitentiam agerestuduit, . . . Jerusalem perrexit, ibique militibus Templi associates aliquandiu permansit. Inde cum licencia eorum regressus trributarius illis ultro factus est. Sic venerandis militibus quorum vita corpore et mente Deo militat, et comtemptis omnibus mundanis sese martirio cotidie preparat, nobilis heros annum vectigal divino instinctu arogavit."

4 Marquis d'Albon, *Cartulaire Général de l'Ordre du Temple 1119?–1150* (Paris, 1913) pp. 5–6, no. 7.

5 William of Tyre, *Chronique*, ed. R. B. C. Huygens (Turnholt, 1986) CCCM LXIIIA Book 14, 1, p. 631. "Erat autem Fulco vir rufus . . . fidelis, mansuetus et contra leges illius coloris affabilis, benignus et misericors."

6 The marriage was in 1129. Baldwin III was born in early 1130.

7 William of Tyre, p. 634.

8 Ibid., pp. 635–37.

9 Ibid., p. 638.

10 Ibn Al-Qalanisi, *The Damascus Chronicle of the Crusades*, tr. H. A. R. Gibb (London, 1932) p. 222.

11 William of Tyre, pp. 640–41.

12 Ibid., p. 641. Since Alice was still in her early twenties, this wasn't that unlikely. But she wasn't the heiress.

13 Please see chapter 20, **The Assassins**.

14 René Grousset, *Histoire des Croisades et du Royaume Franc de Jérsualem* Vol. II (Paris, 1935) pp. 21–22; Ibn al-Qalanisi, pp. 259–60.

15 Malcolm Barber, *The New Knighthood* (Cambridge, 1994) p. 8.

16 Marquis d'Albon, *Cartulaire Général de l'Ordre du Temple 1119?–1150* (Paris, 1913) p. 44, charter no. 61.

17 Richard, p. 163.

18 Barber, p. 35.

19 William of Tyre, p. 683, "sed ad diversa incaute nimis tendentes, fugientium spoils magis quam stragi hosium insistebant imprudenter."

20 Ibid., "vir eximus, frater militia Templi Odo de Monte Falconis, omes morte sua merore et gemitu conficiens."

21 William of Tyre, pp. 710–11.

CHAPTER TWELVE

The Temple in Jerusalem

When the first crusaders conquered Jerusalem, they were eager to find and restore all the sites from the life of Jesus as well as places important in the Old Testament. The problem was, they weren't sure where the places had been. By a process that was part tradition and part guesswork, they decided that the Dome of the Rock was the Holy Sepulcher or Temple of the Lord and the nearby mosque of al-Aqsa stood on the ruins of the Temple of Solomon, although it might have been Solomon's palace. Something "Solomon" was close enough. In the thirteenth century, Jacques de Vitry guessed that it had been named the Temple of Solomon simply to distinguish it from the other building.[1]

King Baldwin I of Jerusalem was the first of the Latin kings to live in the mosque. He seems to have been a terrible tenant. The chronicler of the First Crusade, Fulcher of Chartres, was embarrassed by the neglect. "It is now a matter of serious regret that the fabric of the roof needs repairing, ever since it passed into the hands of King Baldwin and our people."[2] By 1119, when King Baldwin II invited the Templars to share the space, it was falling down and bits of the building had been used for other projects, like the rebuilding of the Church of the Holy Sepulcher.[3]

The new rulers of Jerusalem were building everywhere. The canons

Temple Mount in Jerusalem. The gold dome at the rear is the Dome of the Rock, and the smaller one against the wall in the front is the al-Aqsa mosque, the site of the Templar headquarters. To the left is the space where the stables would have been. *(Albatross)*

of the Holy Sepulcher built the Church of the Ascension on the Mount of Olives. Like many churches, both in the Holy Land and in the West, it was octagonal in imitation of the Dome of the Rock.[4]

The Templars started refurbishing their mosque as soon as they could afford to hire the workers and materials. They built a new cloister, a new church, and the buildings necessary for group living, such as storage sheds, granaries, and a bathhouse.[5]

They didn't need to dig down to create the stables, though. That had been done during the Fatimid rule of Jerusalem. At least the Fatimids had cleared out the vaults of the ancient palace.[6] Whether the vaults had been built by Solomon or King Herod or someone else, they were ideal for the number of warhorses, packhorses, and camels that the Templars needed. In around 1170 Jewish pilgrim, Benjamin of Tudela, noted that three hundred knights lived in the Temple of Solomon. He also mentioned the stables, which he also thought were from the time of Solomon.[7]

Over the years the Templars were continually making repairs on the buildings. Nearby, they started building a new church. They also did work on the exterior walls of the Temple Mount and the Single Gate, leading to the stables, as well as the Hulda Gate, through which one could go into the underground rooms of the mosque.[8]

A thirteenth-century pilgrim described the Temple Mount: "On the right, as you came through the gates, was the Temple of Solomon, where the brothers of the Temple lived. Directly between the Precious Gates and the Golden Gates was the church of the Temple Domini. This was high up, above steep steps. Going up them, you came to another Pavement, . . . paved over its whole extent with marble and entirely surrounding the Temple church. The church was completely circular."[9]

If the Templars spent time in digging down to what they thought would be the secret inner chambers of Solomon's Temple as some people have suggested, they don't appear to have left any evidence of it. If Solomon had left a treasure, the Fatimids would have found it during their excavations. In their first years in al-Aqsa mosque, the Templars probably had all they could do just to keep the place from falling down on their heads.

While many of the surviving Templar and Hospitaller churches in the West are round or octagonal, both military orders also constructed more traditional churches. The Templar castles at Tortosa and Chastel Blanc were rectangular, as were many in England and France.[10]

When **Saladin** conquered Jerusalem in 1187, one of the first things he did was to eradicate any trace of the Templars. This meant tearing down the church they had just finished building and clearing out the space around and within the al-Aqsa mosque so that it could be used again. "East of the *qibla* they had built a big house and another church. Saladin had the two structures removed and unveiled the bridal face of the *mihrab*. Then he had the wall in front of it taken down and the courtyards around it cleared so that the people coming in on Friday should have plenty of room."[11]

I wonder if the people who think that the Templars found arti-facts in Jerusalem have been confusing it with the building done at Chateau Pelerin (Athlit). When they were digging the foundations for the church there, they uncovered a number of Phoenician coins. The chronicler at the time was intrigued by these pieces of money with unknown markings on them.[12] The chapel there was twelve-sided.[13]

The Knights of the Temple of Solomon only had the Temple for sixty-eight years. After the loss of Jerusalem, they moved their head-quarters to Acre.

1 Jacques de Vitry, *Histoire Orientale*, tr. Marie-Genviève Grossel (Paris, 2005) p. 179.

2 Quoted in Adrian J. Boas, *Jerusalem in the Time of the Crusades: Society, Landscape and Art in the Holy City under Frankish Rule* (London: Routledge, 2001) p. 79.

3 Ibid.

4 Denys Pringle, "Architecture in the Latin East, 1095–1300," in *The Oxford Illustrated History of the Crusades*, ed. Jonathan Riley-Smith (Oxford: Oxford University Press, 1995) p. 167.

5 Boas, p. 91.

6 Ibid., p. 93.

7 Benjamin of Tudela, in *Travels in the Middle Ages: The Itinerary of Benjamin of Tudela*, tr. A. Asher (Malibu: Panglos Press, 1987) reprint of 1840 edition, p. 83.

8 Boas, p. 48.

9 *Crusader Syria in the Thirteenth Century: The Rothelin Continuation of the History of William of Tyre with part of the Eracles or Acre Text*, tr. Janet Shirley (Ashgate, Aldershot, 1999) p. 17.

10 Pringle, p. 169.

11 Ibn al-Athir, in *Arab Historians of the Crusades*, ed. and tr. Francesco Gabrielli (Dorset, 1969) p. 164.

12 Oliver of Paderborn, *The Capture of Damietta*, tr. John J. Gavigan (University of Pennsylvania Press, 1948) chapter 5, p. 18.

13 Pringle, p. 169. There *could* be all sorts of mystical reasons for this or it could have something to do with the land the castle was built on, a promontory sticking into the sea.

CHAPTER THIRTEEN

The Popes Get Involved
(You Knew They Would)

O ne of the modern complaints about the Templars, and the basis
for many of the conspiracy theories about them, is that they
were solely under the direction of the pope, owing allegiance to no local bishop or lord. They've been made out to be a sort of papal mafia,
free to carry out secret missions to further some dark Vatican agenda.

It is true that the Templars were free of control by the local bishops. However, this is also true of the **Hospitallers**. Also, many of the
great monastic orders, such as the Cistercians, the Franciscans, and
the Cluniacs, were under the sole authority of the pope. All of these
orders had houses in many territories and this liberation from local
bishops was an attempt to keep the monks from becoming involved in
local politics. It didn't always work but that was the plan.

Let's look at the privileges that various popes gave to the Templars and other orders.

The first papal bull, or confirmation of privileges, for the Templars was issued by Pope Innocent II on March 29, 1139, ten years after
the **Council of Troyes** approved the Templar Rule. The delay in doing
this was entirely due to lack of interest. Innocent had spent most of his
papacy wandering through France because the Romans had elected
another man, Anacletus II, as pope and they refused to let Innocent

into Rome. He didn't get back there until Anacletus died.[1] The Templars weren't all that high on his agenda.

By tradition, papal bulls are known by the first few words in them. The bull of 1139 was titled *Omne Datum Optimum* or "every good gift." The gift in question is the Templars themselves, whom God had turned from lives of secular violence to the protection of Christianity.[2]

Normally such pronouncements from popes for monastic orders covered topics such as freedom from paying tithes to local bishops, the right of the monks to elect their own abbots, and other matters that freed the monastic orders from local domination. This liberty was extremely important as many monasteries and convents had become little more than outposts for the noble families of the region and their property was all too often used for the good of the clan, not the Church.

Omne Datum Optimum had somewhat different wording from the usual monastic grant. Most monks were not told, "You labor without fear in fighting the enemies of Christ. . . . Those things that you take from their spoils you may in all confidence convert for your own uses, and we forbid that you should be forced to give a part of them to anyone against your will."[3] Basically, this meant that the Templars could keep whatever they could grab from the **Saracens**. The average European monastery rarely, if ever, raised an army or plundered towns.

Booty was certainly a great motivator for soldiers and a handy way of getting operating funds, but this was to cause resentment later. The Templars were sometimes accused of letting their desire for plunder overcome common sense. A classic example is when William of Tyre accused Grand Master Bernard of Tremelay of charging into the city of Ascalon first and not letting anyone but Templars follow him because he didn't want to share. We don't know Bernard's side of this because he and all his men were killed in the charge.[4]

Other privileges were more conventional. The Templars were put under the protection of the Holy See. Any crimes they might be accused of were to be judged by the pope alone.[5] The men were to live a monastic life, "in chastity, without personal goods," and obedient to the master of the order. Only the master had the right to change anything in the Rule. No brother was to be allowed to leave the Templars for another religious order.[6] These privileges were shared by other monastic orders.

Innocent added his personal support for the order by donating an annual gift of one mark of gold.[7]

One thing that the Templars were not allowed to do was preach. This must have been comforting to the local priests and bishops.[8] Templars could have their own chapels but the implication is that Mass would be said by a local priest. However, an exception was when they went on their recruiting tours. At least there are many records indicating that they did preach in their efforts to gain new members.

The Hospitallers already had a similar charter, minus the booty, as early as 1113. In it they were given papal protection, freedom from local tithes, and the right to elect their own master.[9]

The right to choose the masters of the commanderies was an important one. The popes and the lay rulers of Europe had been fighting over this for many years. Princes wished to nominate their own candidates as abbots or bishops. Often these were relatives or men to whom they owed favors. The popes and many of the local churchmen were opposed to this for many reasons, the least of which was that the character and intelligence of the upper clergy went down when kings chose them. Bishops were supposed to be elected by the people and clergy of their communities, as was the pope. In practice, this was rarely the case and the popes were never able to completely free the election of bishops from the control of the lay rulers. But with multinational monastic orders, such as the Cistercians, Franciscans, Hospitallers, and Templars, they had much more success.[10]

All of these orders were resented at one time or another because of these privileges. But in 1144 the Templars received one more that really had local bishops and priests seeing red.

This bull is known as *Milites Templi* (Knights of the Temple). It acknowledges that keeping a monk in horses and armor costs a lot more than robes and sandals. Therefore the pope, Celestine II, encouraged all the faithful to donate as much as they could. Even more, to those who were willing to donate an annual amount, the pope would allow them to reduce by one-seventh the amount of any penance imposed on them.[11]

This part was acceptable to the bishops and priests, who could always just up the penance by a seventh if they felt like it. The serious problem came next:

> When the brothers of that Temple who have been sent to receive the contributions enter a city, castle or village, if any place should be under an interdict, churches should be opened once a year to greet them in a friendly manner in honour of the Temple and in respect for these knights, and divine offices should be celebrated without the presence of excommunicants.[12]

Popes and bishops had two weapons to convince Christians to obey Church law. The first was excommunication. That meant that the individual offender could not enter a church or receive the sacraments. It also meant that no other Christians could associate with him. It was hoped that the social problems this would cause would bring the person around.

The second was interdict. This was particularly useful against kings and other important people who found excommunication no more than an annoyance. The idea was to punish the people of the land for the sins of the ruler. So in a country under interdict, no masses could be said and no one married. People could not go to confession or receive communion. All that was permitted was baptism and, for those not personally excommunicated, last rites.[13]

What Pope Celestine was allowing meant that the people in a town under interdict could rush in once a year and take care of their sacramental needs. It also meant that the Templars received the little thank-you donations for this that would normally have gone to the local priests and which they hadn't been able to collect with the churches all closed.

One can see how this might cause bad feeling between the Templars and the local clergy. This only increased when the Templars acquired churches of their own, in direct competition with the native priests.

The right to build their own churches came the next year with the next pope, Eugenius III. In 1145, he issued the bull *Militia Dei* (Knighthood of God). Eugenius knew that this wouldn't go over well with the regular clergy, so he tried to sugarcoat the message to them:

> We believe that it does not escape the notice of your fraternity how useful to the eastern church, . . . how pleasing to God is the knighthood of God, which is called of the Temple. . . . And since they live in a religious manner and strive lovingly to attend divine services, we concede to them the right to recruit anywhere priests suitable for their service who are properly ordained and who have been granted permission by their bishop. To these brothers wishing to provide for this more fully *and not in any way wishing to diminish your parochial rights or remove tithes or offerings of burials* we grant them permission to build oratories in place adjacent to it [the Temple], where the household lives, in which to hear the divine services and indeed it is almost fatal to the souls of religious brothers to mingle with crowds of men and to meet women on the occasion of going to church.[14] (italics mine)

These three bulls are the main grants given to the Templars by the popes. For the most part, they contain nothing that other orders hadn't received. Especially in the twelfth century, the main focus of the popes in regard to the Latin kingdoms was to get men and money enough to keep the lands won by the first crusaders. The popes clearly state that the work of the Templars is for the preservation of the Christian states in the Holy Land.

However, it seems that both the Templars and the Hospitallers took advantage of their privileges. At the Third Lateran Council in 1179, at which Pope Alexander III presided, the complaints of the clergy were addressed. Both military orders were accused of accepting churches from laymen and of allowing people who had been excommunicated to receive the sacraments in their churches and to be buried in their cemeteries. Both orders had also hired and fired priests without the consent of the local bishop. In short they were sapping the authority of the regular clergy.[15]

The council decreed that the Templars and Hospitallers were to stop this at once or they would find themselves under interdict.[16]

This was not the last time that the military orders would be criticized for taking advantage of papal exemptions. The complaints in 1179 were against both the Hospitallers and the Templars but in 1207, Pope Innocent III felt the need to write to the Templars, specifically that they "are so unbridled in their pride that they do not hesitate to disfigure their mother, the church of Rome, which by its favours has not ceased to cherish the brethren of the knighthood of the Temple."[17]

One of the statements made about the Templars in some fiction and even in supposed nonfiction and documentaries, is that they had some sort of hold over the papacy that allowed them to get away with a great deal. There is nothing in the records that indicates this at all. The Templars were only one of several monastic orders that answered directly to the pope. And, as the council decrees and the letter from Pope Innocent show, if they abused their privileges, they would be slapped down.

It's quite possible that some, even many, of the Templars were arrogant and took advantage of the grant of opening their churches to those under interdict. They certainly did all they could to get funds.[18] Pride and greed were the two sins most often attributed to both the Templars and the Hospitallers. This problem grew directly from the gifts that the popes had bestowed on them in order to ensure the safety of pilgrims to Jerusalem.

But as to some dark and secret alliance between the papacy and the Templars, that is never even hinted at, not during their two hundred years of existence, not at their trial, not even after the trial.

Once again, twentieth-century writers seem to be the source of this myth.

1 This happened all the time. For a history of the medieval papacy see I. S. Robinson, *The Papacy 1073–1198, Continuity and Innovation* (Cambridge University Press, 1990), and Walter Ullmann, *A Short History of the Papacy in the Middle Ages* (Routledge, 2003). Anacletus came from a Jewish family but that wasn't the reason he wasn't accepted by northern Europe. It was politics.

2 *"Omne Datum Optimum"* in *The Templars*, tr. and annotated Malcolm Barber and Keith Bate (Manchester University Press, 2002) pp. 59–64. A very handy book for the most important Templar documents in translation.

3 Ibid., p. 60.

4 William of Tyre, 17, 27, pp. 797–99.

5 This was a large bone of contention when **Philip the Fair** ordered the **arrest and trial of the Templars** without the permission of Pope Clement V.

6 Barber and Bate, p. 61. This last was not followed when Master Everard de Barres left the Templars to join the Cistercians in 1153.

7 Charles-Joseph Hefele and Dom H. Leclercq, *Histoire de Conciles* Vol. V (Paris, 1912) p. 713.

8 Barber and Bate, p. 63.

9 *Cartulaire General de l'Ordre des Hospitaliers de S. Jean de Jerusalem 1100–1310*, Vol 1, ed. J. Delaville Le Roulx (Paris, 1894).

10 Although several of the Grand Masters of the Temple seem to have been elected because of their connections to rulers. See the two chapters on the Grand Masters.

11 I suppose this was rather like getting a tax break for charitable donations today.

12 Barber and Bate, p. 65.

13 I am grateful to Prof. James Brundage for clarifying interdict for me. His books *Law, Sex and Christian Society in Medieval Europe* (Chicago: University of Chicago Press, 1987) and *Medieval Canon Law and the Crusader* (University of Wisconsin, 1969) are both tremendously useful and interesting.

14 Barber and Bate, p. 66.

15 Hefele-Leclercq, p. 1095, "robur episcopalis authoritatis enervant."

16 Ibid., "Si vero Templarii sive Hospitalarii as ecclesiasticum interdictum venerint."

17 Quoted in Alan Forey, *The Military Orders* (London, 1992) p. 203.

18 Please see chapter 24, **Templars and Money**, for more on this.

❧

CHAPTER FOURTEEN

The Second Crusade

For some time the leaders of the crusader states had been telling anyone who would listen that they needed help, not just money, but manpower. The response was slow until the fall of the city of Edessa to the Seljuk atabeg Zengi in 1144. Edessa was the first of the crusader states to be settled. It had always been a Christian town and was still populated mostly by Eastern Christians. It was also the farthest east of the crusader lands, in an area difficult to defend and far from aid.

The shock of losing Edessa seemed to come at the right time to push the king of France, Louis VII, then in his mid twenties, to declare that he would take the cross. A couple of years before, in an altercation with Thibaud, count of Champagne, Louis had been carried away with youthful energy and set fire to a church in the town of Vitry. That was bad enough, but the church happened to be full of the townspeople, who had gone there for refuge.[1] About thirteen hundred people were burned alive.

Louis was a sensitive person and this weighed on his conscience. "Some say that the king, touched by pity and flowing with tears . . . soon decided on undertaking a pilgrimage to Jerusalem."[2]

Of course, Louis didn't act on this at once. But when Edessa was taken, and Pope Eugenius III issued a bull calling for the West to come to the aid of the Latin kingdoms, Louis was the first one to sign up. At his Christmas court in Bourges in 1145, he told his followers that he was going to answer the call.

The response was a big yawn and a return to holiday fun.

Louis didn't have the charisma to convince his friends to leave their homes for an arduous journey east. He needed someone to fire up the troops.

Pope Eugenius wanted to be the one to do it. He hoped to come to France and preach the crusade as his predecessor, Urban II, had done in 1095, but he was having some trouble with the population of Rome, who had thrown him out and reestablished the Senate, so the pope turned to his mentor, **Bernard of Clairvaux**.

So, on Easter of 1146, Louis and his court gathered at the Church of Mary Magdalene at Vézelay, France, to hear Abbot Bernard preach the crusade. Pope Eugenius had gladly sent along the requisite papal letters promising the remission of sins for any who went with the king and also protection for the families who stayed behind.[3]

Bernard's well-known gift of persuasion worked. The crowd was so thick that they knocked over the platform the king and abbot were standing on but, miraculously, no one was hurt. The enthusiasm was such that even the queen, Eleanor of Aquitaine, took the cross along with the wives of many of the nobles and at least one of Louis' unmarried female cousins.[4]

As preparations began for the great expedition, Abbot Bernard learned that another time-honored crusading custom was being observed: the massacre of Jews in the Rhineland. He rushed to Germany to put a stop to this. While he was there, he managed to convince the Holy Roman Emperor Conrad III of Germany to mount his own expedition.[5] In his fifties, Conrad was originally not interested in a trip to Jerusalem; he'd already been there.[6] He also had enough problems in his own land. But Bernard was too publicly insistent.

Templars were most involved with the French army. The master of the **Temple in Paris**, Everard de Barres, was prevailed upon to help with organizing the expedition. By April 1147, just before the king and his army left, Everard had gathered together 130 Knights of the

Temple, "wearing the white cloaks" to accompany the king and queen.[7] That means there were at least three times as many sergeants and servants of the Temple in Paris at the time, as well. That may have been the largest number of knights in one place outside of the Latin kingdoms and it must have been an impressive sight.

The Templars received donations great and small at this time, but not as many as one might think. In one charter, Bernard of Balliol gave the order land in England that he had received from Henry I. That was a good haul. But the only other charters from this time recorded in Paris are from Bartholomew, a dean of Notre Dame, who gave the Templars sixty sous, and from a woman named Genta, who gave them a mill, but only after she was dead.[8] She lasted a long time.

Despite the fact that Roger of Sicily had offered ships to take the French to the Holy Land, Louis and his army decided to take the land route, as the First Crusade had done. They left Paris on June 11, 1147, and arrived a few days later in Metz, where the general muster took place.[9]

THE TEMPLARS AND THE ARMY OF THE FRENCH

The Germans under Conrad had gone on ahead of the French crusaders and that created some problems for Louis and company, as the inhabitants of the lands they went through were running out of supplies and goodwill by the time the French arrived. Odo of Deuil, a monk from St. Denis who accompanied Louis, complains that the money changers cheated them and that the citizens refused to sell goods at a fair price. "Therefore, the pilgrims, unwilling to endure want in the midst of plenty, procured needed supplies for themselves by plunder and pillage."[10]

Master Everard de Barres wasn't present when this happened. He had been sent ahead to Constantinople, with other ambassadors, to help smooth the way for the demanding pilgrims.[11]

It was a difficult task. Odo blamed the Greeks for being greedy and treacherous but I imagine that even readers in his own time might have wondered what they would do if overrun by armed "pilgrims" who were furious at not being fed and sheltered at what they considered a fair price.

Everard won a great deal of praise for his calming of the situation when the French were attacked as they approached Constantinople. The emperor, Manuel, was smart enough not to let the crusaders inside the city but allowed them to camp outside and set up a market for them. He did invite Louis and Eleanor and few nobles in for an audience but was clearly relieved when the expedition left.

JOURNEY TO ANTIOCH

Once the French left Constantinople the Templars formed the front and rear guard for the army.[12] Everard must have felt that he was herding cats. It wasn't just Queen Eleanor and her women, although a later chronicler blamed them for coming along at all. "The wives could not manage without their maids, and thus in that Christian army, where chastity should have prevailed, a horde of women was milling about."[13]

There were also hundreds of hangers-on among the soldiers: pilgrims, craftsmen, families of the soldiers, camp followers, and others. These people, including the young and rowdy knights, had no discipline and many were weakened by illness and the weather, which was turning cold and rainy as winter approached.

The worst of the early setbacks occurred in January 1148 at Cadmus Mountain, in what is today western Turkey. If anyone still supposed that a pilgrimage was a good way to evade punishment for their sins, this would have convinced them that purgatory could provide nothing worse. They may have thought it easier to spend a few centuries there than endure another day on the crusade.

The army was already weakened by cold, lack of food, and disease when they came to Cadmus. The vanguard of the army crossed the mountain and began to set up camp on the other side. The rest followed, slowed by pack animals and panicky noncombatants. They climbed a narrow ridge up the side of the mountain with a steep drop on one side. Odo of Deuil describes the scene.

> Here the throng became congested while ascending, pushed forward, then crowded close together, stopped, and, taking no thought for the cavalry [*equo,* perhaps the horses] clung there instead of going ahead. Sumpter horses slipped from the steep cliffs, hurling those whom they struck into the depths of the chasm. . . . Moreover, the Turks and Greeks, their arrows preventing the fallen from rising again, thronged against the other part of our army and rejoiced at this sight, . . . They crossed against us, since they no longer feared the vanguard [that was already on the other side of the mountain] and did not yet see the rear guard. They thrust and slashed, and the defenseless crowd fell like sheep.[14]

One can imagine the horror of this, the rain making the path slick, the people pushing at each other, screams of horses and humans as they fell into the abyss. Added to this was the terror of the arrows flying toward them in the dimming January light.

Odo was sent back to find King Louis and tell him what was happening. The king and his men rushed to help but had to pass through the enemy in order to do so. Louis lost his horse and barely escaped. It was not a good day for the French.

It was generally considered that Geoffrey of Rancon, who was leading the vanguard, was responsible for the disaster. He had been told not to cross the mountain pass but to protect the body of the army.[15] Geoffrey was one of the queen's men, so she was also criticized and some said it was she who told Geoffrey to go on so that she and her ladies could settle in for the night. This is something that we'll never know the truth of. I imagine that everyone did what made sense to them at the time without realizing what might happen.

Actually, the only ones who came out of the episode looking good were Everard de Barres and the Templars. "The Templars and the Master of the Temple, Lord Everard of Barres, who should be revered for his piety and who furnished the army an honorable example . . .

protected the people as courageously as possible."[16] Actually, at the time, Everard was only master of the Temple in Paris. Robert of Craon was still master in the Holy Land. But as far as Odo was concerned, Everard was the one calling the shots.

The next day it was decided that the Templars would lead the army the rest of the way and that everyone would obey them, even the king. This worked well enough that the army made it to Adalia on January 20, 1148. To survive, many of the horses were slaughtered for stew. Only the Templars refused to kill their warhorses, although the men were starving. This also proved important, as it meant that the Templars were able to fight off another Turkish attack and convince the Turks that the army was stronger than was really the case. [17]

After this adventure, Louis was convinced to finish the journey to Antioch by boat.

ANTIOCH INTERLUDE

Louis and Eleanor's stay in Antioch doesn't immediately concern the Templars, but it did affect the course of the crusade and, indirectly, the future of France. They were welcomed to Antioch by Raymond, Eleanor's uncle, who had been brought from Poitiers ten years earlier to marry Constance, the heiress of Antioch, who was then aged about nine.[18] Constance, by the way, was Louis' second cousin, so it was a big family reunion.

Odo of Deuil lets us down as to what happened next; he stopped his chronicle before the arrival at Antioch. John of Salisbury was in Rome at the time and reported the gossip. "The king became suspicious of the familiarity of the prince with the queen and his nearly constant conversation with her."[19] Soon Louis decided he had stayed long enough at Raymond's court and prepared to head on for Jerusalem, but Eleanor had had enough. She told her husband that she'd wait for him in Antioch. Louis, known for having a short fuse, forced her to come with him.[20]

Although there is no evidence that the queen committed adultery, this story has entered the legend of Eleanor of Aquitaine, a person who is the center of as many myths and legends as the Templars. Personally, I doubt it. Eleanor may well have flirted with her uncle but she would have found it hard to do much more. She was surrounded by servants and companions most of the time. Also this episode was not mentioned three years later when Eleanor and Louis finally divorced. For Raymond's part, he would have remembered that he only held Antioch through his wife and not wanted to risk losing it. But hormones have often overwhelmed common sense. An affair is possible, but not proven. That didn't stop the rumors from flying, of course. As with the **Trials of the Templars**, sex always spices up a story.

Thinking that everything was fine, Everard de Barres left the king and his party and went to Acre to try to get together money to lend to

Louis and Conrad entering Antioch. A late and fanciful depiction of the Second Crusade.
(The British Library)

Louis.[21] The king had not counted on losing horses, property, or battles and found himself a bit short on cash. He was forced to write home to Suger, abbot of St. Denis and regent while he and the queen were gone. The letters sound very much like a college student who has just discovered the price of books and beer. "I couldn't have known how much it would cost in so short a time," he writes.[22]

Louis wound up owing the Templars thirty thousand *solidos*, about half his yearly income.[23] And he owed others beside the Templars. A special tax had been levied to pay for the expedition but, as leaders have discovered since, wars always run over budget, especially if you lose. This seems to have been the first time that a king of France entered into an economic arrangement with the Templars. It was the start of a long and, ultimately, fatal relationship.

DISASTER AT DAMASCUS

While Louis was fretting at Antioch, Conrad of Germany was back in Constantinople, recovering from illness. Meanwhile Alphonse Jordan, count of Toulouse, who had been born in the Holy Land, arrived at Acre by ship with his forces.

After he recovered, Conrad arrived in Jerusalem a little ahead of the others. He stayed "in the palace of the Templars, where once the royal house, which is also the Temple of Solomon, was built."[24] After playing tourist for a while, Conrad went back to Acre, where he tried to convince his fed-up knights to stay long enough to attack Damascus. "For he had agreed with the king of that Land [Baldwin III] and the patriarch and the Knights of the Temple to take Damascus."[25]

We have accounts as to what happened next both from the Christian chroniclers and from Ibn al-Qalanisi, who was in Damascus at the time. Both sides agree that there was a truce in effect between Jerusalem and Damascus. Nur ad-Din, Zengi's successor, who had captured Edessa, was Sunni and answered to the caliph of Baghdad, while the majority of people in Damascus were Shi'ite and supported the Fatimid caliphs of Egypt. The Damacenes feared Nur ad-Din as much as the crusaders did. So there is some confusion about why Louis and Conrad were advised to invade the city.

It was a warm day in late May 1148 when the army set out. King Baldwin III was in the lead, since he knew the way, followed by Louis, with Conrad bringing up the rear.[26] They decided to besiege the city by going through the orchard that stretched out for miles to the west and north and up to the city walls. William of Tyre, who was in school in France at the time, says that they picked this route "so that the army would not lack for the convenience of fruit and water."[27]

The army had no chance to picnic, however, as it was attacked first by the peasants tending the orchards and then by cavalry from the city. However, the crusaders managed to reach the river and set up camp.[28] The next day there was a fierce battle. The end was undecided but the citizens of Damascus seemed to be getting the upper hand.

Now the two chronicles disagree. Ibn al-Qalanisi says that the Christians hid out in their stockades for a day or so because the defense was so strong that they couldn't go out without being bombarded by stones and arrows. Then, upon learning that Nur ad-Din was on his way to relieve the city, they went home.[29]

William gives a much more complicated explanation. He says that the citizens of Damascus bribed "certain of our nobles" to convince the army to move to the other side of the city where there was no water or fruit but a plain that was clear of trees and where the walls of the city were not as strong. The kings and the emperor were convinced. But when they got to the plain, they began to run out of food and when they tried to return to the orchard, they found that all the paths had been barricaded. Cut off from supplies, they were forced to return to Jerusalem.[30]

The end was the same in both versions. Damascus was not taken by the crusaders. Personally, I think that Ibn al-Qalanisi is probably closer to the truth. Baldwin, Louis, and Conrad found themselves outnumbered with rumors of more defenders arriving soon. The story of bribery sounds too much like an excuse. One reason I think so is that there is no record of these nobles who purposely gave bad advice ever being punished.

William doesn't name names, but someone in the disgruntled army must have decided to blame the Templars for the failure. John of Salisbury heard of it in Rome shortly after. He writes, "Some say that the Templars were responsible; others that it was some who wished to return home; but the king always took pains to exonerate the brothers of the Temple."[31]

In 1147, the year before the king of France and the emperor of Germany were beaten at Damascus, English and Flemish crusaders had landed in Iberia and taken the city of Lisbon. The Templars fought with King Alfonso and received both honor and all the church property in the city of Santarem.[32] German armies moved eastward into pagan lands with the cross and the sword.[33] Both these aspects of the Second Crusade were successful in terms of expanding the borders of Christendom. But what people remembered then, as most do now, was that the two greatest kings in Europe came back without having accomplished anything.

The crusade was a dismal failure so someone had to be blamed. Odo of Deuil felt that the Greeks had sabotaged the kings.[34] Others, like William of Newburgh, writing many years later, thought that the crusaders were too weighed down by sin to deserve to win. Henry of Huntington, who wasn't there either, agreed. He thought that they indulged in "open fornications, and even in adulteries . . . and finally in robbery and all sorts of evils."[35]

But it was more satisfying to make someone other than the crusaders guilty of their failure. Conrad was sure it was treachery. He mentioned the Templars, but also Baldwin III or the princes of Syria.[36]

People seemed to remember the Templars most. For all their hard work, despite their successes in Spain, they were still criticized. Why? I suspect that Bernard of Clairvaux and the Templars themselves had done their propaganda too well. They were the knights of Christ, pure and invincible. They should have been able to surmount any obstacle, even a disorganized and bickering army coming from Europe and feuding families in the East.

The trouble with being a hero is that you're not allowed an off day.

---

1 Yves Sassier, *Louis VII* (Paris: Fayard, 1991) p. 113.

2 Guillaume de Nangis, *Chronique*, ed. M. Guizot (Paris, 1825) p. 25.

3 Odo of Deuil, *De perfectione ludovici VII in orientum*, ed. and tr. Virginia Ginerick Berry (New York: Norton, 1948) pp. 8–9.

4 Ibid., p. 76. The unnamed cousin was saved by her relatives from being given in marriage to a Greek lord. This is one of those episodes that I really wish there were more information on.

5 Adriaan H. Bredero, *Bernard of Clairvaux: Between Cult and History* (Grand Rapids, MI: Eerdmans, 1996) p. 24.

6 Hans Eberhard Mayer, *The Crusades* (Oxford: Oxford University Press, 1988) p. 98.

7 *Cartulaire Général de Paris, Tome Premier 528–1180*, ed. Robert de Lasteyrie (Paris, 1887) charter no. 334, p. 307, "alba clamide inductis."

8 *Cartulaire Général*, nos. 321, p. 297, and 270, p. 265.

9 Sassier, pp. 162–63.

10 Odo of Deuil, Book III, p. 41, "Peregini ergo, in rerum abnudatia penuriam non ferentes, praedis et rapinus sibi necssaria conquirebant."

11 Ibid., Book II, p. 29.

12 Malcolm Barber, *The New Knighthood* (Cambridge, 1996) p. 67.

13 William of Newburgh, *The History of English Affairs, Book I*, ed. and tr. P. G. Walsh and M. J. Kennedy (Warminster: Aris & Phillips, 1988) pp. 128–29.

14 Odo of Deuil, pp. 116–17.

15 Ibid., pp. 122–23. Well, this is what Odo says.

16 Ibid., pp. 124–25.

17 Ibid., pp. 134–35.

18 Please see chapter 10, **Melisande, Queen of Jerusalem**.

19 John of Salisbury, *Historia Pontificalis*, tr. and ed. Marjorie Chibnall (London: Thomas Nelson, 1956) p. 52, "familiaritas principis ad reginam et assidua fere sine intermissione colloquia regi suspicionem dederunt."

20 Ibid., p. 53.

21 Sugerii Abbatis S. Dionysii, "Epistola" PL Letter 50, col. 1374–1375 "Dilectioni vestrae mandamus quaetenus ea qua Ebrardis magister Templi vobis mandaverit, certa habeatis. Nos siquidem ab Antiocha admuto pecuniam nobis necssariam seto Idus Maii Acaron misimus."

22 Sugerii, Letter 58, col. 1378, "Non enim video nec videre possum quomodo etiam per parvi temporis spatium in partibus illis permanere vel moran facere potuissem, nisi eorum praecedente auxilio et sustentations." There's more but you get the gist.

23 Sugerii, Letter 71, col. 1585. For fraction of income see Barber, p. 67.

24 Otto of Freising, *The Deeds of Frederick Barbarossa*, tr. Charles Christopher Mierow (New York: Norton, 1953) p. 102.

25 Ibid. It's interesting that Otto doesn't mention Melisande, who was still very much in charge in Jerusalem.

26 William of Tyre, Book 17, 3, p. 763. "Primusitaque cum suis Ierosolimorum rex, eo maxime quod locaram periciam . . . secundum et medium locum rex Francorum . . . tercium . . . imperator."

27 Ibid., Book 17, 3, p. 763, "tum ut expeditionibus fructum et aque non deesset commoditas."
28 Ibn al-Qalanisi, The Damascus Chronicle of the Crusades, ed. and tr. H. A R. Gibb (Dover, 2002; reprint from 1832) pp. 283–84.
29 Ibid., pp. 284–87.
30 William of Tyre, Book 17, 5–6, pp. 765–67.
31 John of Salisbury, p. 57, "quod alii Templariis diu imposuerunt; alii vero his quos amor parie revocabat; sed rex fratres Templi semper studiut excusare."
32 Quoted in Giles Constable, "The Second Crusade as Seen by Contemporaries," Tradition Vol. IX (New York: Fordham University Press, 1953) p. 235.
33 Mayer, pp. 99–100.
34 Odo of Deuil, pp. 109–45. Actually, the treachery of the Greeks is a thread running through the whole of Odo's chronicle.
35 Constable, p. 273.
36 Ibid.

PART TWO

The Glory Years

❖

CHAPTER FIFTEEN

Grand Masters
1136–1191

ROBERT THE BURGUNDIAN (DE CRAON), C. 1136–1149

The successor to Hugh de Payns, Robert of Craon is also known as "the Burgundian," but he seems to have roamed about a bit. He was certainly living at the court of **Fulk of Anjou** in the 1120s. Anjou has never been part of Burgundy. Some say that Robert was married but he left his wife to join the Templars. He may have stayed in Burgundy for a while before going overseas or he may have returned in 1133, when he accepted the gift of a village near the commandery of Bure on behalf of the Templars. At that time, he was listed as seneschal of the order.[1] He became Grand Master in 1135.[2] He was still in France a while later when he accepted the service of several men to be supported by Lord Bertrand de Balm.[3]

As you can see, the life of most Templars before they entered the order was rarely important enough to be noted with any certainty. Most of the evidence comes from charters that these men witnessed for others.

Robert was master during the time when many of the important papal concessions were made to the Templars, so his years in the West may have been useful. In 1139, Pope Innocent II in his bull *Omne Datum Optimum* informed the bishops that the Templars were under his protection.[4] That was also the year in which Robert led a "singularly rash and disastrous raid in the neighbourhood of Hebron"—the first engagement we know of in which the Templars participated.[5]

Robert also seems to have been the master who negotiated the agreement for a final settlement of the will of Alfonso I of Aragon and Navarre, in which he divided his kingdom among the Templars, the **Hospitallers**, and the canons of the Holy Sepulcher in Jerusalem.[6] The final agreement is addressed to him. All in all, he seems to have been the administrator that the order needed during the first years of its expansion, even though his military ability left something to be desired.

EVERARD DE BARRES, 1149–1152

Everard de Barres had the misfortune to be the master of the Temple in Paris in 1147, when King Louis VII decided to set off on the **Second Crusade**. The story of his experiences during that expedition is told in chapter 14.

Everard was elected while serving in the Holy Land, perhaps because of his exemplary behavior in protecting the pilgrims, including King Louis and Queen Eleanor. In warfare, diplomacy, and piety he showed himself to be a model Templar.

After his election, he returned with Louis to France.[7] But Everard decided that he was not suited to Templar life. Perhaps he felt he'd had enough of the politics of the job. His motivations are not recorded but he retired from the order soon after coming back to Paris, despite the pleas of his seneschal to return to Jerusalem. It has been said that Everard eventually joined the Cistercians but I have not been able to find proof of this. I shall continue looking.

An odd side note on Everard is that he shows up in an epic written

three hundred years after his death. In the poem, *Saladin,* composed
in the middle of the 1400s, Everard's son, William de Barres, goes to
Jerusalem with King Philip II in 1191 and there meets his father, the
master of the Temple.[8] Now, Everard was long dead by 1191 and there
is no record of his ever having a son named William. But it is intriguing that this fairly obscure Grand Master should suddenly surface in a
work of fiction.

BERNARD OF TREMELAY, 1153

Bernard of Tremelay may have come from the Dole region of Burgundy.[9] That's all we know of him. He was elected Grand Master after
Everard de Barres decided to leave the Templars. It's not certain at
what time he took over the position or even if he was in the East at the
time of his election. However, he arrived in time for the battle of Ascalon, although he must have wished he hadn't.[10] On the night of
August 15, 1153, the king of Jerusalem was leading a force in an attempt
to take the city-fort of Ascalon from the Egyptians. During the attack
a wall of the city was breached. Bernard rushed to the spot and led the
Templars through the hole in the wall and into the city.

William of Tyre says that the Templars rushed in and refused to
let others follow since they wanted the booty for themselves. This gave
the Moslems time to reblock the wall. The Templars were trapped inside and all of them killed. The next day their bodies were hung from
the towers of Ascalon.[11] William was not there at the time and Ibn
al-Qalanisi, writing from the point of view of the citizens of Ascalon,
only mentions that the wall was breached. "At length the way was
opened to them to deliver an assault upon it at a certain point in the
city wall. Having battered it down, they rushed into the town, and a
great host were [*sic*] killed on both sides."[12] Of course, al-Qalanisi
wasn't there, either. So the only thing we can be certain of is that Bernard died in the fighting. The Templars were again without a Grand
Master.

ANDREW OF MONTBARD, 1154–1156

The fifth grand master of the Templars is one of the most illustrious, not because of anything he did but because of his connection to one of the best-known men of the twelfth century.

It's not certain when Andrew of Montbard was born, but he was the sixth child of Bernard, lord of Montbard, and his wife, Humberge. Two of his older brothers, Miles and Gaudry, joined the monastery established by their nephew **Bernard of Clairvaux**.[13] It's possible that Andrew may even have been younger than his famous nephew.

It's amazing that Andrew managed to hold out so long against the family pressure to enter monastic life. Bernard managed to convince all but one of his brothers and most of his uncles and cousins to join him at his abbey of Clairvaux. Eventually Andrew decided that he should also embrace the religious life. But rather than becoming a cloistered monk, spending his days in prayer, he decided to join the Templars. Whether it was his own idea or he was nudged by Bernard, I don't know. It's known that the two men were close and Bernard seems to have approved of his uncle's choice.[14]

There is some confusion about when Andrew went to Jerusalem. Sometime before 1126, **Baldwin II**, king of Jerusalem, sent two messengers to Bernard of Clairvaux. He explained that they were brothers of the Temple who wanted to get confirmation from the pope for their order and also a **Rule** to live by. The king begged Bernard to use his influence with the pope and the "princes of Christendom" to aid them. The two men sent by Baldwin were named Andrew and Gundemar.[15] This was before the trip made by **Hugh de Payns**.

Some authors have assumed that the Andrew mentioned was Andrew of Montbard. However, this isn't likely. Bernard's uncle wouldn't have needed a letter of introduction to his own nephew. Also, there's no mention of Andrew of Montbard in connection with the Templars before the 1140s. In 1148 "Ándreas de Muntbar," seneschal of the Templars, witnessed a gift from Barisan d'Ibelin to the Order of St. Lazarus.[16] That's the first mention of him that I've found.

It's more likely that Andrew joined the order in the rush to enlist after the **Council of Troyes** and by the 1140s had made his way up the ranks to become seneschal of the order.

Andrew apparently kept his nephew up-to-date with matters in Jerusalem, as two letters from Bernard to Queen **Melisande** prove. In the first, written sometime in the 1140s, Bernard tells her, "And if the praise of my dearest uncle Andrew is true, and I believe him implicitly, you will rule by the mercy of God both here and in eternity."[17]

The second letter voices Bernard's concern over reports he has received concerning Melisande's behavior, perhaps having to do with her unwillingness to give up power once her son, Baldwin III, had come of age. However, Andrew has written to Bernard to say that the gossip is false. "My uncle Andrew has happily intervened, and I can in no way disbelieve him. He writes saying better things of you, that you have behaved peacefully and mildly. You rule wisely and with wise counsel; have loved the brothers of the Temple and are friendly with them."[18]

At the same time, Bernard wrote to Andrew himself, lamenting the internal problems that were afflicting the Kingdom of Jerusalem. Andrew may have believed that Bernard's influence and charisma could bring the squabbling crusader families together, for he asked his nephew to come to Jerusalem. Bernard dithers on quite a bit before deciding that he really can't make a trip like that, even though he would dearly love to see Andrew again.[19]

He never did. Abbot Bernard died at Clairvaux in 1153, a year before Andrew became Grand Master.

Andrew may have been the seneschal of the Templars when he wrote these letters or still only a knight brother. It is clear that he was in the confidence of the queen and, like Philip of Nablus, who had not yet joined the order, was one of her supporters. Both Andrew and Philip appear as witnesses on Melisande's donations to St. Lazarus in 1150 and 1151.[20]

In the struggle between Melisande and her son, Andrew seems to have supported the queen and her younger son, Almaric. However, he was able to stay on the good side of Baldwin III, as well.[21] In 1155

Andrew witnessed one of Baldwin's charters to the abbey of Santa Maria of Josaphat and was a frequent witness to other charters of the king.[22]

Andrew was certainly a part of the **Second Crusade** from 1148 to 1150 and seneschal of the order by the end of it. In about 1150, he writes a plaintive letter to **Everard de Barre**, the Grand Master, who has returned with King Louis VII to France. Things are not going well in the Holy Land. Andrew tells Everard, "we are constrained on all sides by lack of knights and sergeants and money, and we implore your paternity to return to us quickly."[23]

Everard did return to Jerusalem, but not for long. Command didn't suit him and he became the first Grand Master ever to retire.[24] He was replaced by Bernard of Tremelay while Andrew of Montbard continued as seneschal.

Andrew's opportunity came in 1154, after the gallant but pointless death of Bernard of Tremelay at the siege of Ascalon.[25]

BERTRAND OF BLANCFORT, 1157–1169

As with many of the Grand Masters, nothing is known of Bertrand's life before he became a Templar. It is possible that he was of the same family who donated property to the Templars of Douzens. The land they gave was in the Aude Valley, north of Limoux in southern France, about twenty-five miles north of the Pyrenees.[26] Actually, the donation was made by someone who held the land for them. They just agreed to it.

Bertrand is not mentioned in any of the seven charters of the Blancfort—or Blanchefort—family to the Templars.[27] A misreading on these charters has led some people, not historians, to attach Bertrand to this family. They saw the name "Bernard de Blanchefort" on the charters of Douzens and, perhaps through wishful thinking, decided that it was just a misspelling of "Bertrand."[28] However, the two names are as different and distinct as "Kelly" and "Kyle" and are not used interchangeably. Bertrand's origins are not certain.

Bertrand had only been Grand Master for about a year when,

along with Odo of St. Amand, another future Templar and Grand
Master, he was captured by Nur-ad-Din at the siege of Banyas in June
1157.[29] He was released at the end of May 1159. So he spent his first two
years as leader of the Templars in captivity.

As Grand Master, he wrote back to Europe, giving the state of affairs and asking for aid for the cause.[30] A few of these letters survive.

The most dramatic event of Bertrand's tenure as Grand Master was
in 1168, when the Templars refused to help King Almaric on his expedition to Egypt. Almaric had long believed that control of Egypt, particularly the port of Alexandria, was essential to the safety of the Kingdom
of Jerusalem. Unfortunately, he had a treaty with Shawar, the sultan of
Egypt. Bertrand refused to allow the Templars to break the treaty.[31] The
campaign was a failure and forced Shawar to seek the protection of his
adversary, Nur-ad-Din, proving Bertrand correct. Relations between
the king and the Templars were not cordial during this time.

Bertrand of Blancfort died in 1169. His successor was much more
inclined to support the king, mainly because he had started out as the
king's man.

PHILIP OF NABLUS, 1169–1171

Philip of Nablus was born in the Holy Land. He was the son of Guy
of Milly and his wife, Stephania "the Fleming." The family probably
came from Normandy.[32] They settled in the town of Nablus in the
early 1100s and established a lordship there. Philip had two brothers,
Guy and Henry the Buffalo.[33]

As a young man, Philip was very much involved in the activities
of the court of **Melisande**, queen of Jerusalem. He supported her during the time she reigned for and with her son, Baldwin III. When
Baldwin decided he was old enough to rule on his own, Philip stayed
on the side of the queen. It was to Philip's town of Nablus that
Melisande retired after Baldwin had taken Jerusalem.

However, once Baldwin and his mother had come to an understanding, Philip began to appear on the king's charters as a witness,

meaning that he again had some position at court. So he must have been able to pacify Baldwin to some extent. In 1153, when the city of Ascalon was finally taken from the Egyptians, Philip was among the noblemen who fought for the king.[34] He must have been there for the disastrous charge that led to the death of Templar Grand Master Bernard of Tremeley (see page 000). But this didn't seem to deter him from joining the order, himself.

Sometime before 1144, Philip married a woman named Isabella. They had three children, Rainier, Helena, and Stephania.[35] Rainier, the only son, didn't survive his father, although he lived at least until 1168, when he witnessed a charter at the abbey of Notre-Dame of Josaphat.[36] In 1148, Barisan of Ibelin confirmed a donation made by Philip's maternal grandfather, Rainier of Rama, to the abbey of St. Lazarus, just outside Jerusalem. Philip was not one of the witnesses. However, the charter was signed at the chapel of the Templars with several of the brothers in attendance.[37]

Philip, still a layman, did witness a charter of Melisande's to the lepers of St. Lazarus in 1150.[38] But, it isn't until 1155 that we find Philip in connection with the Templars. In that year Prince Almaric confirmed a donation made by Philip, his brothers, and his wife and children, again to St. Lazarus. This donation was made in Jerusalem and may have been made at the Templar chapel, as the one of 1148 was. Here Andrew of Montbard, now Grand Master, and several other Templars are witnesses.[39]

This is not an indication that Philip was planning to join the order, for the Temple was used as a central meeting point in Jerusalem for many business transactions. It does assume that Philip was at least on speaking terms with the Templars.

Melisande died in 1161 and around that time, Baldwin III arranged for Philip to give Nablus to the Kingdom of Jerusalem. In exchange, Philip became lord of the Transjordan. It's not clear if this was a reward or a demotion. The Transjordan is the area to the east and south of the Dead Sea. Much of it is in modern Jordan. Part of Philip's territory probably included what is now the city of Amman and stretched down to the Red Sea.[40] It was larger than Nablus, but definitely frontier territory, on the caravan route between Alexandria and Baghdad. King Baldwin realized that the tolls the caravans and the Bedouins paid for a safe crossing were too lucrative to give up to Philip, so he kept them for himself. Philip got everything else, though, including the responsibility of defending the Syriac natives of the area from attack.[41]

Philip's decision to join the Templars is starting to make more sense.

Nevertheless, for a time at least, Philip of Nablus became Philip of Transjordan.

Two years later, Baldwin III died. As he had no children, his brother, Almaric, became king of Jerusalem. Almaric had been on Melisande's side in the battle for the throne and he was friendly toward the man who had not deserted her. He must have been attached to the whole family, for Philip's brother, Guy, was made seneschal of the kingdom.[42]

Philip joined the Templars on January 17, 1166, "probably on the death of his wife."[43] When he did so, he gave the northern part of the Transjordan to the order, including Amman and the area around it.[44] It must have been difficult for him to stay behind when the Templar master, Bertrand of Blancfort, refused to accompany King Almaric on his 1168 expedition to Egypt, for his lands bordered on those that Almaric wanted to conquer.

It was also about the time that Philip's daughter Helena died. It would be natural that being in the Templars would be important to a man who had lost so many people he loved. He could continue to serve his king but also his prayers and sacrifice could help the souls of his wife and daughter.

Philip did take part in the campaign in Egypt against the Kurd Shirkuh and his nephew **Saladin**.[45] When Bertrand of Blancfort died, it's possible that King Almaric influenced the election of Philip as Grand Master. On the other hand, the brothers of the Temple may have thought it would be a good idea to have a leader who got along with the king. There's no way to tell.

But Philip was Grand Master for only a short time. His loyalty to the king was stronger than his devotion to the Templars. He resigned in 1171 in order to return to the service of King Almaric, as an envoy to Constantinople. He apparently died there in April of the same year.[46]

Philip's family continued in their support of St. Lazarus. In 1183, Philip's grandson Humphrey of Toron gave the lepers twenty bezants a year for the soul of Lord Philip. No Templars were witnesses to this, but a Brother Guido **Hospitaller** was in attendance.[47]

Philip's career is not that unusual for a Grand Master, although only Everard de Barres also resigned. But he is not the only one to have been elected because he had a good working relationship with the secular rulers.

ODO OF ST. AMAND, 1171–1179

Odo (or Eudes) of St. Amand started his career in the court of King Baldwin III. On June 19, 1157, he was the king's marshal. Along with several other important members of the court and some Templars, he was taken prisoner by Nur-ad-Din at the siege of Banyas.[48]

On April 25, 1164, Odo of St. Amand was not listed as a Templar when he witnessed a charter of Almaric, king of Jerusalem, along with Philip of Nablus and others.[49] Soon after, as the king's butler, he was sent to Constantinople to escort Almaric's fiancée, Princess Maria, the grandniece of the emperor, back to Jerusalem. So, in 1165, Odo was clearly one of Almaric's trusted officials.[50]

It's not certain when Odo joined the Templars. It had to have been after Almaric's wedding. I wonder if he was chosen to be Grand Master by the king before he had even become a Templar. If so, like Henry II's nomination of Thomas Becket as archbishop of Canterbury at about the same time, it turned out badly.

For whatever reason, Odo of St. Amand became Grand Master on the retirement of Philip of Nablus. Odo's first challenge came from a "renegade Templar," a man named Malih, who was brother of the king of Cilician Armenia. Malih had apparently converted from the Eastern to the Western Christian beliefs and joined the Templars. This is the only mention I know of a native Christian becoming a Templar. At any rate, he didn't stay one for long. When his brother the king died, Malih went to Nur ad-Din for help. With the men he was given, Malih took the throne of Armenia from his nephew and threw the Templars out of the kingdom.[51]

It wasn't an auspicious beginning for Odo. Things got worse.

Some time later an envoy came to Jerusalem from the sect of the **Assassins**. He told King Almaric that the Assassins were tired of paying tribute to the Templars and **Hospitallers**. Instead, they would like to become Christian. William of Tyre says, "The king greeted the legates with a glad heart and granted the request, like the intelligent man he was."[52] I reserve judgment on that, but, again according to William of Tyre, the envoy was on his way back to Assassin territory when he was attacked and killed by a group of Templars.[53]

Upon learning that the Templars had ruined his treaty, King Almaric was furious. He went to his old friend Odo of St. Amand and demanded that the men in question be turned over to his justice.

Odo refused, saying that Templars could only be judged by the master and the pope. He sent word to Almaric that he had given the leader of the murderers, Walter of Mesnil, a penance and would send him to the pope for sentencing. This did not sit well with Almaric, who took a force to Sidon, where Walter was being held. He had the man dragged out, put in chains, and sent to Tyre. Presumably he died there.[54]

The friendship between Odo and King Almaric was at an end.

This story has often been repeated but it seems very strange to me. Some people say that it must, at least in part, be true because Walter Map wrote the same story at about the same time in England. However, in 1179, only two or three years after this was supposed to have happened, there was a council in Rome. Two of the delegates were William of Tyre and Walter Map.[55] Now Walter didn't say in his account, "I got this story over lunch with William." But it's just possible that William vented his annoyance about Odo's actions in this willing ear.

Odo might have been in a lot more trouble over this episode but Almaric died soon after this, leaving his son, Baldwin IV, a sick boy of thirteen, to handle the problem.

Since William, archbishop of Tyre, wrote almost the only chronicle of this time, we are often stuck with his prejudices. William was not a fan of Odo's. He thought the Templar master arrogant and didn't attempt to show him in a good light. However, I don't think he would make up all of the stories about Odo. I'm just not sure which parts are true.

In 1179 in an encounter with **Saladin**, Odo "led a charge of knights that by its sheer force so divided the Christian ranks that the battle was lost."[56] William certainly blamed him. "Among those of our men captured here was Odo of St. Amand, the Master of the Knights of the Temple. He was a bad man, proud and arrogant, having the spirit of fury in his nostrils. He neither feared God nor respected men."[57]

William adds with relish that Odo died in captivity in Egypt a year later.

It's not good to make an enemy of a man with a pen.

ARNOLD OF TORROJA, 1181–1184

Arnold was an experienced Templar who had been master of "Provence and parts of Spain" since 1167.[58] He came from Catalonia and may have entered the order there but all information on him comes from his years in Provence.

Even before he joined the Templars, Arnold gave the order vineyards and other property from his family estates near Lerida. His brother, Raymond, was also a patron of the Templars although he did not become one.[59] Arnold was a Templar by 1173, when he was present to receive a donation from Pons of Molièes of two serfs, part of the rent of a villa, and some forestland. Arnold is listed first in the charter, but still as a "knight of the Temple" not an official of the order.[60] By 1179, he is definitely the master of the Knights of the Temple in Provence and parts of Spain, according to a bull from Pope Alexander III confirming all the property of the Templars in Provence and Spain.[61]

The date of this confirmation is March 1179, which makes me wonder if Arnold was a Templar representative to the Third Lateran Council, taking place that month. Odo of St. Amand was busy fighting Saladin. Perhaps no one else could be spared from the East. As I mentioned above, William of Tyre was there, along with the bishops of Bethlehem and Caesarea.[62] One of the laws decided at this council concerned the complaints of the bishops about how the Templars, Hospitallers, and other exempt orders were abusing the privileges the popes had given them.[63] What better time for Arnold to make sure that the rights of Templars in Spain were all spelled out?

And, when the Templars may have been looking for a Grand Master who hadn't been attached to the court of Jerusalem, Arnold would have been a good choice. He was someone who had done well in another area in which fighting was going on and he knew how to deal with the authorities.

Whatever the thinking, Arnold was elected.

One of his first and more unpleasant duties was to be part of a group that included the master of the Hospitallers, the patriarch of Jerusalem, and various nobles that went to Antioch in about 1181 to convince the prince of the city, Bohemond, to give up the mistress he had moved in with and return to his wife. Bohemond promised to do everything the committee asked, but as soon as they were gone, went home to his mistress and threw the noblemen out of town instead. He was excommunicated and Antioch put under interdict but the prince was not daunted.[64] So much for the fear of hell.

Whatever the Templars were expecting when they elected Arnold, there isn't much mention of what he did as Grand Master. In the three years Arnold served, Saladin made further inroads into the Latin kingdoms and poor Baldwin IV became more and more debilitated as his leprosy progressed. As things got worse, Arnold, along with Heraclius, the patriarch of Jerusalem, and Roger des Moulins, master of the Hospitallers, went on a tour of Italy, France, and England in an attempt to get more support for the East.[65]

Arnold never returned to Jerusalem. He died in Verona in 1184, just before the storm broke.[66]

GERARD OF RIDEFORT, 1185–1191

After the professional competence of Arnold of Torroja, the Templars went back to someone with more personality than sense (in my opinion).

Gerard of Ridefort was either Flemish or Anglo-Norman. He came to Jerusalem to seek his fortune and by 1179 was marshall of the Kingdom of Jerusalem.

According to one story Gerard had first served Count Raymond of Tripoli. As a reward, he expected to be given an heiress in marriage. However, Raymond decided to have the woman Gerard had selected marry a Pisan merchant instead, possibly one he owed money to. Gerard was understandably piqued, especially because a Pisan merchant didn't have the social status of a landless knight. It was a dreadful insult. Sometime later, rather than try for another heiress, Gerard joined the Templars.[67] This story may not be true, but Gerard did have a deep dislike for Raymond of Tripoli.

The new Templar immediately got involved in local politics. It happened that Raymond of Tripoli had been declared guardian for the child king Baldwin V, successor to the leper Baldwin IV. Little Baldwin died before he turned six. His mother, Sybilla, the daughter of King Almaric, was considered by many to be the heir to the throne. Others, including Raymond of Tripoli, thought that he could do a better job. Guess which one Gerard supported?

Along with the patriarch of Jerusalem, Gerard saw to it that Sybilla was crowned ruler along with her husband, Guy of Lusignan. But the Latin kingdoms were now divided and Saladin, whose power was growing, would make the most of this.[68]

The first sign of the rift was when Gerard encouraged King Guy to take an army up to Tripoli and make Raymond obey him. Wiser heads prevailed but Raymond had already made a treaty with Saladin in anticipation of an invasion by Guy.

By the spring of 1186, Guy and Sybilla were willing to make peace with Raymond. Gerard, Roger, the Hospitaller master, along with several others were sent to see if Raymond would make peace. At the same time, Saladin's eldest son, al-Afdal, took advantage of the truce with Raymond to bring some men into Tripoli. There are various explanations for this, depending on which side is telling the story. In the end, Gerard learned about the Moslem incursion and went to the nearest Templar house, where he gathered up some eighty knights, along with ten Hospitallers and forty men from the royal garrison.[69] According to the chroniclers, both the Hospitaller master and the marshal of the Temple tried to stop Gerard from attacking. He overruled them.

It was called the Battle of Cresson Springs. Roger des Moulins, master of the Hospital, was killed, as were all the royal soldiers and most of the Templars.[70]

Gerard of Ridefort survived.

The next day a few men, including Gerard and the archbishop of Tyre, went to see about burying the bodies. Halfway there, Gerard turned back, "so painful and grievous were his wounds from the day before."[71] Count Raymond had to come out to help with the cleanup, "very sorrowful and greatly angered at the events of the day before, and all because of the pride of the master of the Templars."[72]

The one good thing that came out of this was that King Guy and Count Raymond were reconciled. Gerard doesn't seem to have had any sort of reprimand from either of them.

The main source for this event is an unknown chronicler who clearly favored Raymond. Perhaps Gerard didn't always advise unprepared attacks. It was his surviving them that made him look bad.

When Saladin learned that Count Raymond had made peace with the king, he attacked the count's main city of Tiberias while Raymond was away. Raymond's wife, Eschiva, sent word to him that she was holding out in the citadel of the city but that things were desperate.

Reading the Moslem and Christian accounts of what happened next, I am struck by the similarity of the reasons for battle, at least according to the authors of that time. King Guy is advised to "go and chase Saladin out of the kingdom at the first opportunity; [because] he was in the early days of his kingship and, if he let himself appear a fool in the eyes of the Saracens, Saladin would take advantage of him."[73] Saladin's advisers told him "to pillage the Frankish territories and to give battle to any Frankish army that might appear in their path, 'Because in the East people are cursing us, saying that we no longer fight the infidels but have begun to fight Moslems instead. So we must do something to justify ourselves and silence our critics.'"[74]

The Battle of Hattin and the loss of the True Cross. *(The British Library)*

So, being men, they took their armies and rode out to save face.

What became known as the Battle of Hattin took place on July 4, 1187. The crusaders were defeated in the space of six hours. King Guy, Gerard of Ridefort, and many others were captured. The True Cross, which was always carried into battle, was either lost or taken by Saladin.[75]

All the Templars taken at Hattin were beheaded—except Gerard of Ridefort.

The Grand Master was held captive for about a year, during which time Saladin's armies rolled over the country, taking Jerusalem and many of the coastal cities. It was said that Gerard traded his freedom for the Templar fort at Gaza. It surrendered at his order.[76]

Once released, Gerard joined King Guy in the attempt to regain the city of Acre. This time he did not survive. He died in battle in October 1191.

Were his rash acts and bad advice responsible for many of the decisions that led to the fall of Jerusalem? It's hard to say. The anonymous chronicler seems to blame him. But if so, then why did the king keep taking him back? Why did the other Templars still obey him? Maybe he was slandered. Or maybe he was such a vibrant and charismatic person that he could get away with a lot.

Now the spotlight moves from the master of the Temple to the two men who still define crusading in the minds of most people, **Saladin** and **Richard the Lionheart**. But first we need to set the stage.

---

1 Marquis d'Albon, *Cartulaire Général de l'Ordre du Temple 1119?–1150* (Paris, 1913) p. 44, charter no. 61.

2 Alfred Richard, *Histoire des Comtes de Poitou* t. IV 1086–1137 (Pau: Princi Negue, 2004) p. 163.

3 Albon, p. 87, charter no. 125.

4 Rudolf Heistand, *Papsturkunden für Templaer und Johanniter* (Göttingen, 1972) pp. 205–10.

5 T. S. R. Boase, *Kingdoms and Strongholds of the Crusaders* (London: Thames and Hudson, 1971) p. 86.

6 Albon, no. 145, p. 102; no. 72, p. 55; no. 324, pp. 204–5. Also see chapter 24, **Templars and Money,** and chapter 8, **Go Forth and Multiply.**

7 Malcolm Barber, *The New Knighthood* (Cambridge University Press, 1994) p. 70.

8 Suzanne Duparc-Quioc, *Le Cycle de la Croisade* (Paris, 1955) p. 203.

9 Barber, p. 74.

10 Please see chapter 16, **Between the Second and Third Crusades (1150–1191)**.

11 William of Tyre, 17, 27, pp. 797–99.

12 Ibn al-Qalanisi, *The Chronicles of Damascus* ed. and tr. H. A. R. Gibb (London: Dover, 2002; reprint of 1935 ed.) p. 316.

13 Barber, p. 71.

14 See below for Bernard's letters to and about Andrew. It's too bad that we don't have Andrew's to him.

15 Albon, *Cartulaire Général de l'Ordre du Temple 1119?–1150* (Paris, 1913) p. 1.

16 "Fragment d'un Cartulaire de l'Ordre de Saint Lazare, en Terre-Sainte," *Archives de l'Orient Latin Tome* II (Paris, 1884) p. 126, charter VI.

17 Bernard of Clairvaux, Opera Omnia Vol. 1 (Paris, 1889) col. 435, letter CCVI, "et si verum est testimonium quod de vobis perhibit charissimus aunclus meus Andreas, cum multum credimus, et hic, et in eaterum Deo miserante regnabatis."

18 Ibid., cols. 374–375, letter CCLXXXIX. "Sane intervenit Andreas charissimus avunculus meus, cui in nulo decredere possimus, scripto suo nobis significans meliora; quod scilicet pascifice et mansuete te habeas; fraters de Templo dilegas et familiars habeas."

19 Ibid., cols. 572–574, letter CCLXXXVIII.

20 "Fragment d'un Cartulaire," 129–130, charters VIII and X.

21 Barber, p. 70.

22 *Chartes de Terre Sainte Provenant de L'Abbaye de N.-D. de Josaphat*, ed. H-François Delaborde (Paris, 1880) p. 70.

23 Quoted in Barber, *Knighthood*, p. 70.

24 Ibid.

25 William of Tyre.

26 *Cartulaire des Templiers de Douzens*, ed. Pierre Gard and Elisabeth Magnou (Paris, 1965) charter 200, pp. 172–73.

27 Douzens charters, A 38, 185, 200, 207; C 4, 5, 6; see also chapter 41, **The Cathars**.

28 Michael Baigent, Richard Leigh, and Henry Lincoln, *The Holy Blood and the Holy Grail* (Random House, 1982) p. 514, note 12.

29 Wiliam of Tyre, book 18, 14, p. 831. Also in al-Qalanisi, *The Damascus Chronicles of the Crusades*, ed. and tr. H. A. R. Gibb (Dover, 2002; reprint of 1932 ed.) pp. 366–67.

30 *Recueil des historiens des Gaule et de la France* Vol. XVI, ed. Bouquet, et al. (Paris, 1878), letters 123, 125, 144, 145.

31 For more on this, please see chapter 16, **Between the Second and Third Crusades (1150–1191)**.

32 Malcolm Barber, "The career of Philip of Nablus in the kingdom of Jerusalem," *The Experience of Crusading, Vol. 2, Defining the Crusader Kingdom* (Cambridge Universtiy Press, 2003) pp. 62–63.

33 I have no idea why he was called that and would give a great deal to find out.

34 William of Tyre, *Chronicon*, Vol. II, ed. R. B. C. Huygens (Turnholt, 1986), book 17, 21, p. 790.

35 Barber, "Philip of Nablus," p. 63. Stephanie had the misfortune to lose three husbands, the last being the Raynald de Chatillon who was personally beheaded by **Saladin**.

36 H.-François Delaborde, ed., *Chartes de Terre Sainte provenant de l'Abbaye de N.-D. de Josaphat* (Paris, 1880) p. 84, charter no. 36.

37 "Fragment d'un Cartulaire," 126–27. One of the witnesses was Andrew of Montbard, future Grand Master.

38 Ibid., p. 129.

39 Ibid., p. 134.

40 Barber, "Philip of Nablus," p. 68.

41 Ibid., p. 69.

42 Ibid., p. 71. No, I don't know what happened to Henry the Buffalo.

43 Barber, *Knighthood*, p. 106.
44 William of Tyre, p. 1146, "dominus Arabie Secunde, que est Petracensi . . . et Syrie Sobal qui locus hodie Montis Regalis . . . utque trans Jordanum."
45 Ibid., 19, 22, p. 893.
46 Ibid., 20, 22, p. 942, "Philippum Neapolitatum, qui iam militia Templi deposuerit magistrum."
47 "Fragment," pp. 146–47, charter no. 29.
48 Wiliam of Tyre, book 18, 14, p. 831. Also in al-Qalanisi, *The Damascus Chronicles of the Crusades*, ed. and tr. H. A. R. Gibb (Dover, 2002; reprint of 1932 ed.) pp. 366–67.
49 "Fragment," p. 140, charter no. 22.
50 William of Tyre, p. 913, book 20, 1.
51 Ibid., p. 949, book 20, 26.
52 Ibid., p. 954, book 20, 30. "Rex autem legationem eorum leto animo et grantator suscipiens, petitionibus eorum, sicut vir discretissimus erat."
53 Ibid., p. 955.
54 Ibid.
55 Peter W. Edbury and John Gordon Rowe, *William of Tyre: Historian of the Latin East* (Cambridge University Press, 1988) p. 23 for Walter Map, *De Nugis Curialem*.
56 John L. La Monte, *Feudal Monarchy in the Latin Kingdom of Jerusalem* (Cambridge, MA: Medieval Academy of America, 1932) p. 219, William of Tyre XXI, xxix.
57 William of Tyre, 1002, book 21, 28. "Capti sunt de nostris Odo de Sancto Amando militia Templi magister, homo nequam, superbus et arrogans, spiritum furoris habens in naribus, nec dem timens nex ad hominem habens reverentiam." I don't know what the part about fury in the nostrils means. Odo may have just had allergies.
58 Dominic Sellwood, *Knights of the Cloister: Templars and Hospitallers in Central-Southern Occitania c. 1100–c. 1300* (Woodbridge: Boydell, 1999) p. 155.
59 Alan Forey, *The Templars in the Corona of Aragon* (Oxford University Press, 1973) pp. 55–56.
60 *Cartulaire des Templiers de Douzens*, ed. Pierre Gérard and Elisabeth Magnou (Paris, 1965) p. 246, charter no. B 74.
61 Rudolph Hiestand, *Papsturkunden für Templer and Johnniter* (Göttingen, 1972) pp. 288–90.
62 Charles-Joseph Hefele and H. Leclercq, *Histoire de Conciles*, Tome V, Part 2 (Paris, 1913) p. 1087.
63 Ibid., pp. 1095–96.
64 William of Tyre, pp. 1015–17, book 22, 7.
65 Barber, *Knighthood*, p. 109.
66 Peter W. Edbury, *The Conquest of Jerusalem and the Third Crusade: Sources in Translation* (Ashgate, Aldershot, 1998) p. 39.
67 Ibid., p. 38.
68 Please see chapter 18, **Saladin**, and chapter 16, **Between the Second and Third Crusades (1150–1191)**, for more information.
69 Edbury, p. 32.
70 Ibn al-Athir, in *Arab Historians of the Crusades*, tr. Francesco Gabrieli (Dorset, 1969) p. 117.
71 Edbury, p. 34.
72 Ibid.
73 Ibid., p. 37.
74 Ibn al-Athir, p. 119.
75 Please see chapter 16 for a more complete discussion of the battle of Hattin, although not too complete because I think it was stupid to begin with and none of them seemed to give a thought to anything beyond their honor.
76 Barber, *Knighthood*, p. 117.

❖

CHAPTER SIXTEEN

Between the Second and Third Crusades (1150–1191)

In 1149, Louis VII and his army returned to France. They had accomplished nothing except to destroy the truce between Jerusalem and Damascus and encourage the Moslems, who now saw that the Western warriors were not all that fearsome.

Things just got worse. On June 29, 1149, the dashing Raymond of Antioch who had charmed his niece, Eleanor of Acqutaine, was killed in battle. Nur ad-Din had his head and right arm sent to Baghdad; the rest of his body was taken back to Antioch for burial.[1] He left behind a wife, Constance, and four young children.[2] Like **Melisande**, Constance was the heir of Antioch so she could rule in her own right. But her cousin, Baldwin III, still had to come up and help with the transition. Then, in May 1150, Jocelyn, count of Edessa in exile, was captured by Nur ad-Din. He died in captivity nine years later. His wife, Beatrice, held out in the fortress of Tel Bashir for some time, but was finally convinced to turn over her lands to the Greeks, who couldn't hold them, either.[3] William of Tyre wrote, "Therefore, for our sins, both counties were scarcely able to survive, lacking good council, under the rule of women."[4]

Nur ad-Din was the real winner of the Second Crusade. Because the citizens of Damascus had been so angered by the attack of the crusaders, they had agreed in 1154 to let the atabeg take over the city.[5] Nur ad-Din was then able to bring all of Moslem Syria under his control.

With the north solidly in control of Nur ad-Din, King Baldwin looked to the south. The town of Gaza had been abandoned and a fortress was built nearby to block the southern route for trade to the coastal city of Ascalon. Ascalon was ruled by the Fatimid caliphs and was essential to trade between Egypt and the Middle East. When the fortress was finished, it was turned over to the Templars to maintain. While William of Tyre is not always kind to the Templars he states that in this case, "These strong and intrepid men have held this trust faithfully and wisely until this very day."[6] Now, Everard de Barres was Grand Master of the Temple at this time, but probably back in France. So it's not clear who was in charge. The records are pretty sparse.

By 1153, it was obvious that Everard wasn't going to come back. So Bernard of Tremelay was elected Grand Master.

Nothing is known of Bernard and his time as Grand Master was so short that there aren't any examples of his administrative ability. His death, however, was an example of both the positive and negative images of the Templars.

According to William of Tyre, King Baldwin hadn't planned on capturing Ascalon. It was an extremely solid fortress. He was just going to annoy the inhabitants by ravaging their orchards.[7] But things went so well that he decided to besiege the city.

Since this was more than he had intended, Baldwin called for reinforcements. All the princes of the land, along with the patriarch of Jerusalem, various bishops and archbishops, the Templars, and the **Hospitallers**, answered the call. With them they brought the True Cross.[8] As the most holy relic in Christendom, it was brought to all the major military engagements. The Templars were always entrusted with its care and protection.[9]

The siege lasted for several months. At one point a group of pilgrims arrived from Europe and were pressed into service as mercenaries.[10] Finally one of the walls of the city was breached. Bernard of Tremelay and the Templars rushed in first. For some reason still debated, no one followed them. The Templars were all trapped inside and killed.[11] Despite this setback, the siege continued and in June 1153, the city fell. The citizens were allowed to leave unmolested.[12]

The capture of Ascalon achieved what the French and German crusaders had not been able to manage. The Latin kingdoms now controlled the entire Mediterranean coast from Egypt up to what is now Turkey. Finally, things seemed be going well again.

However, it wasn't to last long. In early 1157, a group of Christians attacked a party of nomadic Turkomen near the town of Banyas, despite a truce in effect. Nur-ad-Din immediately brought his army to besiege the town. In the ensuing battle the Frankish army was defeated. King Baldwin barely escaped and several of the leaders were taken hostage, including the king's marshal and future Templar, Odo of St. Amand, and the current Grand Master, Bertrand of Blancfort.[13]

Baldwin III spent the next few years shoring up defenses around his kingdom and making alliances that would protect the territory of Jerusalem from Nur ad-Din. His work was cut short, however, by his death in 1163. William of Tyre swears that the king was poisoned by the doctor who gave him a tonic against the approaching winter. But William is suspicious of the custom in the East of trusting "Jews, Samaritans, Syrians and Saracens," whom he felt were "absolutely ignorant of the science of medicine."[14]

Since Baldwin had no children, his brother, Almaric (or Amaury), became king. There was a slight glitch about the succession because Almaric had married his third cousin, Agnes. This was considered incest, although if she had been his fourth cousin, it would have been okay. However, Almaric obligingly let the marriage be annulled as long as their two children, Sybilla and Baldwin, were considered legitimate.

Don't feel too sorry for Agnes. Almost immediately she married her childhood sweetheart, Hugh of Ibelin.

William of Tyre knew King Almaric well and gives a very interesting portrait of him. Like most of the Frankish kings, he was blond. He was slightly above medium height, say about five feet and six to eight inches. He had a bit of a speech impediment, which made him uncomfortable speaking in public. Although he didn't overeat or -drink, he was much too fat "so that he had breasts [that] were like a woman's, hanging down to his belt."[15] Almaric was only in his late twenties! William also thought Almaric was greedy, not very congenial, and a seducer of married women. And this is someone that William worked for and supposedly liked!

Almaric was, however, a strong ruler who insisted on justice within the kingdom. His most important accomplishment was the *Assise sur la liege*. This pronouncement made all the small landholders and minor lords subject ultimately to the king. In a dispute, the needs of the king outweighed those of the liege lord.[16]

What the Templars thought of Almaric may have been worse than William's opinion, although they didn't record it. Most of Almaric's reign was spent in trying to conquer Egypt and in keeping Nur ad-Din's lieutenant, Shirkuh, from encroaching on his kingdom. In 1165, Shirkuh captured a castle that was in the guardianship of the Templars. Almaric believed that they had made a deal with the Saracens and had twelve Templars hanged.[17] Since the disciplining of Templar brothers was the business of the Grand Master and the pope, this did not go down well with the current Grand Master, Bertrand of Blancfort. ·

At this time, the Shi'ite sultan of Egypt, Shawar, was also having problems with the Sunni Shirkuh.[18] So Almaric sent an envoy to Cairo to negotiate a treaty with Shawar against the common enemy. It was led by Hugh of Caesarea, who spoke Arabic, and the Templar Geoffrey Fulcher.[19] Geoffrey never became Grand Master but was the procurator of the order, something like an attorney. He was also an accomplished diplomat who was in contact with rulers in the West.[20]

The men concluded a treaty and, for a time, Moslem and Christian joined forces. However, in 1168, Almaric decided to invade Egypt again. His excuse was that Shawar had switched his allegiance to Nur ad-Din, or at least that there were rumors to this effect.[21] As the leader of the Templars, Bertrand of Blancfort refused to allow his men to join the expedition, especially to break a treaty that a Templar had helped broker. It seemed wrong to the Templars to attack a friendly kingdom that relied on them. Bertrand felt it was against the terms of the treaty and against the laws of religion.[22]

Now, William thought that the real reason Bertrand refused to go was because the man who had suggested the invasion was the commander of the Hospitallers, Gilbert d'Assaily.[23] I couldn't say. But the bad blood between the Templars and the king was building.

The Templars were fighting the Third Crusade long before the ultimate crusader king, **Richard the Lionheart**, decided to come to the Latin kingdoms and liberate Jerusalem. The First Crusade had succeeded in part because the Europeans happened to arrive when the various Moslem states were busy fighting each other. They were never to be that lucky again.

By this time Shawar had been defeated and Damascus and Egypt had been united under one man, Salah-ed din Yusef ibn Ayub, or **Saladin**. And the crusader kingdoms were in disarray. They were fighting among themselves worse than usual and, instead of a strong warrior, they had only a boy as king, Baldwin IV. And Baldwin was a leper.

One of the saddest stories of the Kingdom of Jerusalem is that of Baldwin IV, only son of Melisande's son Almaric. When Baldwin was nine years old his tutor, William of Tyre, saw the first signs of leprosy in the child. He says that he noticed that when Baldwin was playing with other boys and they were poking and pinching each other, as boys do, Baldwin seemed to be extremely brave about it. Then he realized it was because the boy couldn't feel the pain.[24]

Baldwin IV led his armies and governed the kingdom until his illness progressed to the point of complete disability. When the "Leper King" died in 1185, the throne went to the son of his sister, Sybilla. King Baldwin V was about six years old and only "ruled" for a few months after the death of his uncle.[25] The child died in 1186.

After Baldwin V's death, his mother, Sybilla, was the rightful heir to the throne, but there was another group that believed Raymond of Tripoli should rule. Sybilla was supported by the current Grand Master of the Templars, Gerard of Ridefort. The Templars and the Hospitallers, along with the patriarch of Jerusalem, were entrusted with the

William of Tyre examining the wounds of Baldwin IV. *(The British Library)*

keys to the chest in which the royal crowns were kept.[26] Gerard convinced the master of the **Hospitallers** to help him open the chest so that Sybilla could be officially crowned.

One objection to Sybilla was her husband, Guy of Lusignan. Guy had made enemies. In return for Raymond's support, Sybilla promised to divorce Guy, if she could be allowed to choose her second husband herself. Raymond and his supporters agreed to this. Sybilla divorced Guy and was crowned queen. Then she married Guy of Lusignan.[27]

So Guy was now king of Jerusalem. He was to rule over the disintegration of the kingdom and the loss of the city.

THERE are many chronicles of the Third Crusade, most written within fifty years of the events. So we have the benefit of many points of view, not only Christian but also Moslem. The role that the Templars played in the events of the time is therefore given from several perspectives. The trick is deciding which one, if any, is accurate.

One writer seems to be impressed by the valor of the Templars during the time leading up to the crusade. At the battle of the Springs of Cresson, which took place two months before the fall of Jerusalem, "a certain Templar, . . . Jakelin de Mailly by name, brought all the enemy assault upon himself through his outstanding courage. While the rest of his fellow knights . . . had either been captured or killed, he bore the force of the battle alone and shone out as a glorious champion for the law of his God."[28] The anonymous chronicler describes the battle as one in which the masters of the Temple and Hospital with their few men faced an army of thousands coming to ravage the land.

However, another chronicler has a different take on the battle. According to him, Saladin had a truce with Raymond, count of Tripoli. The Saracens, under the command of Saladin's son, came into the county, harmed no one, and were leaving when the master of the Temple, Gerard of Ridefort, insisted that they attack. Raymond had forbidden anyone to break the truce. "The master of the Temple was a good knight and physically strong but he treated all other people wrongly as he was too presumptuous."[29]

According to this chronicler, Gerard convinced the others to attack. The result was disaster. The master of the Hospital, Roger des Moulins, had his head cut off along with all the knights of the Temple. Only three escaped, one being the master of the Temple, Gerard de Ridefort.[30]

Oddly, Gerard was allowed to continue to give advice to King Guy. His next counsel led to the disaster known as the Horns of Hattin and the capture of Jerusalem by **Saladin**.

---

1 William of Tyre, *Chronichon*, ed. R. B. C. Huygens (Turnholt, 1986) book 17, 10, p. 772.

2 Ibid. Constance was the cousin of Baldwin III, who had been married at the age of nine, much to the shock of her mother, Alice.

3 M. W. Baldwin, ed., *The Crusades: The First Hundred Years* (Wisconsin University Press, 1969) pp. 533–34.

4 William of Tyre, book 17, 11, p. 775. "Sic igitur peccatis nostris exigentibus utraque regio, melioribus destituta consiliis vix in se subsistens, femineo regebatur imperio."

5 Jonathan Riley-Smith, *The Crusades* (New Haven: Yale University Press, 2005) p. 105.

6 William of Tyre, book 17, 12, p. 776.

7 Ibid., book 17, 21, p. 789. Isn't it interesting how often the need for fresh fruit comes into these campaigns?

8 Ibid., book 17, 21, "lignum dominice crucis vivificum et venerabile secum habentes."

9 Laurent Dailliez, *Régle et Status de l'Ordre du Temple* (Paris: Dervy, 1996) p. 1 38, rule no. 122, "Quant l'en porte le verais crois en chevauchée, le Comandour de Jerusalem et les X chevaliers la doivent garder nuit et jour."

10 William of Tyre, book 17, 24, p. 793.

11 Please see chapter 15, **Grand Masters 1136–1189**.

12 William of Tyre, book 17, 30, p. 803. This is confirmed by the Arab historian al-Qalanisi in *The Damascus Chronicles of the Crusades*, ed. and tr. H. A. R. Gibb (Dover, 2002; reprint of 1932 ed.) pp. 316, "and all of them who could depart left the city and proceeded by land or sea to Egypt and elsewhere."

13 Ibid., book 18, 14, p. 831.

14 Ibid., book 18, 34, p. 859, "phisicarum rationum prorsus ignaris."

15 Ibid., book 19, 3, p. 868, "ut more femieo mamillas haberet cigulotenus prominentes."

16 Hans Eberhard Mayer, *The Crusades* (Oxford University Press, 1988) p. 117.

17 Hellen Nicholson, *The Knights Templar* (London: Sutton, 2001) pp. 62–63.

18 For more on this situation, please see chapter 18, **Saladin**.

19 William of Tyre, 19, 18, p. 887.

20 Malcom Barber, *The New Knighthood* (Cambridge, 1994) p. 96.

21 William of Tyre, 20, 5, p. 917.

22 Ibid., 20, 5, p. 917. They were *so* naïve!

23 Ibid.

24 Ibid.

25 John L. La Monte, *Feudal Monarchy in the Latin Kingdom of Jerusalem 1100–1291* (Cambridge, MA: Medieval Academy of America, 1932) p. 33.

26 Ibid., p. 34.

27 Peter W. Edbury, *The Conquest of Jerusalem and the Third Crusade: Sources in Translation* (Ashgate, Aldershot, 1998) pp. 154–55.

28 *The Chronicle of the Third Crusade*, ed. and tr. Helen J. Nicholson (Ashgate, Turnholt, 1997) p. 25.

29 Edbury, p. 32.

30 Ibid.

CHAPTER SEVENTEEN

Who Were the Saracens, Anyway?

In the first paragraph of the Latin **Rule** of the Templars, the order's purpose was stated thus: to "defend the poor and the churches" of the Holy Land.[1] The Rule never actually says against whom, but it was understood that the greatest danger to the poor and the churches came from the Saracens.

But who were the Saracens? It's not certain where the word came from but it was in use by the time of the Romans to refer to the people of the Arab peninsula and, by association, it came to mean Moslems.[2] It was a handy term for the crusaders to use since they were fairly vague on variations of belief and ethnic origins in the Near East.

The people of the area were, and still are, a mix of every migration of the world. The Near East is the pathway connecting Europe, Africa, and Asia, and even armies on their way to conquer something else had to go through it to get there. The first people to venture out of Africa went through on their way to populating the rest of the earth. The area has been ruled by Hittites, Phoenicians, Greeks, Persians, Jews, Romans, and Arabs. So by the end of the eleventh century the strip of land from Suez to Constantinople contained Armenian Christians, Jacobite Christians, Greek Orthodox Christians, Orthodox Jews, Karaite Jews, Samaritans, Arab Moslems, Persian Sunni Moslems, Druze, Egyptian Shi'ite Moslems, and the new guys, the Turks, who were ultraorthodox Sunni. And that's just the religions. The coming of the Franks was no more than a new ingredient to the mix.

However, one problem the Western invaders had was that they weren't up on all these variations. They didn't understand that the Jacobite Christians were less oppressed by the Moslems than by the Byzantines, or that the Shi'ite city of Damascus preferred dealing with Christians than coming under the dominance of the Sunni caliphs of Baghdad.

In some ways, the Templars as a group learned the ropes sooner than the new princes and counts of the crusader kingdoms. In his autobiography, de Usama ibn Munqidh, emir of Shaizar, relates a tale about visiting the church that had been made next to the **Temple in Jerusalem** (the Templars' headquarters—before and after the crusades, the mosque of al-Aqsa). "Whenever I went into the mosque, which was in the hands of the Templars who were friends of mine, they would put the little oratory at my disposal, so that I could say my prayers there."[3] Usama was not particularly fond of the Franks but he saw and judged them as individuals and did have friends among them, including Templars.

The Templars and Hospitallers also had groups of Moslems who paid tribute to them. For instance the **Assassins** paid two thousand bezants a year to each order. In 1230, the two military orders joined forces to exact retribution from the town of Hamah, which refused to pay.[4]

However, the main contact that the Templars had with the "Saracens" was in battle. Among the Turks, their first opponents, they came up against three very different leaders: Zengi, Nur ad-Din, and Saladin.

ZENGI (IMAD AL-DIN ATABEG)

The first of the great Turkish adversaries of the crusaders was known to the Franks as Zengi (Zangi, Zanki), atabeg of Mosul. For most of his early career Zengi, working for the Sunni caliphs of Baghdad, concentrated on defeating the Shi'ites of Egypt and Damascus.[5] His first known contact with the Templars was in 1137 near Montferrand, in Tripoli.

At that time Zengi had come to the defense of the Moslem fortress of Homs, and defeated Pons of Tripoli, who died in the battle. As a result, King Fulk came north with a force that included several Templars. The Norman historian Orderic Vitalis relates the story of the battle and its aftermath:

> Countless thousands of the Pagans fell, but by the will of God, whose judgments are just and right, almost the whole Christian force crumbled and all except thirty knights were slain. Only the king himself escaped, with ten of his household knights and eighteen knights of the Temple, and fled to a castle . . . called Montferrand where they stoutly resisted, although besieged for some time. . . . Zengi, although he had lost thousands of his men by the swords of the Christians, was nevertheless elated at winning the victory he had hoped for.[6]

At this point, Zengi was more concerned with conquering Shi'ite towns than attacking the Franks. But, since he was in the neighborhood, the opportunity was too good to pass up. He hadn't had much luck with the Shi'ite town of Hims, and so the defeat of Fulk and his army was especially satisfying. He then besieged the remnant of the army at Montferrand and had reduced them to eating their horses and dogs, when a relief force appeared.[7]

The Chronicles of Damascus reports that Zengi was still the victor, even though he had to leave the field:

> It became necessary under the circumstances to grant the besieged their liberty, and he made an agreement with them, on the grounds that they acknowledged his suzerainty, and stipulated for a sum of fifty thousand dinars, which they should pay him forthwith.[8]

Orderic doesn't mention a payment or that King Fulk agreed that Zengi should be his lord. He states that the two men agreed to an exchange of prisoners and that Fulk, not knowing that relief was on the way, surrendered the castle in return for freedom.[9]

It's interesting to me that both the Moslem and Christian accounts use the same language and that both Zengi and Fulk are fighting by the same conventions. Foot soldiers are killed; leaders and noblemen held for ransom. However far apart the worlds may seem to be, these are men of the same warrior culture. The fact is that they are part of a long tradition of Romans, Greeks, and Persians invading each other over many centuries. Even though Fulk was of German stock and Zengi Turkish, they had each grown up in a society in which the rules of war were identical.

Zengi then turned his attention back to his main objective of gaining control of Shi'ite towns. In 1139 he began to prepare for the siege of Damascus. After some time and several bloody battles outside the walls of the city, the leaders of Damascus sent to Fulk of Jerusalem for aid. Fulk agreed and made a treaty with the city.[10] On hearing this, Zengi backed off, contenting himself with raids on smaller villages, both Moslem and Christian, from which he looted "an innumerable quantity of horses at pasture, sheep and goats, cattle and furnishings."[11]

You see what I mean about the rules of war. That's exactly what the Christian forces were doing.

Even though he was more concerned with uniting the Moslem towns under Sunni government, Zengi still attacked Christian outposts. The Templar castle near the Jordan River was built as a result of Zengi's massacre of six monks who were living in a church there.[12]

While he never was able to take Damascus, Zengi's greatest triumph was the conquest of the city of Edessa on Christmas Eve 1144. This was the event that led to the **Second Crusade**.

NUR AD-DIN

The son of Zengi, Nur ad-Din (Nur al-Din, Nurandin) was a fit successor to his father and a daunting opponent to the crusader states. In appearance he was "a tall, swarthy man with a beard but no moustache and a pleasant appearance enhanced by beautiful, melting eyes."[13]

Unlike Zengi, who was basically interested in the political conquest of Shi'ites as well as Christians, Nur ad-Din saw his mission as the elimination of the Latin kingdoms and the return of Jerusalem to Moslem control. He left a number of inscriptions on public buildings that emphasize this. One sign of his determination to return to a pure form of Islam is that the language of these inscriptions is Arabic, not Turkish or Persian, like those of his father.[14] He has been credited with reintroducing the idea of jihad, or religious war, into the Moslem world.[15]

His most remarkable feat was in 1154 when he took over the government of Damascus through propaganda rather than force. The leaders of Damascus feared him enough to make an alliance with the Franks but the people of the town had been listening to stories, songs, and sermons about how Nur ad-Din was a "true *mujahid*" and the only one who could assure a victory for Islam.[16] They decided to overthrow their leaders and invite Nur ad-Din in.

Nur ad-Din died in Damascus on May 15, 1174. Despite the nearly thirty years of war between him and the Latin states, William of Tyre still wrote that "he was of great renown, a just prince, persecutor of the Christian faith, cunning and prudent and religious according to the traditions of his people."[17]

Nur ad-Din would be succeeded not by the son he left behind, but by the leader who, for the West, is the archetypal Saracen, the Kurd **Saladin**.

---

1 "Paupers aut Ecclesias defendere," in Laurent Dailliez, *Règle et Status de l'Ordre du Temple* (Paris: Dervey, 1996) p. 324.

2 Oxford English Dictionary (Oxford University Press, 1971) p. 2639.

3 "Usama," in Francesco Gabrieli, *Arab Historians of the Crusades* (New York: Dorset, 1989) tr. from Italian by E. J. Costello p. 79.

4 Ph. Gourdin and G. Martinez-Gros (dirs) *Pays d'Islam et monde latin 950–1250* (Tourai, 2001) p. 263.

5 Abua'lá Hamzah ibn Asad Ibn al-Qalanisi, *The Damascus Chronicles of the Crusades*, tr. H. A. R. Gibb (New York: Dover, 2002). p. 227ff.

6 Orderic Vitalis, *The Ecclesiastical History of Orderic Vitalis* ed. and tr. Marjorie Chibnall (Oxford University Press, 1978) Vol. VI, book XIII, v. 94, pp. 496–97.

7 Ibid.

8 Ibn Al-Qalanisi p. 243.

9 Orderic Vitalis, op. cit., pp. 500–03.

10 Ibn Al-Qalanisi, pp. 259–60.

11 Ibid., p. 262.

12 Malcom Barber, *The New Knighthood* (Cambridge University Press, 1996) p. 89.

13 Ibn Al-Athir, in Gabrieli p. 68. Ibn Al-Athir (555/1160–630/1233) wrote a history of the Moslem world. He was fourteen when Nur ad-Din died.

14 Yasser Tabbaa, "Monuments with a Message: Propagation of Jihad under Nur Al-Din," in Vladimir P. Gross, ed., *The Meeting of Two Worlds* (Kalamazoo, MI: Medieval Institute, 1986) p. 224.

15 Ibid., pp. 223–37.

16 Gourdin and Gros, p. 195.

17 William of Tyre, *Chronicon*, ed. R. B. C. Huygens (Turnholt, 1986) 20, 31, p. 956. "Noradinus, maximus nominis et fidei christiane presequutor, princes tamen justus, vafer et providus et secundum gentis sue traditiones religiosus."

CHAPTER EIGHTEEN

Saladin

In medieval and modern legend, he was the most chivalrous of all those involved with the crusades. He was mighty and merciful, wise and brave. He was also the man who destroyed the dream of a Christian Jerusalem and started the slow retreat of the Latin kingdoms.

In the west he is known as Saladin.

Salah-ed din Yusef ibn Ayub was born in the year 1138.[1] His family was of the Rawadiya clan of Kurds who had migrated to Baghdad and entered the service of the caliphs. They were devout Sunni Moslems and Yusef, that is, Saladin, was a shining example of the ideal warrior for orthodox Islam.

Saladin's father, Ayub, was governor of the town of Baalbek in Syria. Saladin was born in Tikrit, north of Baghdad, and spent his childhood in Mosul.[2] In 1152, at the age of fourteen, he entered the service of Nur ad-Din, the son of Zengi, who had captured Edessa, precipitating the **Second Crusade**.[3]

Shi'ite Damascus was often a reluctant ally of the kings of Jerusalem against the incursions of the newly converted Sunni Turks. When, in 1157 Nur ad-Din took Damascus the only major Shi'ite stronghold left was Egypt. The country had been weakened by internal battles for power. The Shi'ite Fatimid dynasty was failing. Around 1162, the vizier to the Fatimid caliphs, Shawar, was unseated in a palace coup. Shawar

fled to Syria and convinced Nur ad-Din to support him in an attempt
to regain power. Nur ad-Din sent his lieutenant Asad al-Din Shirkuh
to lead the army. With him Shirkuh took his nephew Saladin.[4]

Shawar was restored to his position in 1164 and Shirkuh and Saladin returned to Syria. However, Shawar was "obsessed by the fear of
a Turkish invasion."[5] Not trusting his Turkish-Sunni allies, he con-
tacted the Frankish king, Almaric, who had already been in negotiations with the Egyptians and asked the king to protect him from
Shirkuh if necessary. The king's representatives to the vizier were
Hugh, lord of Caesarea, and Geoffrey Fulcher, a Templar.[6]

Almaric agreed to join forces with Shawar. The combined armies
were able to roust Shirkuh from the town of Balbis, which he had recently taken. But, while Almaric and his men were in Egypt, Nur
ad-Din took advantage of the situation and attacked the Latin city of
Banyas.[7] This was typical of the problems of the Latin kingdoms.
There were too many fronts to defend.

In 1167, King Almaric and Vizier Shawar again met Shirkuh in
battle. In this battle Saladin distinguished himself, capturing the envoy, Hugh of Caesarea, and many others.[8] However, after defending
the city of Alexandria during a long siege, Saladin and his uncle were
forced to retreat once again.

Finally in 1168, Almaric was told that Shawar was sending messages to Nur ad-Din, asking for his help to maintain power in Egypt.
It is not at all certain that this was true. According to William of
Tyre, the Templars refused to take part in this expedition because they
didn't believe Shawar had broken the treaty. He also suggests that the
Templars were annoyed because the invasion was the idea of Gilbert
d'Assaily, the master of the Hospital.[9] William always had mixed feelings about the Templars.

Whatever the reason, Shawar was seriously weakened by the Christian attack. After he had made another truce with Almaric, the king
retreated back to Jerusalem, leaving the way open for Shirkuh and
Saladin.

Shawar greeted the Turks as rescuers but Shirkuh was highly
suspicious of a man who made treaties with idolaters against other

Moslems. He felt that this was because the caliphs of Egypt were, in his mind, Shi'ite heretics. Therefore, he decided to oust the vizier.[10]

Saladin was dispatched to arrest Shawar. The vizier was beheaded and his head sent to Cairo. Shirkuh was made vizier in his place.[11] The Fatimid caliphs were kept as puppet kings for the time being.

Saladin's biographer states that Shirkuh "was a great eater, excessively given to partaking of rich meats. He suffered many bouts of indigestion."[12] On March 22, 1169, Saladin's uncle died, perhaps after a particularly rich meal, and Saladin became vizier of Egypt. He never looked back. In 1170 he captured Gaza, a frontier town long held by the Templars.

Like Nur ad-Din, Saladin was devoutly orthodox and believed it was his duty to rid the Holy Land of infidels. Like the Christians, he also believed it necessary to either convert or silence heretics within his own faith, like the Shi'ites. One of his first tasks in Egypt was "strengthening the Sunni cause and planting in the local population pious learning, law, Sufi practice and [true] religion."[13] This included the crucifixion of the Sufi heretic al Suhrawadi in 1180 because "it was said that he rejected the Holy Law and declared it invalid."[14]

When the last Fatimid caliph died in 1171, Saladin replaced him. His dynasty would be known as the Ayyubids, after Saladin's father, Ayub.

Once established in Egypt, Saladin put his energy into driving out the Franks and in establishing his independence from Nur ad-Din without causing an outright rupture in their relations. He was aided in both these things by the deaths in 1174 of both Nur ad-Din, on May 15, and King Almaric, on July 11.[15] Nur ad-Din's heir was a young boy. Almaric's was the thirteen-year-old Baldwin IV, who had suffered from leprosy since the age of nine. Neither was able to provide the leadership needed, although poor Baldwin tried.

Saladin seems to have felt that he was the spiritual heir of Nur ad-Din. He took over the city of Damascus and married Nur ad-Din's widow. Now he controlled both Egypt and Damascus. He was able to attack the Latin kingdoms from both the east and the west.[16] Jerusalem braced for the blow. Instead, to the great relief of the Christians,

Saladin. *(Art Resource, NY)*

Saladin turned east to finish taking over the lands that Nur ad-Din had left to his young son, including the cities of Mosul and Aleppo.

In 1180, Saladin made an alliance with the Seljuk sultan of Anatolia, Kilij Arslan II, in order to fight against the town of Mosul.[17] He married one of his daughters to Kilij's son, who slowly pushed his father out of office and proved a strong supporter of his father-in-law.

While still working to capture Mosul, Saladin was able to take Aleppo, which he gave to his brother, al-Adil, to govern.[18]

Mosul still held out, so, in 1185, Saladin made a four-year truce with young Baldwin, despite his earlier reservations about those who make treaties with infidels in order to fight other Moslems.

What happened next depends on one's point of view. But, in one of the unpredictable quirks of history, the fate of Jerusalem may have been decided by the actions of one hotheaded man.

Once upon a time there was a knight named Reynald de Chatillon. He was good looking and adventurous, but poor. So, perhaps seduced by romance tales popular in France, he came to Antioch in the 1150s to seek his fortune. Amazingly, he found it in the person of Constance, princess of Antioch. She had been the little girl married at the age of nine to Raymond of Poitiers. Raymond was dead and Constance was not inclined to marry again for the good of the realm. Instead, she chose Reynald.[19]

He wasn't popular with his in-laws. When Reynald was captured by Nur ad-Din in 1160, no one bothered to ransom him.[20] By the time he was freed in 1176, his wife had died. Since she was the heiress of Antioch, Reynald had no claim on her property. The soldier of fortune was once again without funds.

Captivity seems to have done nothing to diminish his charm. The next year Reynald married Stephanie of Milly, the daughter and heiress of Templar Philip of Nablus. Through her, Reynald gained control of the province of Outrejordan.

According to most of the chronicles, Reynald felt that the truce with Saladin didn't apply to him. He behaved much like the Moslem raiders had in the first part of the century. He attacked pilgrims on their way to Mecca, burned towns, and, as the last straw, in 1187 he pillaged a Moslem caravan going from Cairo to Baghdad. "He seized it treacherously, maltreated and tortured its members. . . . They reminded him of the truce, but he replied, 'Tell your Mohammad to release you.'"21

Reynald was handsome, charming, adventurous, and stupid.

This either gave Saladin the excuse he'd been looking for or tried his patience for the last time. It was probably a little of both.

By 1187 Baldwin IV had died. His replacement was his sister, Sybilla, and her husband, Guy of Lusignan. Guy was another adventurer and not universally popular. He and his supporter, Templar Grand Master Gerard of Ridefort, had problems with Count Raymond of Tripoli that were serious enough for Raymond to make his own truce with Saladin.22 But, when Reynald absolutely refused to return the booty he had taken from the caravan, even though King Guy insisted, everyone knew that Saladin had the perfect reason to attack.

The result was the disastrous battle of the Horns of Hattin on July 4, 1187.23

Among the men captured at Hattin were King Guy, Master Gerard of Ridefort, a large number of Templars and Hospitallers, and Reynald de Chatillon. The worst loss to the Christians, though, was the True Cross, carried into battle in a gold reliquary.

Saladin had the important prisoners brought to his tent. He offered King Guy a cup of water. When the king had finished drinking, he handed the cup to Reynald. Saladin was furious. "This godless man did not have my permission to drink!" he roared. "And I will not save his life in that way."24 With that he took his sword and beheaded Reynald of Chatillon himself.25

It must have been very satisfying, if damaging to the carpets.

King Guy and Gerard of Ridefort were ransomed but the rest of the Templars and Hospitallers were also beheaded. "He had these particular men killed because they were the fiercest of all the Frankish warriors, and in this way he rid the Muslim people of them."26

After this, Saladin was able to roll across the country practically unhindered. He took Acre on July 10, Ascalon on September 4. Although Queen Sybilla defended the city of Jerusalem as best she could, there were no more fighting men left. Saladin captured it on October 2, 1187. He allowed the people of the town to pay their own ransoms. The patriarch of Jerusalem asked the Hospitallers for thirty thousand bezants to cover the ransoms of seven thousand poor people. That was delivered, but some people were still unredeemed. The Templars, Hospitallers, and the burgesses of Jerusalem were asked to donate more and they did, "but they didn't give as much as they should have."[27]

Even the Christian chroniclers remarked on the generosity of Saladin and that of his family in their treatment of the people of Jerusalem. Saif al-Din, Saladin's brother, asked for the freedom of one thousand more people and, on his own, Saladin freed thousands more.[28] However there were many who could not pay and they were sold as slaves.[29] One Moslem chronicler relates the fate of the women of the city with delight. "How many well-guarded women were profaned, . . . and miserly women forced to yield themselves, and women who had been kept hidden stripped of their modesty, and serious women made ridiculous, . . . and virgins dishonoured and proud women deflowered . . . and untamed ones tamed and happy ones made to weep!"[30]

On all sides, it seems chivalry only goes so far.

Then Saladin set out to purify the city. "The Templars had built their living quarters against al-Aqsa, with storerooms and latrines and other necessary offices, taking up the area of al-Aqsa. This was all restored to its former state."[31]

When Europe learned of the fall of Jerusalem the pope, Urban IV, is said to have died from the shock. Henry II of England and Philip II of France were convinced to call a truce in their constant battles and establish a tax, known as the Saladin tithe, to finance armies to retake the city.[32]

Eventually Frederick Barbarossa, the Holy Roman Emperor, Philip Augustus, king of France, and **Richard the Lionheart**, king of England, came to retake the Holy Land. In the chronicles of the Europeans, Saladin is a dangerous but magnanimous ruler. In the chronicles of the Moslems, Richard is a dangerous but cultivated ruler. Perhaps both sides felt that their respective heroes deserved a worthy opponent. Each seems to have been more respected by their enemies than their own side.

I have often heard and read that, when Richard was ill, Saladin was so gracious as to send his own doctor to the king. However, in going through the firsthand accounts from both sides, I haven't found any reference to it. What I did find was a comment from Ba'ha al-Din that Richard asked Saladin for fruit and ice, as he craved them. The sultan "was supplying him with [these,] while intending to gain intelligence by the to-and-froing of the messengers."[33]

Saladin was in his early fifties at the time of the crusade and his beard had turned white. Richard was in his early thirties and Philip some ten years younger. The sultan must have felt that he was going to war against schoolboys. Richard seems to have surprised him with his military and diplomatic skill. Reading through the chronicles, especially the interminable negotiating through envoys, interspersed with skirmishes, I get the impression that this was a contest between equals. Both men fought in the name of a religion that each believed in. They had the same rules and much the same battle tactics.

Whether they were gentlemen or barbarians is entirely a matter of opinion.

Eventually Saladin accepted a division of the country and allowed Christian pilgrims to come again to Jerusalem. He returned to Damascus to resume the governing of his far-flung territory. In late February 1193, he fell ill and, despite all the efforts of his doctors, died on March 3, at the age of fifty-five.[34] He left many children and grandchildren, but his dynasty would only last three generations. Without his guiding influence, brothers and cousins would fight each other until they were overcome by the Mamluks, the equivalent of the palace guard of Egypt.

Saladin was such a grand figure that he was respected as well as feared in the West. Unlike the Templars, he was the subject of romance literature. By the fifteenth century, there were several stories about him, including how he had made a journey to France as a young man and had an affair with the queen of France.[35]

It seemed impossible to some that such a magnificent man could be totally from another culture. The author of the thirteenth-century romance "The Daughter of the Count of Pontieu" decided that he must have had some European ancestry. In the story, the heroine is kidnapped by a Saracen king who treats her well and by whom she has children. However, she longs to return to Christian lands and finally escapes. One of the children she leaves behind becomes the grandmother of the "chivalrous Saladin."[36] Of course there is no truth to the story. But it does show how the legend of the "chivalrous Saladin" penetrated even in the lands of his enemies.

The legend survives to this day.

1 Stanley Lane-Poole, *Saladin and the Fall of the Kingdom of Jerusalem* (New York: G. P. Putnam's Sons, 1898) p. 6.
2 Baha' al-Din Ibn Shaddad, *The Rare and Excellent History of Saladin*, tr. D. S. Richards (Ashgate, Aldershot, 2002) p. 17.
3 Hans Eberhard Mayer, *The Crusades* (Oxford University Press, 1988; 2nd ed.) p. 121.
4 Ba'ha al-Din, p. 17.
5 Ibid., p. 18.
6 Malcolm Barber, *The New Knighthood* (Cambridge University Press, 1994) p. 96.
7 William of Tyre, *Chronicon*, ed. R. B. C. Huygens (Turnholt, 1986)19, 5–11, pp. 872–79. Banyas had been an **Assassin** town but they had turned it over to the Franks rather than let the Sunni have it.
8 William of Tyre, 19, 25, p. 899.
9 Ibid., 20, 5, p. 918.
10 Ba'ha al-Din, p. 44.
11 Ibid. They were always sending heads to Baghdad or Cairo. Don't you wonder what they did with them all?
12 Ibid., p. 45.
13 Ibid.
14 Ibid., p. 20.
15 William of Tyre, 20, 31, pp. 956–57.
16 Mayer, p. 124.
17 Ibid., p. 125.
18 Ba'ha al-Din, p. 63.
19 This story is in most histories of the crusades, as well as William of Tyre. One of the best summaries of his life is in René Grousset, *Histoire des Croisades et du Royaume Franc de Jérusalem* (Paris, 1935) p. 699ff. For more on Constance, see chapter 10, **Melisande, Queen of Jerusalem**.
20 Mayer, p. 115.
21 Ba'ha al-Din, p. 37.
22 Barber, p. 113.
23 Please see the reference to the Third Crusade elsewhere in this book.
24 Imad ad Din, in *Arab Historians of the Crusades*, tr. Francesco Gabrieli (Dorset, 1969) p. 124.

25 Ibid. Ba'ha al-Din, p. 75, says that Saladin only cut off his arm and others finished him off. It turned out the same for Reynald.

26 Ibid., p. 124. Other chroniclers agree that the members of the military orders were killed, but only this one gives a reason.

27 *Chronique d' Ernoul et de Bernard le Trésorier*, ed. m. L. De Mas Latrie (Paris, 1871) p. 226, "et li Temples et le Hospitaus i donna; mais n'i donnerent mie tant come il deussent."

28 Ernoul, p. 228. This was written long after the event. It may or may not be true, but it does show that the West saw Saladin as a chivalrous man.

29 Ibn al-Athir in Gabrieli, p. 163.

30 Ibid.

31 Ibid., p. 144.

32 Mayer, pp. 139–40.

33 Ba'ha al-Din, p. 228.

34 Ibid., p. 244.

35 Suzanne Duparc-Quioc, *Le Cycle de La Croisade* (Paris, 1955) pp. 170–205.

36 *La Fille du Comte de Pontieu* (Paris: Société des Anciens Textes Français, 1923) p. 50, "ensi com verités tesmoingne, de cele fu nee le mere au courtois Salehadin."

CHAPTER NINETEEN

Richard the Lionheart

He was lofty of stature, of shapely build, his hair halfway between red and yellow, his limbs straight and supple. His arms were somewhat long and, therefore, better fitted than those of most men to draw or wield a sword. He also had long legs in keeping with the character of his whole frame. . . . He far surpassed other men in courtesy and the greatness of his strength."[1]

Richard I, count of Poitou and king of England, better known as "the Lionheart," is another figure whose legend has obscured his real history. Like the Templars, Richard's legend began in his own lifetime and continued to grow long after his death.

Richard was born at Oxford on September 8, 1157.[2] His mother, Eleanor, was countess of Poitou and duchess of Aquitaine in her own right as well as having been queen of France before she became queen of England.[3] His father, Henry Plantagenet, was descended through his mother, Matilda, from William the Conqueror and through his father, Geoffrey of Anjou, from the devil.[4]

The story is that a distant ancestress of Richard was Melusine, a demon in disguise who married a count of Anjou. She seemed perfectly normal except for a habit of leaving church halfway through the Mass. One day, suspicious vassals forced her to stay in the church for the consecration of the Host, at which point, she shrieked and vanished forever, leaving a startled husband and children behind. The Plantagenets always seemed very proud of her. However, this same story was told about a number of medieval families as well as being a popular theme in fiction so they were not unique in their fascinating ancestry.

Nevertheless, according to a contemporary, Richard was known to have said, "It's not strange that, with such a family history, the children are always attacking their parents and each other for they all came from the devil and to the devil they will return."[5]

But Richard also had strong ties to the early crusaders and to the Latin kingdoms. His great-grandfather **Fulk of Anjou** had started a second life as king of Jerusalem when he married **Melisande**, the heiress to the kingdom. And his mother's uncle, Raymond of Poitiers, had done the same thing when he married the heiress of Antioch.[6] And, of course, his mother Eleanor had scandalized half the continent with her adventures with her first husband, Louis VII of France, on the **Second Crusade**.

Richard was the third son of Henry and Eleanor. The first, William, had died as a baby. The second, Henry, was being groomed to be the next king of England. Richard was to inherit his mother's lands. Therefore, he spent much of his time in Poitou and Aquitaine. This territory was not only larger than England, but much more prosperous and produced much better wine. I don't blame Richard for being attached to it.

One often repeated story is that Richard passed less than a year of his life in England. That's not exactly true. He spent less than a year in England as king. In his early years he went back and forth across the channel several times. His parents probably left him with his nanny, Hodierna, much of the time. She may have come from the Oxford area. He was certainly fond of her, and when he became king he gave her a large pension that allowed her to retire to Wiltshire in style.[7]

Like most of the Anglo-Norman nobility, Richard never learned to speak English. He did, however, learn to read and write French and Provençal and "was sufficiently well-educated in Latin to be able to crack a Latin joke at the expense of a less learned Archbishop of Canturbury."[8]

He became king in July 1189 at the age of thirty-two. His elder brother Henry had died. At the time Richard was at war with his father and not on great terms with his younger brothers, Geoffrey and John. His mother had been imprisoned by his father for several years as a result of her plots against him. Maybe there is something to the demon story.

The year before he assumed the throne, Richard had been one of the first to answer the summons of Pope Gregory VII for the Third Crusade. As king, he not only still had to fulfill this vow but also to honor that of his father, Henry II, who had also promised to go.[9]

But before that he went to Westminster for his official anointing and coronation. On September 13, 1189, he became Richard I of England. He then immediately set about collecting as much money as he could to finance his expedition to the Holy Land.[10] "He put up for sale everything he had—offices, lordships, earldoms, sherriffdoms, castles towns, lands, the lot."[11] He was also able to collect the tax that Henry II had started, known as the "Saladin tithe," which shows that the people of Europe knew who had taken Jerusalem from them. This was not always paid cheerfully, especially by the clergy, but Richard knew how to convince them. Both he and his father made the Templars his tithe collectors.[12] This didn't endear people to them.

The intense demand for money from the people of England, along with the usual crusading fervor, may have been responsible for an outbreak of violence against the Jews in England. It seems to have started when some Jews arrived at Richard's coronation with gifts and were told they couldn't come in. Women and Jews had not been invited. The crowd outside, who apparently also hadn't been invited in, attacked the Jews, killing some of them. This led to a general riot in London. Jewish homes were ransacked and burned and many people murdered.[13]

Richard was not particularly pro-Jewish, but all the Jews of England were under the king's special protection and had been since they first came to England in the time of William the Conqueror. They were also a great source of revenue. He was furious about the attacks and tried to stop the destruction but, over the next few months, the violence spread to other towns of England.

This culminated in a horrifying massacre on Friday, March 16, 1190, *Shabbat ha-Gadol,* during which 150 people were killed in the city of York when they took refuge in a tower there. The chronicler William of Newburgh lived nearby and reports, "And there were not lacking among the mob many clergymen, among whom a certain hermit seemed more vehement than the rest . . . frequently repeating with a loud voice that Christ's enemies ought to be crushed."[14] The instigators seem to have been friends of the bishop of Durham, Richard Malebysse and William Percy. Richard saw that the men were fined and had their lands taken away.[15] No one seems to have offered to help the Jews rebuild.

By the time this happened, Richard had already left England.

On the way to the eastern Mediterranean as part of the Third Crusade, Richard decided to forge an alliance with Sancho VI, king of Navarre, and became engaged to his daughter, Berengaria.[16] This immediately proved a problem with Philip II, king of France and Richard's stepbrother. Richard had been engaged to Philip's sister, Alix, for most of his life and Alix had been raised at the English court, effectively keeping her from meeting anyone new.

The two kings met on Sicily and Philip was bought off. Queen Eleanor, who was in her late sixties at the time, brought Berengaria to Richard and they were married in Cyprus May 12, 1191. Richard seems to have spent most of the time before the wedding conquering the island. It later proved to be too much trouble to maintain so he sold it to the Templars.[17] The Templars also found Cyprus difficult to hold and so it was passed on to Guy of Lusignan, the widowed husband of Sybilla, queen of Jerusalem.

King Philip and Richard finally arrived at the city of Acre, which had been taken by Saladin four years before. They joined the besiegers and, after a long and horrible winter, the city finally fell.[18]

Here two things happened that would come back to haunt Richard. The first was something that seemed minor at the time. Leopold,

Richard the Lionheart takes Acre, from *Les Grandes Chroniques de France*. Note that the other lords are not shown. (*The British Library*)

duke of Austria, had been fighting at Acre longer than the two kings. When the city fell, he had his standards raised along with those of Richard and Philip. Richard, believing that Leopold intended to take a third of the booty, had them torn down. He and Philip had already decided on a fifty-fifty split. Leopold was naturally offended by this and decided to take his soldiers and go home. With him, he took a grudge against Richard.[19]

The second thing was much more immediately damaging to Richard's reputation. He had captured nearly three thousand Moslem citizens of Acre who were being held for a ransom of one hundred thousand bezants. At some point he decided that **Saladin** wasn't going to pay. Richard wanted to leave Acre but couldn't until the captives were got rid of. So one morning he took them outside the city and slaughtered them all.[20] Both the Arab and Christian chroniclers agree that this happened. The Arab chronicler states:

> Many reasons were given for this slaughter. One was that they had killed them as a reprisal for their own prisoners killed before them by the Muslims. Another was that the King of England had decided to march on Ascalon and take it, and he did not want to leave behind him in the city a large number [of enemy soldiers]. God knows best.[21]

Whatever his reasons, this act did not reflect well on Richard, among his own people or the Moslems. Even the king's chronicler, the poet Ambroise, who thought Richard was practically perfect, seems to stutter over this event. "And Richard, the king of England, who had on earth killed so many Turks, did not wish to be bothered any longer, and so to lesson the pride of the Turks and to dishearten their beliefs and to avenge Christianity . . ." he had them killed.[22]

It must have sounded pretty thin even to him.

Richard soon realized that, even if he took Jerusalem, he couldn't hold it. In 1191, he made a three-year truce with Saladin and set out for home.[23] While he had some success in securing the coastal cities, the Holy City, the goal of the crusade, remained in Moslem control.

On the way back he was forced by shipwreck to travel through the lands of Leopold of Austria. He and his companions went in disguise, as simple pilgrims returning from the Holy Land. However, they weren't very good at disguise. The men were far richer than the usual pilgrims and always wanted to get the best accommodations. Richard was recognized and captured by Leopold's men. He spent the next year and a half in the custody of the Germans, first Leopold and then the Holy Roman Emperor, Henry VI. The pope immediately excommunicated Leopold but this doesn't seem to have made much difference to anyone.[24]

Richard's behavior during this time amazed both friend and foe. He passed his days writing poetry, playing jokes on his guards, and charming one and all.[25]

Henry VI put Richard up for ransom. This was one of the things that was Not Done among Christian rulers, but if the pope couldn't stop Henry, no one else could, either.

Richard's youngest brother, John, had no interest in seeing him come home so it fell to Eleanor to raise the money, one hundred thousand pounds. This was more than the annual income of the king and had to be found in a country that had just collected a huge amount to finance the crusade.

No one should underestimate the power of a mother whose favorite son is being held captive. Eleanor tore off letters to Pope Clement III, reminding him that the king of England was also "the soldier of Christ, the anointed of the Lord, the pilgrim of the cross."[26] She took charge of raising the cash. Taxes were assessed at 25 percent on all moveable goods. Churches were told to surrender all their gold and silver. The Cistercian and Gilbertine orders may have thought they would be spared for they didn't believe in such extravagance, using plain ornaments in their churches. Eleanor told them they could hand over that year's wool crop instead.

She then took the treasure and the hostages that Henry VI had also demanded and set out for Germany, arriving at Richard's prison in Speyer on January 17, 1194.[27] She was seventy-one years old. Richard was released a month later. She then returned to England with him, where he had a ceremonial wearing of the crown, just to remind everyone that he was back and in charge.[28] Oddly, his wife, Berengaria (remember her?) was not with him. She had stayed on the continent. Eleanor was at his side for Richard's triumphant return.[29]

The rest of Richard's reign was spent in mopping up the mess caused by his baby brother, John, and Philip of France. They had done their best to carve out as much as they could from Richard's property while he was away. John had even insisted at one point that Richard was dead and that he, John, should be king. Eleanor had put her foot down on that one but, even so, there were rebellions in Richard's southern territories and he soon left England, never to return.

The story of Richard's death is also the stuff of legend. The bald facts are that he was shot in the shoulder while besieging the castle of

Chalus-Chabrol in the Limousin area of southern France. Twelve days later he died of complications from the wound. It was April 6, 1199. He was forty-one years old.

Almost before he was buried (at the convent of Fontevraud, where his mother, Eleanor, was spending her last years) the rumors were flying. It was said that Richard had been besieging the castle because he had heard there was a treasure there and wanted it for himself. This was made more reprehensible because it was Lent and the church had forbidden war during the Easter season.[30]

The treasure might have been a group of golden statues left by the Romans or a hoard of coins or just a lot of gold and silver.[31] No one could agree. The interesting thing is that none of the stories mention what happened to the "treasure" after Richard died trying to get it.

While Richard did indeed die while fighting during Lent and it may have been divine judgment, the treasure story seems to have come from the same sort of wishful thinking that led to the tales of a Templar treasure. Richard was putting down a rebellion of the viscount of Limoges and Chalus-Chabrol was one of several castles that Richard was besieging.[32] There wasn't anything special about it. Like many kings who led their own armies, Richard died in battle.

He is remembered as a hero, a barbarian, a protector of the poor, a greedy and absent king, and a valiant knight. Like many people, my first introduction to Richard was at the end of *Robin Hood* when Good King Richard comes home to save his country from Bad Prince John. It's hard to shake a glorious image like that.

But it is just an image. Robin Hood is a legend and the Richard of the story is legend, too. Despite not being able to retake Jerusalem, the crusade was Richard's finest hour. He must have been to some extent a charismatic person. He certainly inspired devotion and respect from his followers and even from some of his enemies.

The burning question seems to be whether he was a homosexual. I don't think there's enough evidence to decide and actually, I don't think it's important. He apparently did have a bastard son in Aquitaine, named Philip.[33] His name wasn't linked to any man in particular, as was the case with Edward II. He and Berengaria spent very little time together and, although they were married eight years, they had no children. But there might have been other reasons for this than his distaste for women. She might have been unable to have children. Richard may have found her unattractive. The fact that he didn't leave an heir was a serious problem for the stability of his kingdom. But even homosexual kings (and queens, I imagine) have done their duty and produced children.

Does it really have anything to do with what Richard accomplished or failed to accomplish?

The only person it might have mattered to was Berengaria. She is one of the lost children of history. After Richard's death, she retired to Le Mans in Normandy, where she founded an abbey. She died there in about 1230.[34]

Richard's wife had as little part in his life as she does in his legend. Richard was definitely a "man's man," a strong warrior, a brilliant strategist, not afraid to get his hands dirty and yet still cultivated, a lover of music and poetry. His exploits on the Third Crusade, his nobility while in captivity, and the dramatic tragedy of his death are all the stuff of high adventure.

As with the Templars, it's hard not to prefer the fantasy of Richard's life to the reality.

---

1 Richard of Aldgate, *Itninerarium Peregrinorum et Gestis Regis Recardi*, tr. A. F. Scott, in *The Plantagenet Age* (New York: Crowell, 1976) p. 4.

2 John Gillingham, *Richard the Lionheart* (New York: Times Books, 1978) p. 24.

3 There are numerous biographies of Eleanor of Aquitaine. Many of them are entertaining but I have found none that are historically satisfying.

4 Gabrielle M Spiegel, "Maternity and Monstrosity: Reproductive Biology in the *Roman de Mélusine.*" In Donald Maddox and Sara Sturm-Maddox, *Melusine of Lusignan: Founding Fiction in Late Medieval France* (Georgia University Press, 1996) p. 101.

5 Giraud de Barri, *De Principi Instructione*, III 27, p. 301, quoted in Laurence Harf-Lancer, *Les Fées au Moyen Age: Morgane et Mélusine, La naissance des fées* (Paris, 1984) p. 399, "non esse mirandum, si de genere tali et filii parentis et sese ad invicem fratres infestare non cessent: de diabolo namque eos omnes venisse et ed diobolum . . . ituros esse." Of course the same thing was supposed to have been said about them by Saint Bernard, in the form of a curse. The history of this legend doesn't belong here but it's lots of fun. By the end of the thirteenth century, Eleanor has been demonized as the Fairy Queen.

6 For the problems this caused, please see chapter 10, **Melisande, Queen of Jerusalem**, and chapter 14, **The Second Crusade**.

7 Gillingham, p. 32.
8 Ibid., p. 33.
9 Jonathan Riley-Smith, *The Crusades* (New Haven: Yale University Press, 2005) p. 141.
10 Gillingham, pp. 129–34.
11 Roger of Howden.
12 Malcolm Barber, *The New Knighthood* (Cambridge University Press, 1994) p. 278.
13 Gillingham, p. 130.
14 William of Newburgh, *The History of English Affairs.*
15 A. L. Poole, *From Domesday Book to Magna Carta 1087–1216* (Oxford, 1955; 2nd ed.) p. 353.
16 Gillingham, p. 139. It's not clear if Richard saw her before the marriage or if he let his mother pick her out.
17 Barber, pp. 119–220.
18 Please see the reference to the Third Crusades elsewhere in this book.
19 Gillingham, p. 176.
20 Ambroise, *Estoire de la Guerre Sainte*, ed. Marianne Ailes and Malcolm Barber (Woodbridge, UK: Boydell Press, 2003) p. 89, ll. 5508–36.
21 Baha' al-Din, in Francesco Gabrieli, *Arab Historians of the Crusades*, tr. from Italian by E. J. Costello (Dorset, 1989) p. 224. I know this is a translation of a translation and am not happy about it, but we take what we can get.
22 Ambroise, ll. 5524–30. "E Richardz li reis de Engleterre, Qui tanz Turs ocist en la terre, Ne volt plus sa teste debatre, Mais por l'orgoil des Turs abatre, Et por lor lei desaëngier, Et por cristïenté vengier."
23 Hans Eberhard Mayer, *The Crusades* (Oxford University Press, 1988; 2nd ed.) p. 149.
24 Gillingham, pp. 223–28.
25 Ibid., pp. 217–40.
26 Quoted in Ralph V. Turner, "Eleanor of Aquitaine in the Governments of Her Sons Richard and John," *Eleanor of Aquitaine, Lord and Lady*, ed. Bonnie Wheeler and John Carmi Parsons (Palgrave NYC, 2003) p. 85.
27 Ibid.
28 Gillingham, p. 242.
29 Turner, p. 86.
30 Gillingham, p 11. This was smart of the church since it was traditional for the nobility to get out of its winter stupor by riding out to fight someone, and this delayed them at least until after Easter.
31 According to Eudes Rigord, Guillaume le Breton, and Roger of Howden, respectively, in Gillingham, pp. 11–13.
32 Gillingham, pp. 9–23. This is an excellent example of how historians study the sources in order to come up with the most probable facts.
33 Gillingham, p. 162. The child must have been born before Richard and Philip II broke up.
34 Anne Echols and Marty Williams, *The Annotated Index of Medieval Women* (New York: Markus Wiener, 1992) p. 79.

CHAPTER TWENTY

The Assassins

The word "assassin" is, unfortunately, so common now, that we rarely wonder where it comes from, why, and when. While the act of hired murder is as old as history and myth, the first people to be called assassins lived in the late eleventh century in what is now Iran.

They did not call themselves Assassins. That name was only given to them by the Syrians when some of them settled in the mountains of Syria in the eleventh century.

The Assassins were founded by Hasan-i Sabbah, a Shi'ite Moslem born around 1060 in the Persian city of Qumm who moved as a child to the city of Rayy, present-day Tehran.[1] Hasan's family were Twelver Shi'ites, not members of the dominant group but well integrated into the society there. In his autobiography, Hasan relates how he came to follow a more radical path:

"From the days of my boyhood, from the age of seven, I felt a love for the various branches of learning, and wished to become a religious scholar; until the age of seventeen I was a seeker and searcher for knowledge, but kept to the Twelver faith of my fathers."[2]

This ended when Hasan met a man who taught him of the Isma'ili heresy, a form of Shi'ite Islam that followed the descendants of Isma'il, the son of the eighth-century imam Ja'far al-Sadiq. Over the centuries the Isma'ilis had developed a very different philosophy and worldview from the mainstream of Islam.[3]

After much study and soul searching, Hasan was converted at last during a serious illness. "I thought: surely this is the true faith, and because of my great fear I did not acknowledge it. Now my appointed time has come, and I shall die without having attained the truth."[4]

Now, in order to understand the place of the Assassins in the Islamic world, both then and now, it helps to know the background of the divisions within the faith.[5]

The two main branches of Islam are the Sunni and the Shi'ites. This split occurred almost immediately after the death of the prophet Mohammed. The first debate was over who should succeed him. Those who wanted to follow his uncle, Abu Bakr, became the Sunni. The Shi'ites followed Mohammed's cousin and son-in-law, Ali, married to his daughter, Fatima. Within a fairly short time, a fundamental difference developed. It was not so much about belief as practice. The Shi'ites felt that it was necessary for individual Moslems to have a teacher (imam) rather than try to interpret the Koran for themselves. The Sunni believed that the head of the community could be chosen by the community and, as long as the main teachings of the Koran were obeyed, there was room for a certain amount of variety in behavior.

The Shi'ites then divided among themselves on who was the most worthy imam. At first they were chosen from the descendants of Ali and Fatima. This group then split over the leadership of the grandsons of the Prophet, Hasan and Husain. Those who believed that Husain was the genuine imam looked to his descendants for leadership until the middle of the eighth century.

The trouble started when the imam at that time, Ja'far, disinherited his elder son, Isma'il, perhaps because he was too fond of wine. The younger son, Musa, was accepted by most of the community, but a few felt that Isma'il should have been chosen.

Isma'il died before his father and that should have ended the matter. However, the Isma'ili refused to rejoin those who followed Musa. Instead, they taught that, even though the "visible" imams no longer existed, there was a line of hidden imams who sent out agents to continue teaching the faithful. When the time was right, the hidden imam would appear to lead a world of justice.[6]

In the meantime, the followers of Musa and his descendants adapted to life under Sunni rule. When the twelfth of their imams, Muhammad al-Mahdi, vanished around 874, his followers decided that he would return in the end times and they needed no one else. They settled in to wait for him and took little interest in earthly politics. They became the Twelvers and they considered the Isma'ili to be the darkest heretics, hardly Moslem at all.[7]

So it was a big leap for the Twelver Hasan-i Sabbah to decide to join the Isma'ili. He left his home and spent several years traveling, learning and eventually preaching the Isma'ili faith.

At this time the Seljuk Turks had taken over a great portion of the Islamic world. They were fiercely orthodox Sunni who did not have the traditional Moslem tolerance for Christians and Jews. They were also determined to force all the Shi'ites to return to the Sunni path. Not surprisingly, there was a great deal of resentment toward them among the Shi'ite communities.

Hasan's Isma'ili sect branched off again to become the Nizari, named after another man whom they felt should have been the true imam. In most of the Moslem documents, the Assassins are known as the Nizari. They eventually made their headquarters in Alamut, in northern Iran, in about 1090.[8] It was at this time that the legends of the sect began.

At first the Nizari were concerned with destroying the power of the Seljuk invaders. They did this by infiltrating the courts of the Seljuk sultans until they could get close enough to them to kill them. It was a point of honor that they face their victims, who were usually well guarded. For this reason, the assassinations were considered suicide missions.[9]

The secrecy and suddenness of the attacks made the Nizari feared and hated throughout the Seljuk and Sunni people. "To kill them is more lawful than rainwater," said one. "To shed the blood of a heretic is more meritorious than to kill seventy Greek infidels."[10] Often the murder of an important dignitary would result in the massacre of local Isma'ili although they were not Nizari. The divisions among Sunni, Twelver Shi'ites, and Isma'ili grew wider.

THE NIZARI BECOME ASSASSINS

It wasn't until the late twelfth century that the crusaders took much notice of the Nizari. At that point they were known by their Syrian name of Hashishiyya, or Assassins. William of Tyre writes of them in the 1180s, "in the province of Tyre . . . is a certain people who have ten castles and surrounding lands and we have often heard that there are sixty thousand of them or more. . . . Both we and the Saracens call them Assassins, but I don't know where the name comes from."[11]

It wasn't until the early nineteenth century that a French historian named Sylvester de Sacy determined that the word "assassin" came from the word "hashish." This led to a number of fanciful stories. One explained that young Nizari men were drugged in order to believe that they had been to heaven and could only return there after achieving martyrdom. Another, repeated even by modern historians, is that they were given hashish to give them the courage to go out and kill.[12]

I first heard this explanation in my college days and even then it seemed odd to me. For one thing, hashish doesn't normally increase aggressiveness, quite the opposite. I kept having an image of giggling men in dark cloaks gliding through palaces, stopping to admire the colors of the gardens and fountains as they hunted down their target. However, most historians today think that the name was given the Nizari as a term of contempt, implying that they were as worthless as those who succumbed to drugs.

It is interesting that, as with the stories of the Templars, the legends of the Assassins are better known than their actual history.

THE ASSASSINS AND THE TEMPLARS

William of Tyre wasn't particularly concerned with the Assassins, as they rarely attacked Christians. As a matter of fact, the Syrian Assassins sometimes allied themselves with crusader lords to fight their mutual enemies. In 1128 the Assassins living in the town of Banyas were threatened by the city of Damascus. Their leader and a few others were crucified on the battlements of the wall of Damascus, "in order that it might be seen how God had dealt with the oppressors and brought signal chastisement upon the infidels."[13] Rather than let the town of Banyas fall to the Damascenes, the Assassins turned the town over to **Baldwin II**, king of Jerusalem.[14]

From about 1152, the Assassins in Syria paid tribute to the Templars of two thousand bezants a year.[15] This may have been brought about in retribution for the assassination of Count Raymond of Tripoli in that year, but the facts aren't certain. Soon after, the **Hospitallers**, now in possession of the fortress of Krak des Chevaliers, on the border of Assassin territory, also demanded two thousand bezants a year.

This leads to another story from William of Tyre, one of the most puzzling concerning the early days of the Templars.

According to William, the leader of the Assassins, whom he called "the old man of the mountain," wished to make an alliance with the crusaders. He sent a representative named "Boabdelle" to Almaric, king of Jerusalem, asking for instruction in Christianity. The catch was that conversion hinged on the remission of the two thousand bezants that the Assassins paid the Templars each year. Almaric was open to the idea, but the Templars were against it. They waylaid the emissary on his way back to Syria and murdered him.[16]

William continues to describe the anger of the king. Almaric tried to put the leader of the attackers, William of Mesnil, in prison. The Templars would have none of this and appealed the matter to the pope. Where it would have gone from there is hard to say, for Almaric died. One of the regents for his son, Baldwin IV, was Raymond, son of the murdered count of Tripoli. He was not interested in punishing those who killed Assassins. So the Assassins remained Moslem and the tribute continued to be paid.

Historians have puzzled over this for many years. Some think William made the whole story up. It's not found in any other records from the time. It seems strange that the Assassins would suddenly wish to convert just to save money. It seems equally strange that the Templars, knights of God, would want to lose the chance to bring so many souls to baptism. William believed that their greed overcame their piety and used this episode as proof of how far the order had fallen since its humble beginnings.

Unless new documents turn up, the truth will never be known. William's story was believed in his own time and it reflects the mixed feelings people had begun to have about the Templars.

The Assassins were still paying tribute in the middle of the thirteenth century when they again tried to have it ended by sending an envoy to King Louis IX of France, who was then in Acre on his crusade.

One theory as to why they felt compelled to pay this tribute instead of fighting was that their normal method of eliminating troublesome leaders wouldn't work with the military orders. The biographer of Louis, Jean de Joinville, explains, "for neither the Templars nor the Hospitallers had any fear of the Assassins, since their lord knew well that if he had either the Master of the Temple or of the Hospital killed, another, equally good, would be put in his place; therefore he had nothing to gain by their death. Consequently, he had no wish to sacrifice his Assassins on a project that would bring him no advantage."[17]

King Louis refused to eliminate the tribute and the masters of the Temple and the Hospital threatened the envoy. He soon returned with gifts for the king in an effort at conciliation.[18] Louis sent gifts in return along with a Syriac-speaking priest, Yves le Breton, who failed to convince the Assassins to convert.[19]

Eighty years after William of Tyre, Joinville saw the Templars as heroes and defenders of the faith in their relations with the Assassins.

While the Christians do not seem to have understood the differences among the sects of Islam, they did have the idea that the Assassins were not Moslem. Joinville says that they did not follow Mohammed but his uncle, Ali.[20] Benjamin of Tudela, a Spanish Jew, also assumed that the Assassins were a group apart. In his tale of his travels through the Middle East in 1169, Benjamin states, "it is four days to the land of Mulahid. Here lives a people who do not profess the Mohammedan religion, but live on high mountains, and worship the Old Man of the land of the Hashishim. And among them there are four communities of Israel who go forth with them in war-time. They are not under the rule of the king of Persia, but reside in the high mountains, and descend from these mountains to pillage and to capture booty, and then return to the mountains, and none can overcome them."[21]

"Mulahid" is a word that Christian commentators also used for the land of the Assassins. They learned it from the Moslems. It means "heretic."

The belief that the Assassins could strike everywhere and anywhere spread throughout the Christian and Moslem world. The French chronicler Guillaume de Nangis tells of how the Old Man of the Mountain sent an assassin to France to kill King Louis IX (Saint Louis). "But, in the course of their journey, God changed his heart, inspiring him to think of peace instead of murder."[22]

The Assassins stopped paying tribute only after the fall of the Hospitaller fortress of Krak des Chevaliers in 1271.[23]

Despite the Western fascination with the sect, the Assassins were much more concerned with the establishment of their theology among other Moslems than they were with the Christians. Eventually, the Assassin strongholds were conquered and the people dispersed during the Mongol invasions of the fourteenth century.

In their time, the Assassins managed to spread terror throughout the Islamic world. No one knew when or where they would strike. Stories were told of the fanaticism of the Assassins and of the immoral lives they led. One frequently repeated tale is of the mother who heard that her son's party had succeeded in assassinating a sultan. She rejoiced that he was now a martyr. When she discovered that he had survived, she put on mourning.

All through history there have been cadres of people who try to change the world through judicious removal of key leaders. The killing of Archduke Ferdinand and his wife is a good example. It resulted in the First World War. Of course, it's not clear if that was what the assassins intended.

It might be noted that Assassins, while prepared to die in the execution of their duty, did not practice random killing but prided themselves on only eliminating their main target. Their history is a complex one composed of faith, altruism, fanaticism, mysticism, and pragmatism.

In many ways, they were not that different from the Templars.

---

1 Bernard Lewis, *The Assassins: A Radical Sect in Islam* (London: Weidenfield and Nicolson, 2001) p. 38.

2 Quoted in Lewis, op. cit.

3 Lewis, pp. 26–27.

4 Quoted in Lewis, p. 39.

5 This is a very quick outline. For more complete information please consult your local librarian.

6 J. J. Saunders, *A History of Medieval Islam* (London: Routledge and Kegan Paul 1965) p. 127. The idea that a secret savior is waiting in the wings is a very old one.

7 Lewis, p. 39; Saunders, p. 127.

8 Marshall G. S. Hogan, *The Secret Order of Assassins: The Struggle of the Early Nizari Isma'ilis Against the Islamic World* (University of Pennsylvania Press, 2005; reprint of 1955 ed.) p. 77.

9 Ibid., pp. 110–13; Lewis, pp. 47–54.

10 Quoted in Lewis, p. 48.

11 William of Tyre, 20, 29. "In provincial Tyrensi . . . est quondam populus, castella decem habens cum surburanis suis, estque numerus eorum, ut sepius audivimus, quasi as sexaginta milia vel amplior. . . . Hos tam nostril quam Sarraceni, nescimus unde nominee deducto, Assissinos vocant."

12 Hogan, pp. 134–37; Lewis, pp. 11–13. Both authors point out the flaws in this theory.

13 Ibn al-Qalanisi, *The Damascus Chronicles of the Crusades*, tr. H. A. R. Gibb (London, 1932) p. 193. Here the Assassins are called "Batani."

14 Ibid., p. 194.

15 Malcolm Barber, *The New Knighthood* (Cambridge University Press, 1994) p. 103.

16 William of Tyre, 20, 29 and 20, 30, pp. 953–54.

17 Joinville, *Life of St. Louis*, tr. Margaret R. B. Shaw (Penguin, 1963) p. 277.

18 Reginald of Vichiers was probably the Templar master at this time. William de Chateauneuf was master of the Hospitallers.

19 Joinville, p. 278.

20 Ibid. Since the Assassins were an offshoot of the Shi'ite and it was the Sunni who followed the rule of Ali, Joinville had it backward, as well as not understanding that all the Moslems followed the teachings of Mohammed.

21 Benjamin of Tudela, *Travels in the Middle Ages*, tr. A. Asher (Malibu: Pangloss Press, 1983; reprint of 1840 ed.) p. 110. I have read nowhere else of Jewish forces fighting with the **Assassins**. If anyone finds a reference, please let me know.

22 Guillaume de Nangis, *Chroniques capétiennes Tomes 1. 1113–1270*, tr. François Guizot (Paleo, 2002) p. 169.

23 Alain Demurger, *Jacques De Molay: Le crepuscule des templiers* (Paris: Biographie Payot, 2002) p. 73.

CHAPTER TWENTY-ONE

The Hospitallers

As their name implies, the Order of the Knights of St. John, or Hospitallers, began as a charitable group, intended to assist pilgrims to Jerusalem who were in need of care and shelter. They seem to have been started sometime in the late eleventh century by some merchants from the Italian town of Amalfi. I say, "seem to" because there are no records of the foundation and because, like the Templars, the Hospitallers invented a mythology of their own in which, in some versions, the order was founded before the time of Christ and the parents of John the Baptist had once been associated with it.[1]

In the 1070s, the most likely time of establishment, Jerusalem was under the control of the Fatimid caliph of Egypt. He allowed pilgrims from the West to come to the city to visit the sites of Jesus' life. The canons of the Holy Sepulcher were Syrian Orthodox Christians, under the control of the Orthodox patriarch of Jerusalem. Pilgrims from Italy felt the need of a place for pilgrims to rest and be cared for where there would be people who spoke their language and practiced their religious rites.[2]

The military side of the hospitallers may have started as an additional service for the pilgrims, especially those going to the Jordan River to wade in the water where Jesus had been baptized. The Hospitallers set up a hostel known as the Red Cistern where pilgrims could get water and stay the night in safety on their way to the river.[3] Naturally, the cistern needed to be protected from raiders and one thing led to another until the Hospitallers had a contingent of knights. However, they never gave up the tradition of hospitality and often stressed that this was their main function.

By the late twelfth century the Templars and the Hospitallers were often spoken of in pairs, as if they were interchangeable. Rulers would send one member from each order on diplomatic missions. But there were several differences between the orders. From the early days of both, the Templars were largely drawn from French-speaking areas and theirs was solely a military order, whereas the Hospitallers were mostly Spanish- and Italian-speaking and focused on the care of the sick and the protection of pilgrims. As the Hospitallers grew, the order attracted more French speakers until it was largely French-speaking.

It's clear that the military side of the order began early. In 1144, Raymond, count of Tripoli, gave the Hospitallers the fortress known as the Krak des Chevaliers. Eventually the Hospitallers acquired more property in the crusader kingdoms than the Templars.[4]

The Templars and Hospitallers are often seen as rivals, even enemies. I think of them more as brothers. Sometimes they got along fine, supporting each other against the rest of the world. Sometimes they were on opposite sides of a question and fought each other bitterly. In the end, the gallant death of the Templar master William of Beaujeu at the siege of Acre is mourned by the Hospitaller Grand Master, "On that day the Master of the Temple also died of a mortal wound from a javelin. God have mercy on his soul!"[5]

Many donation charters gave property equally to the Templars and Hospitallers. The most astonishing of these is that of Alfonso I, king of Aragon and Navarre, made in 1131 in which he left his entire kingdom to the Templars, Hospitallers, and the Church of the Holy Sepulcher.[6] They weren't allowed to keep the kingdom; the heirs that Alfonso had ignored protested and a settlement was arranged. But it shows dramatically how even at that early date, the two orders were united in popular thinking and connected with the Church of the Holy Sepulcher. It didn't help in telling them apart that both the

Templars and the Hospitallers often built their churches with a round nave, in imitation of the Church of the Holy Sepulcher.[7]

The Hospitallers even loaned money, just as the Templars did. On the **Second Crusade**, Louis VII of France borrowed from the French Templar master, Everard de Barres, and also the Hospitaller master, Raymond du Puy.[8]

The Hospitallers also came in for their share of criticism, especially from that late-twelfth-century defender of the secular clergy, Walter Map. He was furious at the privileges granted to both the Templars and the Hospitallers at the Third Lateran Council. Walter saw both orders as equally wicked. "By many tricks they supplant us and keep us from the churches."[9] He felt that they lured impoverished knights into joining the orders by refusing to give them money unless they signed up. In that way they kept donations from coming to local parishes. There is no evidence that this charge was true.

Even popes would occasionally chide the Hospitallers. In 1209, Innocent III scolded them for keeping concubines and "shamefully involving themselves in secular affairs as if they were laymen."[10]

There is a general belief that the Templars and Hospitallers were constantly in competition and rarely on good terms. While they did have their differences, particularly over land, on the whole they seem to have worked together quite well. During the crusade of **Richard the Lionheart** the Templars and Hospitallers switched each day from the rear guard to the vanguard of the army.[11] Also the **Rule** of the Temple makes it clear that, in a pinch, the Templar knight should make for the nearest unit of Hospitallers:

> Rule 167. "And if it happens that any brother cannot go towards his banner because he has gone too far ahead for fear of Saracens who are between him and the banner, or he does not know what became of it, he should go to the first Christian banner that he finds. And if he finds that of the Hospital, he should stay by it and should inform the leader of the squadron."[12]

The main issues that divided the two orders were political. Although in theory they were supposed to be outside of local squabbles, in reality it was impossible not to get pulled into them. One of the nastiest was when the orders became involved in the constant rivalry between the Italian city-states of Genoa and Venice. The city of Acre was largely divided among the military orders and the Italians, with a small area for other religious groups and the English. In a struggle that went on between 1256 and 1258, over some property that was owned by the monastery of St. Sabas, the Hospitallers supported the Genoese and the Templars the Venetians.[13] This more than once led to blows between the knights.

The most dramatic divisions had to do with the several conflicts over who was to inherit the crown of Jerusalem. One of these took place later in the history of the Latin kingdoms, long after Jerusalem had been lost. In 1277, the claimants were Hugh III, king of Cyprus, descended from Sybilla, the sister of Baldwin IV, and Charles of Anjou, the brother of the king of France, who had bought rights to the throne from Maria of Antioch, Hugh's cousin.[14] The Hospitallers supported Hugh; the Templars supported Charles. One reason the Templars did this is that the Grand Master, William of Beaujeu, was related to Charles.

The Hospitallers had one edge over the Templars: when the criticism got too hot, they could retreat into their hospices. They seem to have done this after the debacle of the **Second Crusade**, although they don't seem to have played a large military role in the expedition in any case.[15]

The idea that the Templars and the Hospitallers were much the same was emphasized in the way they were viewed by chroniclers. "So the Hospitallers and the Knights Templar armed themselves taking with them a great many very strong Turcopoles."[16] King Richard orders "the Templars and the Hospitallers to come to him."[17] "Count Raymond of Tripoli wanted the fortresses and castles to be in the keeping of the Temple and the Hospital."[18] The Templars and Hospitallers are given joint custody of the town of Messina, until it can be decided who should have it.[19]

This is reflected in the number of times that an envoy included a

Templar and a Hospitaller apparently as witnesses or perhaps even bodyguards. They are rarely named; they are simply seen as representatives of their orders. The popes, including **Clement V**, customarily had one Templar and one Hospitaller as chamberlains. The papacy used the brothers indiscriminately as messengers and relied on loans from both orders to shore up papal finances.[20]

Even negative remarks were aimed at the military orders as if they were all the same. Pierre Dubois, one of **Philip the Fair**'s employees, wrote that the Templars and the Hospitallers should be able to live off their lands in the Holy Land and Cyprus and donate the money they gained in the West to start schools for missionaries and pay for mercenaries to fight.[21]

It's possible that in 1307 King Philip the Fair was interested in condemning the Hospitallers as well as the Templars, or it may be that the Templars were just more accessible. When **Jacques de Molay** was summoned to meet with Pope Clement V and the king, the master of the Hospitallers, Fulk de Villeret, was supposed to be there as well. But he was "stopped in his way at Rhodes by the Saracens . . . and could not come on the date set and was given a legitimate excuse by the messengers."[22] Whew!

So Fulk escaped the fate of Jacques de Molay and the Hospitallers actually gained something by the dissolution of the Templars at the **Council of Vienne**, since most of the Temple property eventually reverted to them, although they had to make deals with the various kings in order to get it.

At the same time that the Templar trials were going on, the Hospitallers were busy organizing the conquest of the island of Rhodes. On August 11, 1308, Pope Clement proclaimed a special crusade to be undertaken by the Hospitallers for the defense of Cyprus and Armenia.[23] He offered indulgences to those who gave to the cause and had boxes put in the churches particularly marked for the Hospital.[24] Fulk de Villeret thought Rhodes was a better goal and so took that island. He was right in that it was easier to hold on to. The Hospitallers would be based at Rhodes until 1522.

Now that they were headquartered on an island, the Hospitallers concentrated on sea power. They hired a fleet of pirate corsairs that were licensed to harry Moslem trading ships and those of the Italians who did business with Moslems. The booty made a welcome addition to their income.[25]

In the fifteenth century the arrival of the Ottoman Turks in the east put the Hospitallers on the front lines again. They had come to terms with the familiar enemies, like the Mamluks. Now they were faced with another batch of newly converted conquerors. Under the sultan, Selim, the Ottoman armies expanded into eastern Europe and attacked Rhodes. The last Hospitaller Grand Master on Rhodes was forced to surrender the island to Selim on January 1, 1523.[26]

The remnants of the Hospital had no base for seven years. In 1530, the Spanish Holy Roman Emperor gave the order the islands of Gazon, Camino, and Malta. From there, the Christians still had dreams of reconquering the Holy Land.[27]

The Hospitallers became known as the Knights of Malta, the name they bear to this day. The next time they were conquered, it would not be by the Moslems but by the natural force known as Napoleon Bonaparte.

For the next two hundred years and more after arriving in Malta, the Hospitallers continued their rear-guard crusade through piracy. Then the French Directorate, still finding its feet after the Revolution, learned that Malta might be taken over by its enemies, the Austrians and the Russians.[28]

They sent Napoleon to take care of matters. He took Malta without a fight. The master and the brothers left on June 17, 1798, taking some of their relics with them. Many other relics and all the records the Hospitallers had inherited from the Templars were among the loot taken by the French soldiers. Much of the loot was put aboard Napoleon's ship *l'Orient*.[29]

Napoleon set off to take his army for a fun summer in Egypt. "On the evening of 1 August the British fleet under Nelson caught up with the French fleet in Aboukir Bay off the north Egyptian coast and defeated it in the battle of the Nile. *L'Orient* was blown up and sunk, with the Order's relics on board."[30]

Just think how many questions could be settled if that ship could be found.

The next years of the former Hospitallers were exceedingly strange and included having Paul I, the Russian tsar and son of Catherine the Great, as Grand Master. That experiment didn't last long.

In 1834 Pope Gregory XVI gave the Knights of Malta a hospital, where they returned to their original duty of taking care of poor and sick pilgrims. In this form the order has spread over the world, and even has Protestant affiliates.[31]

Why did the Hospitallers survive when the Templars didn't? I believe that it was because of the things that made them different. They always said that the care of the poor and sick was their first responsibility. When times got tough, they had that to fall back on. While, like the Templars, they were involved in banking, they did not have such high-profile depositors. So the average person did not associate the Hospitallers with untold wealth.

Perhaps the Templars might have been saved if they'd simply founded a few hospitals. . . . Perhaps not.

---

1 Helen Nicholson, *The Knights Hospitaller* (Woodbridge, UK: Boydell and Brewer, 2001) p. 3.

2 William of Tyre, *Chronicon*, ed. R. B. C. Huygens (Turnholt, 1986) book 18, 4–5, pp. 814–17.

3 Malcolm Barber, "The Charitable and Medical Activities of the Hospitallers and Templars, Eleventh to Fifteenth Centuries." The Whichard Lecture, March 23, 2000, p. 6. Text at: http://www.ecu.edu/history/whichard/MBarberCharitable.htm

4 Joshua Prawer, *The Crusaders' Kingdom: European Colonialism in the Middle Ages* (London: Phoenix Press, 1972) p. 260.

5 Quoted in Nicholson, p. 37 (Cartulaire 4, no. 4157) tr. Edwin James King, *The Knights Hospitaller in the Holy Land* (London, 1931) p. 301.

6 The text of this charter is translated in Malcolm Barber and Keith Bate, *The Templars: Selected Sources translated and annotated* (Manchester University Press, 2002) pp. 161–62. See also chapter 8, **Go Forth and Multiply**.

7 Nicholson, p. 6.

8 Suger, abbot of St. Denis. *Omnitt Opera*, p. 27.

9 Walter Map, *De Nugis Curialium* tr. Frederick Tupper and Marbury Ogle (London: Chatto and Windus, 1924) book xxiii, p. 44.

10 Alan Forey, *The Military Orders* (London: McMillon, 1992) p. 199.

11 Helen Nicholson tr., *The Chronicle of the Third Crusade* (Ashgate, Aldershot, 1997) pp. 240–62.

12 J. M. Upton-Ward tr., *The Rule of the Templars* (Woodbridge: Boydell, 1992) p. 60.

13 Malcolm Barber, *The New Knighthood* (Cambridge University Press, 1994) p. 155.

14 Nicholson, p. 37. For more on Charles of Anjou please see **The Templars and the Saint**.

15 Ibid., p. 20.
16 Helen Nicholson tr., *The Chronicle of the Third Crusade* (Ashgate, Aldershot, 1997) p. 258.
17 Ibid., p. 370.
18 Peter W. Edbury tr., *The Conquest of Jerusalem and the Third Crusade* (Ashgate, Aldershot, 1998) p. 14.
19 John Gillingham, *Richard the Lionheart* (New York: Times Books, 1978) p. 153.
20 I. S. Robsindo, *The Papacy 1037–1198* (Cambridge University Press 1990) p. 243.
21 Forey, p. 218.
22 Guillaume de Nangis, *Chroniques capétiennes Tome II 1270–1328*, tr. François Guizot (Paris: Paleo, 2002).
23 Sylvia Menache, *Clement V* (Cambridge University Press, 1998) p. 105.
24 Ibid., p. 109.
25 Nicholson, p. 57.
26 Ibid., p. 67.
27 Ibid.
28 Ibid., p. 135. The Austrians were especially angry because the French had decapitated Marie Antoinette, who had been born an Austrian princess.
29 Ibid., p. 136.
30 Ibid.
31 Ibid., p. 144.

CHAPTER TWENTY-TWO

Grand Masters 1191–1292/93

ROBERT OF SABLÉ, 1191–1193/94

Robert of Sablé came from Anjou, the core of the lands that **Richard the Lionheart** controlled before he became king of England. Robert was a follower of the Lionheart who supported the revolt of Richard and his elder brother Henry, "the Young King," against their father, Henry II.[1] He was in Richard's entourage when the new king went on crusade and served both as treasurer of the king and as a messenger during the crusade.[2]

He must have been a very recent member of the Templars when he was elected to succeed Gerard of Ridefort, who was killed at the 1191 siege of Acre. The *Eracles* chronicler states, "Afterwards, the Templars elected a man of high birth who was in their house, named Brother Robert of Sablé as their master."[3] The way they express it, he may just have been visiting at the time.

On the way to the Holy Land, Richard had taken a few days off to conquer the island of Cyprus. He really didn't need another island and so he offered to sell it to his friend Robert and his Templars. He asked only one hundred thousand bezants for the whole thing, a real bargain.[4] The Templars didn't have that much money so they gave the king a down payment of forty thousand bezants' worth of property and sent some men to Cyprus to tell the natives about the deal and collect the taxes.

This turned out to be a big mistake.

[T]hey thought they could govern the people of the island in the same way they treated the rural population in the land of Jerusalem. They thought they could ill-treat, beat and misuse them and imagined they could control the island of Cyprus with a force of 20 brothers. The Greeks hated their rule and were oppressed by it. . . . They rose in rebellion and came to besiege them in the castle of Nicosia. When the Templars saw such a multitude of people coming to besiege them, they were greatly taken aback. They told them that they were Christians, just as they were, that they had not come there by their own strength, and that, if they would let them quit the island of Cyprus, they would go willingly.[5]

The Cypriots, still smarting from the injuries inflicted by Richard's army, preferred to take revenge on the Templars. However, the twenty brothers managed to defeat the mob and get back to Acre, where it was decided that Cyprus wasn't worth the manpower needed to tame it.

Robert of Sablé went to Richard and asked him to return the deposit and take his island back. Richard said he'd be happy to take back Cyprus but he had decided that the property the Templars had given him in payment wasn't worth what they had said and so he wasn't going to give it back.[6] In those days there was no grace period to rethink a purchase so the Templars just had to grin and bear it.

Richard then sold the island to Guy of Lusignan. Guy had been king of Jerusalem through his wife, Sybilla. Sybilla and their two daughters had died around 1190, presumably in an epidemic. The crown, such as it was, since Jerusalem had fallen to Saladin in 1187, passed to Sybilla's sister, Isabelle.[7] Guy had never been all that popular with anyone but Sybilla. He went to Richard and offered to buy the island on the same terms as those given to the Templars. Guy then borrowed money from some merchants in Tripoli and paid Richard, who had now managed to sell the island twice.[8]

Guy remarried and his descendants ruled Cyprus for the next three hundred years.

I don't know if the relationship between Richard and Robert of Sablé cooled after this. Kings can get away with a lot. In 1192, when Richard decided to return to England, he asked Robert for ten knights and four sergeants to guard him on the trip.[9] Forced to travel through the land of his enemy, Leopold of Austria, Richard was taken captive and held two years before his ransom could be paid.

Robert did not neglect the administrative side of his job. In 1191 he made sure that the new pope, Celestine III, confirmed all the rights that previous popes had granted the Templars.[10] Other than that, his time as Grand Master was one of the more tranquil ones.

Robert de Sablé died on September 28, in either 1193 or 1194.

GILBERT ERAIL, 1194–1200

Gilbert was another career Templar. He had served in Jerusalem, where he was grand commander of the city in 1183.[11] He then went to Spain, where he was living when he learned of his election as Grand Master.

One of the first things Gilbert did in 1194 was to get a papal confirmation of the privileges of the order.[12] This was something that no Templar master ever took for granted. Those privileges were the base of the Templar economy.

He was in Acre by March 5, 1198, perhaps before.[13] During his tenure the Templars became involved in property disputes with the Hospitallers over rights in the town of Vilania. This became so intense that the matter had to be settled by the pope, Innocent III.[14]

When Gilbert was excommunicated by the bishop of Sidon, Innocent stepped in again, saying that only he could excommunicate Templars.[15] I haven't been able to find out what Gilbert had done to offend the bishop but I'm sure he was glad that he had been to renew the regulation that only the pope could excommunicate a Templar.

Gilbert died on December 21, 1200. His time as Grand Master seems to have been one of consolidation after the loss of so much land to **Saladin**. The fleeting mentions of his arguments with others in Acre are tantalizing but they don't seem to have been interesting enough for chroniclers to make much of them.

PHILIP OF PLESSIS, 1201–1209

Philip was another Angevin who came to the Holy Land with Richard I. He was a younger son who had already married and had sons of his own when he left on crusade. He encouraged fighting rather than making truces with the Moslems.[16] While Innocent III supported him, the pope also wrote that he had succumbed to the sin of pride and abuse of his privileges.[17] Philip died November 12, 1209.

WILLIAM OF CHARTRES, 1210–1219

William of Chartres is also known as William of Puiset. He was from a family that had a tradition of supporting the crusading movement. Before becoming Grand Master he was wounded in an ambush by the Armenians under Leo, Roupenid prince of Cilicia.[18] In 1215 William was one of the signers of an agreement concerning property rights among the Templars, Hospitallers, and the Order of Santiago, brokered by Pope Alexander III.[19] He was also the Grand Master during the first part of the Fifth Crusade in which the Christian armies under Andrew of Hungary and the excommunicated Frederick II attempted to defeat Egypt.[20] William's father, Count Milo of Bar-sur-Seine, and his brother, Walter, both fought and died on that same crusade.[21] William became ill while with the crusaders in Damietta and died August 26, 1219.

PETER OF MONTAIGU, 1219–1231

Peter of Montaigu was probably elected in an emergency meeting of the order at Damietta, following the death of William of Chartres. Like William, Peter's family was very much involved in the religious life of the East. Peter's brother, Guérin, was Grand Master of the Hospital, giving a whole new meaning to the fraternal rivalry between the two orders. One of his uncles was Eustorge, archbishop of Nicosia.[22] Another uncle, Bernard, was bishop of Puy, in the French Alps. Peter also had a cousin who didn't enter the religious life but married on Cyprus and died there, fighting imperial troops.[23]

Although his family was from the Auvergne region of France, Peter spent his early career in Spain and Provence, becoming master of the Templars of the region in 1206.[24] He distinguished himself in battle in Spain, especially at the battle of al-Aqsa, where he and his Templars arrived in time to save the day.[25]

The Fifth Crusade was another resounding defeat and Peter was one of those who had to mop up. He wrote a letter of frustration to the preceptor in England, Alan Martel. In it he describes the misery of the army when the Egyptians opened the sluice gates in the Nile Delta, cutting off the supply routes. "Destitute of provisions, the army of Christ could neither proceed further nor retreat nor flee anywhere, . . . It was trapped like a fish in a net."[26]

The letter ends like most from the crusades, with a plea for more funds.

Peter was also caught up in the struggle between the Holy Roman Emperor, Frederick II, and the popes. This was the old battle between the temporal and spiritual powers. Italy was part of Frederick's inheritance, which brought him into conflict with the Papal States. Then he married Isabelle, the heiress to the throne of Jerusalem, which gave him some interest in retaking the city. Frederick managed to be excommunicated by a number of popes, dying unrepentant in 1250.

When Frederick arrived in Acre, after the defeat of the army at

Damietta, the Templars and the Hospitallers refused to follow him, since he was shunned by the Church. This eventually led to a nasty scene in which, according to some, Frederick accused the Templars of trying to murder him.[27] They accused him of treachery.[28]

Although Frederick soon left Acre, he got his revenge on the Templars and the Hospitallers by confiscating all their property in Italy and imprisoning many of the brothers there. The property still hadn't been returned when Peter died in 1231. The treaty of reconciliation between Frederick and the pope wasn't made until 1239, when Armand of Périgord was Grand Master. As we shall see, this may not have been accidental.

ARMAND OF PÉRIGORD, C. 1231–1244

Armand of Périgord probably came from Guienne, in the south of France. He had been Templar preceptor in Sicily and Calabria before becoming Grand Master and it was widely believed that his election was influenced by the Holy Roman Emperor, Frederick II, who controlled Sicily at that time.[29] However, there seems to be no proof of that.

Most of Armand's career as Grand Master was spent in skirmishes with both Moslem and imperial forces. Frederick had arranged through negotiations for the Christians to have most of Jerusalem back, as well as signing an eight-year truce with the sultan of Cairo.

Armand did nothing to uphold the truce. The most notable of his actions resulted in another Templar slaughter. In 1237, against the advice of Walter, count of Jaffa, he led a band of knights against Moslem troops who were "foraging in the region between Atlit and Acre." The Templars were badly defeated. Only the Grand Master and nine of his men escaped.[30]

Armand slowly learned the reality of life in the Latin kingdoms, what was left of them. He began to understand the complexity of the relations among the descendants of **Saladin**. They were arguing over who had the best claim to the Ayyubid kingdoms; choosing up sides, and fighting each other, just as the Christian lords did. And there were some who were willing to ally themselves with the Christians in order to defeat their brothers and cousins. In 1237, Armand believed it would be possible to divide and conquer the Ayyubids.[31]

In November 1239 another force of fresh blood arrived from the West, this time under the command of Thibaud, count of Champagne. The knights he brought with him were eager for battle and plunder and annoyed by the hard-learned caution that the masters of the Temple and Hospital showed. Henry, count of Bar, announced that he hadn't come all this way to sit around and that he and his men were riding out the next day to "forage."

> They [the Masters] knew very well that neither their intentions nor their motives were good, that they were inspired by envy, malice, pride and greed. . . . They told them [the knights] clearly that if they rode to war as they intended, they would well be . . . killed or taken prisoner, to the great shame and harm of Christendom. The foragers replied forcefully that they would do nothing of the kind; they had come there to fight unbelievers and did not mean to keep putting off any encounter.[32]

Henry and his men sallied forth to the plain near Gaza where they had heard that the local people had sent many of their animals for safekeeping. They decided to camp awhile, have dinner, sleep, and then sneak out in the morning and capture the horses. "Such was their pride and their arrogance that they felt little or no concern about their enemies, into whose land they had thrust so far forward and who were very near them. Then they learned indeed that Our Lord will not be served in that way."[33]

The sultan Al-Adil Abu Bakr II happened to be in Gaza and learned of the slowly approaching raiding party. He summoned all fighting men from the region and they went to meet the invaders. By morning, some of the crusaders were getting nervous and decided to turn back. But Henry of Bar and many others decided to fight.

They were surrounded and annihilated. Any survivors were taken to Cairo and sold into slavery.[34]

Although the Rothelin chronicler, living in Acre, felt that the men got what they deserved, some in Europe saw it differently. Both the Templars and the Hospitallers were criticized for failing to support Henry of Bar.[35] There was even a poem, supposedly written by the enslaved count of Monfort and smuggled to the West.

> *If the Hospitallers*
> *Templars and brother knights*
> *Had shown our men the way,*
> *Had ridden as they should,*
> *Then all our chivalry*
> *Would not in prison lie.*[36]

Perhaps it was to quell these negative views of the order that a year later Armand, on behalf of the Temple, gave the master and the brothers of St. Lazarus the rents from property they owned in the English quarter of Acre.[37]

The settlers from the West had learned a lot about Near Eastern politics in the five generations they had been there. In the 1240s they were keenly aware of the struggle that was going on among the heirs of Saladin in Egypt and Damascus. The Templars supported Damascus; the Hospitallers, Egypt. In 1244, the Templars, under Armand of Périgord, apparently convinced the Christian forces to support Damascus with military aid. The combined armies marched into Gaza and, on October 18, were soundly defeated at the battle of La Forbie (Harbiya).[38]

Among the dead were Peter, the archbishop of Tyre, and the bishop of St. George of Ramla. Walter of Châteauneuf, master of the Hospitallers, was captured. He didn't regain his freedom until 1250.

Armand of Périgord was also captured at La Forbie. He died in prison; no one knows when.

WILLIAM OF SONNAC, 1247–1250

William of Sonnac was the preceptor of Aquitaine when he was chosen as the new Grand Master. Before that he had been the commander of the Templar house at Auzon.[39] Since no one was certain if Grand Master Armand was dead, William may have felt that he was always just an acting Grand Master. If so, it was one hard act.

William accompanied **King Louis IX** on his expedition to Egypt, where the Grand Master was forced into a battle in the town of Mansourah, in which Robert, the brother of the king, was killed. Everyone agreed that the attack was a mistake, with most of the blame going to Robert. Jean de Joinville, seneschal of Champagne, says, "The Templars, as their Grand Master told me later, lost on this occasion some two hundred and eighty men-at-arms, and all mounted."[40] There seems such a weight of despair in that simple statement. In all the years of the Templars, the total number of knights in the East never averaged more than three hundred. Even assuming that many of the dead were sergeants, the Templars had still lost more than a quarter of their fighting men.

William, who had already lost the use of one eye in an earlier encounter, was blinded and killed in battle in Egypt on February 11, 1250.

RENAUD OF VICHIERS, 1250–1256

When William of Sonnac was killed, Renaud of Vichiers was marshal of the order. Not only was there no time for a proper election, there also weren't enough Templars left alive to hold one. Renaud took over until their return from Egypt to Acre where enough men could be collected.

When King Louis of France and many of his noblemen were held for ransom, Renaud took it upon himself to allow Jean de Joinville to take money from the chests that the Templars were holding for various depositors, in order to free the king.[41]

When the king and the remnants of the army returned to Acre, "the king, on account of the consideration the Temple had shown him, helped make him Master of the Temple."[42] There may not have been much protest from the remaining Templars. Renaud had done well under terrible circumstances.

Louis seemed to think that made the score even between them. He certainly showed Renaud no further favors. In 1251 Renaud sent his marshal, Hughes de Jouy, to negotiate an agreement with the sultan of Damascus to share a rich farming region between the two lands. When Hughes came back to Acre to have King Louis IX ratify the treaty, Louis was furious that it had been done without his authority. He had the Templars parade barefoot through the camp to his tent. Renaud was forced to hand the treaty back to the sultan's representative and say loudly that he regretted acting without the king's permission. Hughes was banished from the kingdom of Jerusalem.[43]

Renaud died January 20, 1256.[44] Louis lasted long enough to lead another ruinous crusade. Renaud is mostly forgotten. Louis was made a saint. I think there should be a recount.

THOMAS BÉRARD, 1256–1273

When Thomas Bérard became Grand Master, he was faced with a terrifying new threat to all the peoples of the Near East and also the lesser but more immediate troubles of the incessant squabbling among the inhabitants of the various sections of Acre.

Most of the quarreling was among the merchants of the Italian city-states Genoa, Pisa, and Venice. They all had financial stakes in Acre and were fierce competitors for trade throughout the eastern Mediterranean.

"In 1258, during the civil disturbance known as the War of St. Sabas, the master of the temple, Thomas Bérard, took refuge in the tower of St. Lazarus when his own stronghold was subjected to crossfire between the Pisans, Genoese and Venetians."[45]

This seems to have been a normal day at the office for Thomas.

But he also had to continue the effort to regain land lost over the past eighty years. In 1260, the Templars and the Ibelin lords attacked a large encampment of Turks near Tiberias. They were routed and many Templars were killed or captured. Among the prisoners were future Grand Masters William of Beaujeu and Thibaud Gaudin. The marshal of the Templars, Stephen of Saissy, survived and, perhaps because of this, Bérard believed that he had showed either cowardice or treachery. He stripped Stephen of his habit and sent him back home.[46] Considering the shortage of manpower, Stephen must have been a pretty poor example of a Templar.

But these were all small matters compared to the long-dreaded arrival of the Mongols in the Near East. Under Genghis Khan, they had already conquered much of China and were now moving into the ancient Persian Empire. Tales of their cruelty flew like crows through the towns in their path. However, since they were considered "pagans" there was hope among the leaders of the Church that they could be brought into the Christian community and would join forces to liberate Jerusalem again. Franciscan missionaries were sent east as the Mongols drew near.

From his vantage point Thomas saw that this was a forlorn hope. He wrote many times to the West, trying to make them see the seriousness of the situation. One letter, sent in 1261 to the Templar treasurer in London, has survived:

Although in our usual way we have previously informed you on many occasions of the terrible and awesome arrival of the Tartars [Mongols] . . . they are now here in front of our walls, knocking at our gates and now is not the time to hide their skirmishes under a bushel bur rather openly to reveal their stupendous and amazing exploits that have shaken Christendom externally with the weapons of great pain and fear.[47]

The letter continues with a recitation of all the lands the Mongols had taken; how the people of Antioch begged to be allowed to pay tribute rather than be destroyed; how the city of Aleppo was flattened. Then Thomas comes to the essential reason for his letter:

> Because of the poverty and weakness of the Christians we do not see the possibility of holding on to the other lands and places unless the Lord show his mercy. . . . May you be in no doubt that unless help comes quickly to us from your countries, whatever our ability to resist the attack and onslaught of such a great horde, there is no doubt that the whole of Christendom this side of the sea will be subject to Tartar rule. Added to this, you should know that because of the important and countless expenses incurred in fortifying our said castles and the city of Acre to improve matters, our house is suffering and has suffered such huge runs on our money that it is recognized that we are in a dangerous financial situation.[48]

Thomas was serious about the dire financial situation. He would have been willing to take out loans from the Italians but they had all left the city. He was ready to pawn the crosses and incense burners and anything else in the house.

While waiting for help, Thomas did everything he could to find cash. In 1261 he negotiated with the archbishop of Nicosia for the payment to tithes owed to the order from land in Cyprus.[49]

He sold Templar land in Lucca to the Franciscans.[50] When the heirs of Saint Francis have more money than the Templars, you know the world is upside down.

Thomas Bérard died on March 25, 1273.[51] After him the sky fell in on the last of the crusader states.

WILLIAM OF BEAUJEU, 1273–1291

The election of William of Beaujeu [or Clermont] as Grand Master was announced by Hugh Revel, the Grand Master of the Hospitallers, in a letter to the count of Flanders. "The good men of the Temple have chosen, as master and governor of the Temple, Brother Guillaume de Beaujeu. . . . The messengers of the Temple have left for France, taking the purse [empty, no doubt] and the news."[52] Master Hugh continues to say that things are bad in the Holy Land and "the funds that the lord king of France requested of the lord pope for the sustenance of the land are now as lost."[53]

It was not an auspicious beginning.

William was born, probably in France, about 1230.[54] He was connected to the family of Beaujeu-Forez, which was distantly related to the royal family of France. William joined the Templars as a young man and was in the East by the time he was thirty when he was captured by the Turks at a battle near the town of Tiberius.[55] Even before that, in 1254, he may have been preceptor of a commandery in Lombardy.[56] In 1272, he is listed as the master of the Knights Templar in Sicily.[57] He was there when he was elected.

Knowing how bad the situation was in Acre, William spent two years "visiting all the houses of the Temple in the kingdoms of France and England and Spain" rather than going to the city at once.[58] His secretary reports proudly that "he amassed a great treasure and then came to Acre."[59]

But would it be enough?

As with many of the other Grand Masters, William came from a family with strong crusading traditions. A relative, Humbert of Beaujeu, had died with Saint Louis at Damietta in Egypt.[60] While William was trying to preserve the last of the Latin cities in the East, his brother Louis, constable of France, died on crusade in Spain with King Philip III.[61]

Despite the outside threats, the Templars still found themselves getting caught up in local politics. Because the lord of Jubail had become a lay brother of the Temple, William took his side in a feud with the bishop and prince of Tortosa. William sent thirty Templars to help the lord of Jubail. As a consequence, "the prince had the house of the Temple in Tripoli knocked down, and cut down the Templars' woods."[62]

After all the fear of a Mongol invasion, the end of the Latin king-doms came from Egypt, just as many of the later kings and crusaders had feared.

William of Beaujeu died at the siege of Acre in 1291, run through with a spear as he rode into battle.[63]

THIBAUD GAUDIN, 1291–1292/93

The next-to-last Grand Master of the Temple had spent many years in the East. He had been captured by the Turks and, after his release, was commander of the ever-diminishing land of Jerusalem.[64] During the siege of Acre, Thibaud and a few of the Templars escaped from the city in ships and went to the Templar castle of Sidon farther up the coast. The sultan sent "one of his emirs, Sanjar al Shuja'i, who besieged the castle on the sea with siege engines."[65] Thibaud "saw his position assaulted and thought he ought not to begin his term of office by abandoning the castle."[66]

But guess what? "He took counsel with the brethren and with their consent he went off to Cyprus, promising them that he should send them relief."[67] I suspect that the anonymous Templar of Tyre went with him or we wouldn't know anything of this. When Thibaud got to Cyprus, he didn't seem all that energetic about getting help for the men left behind. Finally, other Templars who had made it to the island sent word back to Sidon that no help was coming.[68]

The castle of Sidon was abandoned to the Mamluk sultan, who had it razed.

Thibaud Gaudin remained in Cyprus and sent back to Europe for more men to replace those who had fallen at Acre. Amazingly, they came.[69]

It's hard to say if, having abandoned two Templar bases, Thibaud could have inspired his men with fighting fervor. But we are not to know, for he died April 16, probably in 1292.[70]

Now the whole mess was in the hands of **Jacques de Molay**, the last Grand Master. His fate deserves a chapter of its own, but first we must return to other views of the thirteenth-century crusades.

1 Malcolm Barber, *The New Knighthood* (Cambridge University Press, 1994) p. 119.

2 Helen Nicholson tr., *The Chronicle of the Third Crusade* (Ashgate, Aldershot, 1997) p. 165.

3 Peter W. Edbury tr., *The Conquest of Jerusalem and the Third Crusade [Eracles]* (Ashgate, Aldershot, 1998) p. 83.

4 Ibid., p. 112.

5 Ibid.

6 Ibid.

7 Hans Mayer, *The Crusades*, tr. John Gillingham (Oxford University Press, 1972) p. 146.

8 Edbury, p. 113.

9 Ibid., pp. 121–22.

10 Rudolf Heistand ed., *Papsturkunden für Templer und Johanniter* (Göttingen, 1972–84) p. 402.

11 Barber, p. 122.

12 Heistand, p. 407. (From Celestine III, who had already given a confirmation to Robert, but it never hurts to be sure.)

13 Barber, 122–23.

14 Ibid., p.125.

15 Ibid.

16 Ibid., p. 123.

17 Ibid., p. 126

18 Ibid., pp. 121–22.

19 Heistand, p. 278.

20 For more on William, please see chapter 23, **The Crusades of Louis IX.**

21 Oliver of Paderborn, *The Conquest of Damietta*, tr. John J. Gavigan (University of Pennsylvania Press, 1948) p. 30, note 16.

22 Ibid., p. 68.

23 "Histoire des Archeveques Latin de l'Île de Chypre," in *Archives de l'Orient Latin Tome II* (Paris, 1884) p. 214.

24 Barber, p. 128.

25 James M. Powell, *Anatomy of a Crusade 1213–1221* (University of Pennsylvania Press, 1986) p. 126.

26 Quoted in Barber, p. 130.

27 Lionel Allshorn, *Stupor Mundi: The Life and Times of Frederick II, Emperor of the Romans, King of Sicily and Jerusalem, 1194–1250* (Martin Secker, 1912) p. 95.

28 Barber, p. 135.

29 Ibid., p. 136.

30 Ibid., pp. 137–38.

31 Ibid.

32 *The Rothelin Continuation of the* History *of William of Tyre*, in *Crusader Syria in the Thirteenth Century*, tr. Janet Shirley (Ashgate, Aldershot, 1999) p. 46.

33 Ibid., p. 48.

34 Ibid., p. 50.

35 Barber, p. 139.

36 Rothelin, p. 53.

37 "Fragment d'un Cartulaire de l'Ordre de Saint Lazare, en Terre-Sainte," *Archives de l'Orient Latin Tome II* (Paris, 1884) pp. 156–57, charter no. 39.

38 John France, *Western Warfare in the Age of the Crusades 1000–1300* (Cornell University Press, 1999) p. 217.
39 Alain Jacquet, *Templiers et Hospitaliers en Touraine: sur les traces des monines chevaliers* (Sutton Saint-Cyr-sur-Loire, France 2002) p. 143.
40 Joinville, "Vie de St. Louis," in *Chronicles of the Crusades* tr. Margaret R. B. Shaw (Penguin, UK 1963) p. 219.
41 Ibid., p. 258.
42 Ibid., p. 267.
43 Ibid., p. 294.
44 Alain Demurger, *Jacques De Molay: Le crepuscule des templiers* (Paris: Biographie Payot, 2002) p. 61.
45 David Marcombe, *Leper Knights* (Boydell, UK 2003) p. 11.
46 *The Templar of Tyre* ed and tr. Paul Crawford (Ashgate, Aldershot, UK 2003) pp. 36–37.
47 Thomas Bérard in *The Templars: Selected Sources Translated and Annotated*, Malcolm Barber and Keith Bate (Manchester University Press, 2002) p. 101.
48 Barber and Bate, p. 104.
49 "Histoire des Archeveques Latin de l'Île de Chypre," p. 237.
50 Fulvio Bramato, *Storia dell'Ordine Dei Templari in Italia Vol. II Le Inquisizioni, Le Fonti* (Rome: Atanò, 1994) p. 131.
51 "Etudes sur les Derniers Temps de Royaume de Jérusalem," in *Archives de l'Orient Latin Tome II* (Paris, 1884) p. 398.
52 "Six lettres relatives aux croisades," in *Archives de l'Orient Latin Tome I* (Paris, 1884) p. 390.
53 Ibid., p. 391.
54 Barber, p. 178.
55 *The Templar of Tyre*, p. 37.
56 Bramato, p. 127.
57 Ibid., p. 146.
58 *The Templar of Tyre*, p. 69.
59 Ibid.
60 Demurger, pp. 64–66. See chapter 23, **The Templars and the Saint**.
61 *The Templar of Tyre*, p. 85.
62 Ibid., p. 72.
63 For a more complete telling of this please see, **The Last Stands**.
64 *The Templar of Tyre*, p. 37.
65 Ibid, p. 118.
66 Ibid.
67 Ibid.
68 Ibid.
69 Barber, p. 291.
70 Ibid., p. 288.

CHAPTER TWENTY-THREE

The Templars and the Saint, Louis IX of France

Louis IX, King of France, whom we now know as Saint Louis, was born in 1214, the second son of Louis VIII and his wife, Blanche of Castile. In 1226, Louis VIII, only twenty-eight, died of dysentery on his way back from fighting heretics in the south of France, leaving Louis IX, a boy of nine, as heir to the kingdom.[1]

Luckily, the regency was held by the dowager queen, Blanche. At twenty-seven years old, she had been married more than half her life and had borne twelve children, of whom seven survived. And, like her redoubtable grandmother, Eleanor of Aquitaine, Blanche was good at ruling. Not only that, but unlike **Queen Melisande** of Jerusalem, all her children were apparently devoted to her. She kept the country in hand until Louis came of age and then, carefully, let him take the reins of government.

The entire family was pious, Louis especially so. He arranged for relics of the Passion of Christ to be brought from Constantinople to Paris: the crown of thorns, a piece of the True Cross, and the sponge soaked in vinegar that the Roman soldiers held to Jesus' lips at the crucifixion. He then built a special church to hold them. The exquisite Sainte Chapelle still stands on the Île de la Cité in Paris.

Then, in 1244, Louis was struck down with an illness that no medicine was able to cure. Sure that he was going to die, Louis "put his affairs in order, and earnestly begged his brothers to take care of his wife and children, who were very young and helpless."[2]

At one point, those caring for him thought he had died, but he rallied. According to the chroniclers, Louis' first words were to the bishop of Paris, William of Auvergne. "I want to take the cross!" he croaked.[3]

When Louis had completely recovered, both his mother, Blanche, and the bishop tried to talk him out of going; "When you took the cross . . . you were ill. . . . Blood had rushed to your brain so that you were not of sound mind," they insisted.[4]

But Louis would not be dissuaded. Word had come of the conquest of Jerusalem in July 1244, by the Khorezmian Turks, who were being pushed west by the advancing Mongols, and the defeat of the Christian forces at Gaza. It seemed to Louis that he had been called to save the Holy Land.

He also convinced his three younger brothers, Robert, Alphonse, and Charles, to come with him along with many of the great lords of the kingdom. The only holdout was Thibaud, count of Champagne and king of Navarre, who had just returned from his own totally disastrous crusade and felt that he'd had enough of foreign travel.[5]

Louis also took his wife, Marguerite of Provence. For the good of the succession, they left behind their two young sons, Louis and Philip, in the care of their grandmother.[6]

The rest of the family set sail from France in August 1248, except for Alphonse, who stayed behind to watch out for the kingdom and to take care of Robert's wife, who was too pregnant for a sea voyage.[7] Both of them followed later.

The family was smart enough not to have all three brothers take the same ship, but each one arrived safely. Louis and his party went first to Cyprus, landing there on September 17. They were greeted by William of Sonnac, the Grand Master of the Templars, who had come from Acre to accompany the king on his crusade.

It was decided to spend the winter in Cyprus. While planning for the campaign in the spring, Louis took time to settle a dispute between the Hospitallers and the Templars.[8]

William accompanied Louis and the army when they shipped out the next summer. It had been decided that Egypt held the keys to Jerusalem and so Louis planned to attack the town of Damietta in Egypt first, thereby cutting off the supply routes north.

The landing was a little tricky. The French army was fired upon as they came ashore in small boats. "It was a sight to enchant the eyes," the chronicler, Jean de Joinville, remembered. "For the sultan's arms were all of gold and where the sun caught them they shone resplendent."[9] Joinville, who seems to have been cousin to almost everyone, including King Louis, was in his early twenties at the time and the crusade was the big adventure of what was to be a very long life.

As they approached Damietta, the French discovered that the gates were wide open and the town deserted. The people of the town had remembered the last time Damietta was besieged by the Franks and they decided they would rather abandon it than go through that again. Even the garrison, under Fakr ad-Din, chose to flee. When the Sultan, on his deathbed, heard of this, he ordered the soldiers hanged.[10]

Louis was delighted. He settled in to the town with his army and his wife. Damietta was a good place to wait out the annual flooding of the Nile and a good base for raids into Egypt.

As winter neared, the army began to move through the Nile Delta toward the town of Mansourah. On December 7 they were attacked by the Egyptian Turks. "But the Templars and the others of ours in the vanguard were not in the least startled or dismayed," Joinville assures his readers.[11]

Of the many things said about the Templars, no one who saw them in battle ever said they were cowards.

But all too soon came the first disaster for the French and the price the Templars paid for it was high.

On February 8, the king's brother Robert, count of Artois, was in the vanguard of the army along with the Templars. They had crossed a river and Louis had told them to wait for the rest of the force before moving on. Instead, Robert and his men raced ahead and began attacking the Saracen camp. They slaughtered everyone they found there, regardless of age or sex.[12]

William of Sonnac, the Grand Master of the Temple, "a good knight, valiant, hardy, wise in war and clear-sighted in such matters, advised the Count of Artois to wait and rally his men."[13] Robert apparently sneered at him and set out. The Templars couldn't let him go off and be killed on his own so they rode with him, perhaps still hoping to convince him to turn back.

Count Robert and the vanguard entered the town of Mansourah and were soon caught in the twisting streets where they became easy targets for the defenders. "At the moment of supreme danger, the Turkish battalion of the Mamluks . . . lions in war and mighty in battle . . . drove them back. The Franks were massacred one and all."[14]

It was said that the Templars lost 280 men at Mansourah.[15]

Louis hoped for a few days that his brother had only been captured and was being held for ransom, but at last he was told that Robert had died. " 'May God be worshiped for all he has given me,' replied the king and then big tears began to fall from his eyes."[16]

The few Templars that were left continued to fight for Louis. Although he had lost the use of one eye previously, William of Sonnac was still at the front of every fight. On February 11 he was at a barricade that he had made out of parts of captured siege machines. The Turks threw Greek fire at the tinder-dry barricade and it caught at once. "The Turks . . . did not wait for the fire to burn itself out, but rushed in and attacked the Templars amidst the flames."[17]

In the course of the battle, William's other eye was put out. He soon died from his wounds.

Until a new Grand Master could be chosen, the marshal of the order, Renaud of Vichiers, took charge.

But there were to be no more glorious battles in Egypt. Louis' army was trapped in the delta, surrounded by enemy soldiers and attacked daily by flies, fleas, and disease. Supply ships sent from Damietta were taken and plundered before they could reach the French. Scurvy broke out among the men. Even the king's diet wasn't enough to protect against it. Louis tried to arrange a truce but it was clear that they were defeated.

Louis sick in captivity *(The British Library)*

The Turks attacked on April 7. By this point Louis not only had scurvy but also dysentery so constant that "they had to cut away the lower part of his underwear."[18] If the king was this bad off, you can imagine the state of the rest of the army. They were routed.

Louis and his two remaining brothers were among those taken prisoner.

Queen Marguerite was at that time in Damietta and close to the end of a pregnancy. It was she who had to decide what to do. Her main goal was the release of the prisoners.

After some haggling, the sultan agreed that the ransom for Louis and his men was the surrender of Damietta and the payment of five hundred thousand livres, or one million gold bezants. It was later reduced to four hundred thousand livres, which was still more than Louis made in a year.

Unfortunately, the next day, the sultan was killed by his bodyguard. This was a setback for the negotiations and the French thought they might be killed, but the new government was willing to accept the terms of the ransom.[19]

An interesting note in Joinville's memoir is that, according to him, Louis was asked to swear an oath that he would deliver the ransom. Part of the oath was, "if the king did not keep faith with the emirs he should be dishonored as a Christian who denies God and his law and in contempt of Him, spits on a cross and tramples it underfoot."[20]

Now, these were two of the main charges against the Templars at their **arrest and trials**. The question is, was this something that really happened and perhaps was spoken of by Louis' family? He refused to take that oath and might have told this to his children proudly. Then Philip IV, Louis' grandson, might have already known about it and thought it a good thing to charge those infidel-loving Templars with.

On the other hand, Joinville lived until 1317, ten years after the arrest of the Templars. He began writing his memoir in 1305, or perhaps earlier, but it wasn't finished until just before his death at the age of ninety-one. Could he have confused the oath Louis refused to take with what he had heard about the Templars?

The Templars had another role to play in the finding of Louis' ransom. When all the money in Damietta was counted up, they were still thirty thousand livres short. The first thought at the court was to get a short-term loan from the Templars. The master having died, Jean de Joinville, the seneschal of Champagne, went to the Templar commander, Étienne d'Orricourt. He refused to give the loan, saying, "You know that all the money placed in our charge is left with us on condition of our swearing never to hand it over except to those who entrusted it to us."[21] The Templars did not have money of their own with them at Damietta.

Joinville was not going to stand for that and the two men were arguing loudly when the marshal of the temple and acting Grand Master, Renaud of Vichiers, came by and suggested that, while the Templars couldn't make a loan of the money, if it were stolen from them there wasn't much they could do about it. He did point out that Louis could repay them from his account in Acre.[22]

And so, thanks to the creative thinking of Renaud of Vichiers, the ransom was paid. Louis handed over Damietta and took his wife and newborn son to Acre.[23] Most of the lords, including Louis' two remaining brothers, went home.

Louis stayed in the East until 1254. His crusade had cost a

king's ransom and thousands of lives. The most that he accomplished was the rebuilding and fortifying of some towns in the Kingdom of Jerusalem.

He seems to have felt that this wasn't enough, for ten years later he began to plan another crusade. This was in response to the arrival of a Templar messenger from Acre, telling of the ongoing conquests of the Mongols.[24]

Again Louis' two brothers went with him, as well as his sons, Philip, who had missed the last crusade, along with Jean Tristan and Peter, who had both been born while on it. He also took his daughter, Isobel, and her husband, another Thibaud of Champagne. This time, Marguerite decided to stay home. Prince Edward of England also agreed to go, but he arrived too late and eventually went to Acre to fulfill his crusading vow.[25]

For Louis did not go to Acre again, nor to Egypt, but to Tunis. He apparently didn't tell anyone about this until his ships had put to sea. The logic behind this is still being debated. Some say that Louis believed that the emir there was willing to convert to Christianity but needed military backing.[26] At one time it was thought that the king's brother, Charles of Anjou, who had since become king of Sicily, suggested the invasion as a means of getting a foothold in Africa.[27] However, it has since been proven that Charles wasn't aware that Louis was planning on going to Tunis and had to change his own plans to accommodate him.[28]

For whatever reason, the crusade was again a dismal failure. The army wasn't defeated by the Moslems, but by the summer heat. They landed in August in North Africa. There was little water and no shelter from the sun. Sickness filled the camp. The first of Louis' family to die was his son Jean Tristan. Then Philip, the eldest son, became sick. Louis, who had never really recovered from his suffering in Egypt, became ill next. Soon he realized that he was dying and so he had himself laid out on a bed of ashes, arms outstretched in the form of a cross. He died August 25, 1270.[29]

Charles of Anjou arrived shortly afterward. He arranged for his brother's body to be rendered and his bones taken home for burial.[30]

Charles conducted the business side of the crusade and arranged a treaty with the emir that was very favorable to Sicily.[31]

That was the last major crusade ever launched by a European king.

Louis' son Philip III survived, but Philip's wife, Jeanne, died from a fall from a horse followed by a stillbirth. One wonders if their son, Philip the Fair, would have been a warmer person if his mother had lived. As a result of the crusade, Louis' brother Peter and his wife also died, as did Louis' daughter and son-in-law.[32]

Almost immediately miracles were reported at Louis' grave. His remaining brother, Charles, built a shrine to him in his palace.

It may be said that the only thing the Templars had to do with Louis' last journey is that they transferred the funds for it.

By all accounts, Louis was almost always on good terms with the Temple. Hundreds of Templars were killed or enslaved in the Egyptian campaign. Their courage and military wisdom were praised. So that doesn't seem a likely reason why Louis' grandson, Philip the Fair, would want to condemn them.

However, the popular feeling that the Templars and the Hospitallers should have fought harder to protect the Holy Land was only increased by the debacles of Saint Louis.

---

1 Margaret Wade Labarge, *Saint Louis: Louis IX Most Christian King of France* (Boston: Little, Brown, 1968) p. 25.

2 *The Rothelin Continuation of the* History *of William of Tyre*, in *Crusader Syria in the Thirteenth Century*, tr. Janet Shirley (Ashgate, Aldershot, 1999) p. 66.

3 Jean de Joinville, "Life of St. Louis," in *Chronicles of the Crusades* tr. M. R. B. Shaw (Penguin, 1963) p. 191; Matthew Paris, *Chronica* tr. Richard Vaughn (New York, 1984) p. 131; *Rothelin*, p. 66.

4 Matthew Paris, p. 131. Matthew wasn't there but Joinville also says that Queen Blanche and Bishop William were upset so this may be the gist of their argument.

5 *Rothelin*, p. 67. For the details of that crusade see the section on Armand of Périgord in chapter 22.

6 Philip was born on May 1, 1245, and so was only three years old when his parents set off on crusade.

7 Guillaume de Nangis, *Chronique* tr. M Guizot (Paris, 1825) p. 156.

8 Paris, p.181.

9 Joinville, p. 201.
10 Jamal ad-Din Ibn Wasil, *Mufarrij al-Kurub fi akhbar Bani Ayyub* in *Arab Historians of the Crusades* tr. Francesco Gabrieli (Dorset, 1982) p. 286.
11 Rothelin, p. 91.
12 Ibid., p. 95.
13 Ibid.
14 Ibn Wasil, p. 290.
15 Joinville, p. 219.
16 Ibid., p. 226.
17 Ibid., p. 232.
18 Ibid., p. 240.
19 Ibn Wasil, p. 298.
20 Joinville, p. 254.
21 Ibid., p. 258.
22 Ibid., p. 259.
23 Marguerite gave birth three days after she learned of Louis' capture. She named the boy Jean Tristan, "triste" meaning sadness. By the time she returned to France, she had had another child and was pregnant again. I think her story is fascinating but, since no Templars were involved, it will have to wait for another time.
24 Jonathan Riley-Smith, *The Crusades* (New Haven: Yale University Press, 1987) p. 208.
25 Labarge, pp. 227–44.
26 Riley-Smith, p. 210.
27 Labarge, pp. 239–40.
28 Hans Mayer, *The Crusades* tr. John Gillingham (Oxford University Press, 1988) p. 282.
29 Labarge, p. 243.
30 Ibid.
31 Nangis, p. 187.
32 Ibid.

CHAPTER TWENTY-FOUR

Templars and Money

"The whole country of the East would have been conquered long ago had it not been for the Templars and the Hospitallers and others who call themselves religious. . . . But the Templars and the Hospitallers and their associates, who are fattened by ample revenues, are afraid that if the country [Egypt] is subjected to Christian laws, their supremacy will come to an end."[1]

These words were put in the mouth of Robert of Artois, brother of Louis IX, by the English chronicler Matthew Paris. Matthew was writing shortly after the end of Louis' useless and very expensive crusade in 1250. Robert is supposed to have said this in response to the advice of the master of the Templars, William of Sonnac, that they should put off attacking the Saracens at the town of Mansourah in Egypt.[2]

It's highly unlikely that Robert actually said these words. Jean de Joinville, who was there, doesn't mention anything of the kind. But Matthew may have been reflecting popular home front opinions on the wealth of both the Templars and the Hospitallers. Matthew was a monk at the English abbey of St. Albans and his only contact with Templars would have been in their role as competitors for lay donations and tithes.

"Everybody knows" that the Templars were rich.[3] They had piles of treasure hidden everywhere. When the order was dissolved, no treasure was found. Therefore, it's still hidden.

There are a lot of assumptions in the above statements. The Templars did have a reputation for being both greedy and miserly, but was it true? Were they rich? What form did their wealth take? What was their financial situation when the order was dissolved in 1312? What's the real story of the Templars and money?

Let's start at the end. On October 13, 1307, the Templars of Baugy, in Calvados, Normandy, were arrested along with the rest of the Templars in France. That same day an inventory was made of their goods. It was done in the presence of the three Templars assigned to Baugy and five officers of the king.[4]

The commandery owned fourteen milk cows, five heifers, one ox, seven calves more than a year old, two bulls, one calf still nursing, one hundred sheep, ninety-nine pigs, and eight piglets. There was a good horse for the commander and four nags to pull carts. There was also a good supply of grain, the harvest just having been finished and tithes paid two weeks before, half a tun of wine, and a supply of beer "for the boys and the workers."[5]

The chapel had the bare minimum of equipment for services: vestments, one chalice, books, and altar linen. The chamber of the commander had some plain silver cups and some wooden ones. He had bed linen and clothes, including a rain cloak. He also had a blue overdress "belonging to the wife of M. Roger de Planes, which was being held for a debt, so said the commander and Bertin du Goisel."[6] The king's men seemed to think that women's clothing in the commander's chamber was suspicious, but there was other clothing belonging to men of the neighborhood so they decided to believe the Templars.

While the Templars in Paris and London may have made major loans to kings, the Templars in the provinces seemed to have functioned as local pawnbrokers.

There was nothing else at the commandery that wouldn't have been found on any well-run farm in Normandy. The three Templars were the only members of the order living there. There were twenty-six servants, including a chaplain, Guillaume Durendent, who doesn't seem to have been a Templar priest since he and the other servants reminded the officials that they still expected to be paid.[7]

All the other inventories of Templar property gave the same results.

The prestigious **Temple in London** had little more than the provincial commandery had. The cellar contained some maple cups, twenty-two silver spoons, some canvas cloths, and four tankards. There were seven horses in the stable, three for farm work. The master had some clothes and bed linen, one gold buckle, and a crossbow without bolts.[8]

The Templars seem to have lived simply. They had plenty to eat and drink but most of their cash went to pay bills or to the headquarters of the order in Cyprus. Even in Paris there were no great caches of jewels or coins. Most of the valuable property was either held as security for loans the Templars had made or was on deposit as in modern banks.

If the Templars really were terribly rich, then where was all the money?

Before speculating on missing pots of gold and midnight runs through the streets, it would be a good idea to try to find out just how much the Templars had.

WHERE DID THE TEMPLARS' MONEY COME FROM?

The first gift to the Templars, according to tradition, was the "Temple of Solomon" itself. "As they had neither a church nor a regular place to live, the king allowed them to live temporarily in a part of his palace, which was on the south side of the Temple of the Lord. The canons of the Temple of the Lord gave them the courtyard that they had that was near the palace, under certain conditions, for the saying of the Office."[9]

The king was **Baldwin II**. He was living at the time (around 1120) in the al-Aqsa mosque and may have planned to have the Templars stay only until they could afford a place of their own. It turned out that the king moved first and let the knights have the whole building.[10] Of course, the building was falling down and needed the roof repaired among other things, so it wasn't quite such a generous donation as it might have seemed at first.[11]

The king and the patriarch of Jerusalem also gave the Templars funds to support themselves, in return for the knights' promise to protect pilgrims on the road against thieves and highwaymen.[12] We don't know what these funds consisted of since the records have been lost but the most likely gifts would have been something that renewed itself, like rents or tithes.

The first donation recorded in Europe is from a certain William of Marseille. This was made before 1124, when the Grand Master, **Hugh de Payns**, arrived from Jerusalem to drum up support for the order. William divided the gift of a church in Marseille and all its property between the Knights of the Temple of Solomon, the Church of St. Marie, and the monks of St. Victor.[13]

A third of a church isn't a bad start. However, the Templars soon sold their share to the bishop of Fréjus in return for eight *sestiers* of wheat, to be paid annually.[14] That is about as much as a donkey could comfortably carry. It wouldn't have been enough to make bread for a man to last a week.

It wasn't until 1127, when Hugh de Payns and his comrades came back to Europe, that the order began to get some serious support.

Hugh went first to **Fulk, count of Anjou**, who had lived with the Templars for a time when he was on a pilgrimage to Jerusalem and gave them thirty livres a year.[15] It is said that King Henry I of England met with Hugh and his comrades in Normandy and gave them gold and silver and sent them on with letters of introduction.[16] There are no records of Henry's exact donations, but it is certain that his successor, Stephen, or to be more accurate, Stephen's wife, Matilda of Boulogne, made one of the first donations of land in England. She gave the Templars a manor and church in the town of Cressyng with all that pertained to it, including woods and fields, ponds and rivers, as well as the toll from mills and also local taxes.[17]

Lords in Flanders, Champagne, Poitou, and Aragon gave similar donations.

After Hugh de Payns went back to Jerusalem, several Templars, perhaps newly recruited, stayed on to spread the word.[18] By 1150, the order had lands in France, Aragon, Castille, Flanders, England, Portugal, the various counties of Provence, and Germany.[19]

An example of typical property is the Templar house in the Rouergue, a fairly remote area near the Pyrenees, which was established in 1140. However the Cistercians and the Hospitallers had arrived there first. Though the Templars established a network of houses, cleared land, and received many gifts, the other orders still had a larger share in most places and there wasn't always enough to go around. The Cistercians of Sylvane and the Templars and Hospitallers fought over the rights to tithes from local churches for over a hundred years. It came to the point that Templars began to be asked to witness donations made to the monks of Sylvane in the hope that the monks wouldn't later contest the gifts.[20] Perhaps this tendency to dispute the rights of others to receive donations was another case that gave the order a reputation for greed.

Southern France was one of the areas in which the Templars became well established. The land had sent many of its noblemen on the First Crusade and the counts of Toulouse and St. Gilles had relatives among the counts of Tripoli. Actually, most of the important centers of Templar commanderies—Flanders, France, Champagne, Aquitaine, and Provence—were the same areas that produced many of the settlers in the Latin kingdoms.

In most of western Europe, the land the Templars owned was used for farming and livestock. The Templar lay brothers, men who donated their services without becoming monks, did much of the farm work. There were also paid servants and, in Spain, even Moslem slaves to do the work.[21] A few of the Templar knights lived at the commanderies, which were usually buildings that had been donated, but many of the houses were run by sergeants. Men of fighting age and ability were immediately sent overseas.

In the British Isles the Templars had farms that produced wheat, oats, rye, and barley. Some of this was for their own use, but some was sold. They also raised sheep and exported wool.[22] They had an edge over lay wool sellers in that they were excused from having to pay customs duty. Of course, the Cistercians had the same exceptions and much larger holdings so the Templars could only capture a small share of the market.[23]

They did make some money by renting out the land they were given to small farmers. In some cases this was in return for a portion of the harvest, but the Templars preferred cash and, especially in good years, it was to the advantage of the farmer to pay a set amount annually.

We have a window into the Temple lands in England from a survey of their property made in 1185. It shows that the Templars owned and rented out many small plots of land. The renters paid in shillings and also in kind. Examples of this are not only ale and "2 capons at Christmas" or "15 eggs at Easter," but also promises to serve on a local jury, reap half an acre of Templar fields, shoe six Templar horses, or plow either in spring or autumn.[24]

Some of the commanderies must have raised horses for the knights overseas. Jean de Joinville comments on the horses loaded in the hold of the ship at Marseille for Louis IX's first crusade.[25] There are other accounts of ships bringing horses for the use of the Templars. The warhorses used by European knights were specially bred to handle the weight of men and armor.[26] However, since most of the horses would have been used by the Templars themselves, breeding them probably didn't produce much income.

The best income-producers of the time were mills and ovens. Many people gave Templars the rights to water mills, and one of the worst battles between the Hospitallers and Templars in the Latin kingdoms was over water and mill rights.[27]

Another source of income was the right to hold fairs. These were markets at which everything from local produce to imported luxury goods were sold. Merchants coming to the fairs had to pay for a spot to set up shop as well as a tax on the goods they brought to sell. The Templars could collect these fees as well as selling their own goods at the fairs without having to pay the same fees.

Again, there were complaints that the Templars were abusing this privilege. In around 1260, in the town of Provins, in Champagne, the local tradesmen complained to the count that the Templars were charging fees to merchants bringing wool into town for the fairs. The merchants reminded the count that for a penny a week, they had always been excused from paying what was basically sales tax. As a result of the fees imposed by the Templars, wool sellers were taking their goods elsewhere. "Sir," they begged the count, "[w]e know truly that if you knew the great damage which you are suffering here from loss of rents, from your ovens, your mills, your fabric manufacturers and your other factories which you have here at Provins, and the great damage which your bourgeois are suffering . . . for God's sake, help us."[28] Unfortunately, we don't know how the count, Thibaud, responded to this poignant plea. Nor do we know how much the Templars earned from their extortion.

Another big source of income was from the privileges given to the Templars by the various popes. The first, given by Pope Innocent II, on March 29, 1139, was that the Templars could keep all the booty they captured.[29] This was a privilege that the Benedictines and Cistercians hadn't even thought of. In Spain especially, this was extremely profitable, although the order was often given land by the kings on condition that they conquer it themselves.[30] Booty also brought in a lot of income in the Holy Land, at least at the beginning. It was because of this that William of Tyre accused Grand Master Bernard of Tremeley of refusing to let anyone but Templars inside the walls of Ascalon when they had broken in. William insisted that Bernard was too greedy to let anyone else have a chance to loot the city.[31]

The pope also gave the Temple the right to build its own small churches and bury its members and "family" in them. The "family" was a very loose term, meaning the relatives of the brothers but also servants, their relatives, and anyone who had become a lay brother or lay sister of the house through a donation.

One of the worst bones of contention between the order and the local clergy grew out of the privilege given by Pope Celestine II on January 9, 1144. Celestine encouraged people to donate to the Temple by allowing them to ignore one-seventh of any penance a priest had given them. That wasn't so bad. It didn't cost anyone anything. The priest could adjust the penance. But then he allowed the Templars to come through villages once a year and open the churches in places that were under interdict. This meant that the Knights of the Temple got the donations that were given at marriages and burials that the local clergy couldn't perform while the interdict lasted.[32] This was literally a godsend for the order.

The biggest donation that the Templars ever received was one-third of a country. They didn't get to keep it, but they traded it back to their advantage.

In 1134, Alfonso I of Aragon and Navarre, known as "the Battler," died without direct heirs. Instead of finding some distant cousin to rule after him, he left the whole kingdom of Aragon to be divided between the Templars, the Hospitallers, and the canons of the Holy Sepulcher in Jerusalem.[33]

Before the celebrations in the commanderies were over, the beneficiaries of the will realized that the nobility of Aragon weren't going to stand for that. They dragged Alfonso's brother, Ramiro, out of a monastery, married him off, and crowned him king.[34] In Navarre, Count García Ramírez took over.

Pope Innocent II tried to get the terms of the will enforced, but it was impractical from the beginning. The Hospital and the canons of the Holy Sepulcher came to terms with the Spanish nobles by 1140. The Templars held out until 1143. Their settlement included castles, a tenth of royal revenues, one thousand *solidos* every year, a fifth of all lands conquered from the Moors, and exemption from some taxes.[35]

So the Templars (and the Hospitallers) had a wide variety of sources of income. But was it enough?

WHERE DID THE MONEY GO?

Critics such as Matthew Paris seem to have had the impression that the Templars and Hospitallers had more than enough money to conquer Saracen lands from Cairo to Baghdad. He and others were certain that the Templars spent all their money on a luxurious lifestyle and oriental decadence. Either that or they were misers, hoarding cash that should go to the struggle to regain the Holy Land.

Were they? What did they spend their money on?

First of all, the Knights Templar did not live like ordinary monks. Each knight brother had to have three horses and tack and one squire, a ration of barley for the horse, and armor, as well as regular clothing.

He needed his own napkin and washcloth.[36] He also had a cook pot and bowl to measure the barley, drinking cups, two flasks, a bowl and spoon made of horn, and a tent, among other things.[37]

The sergeants got most of the same things as the knights, except for the tent and cook pot. They were allowed one horse each.

The average cost of a warhorse during the twelfth and thirteenth centuries was thirty-six livres.[38] That's more than the value of a good-sized manor. There are many stories about poor knights who sold or mortgaged their patrimony for a good horse. Most Templar knights brought at least one horse with them when they entered, but horses were just as often casualties of war as men and both were costly to replace.

The Templars also hired Turcopoles to fight with them. These men were Christian Syrians or sons of Greeks and Turks. They were trained as mounted archers in the Eastern style. Some of them were brothers of the order but most were paid mercenaries. The Templars had a master in charge of them, called a Turcopolier, who also was commander of the sergeant brothers in times of combat.[39]

Added to these, there was the cost of shipping men and equipment from West to East. By the middle of the thirteenth century, the Templars had some ships of their own, but they were costly to maintain, even if they took on paying passengers.

Also, not all of those donations came without strings.

For example, in April 1145, two women of Arles, Maria and Sclarmandia, and, oh yes, their husbands and all their children, sold property to the Templars. They were very specific about the money they would receive as a "gift" in return: 250 sous of Melgueil in new money and 150 sous in small change.[40]

Generally, the charters aren't as up front about sales as this one was. Most people wanted it to appear that they were giving property or rights for the good of their souls. For instance, in 1142, a man named Arnaud gave the Templars "willingly, of my own accord all that I have or should have in the town of Burcafols."[41] He adds that he does this "for the love of God and the remission of my sins and those of my family and to receive life everlasting, Amen."[42] It's only in the final sentences that it's mentioned that the Templars are giving him fourteen livres *morebetani* and ten sous and a carton of wheat of the measure of Toulouse.[43]

Many times the price of the property being "donated" is called a "charity." In 1152, Bernard Modul received forty sous from the Temple as charity for some land his brother had given the Templars of Douzens. Apparently Bernard also had a claim to the land. In return, Bernard released his claim.[44]

Reading through the surviving charters, it appears that a large part of the "donations" to the Templars were actually sales.

Also, the Templars accepted what were called "corrodians." This system was something like the retirement homes that take a large fee up front and promise to house and feed the residents until they die. An early example of a Templar corrody comes from 1129. Pierre Bernard and his wife gave themselves and their property to the Temple. In exchange for this, the Templars promised to feed and clothe them for the rest of their lives. Pierre and his wife weren't that old at the time, for they put in a clause about the care of their children, "if we have children."[45] That meant that, while the Templars did get everything the donors owned, they might well be supporting the family for two generations.

In some cases the corrodies also included a set amount of money to be paid by the Templars every year along with "a tallow candle nightly, firewood as needed, and a groom assigned by the preceptor to serve them."[46]

The Rule of the Templars implies that there are times when they expected to run short of ready money. "When the time after Easter comes for the great expenses that the houses have to pay from the harvests, and the commanders tell the Master that they don't have enough meat, the Master may go to the brothers and ask their advice. And if the brothers agree to give up meat on Tuesday, then they may do without. But when the wheat is harvested, then the meat should be restored."[47] Although the Templars tried to get rents in money, most of the time they seem to have been land rich and cash poor.

BANKERS TO THE KINGS

Outside of their military activity, the Templars are best remembered as financiers, holding the treasuries of England and France in their commanderies, making loans to all the best families of Europe, and transferring large amounts of funds from one end of the continent to the other.

The Templars seem to have gotten into the banking business almost by accident. It started with King Louis VII of France. On his expedition to Jerusalem in 1148, he ran short of money and borrowed from the Templars. He had to write home to his regent, the abbot Suger, telling him to pay the Templars in Paris "thirty thousand *sous* in the money of Poitou."[48] Fortunately, Suger came through with the cash.

When Louis came home, he placed the royal treasury, what was left of it, in the safekeeping of the Templars in Paris.[49] He made a Templar, Theirry Galeran, royal treasurer.[50] Galeran had been in Louis' service for many years and had gone on the crusade with him.

From that time, the French royal treasury was generally in the care of the Templars. Under Louis' son Philip Augustus, the treasurer of the Temple took in and counted the money the king received, under the watchful eyes of six of the burgesses of Paris and a M. Adam.[51] The Templar brothers Giles and Hugh seem to have filled the same office under Saint Louis.[52] Right up through the early years of King **Philip the Fair**, the Templars not only held the treasure for the king, but also kept an account of creditors and debtors and the amounts owed.[53]

However, the Temple in Paris was never more than a holding place for cash. The treasurer of the Templars was not normally a royal official. He did not have any part in financial planning nor did he audit accounts. The Temple took money in, stored it, and paid it out.[54] Most of the time the Templars were more like warehouse guards than bankers.

Statements were sent to the kings (and other clients) three times a year, at Candlemas (February 2), Ascension (forty days after Easter; the date changed), and All Saints' Day (November 1). There are only a few fragments of these statements for the French kings. From one fragment we learn, however, that, in 1202/03 the provosts of Paris deposited 18,000 livres in the care of Brother Haimard at the Temple. The bailiffs deposited 37,000 livres with Brother Haimard and a further 5,000 livres with Brother Guérin.[55] In 1292 at Candlemas, the treasury took in 72,517 livres, 19 sols, and 7 denarii. Expenses were 125,000 livres, 1 sol, and 0 denarii. At Ascension, it took in 121,806 livres, 18 sols, and 3 denarii and paid out 111,073 livres, 9 sols, and 3 denarii.[56]

If it was good enough for the king of France, it was good enough for the nobility, too. Louis IX's brother Alphonse of Poitiers had all his revenues sent directly to the Temple in Paris.[57] Alphonse even sent unrefined silver to the Temple from his mines in Orzals through the commander in Rouergue.[58]

The Templars even obliged by carrying depositors' funds for them while on crusade. When Louis IX went on his first crusade and was unfortunate enough to be captured, Jean de Joinville broke into the money boxes belonging to some of the noblemen (over the protest of the Templar guarding them).[59]

There is some record of kings in other countries using the Temple as a safe place to keep their cash. In 1203, King Emeric of Hungary received a quantity of silver from Archbishop Urane and deposited it with the Templars.[60]

The Templars must have had some sort of holding fee for this, but they couldn't and didn't charge interest on loans and they also didn't lend money left in their keeping.

It isn't clear how much of the Templar income came from banking. They kept money for people at their commanderies and moved it from one side of the sea to the other. They made loans, especially to royalty. But kings are notoriously slow to repay. It seems that most of the money kept in Paris and London belonged to depositors. When Hubert de Burgh, the justiciar of King Henry III of England, fell from power, Henry tried to appropriate the money that Hubert had deposited at the Temple. The master refused to turn it over without Hubert's permission.[61] Hubert was "convinced" to give it.

There are several other cases where depositors' money was stolen by the kings or nobleman. In 1263, Prince Edward went to the New Temple and "broke open a number of chests and carried off a large sum of money belonging to others."[62]

Banking may have been more high profile than lucrative, and the dangers involved in transporting valuables were high. There is no indication that the Templars ever had mounds of cash and treasure for their own use, especially not in the London and Paris houses.

The Templars did not invent modern-style banking. For centuries Jews had been arranging among themselves to deposit funds at one place and pick them up at another. Most monasteries accepted goods for safekeeping and also loaned money at interest, despite prohibitions on usury.[63] The Italian city-states, particularly Venice, Genoa, and Pisa, had a trading empire that including banking. The Templars were simply one group among many.

The difference is that the Templars were trusted by royalty, particularly the kings of France and England, to handle their business affairs. The Temple commanderies in both London and Paris served as the royal treasuries. This meant that the treasure stored there belonged to the king. It could be retrieved at any time. The Templars took a fee for guarding it but they didn't dare use it to invest in other loans or enterprises.

Sometimes the Templars themselves needed to transmit funds. In 1304, Walter de la More, Templar master of England, needed to travel to see the Grand Master. He paid a sum to a group of Florentine bankers, the Mari, who had an office in London. Walter was supposed to retrieve it at the Mari bank in Paris but the Paris officers of the company had skipped town.[64] No reason is given as to why Walter hadn't handled the matter through the Temple, but it's possible that he wasn't sure there would be enough cash in the Paris commandery to take care of his needs.

The Templars did indeed have a lot of property in western Europe, but they usually didn't receive rent for it in money, but in produce. Part of their earnings went to feed the poor and themselves. Also, one-third of everything that was taken in went to the East to maintain the fighting force.

* * *

For years some people have been assuming that somehow in 1307 all the commanderies in France got wind of the impending arrests and either hid or removed everything of value. Then they all just went to bed and waited for the king's men to come for them. I find this hard to believe. First of all, it implies an amazing lack of self-preservation among the knights. But mostly, it seems very unlikely that all the bustle of collecting and sending away valuables could have been accomplished without someone noticing. The streets of Paris were narrow and crowded. Carts big enough to carry tons of treasure couldn't have made it through. Also, there were city gates that were shut every evening and guarded. If anyone had tried to get out with a large amount of goods, they would have been stopped and the boxes searched. If the Templars had tried to get away by the Seine River, they still would have had to cross town to do it.

The entire city would have heard them.

Finally, the supposed treasure not only has never been found but it has never even been described. All these things together make me think that nothing left Paris from the Temple before the arrests.

The treasure of the Templars, if there was any, wouldn't have been in London or Paris in any case, but in Cyprus in the Templar headquarters. On the day of their arrest in Cyprus, an inventory was taken of Templar goods. At Nicosia, along with a lot of crossbows and foodstuffs were 120,000 white bezants (coins made of a mix of silver and some gold). That seems like a lot to me but legends begin early, and a near contemporary chronicler insists that "no one knew where in the world they hid the rest, nor has anyone been able to find out."[65]

---

1 Matthew Paris, *Chronicles*, ed. and tr. Richard Vaughan (Gloucester: Sutton, 1894) p. 241.
2 Please see **The Templars and the Saint** for more on this episode. For William, see **Grand Masters 1191–1292/93**.
3 Please see **How to Tell if You Are Reading Pseudohistory**.
4 Georges Lizerand, *Le Dossier de l'Affaire des Templiers* (Paris, 1923) p. 47.
5 Ibid., p. 50, "cervoise pour les garsons et pour les ouvriers."

6 Ibid., "qui est a la fame mons. Roger de Planes et est en gages, si comme le cammandoour et Bertin deu Couisel disoient."

7 Ibid., p. 52.

8 Evelyn Lord, *The Knights Templar in Britain* (London, 2002) pp. 27–30. I find it very responsible of the master not to keep a loaded crossbow in the house.

9 William of Tyre, *Chronique*, ed. R. B. C Huygens (Turnholt, 1986) 12, 7, p. 553. "Quibus quoniam neque eccesia erat neque certum habebant domicilium, rex in palatio suo, quod secus Templum Domini ad australem habet partem eis ad tempus concessit hibiaculum, canonici vero Templi Domini plateam, quam circa predictum habebant platinum, ad opus officiarum certis quibusdam conditionibus concesserunt."

10 This often happens. Baldwin moved into what was called the "Tower of David." Since he had four daughters, he may have been looking for a place with more bathrooms.

11 Adrian J. Boas, *Jerusalem in the Time of the Crusades: Society, Landscape and Art in the Holy City Under Frankish Rule* (London: Routledge, 2001) p. 79. Boas quotes the chronicler, Fulcher of Chartres. "Because of our lack of resources we were not able even to maintain this building in the condition in which we found it. For this reason it is mostly destroyed."

12 William of Tyre, 12, 7, p. 554.

13 Marquis d'Albon, *Cartulaire de l'Ordre du Temple* (Paris, 1912) p. 2.

14 Ibid.

15 Please see chapter 11, **Fulk of Anjou.**

16 Thomas W. Parker, *The Knights Templars in England* (University of Arizona Press, 1983) p. 15.

17 D'Albon no. 124, p. 87.

18 Please see chapter 8, **Go Forth and Multiply.**

19 D'Albon listed every charter he could find from 1119 through 1150. The compilation is 500 pages.

20 Paul Orliac, *La Cartulaire de La Selve, La Terre, Les Hommes at le Pouvior en Rouergue au XIIe Siècle* (Paris, 1985) p. 76.

21 Alan Forey, *The Templars in the Corona of Aragon.*

22 Parker, pp. 52–53.

23 Ibid., p. 56.

24 Malcolm Barber and Keith Bate, *The Templars: Selected Sources Translated and Annotated* (Manchester University Press, 2002) pp. 184–90.

25 Jean de Joinville, *Histoire de Saint Louis* tr. M. Natalis de Wailly (Paris, 1865) p. 57.

26 R. H. C. Davis, *The Medieval Warhorse* (London, 1989) pp. 65–97. Page 62 also has a neat illustration of how the horses were boarded on the ships.

27 Helen Nicholson, *The Knights Templar* (London, 2001) p. 183.

28 Nicholson, p. 191. One interesting thing about this is that the wool the merchants were selling was still on the sheep. They were being charged for selling wool futures.

29 *Omne Datum Optimum*, in d'Albon, p. 376. "Ea etiam que de eorum spoiliis ceperitis, fidenter in usus vestros convertatis, et, ne de his, contra velle vestrum, portionem alicui dare cogamini, prohibemus."

30 Alan Forey, *The Templars in the Corona of Aragon* (Oxford University Press, 1973) p. 25ff.

31 William of Tyre, 17, 27, pp. 797–99.

32 *Milites Templi*, in Rudolf Heistand, *Papsturkunden für Templar und Johanniter* (Göttingen, 1972) p. 215, "si forte locus ipse indterdictus sit, . . . in anno aperiantur ecclesie et et exclusis excommunicates divina official celebrentur."

33 Forey, p. 17.

34 Joseph F. O'Callaghan, *A History of Medieval Spain* (Cornell University Press, 1975) pp. 233 and 258. Ramiro did his duty, had a daughter to inherit, and returned to the monastery.

35 Forey. p. 22.

36 Contrary to popular opinion, people in the Middle Ages did wash.

37 Laurent Dailliez, *Régle et Statuts de l'Ordre du Temple* (Paris, 1972) p. 143, rule no. 140.

38 Charles Gladitz, *Horse Breeding in the Medieval World* (Dublin: Four Courts Press, 1997) p. 158.

39 Dailliez, p. 152, rules no. 169 and 170.

40 D'Albon, p. 227, no. 352, "ccl solidos Melgoriensis nove monete et cl solidos de numis."

41 *Cartulaire des Templiers de Douzens* ed. Pierre Gérard and Élisabeth Magnou (Bibliothéque Nationale, 1965) p. 114, no. 121.

42 Douzens, p. 115, no. 121.

43 Ibid.

44 Ibid., p. 51, no. 41.

45 Ibid., p. 269, no. 11.

46 Parker, p. 23.

47 Dailliez, p. 130, rule no. 96.

48 Sugerii Abbatis S. Dionysii, *Opera*, Episotolae LVII and LVIII, columns 1377–1378. "Debet autem eis reddere triginta milia solidorum Pictaviensis monetae, de quisbus licet mihi bonum responsum dederit."

49 Achille Luchaire, *Institutions Françaises* (Paris, 1892) p. 588.

50 Sugerii, column 1402, in a letter from the Archbishop of Sens. "Vidimus enim fratrem Geleranum, qui custodiet Parisiu domum Templi, redeuntem a dominus rege."

51 Ferdinand Lot and Robert Fawtier, *Histoire des Institutions Franaise au Moyen Age: Tome II— Institutions Royale* (Paris, 1958) p. 188

52 Luchaire, p. 589.

53 Ibid.

54 Bryce Lyon and A. E. Verhulst, *Medieval Finance* (Brown University Press, 1967) p. 41.

55 John W. Baldwin, *The Government of Philip Augustus: Foundations of French Royal Power in the Middle Ages* (California University Press, 1986) p. 166.

56 Lot and Fawtier, p. 191. Until everything was put on the decimal system, the *l*, *s*, and *d* became the shorthand for "pounds, shillings and pence" in England, just in case you ever wondered.

57 Boutaric, *Louis IX et Alphonse de Poitiers* (Brionne, 1879) pp. 181–312. There is no indication that the Templars were financial advisers. They simply took in the money and kept accounts.

58 Boutaric, pp. 208–10. The records don't say who refined the silver.

59 Jean de Joinville, "Life of St. Louis," in *Chronicles of the Crusades* tr. M.R.B. Shaw (Penguin, 1963) p. 259.

60 Thomas of Spalato, *ExThomae Historia Pontificum Salonitanorum et Spalatinorum* in *Monumenta Germania Historia Scriptores* ed. G. H. Pertz. Vol. 29, p. 577.

61 Parker, p. 60. From his prison cell, Hubert gave the required permission. What a good sport!

62 Ibid., p. 61.

63 Bernard of Clairvaux.

64 Demurger, p. 121.

65 Amaldi, quoted in Alain Demurger, *Jacques de Malay: Le crepuscule des templiers* (Biographie— Payot, Paris, 2002) p. 319, note 27. "Il resto havevano nascoso cosi secramente che alcun del mondo non ha possuto saver niente di quello." Demurger adds, "Courage treasure seekers! It's to Cyprus one must go!"

The Temple in Paris

The closest one can come today to the Temple compound in which **Jacques de Molay** and the other Templars were arrested is to take the Paris Metro (line 3) to the stop labeled "Temple." But don't expect to find anything of the Templars there. The buildings were destroyed during or shortly after the French Revolution. "Of the imposing group of its monuments, church, donjon, cloister and monastic buildings, and constructions of all sorts, homes and houses of commerce that were encircled and sheltered by its vast enclosure, not one stone remains."[1]

When did the Templars first have a building in Paris?

The commandery of the Knights Templar in Paris is first noted during the time of Louis VII. A woman named Gente, the daughter of the physician of Louis VI, donated a water mill, under the Great Bridge in Paris, to the Templars. Unfortunately, we can only date this within the years 1137 and 1147.[2] The Templar who acchepted the gift was Everard de Barres, master of the Temple in Paris and later Grand Master.

King Louis made a gift to the Temple in 1143, of twenty-seven livres to be paid once a year. However, the donation charter doesn't specify that this is to the Temple in Paris, only to the Templars. Neither does a donation made to the Templars in 1145 by Bartholomew, deacon of Notre Dame.[3] It's frustrating, but part of historical research is not to assume anything, so while it makes sense that there would have been a commandery, there is still no proof.[4]

A meeting with the king outside the Temple walls in Paris. The
pointed towers in the background are the Louvre. *(Art Resource, NY)*

Finally, in 1146/47, there is a record of a donation from Simon, the
bishop of Noyon, to the Templars. It states clearly that this was done
at the Temple in Paris, in the presence of the master and the "convent
of knights." Now we can be certain that there was a building in Paris
where the Templar master for France and the knights lived.[5] Whether
it is the same as the one that became the center of the Templar compound in Paris still isn't sure, but we're closer.

In August of 1147, there was a great gathering of Templars. Pope
Eugenius III was in town and preparations were being made for the
Second Crusade. Lord Bernard of Balliol gave the Templars lands
that he possessed in England. This was witnessed by the pope, King
Louis VII, several archbishops, and 130 brothers of the Knights Tem-
plar, "wearing the white cloaks."[6] This means that there were that

many nobly born knights of the Temple in Paris. Since the fighting force in Jerusalem at that time averaged from three to six hundred it's a good bet that these knights had arrived from all over France, and perhaps England, before they left for the East.

If we had the charters of the Temple itself, a lot of the mystery surrounding the order would be cleared up. As it is, the next major gift in Paris that we know of was not until 1172, when Constance, sister of King Louis, gave the Templars a house in Champeaux. In this case, nine Templars of the house in Paris are listed by name.[7]

By the end of the twelfth century, the Temple in Paris was being used for the royal treasury. Louis' son Philip II (Philip Augustus) used the Temple as a depository for taxes and other revenues. His officials then drew money out for personal expenses for the king and his family.[8]

This was continued under his son, Louis VIII, and grandson, Louis IX.

Even though the kings had their own palace, many times the entire royal family chose to stay at the Templar commandery while they were in Paris. Philip III stayed there with his wife and children in 1275 and again in 1283 and 1285.[9] In order for the Temple to house the king and court, they would have needed a spacious guest house within the grounds.

The Temple in Paris also served as a safe place to keep royal documents, such as treaties. In 1258, Henry III of England agreed to renounce his claims to Normandy, Maine, Anjou, Touraine, and Poitou, about a quarter of the territory of modern France. The treaty was deposited at the Temple. In return, Louis promised to pay a certain amount to Henry, to be deposited to Henry's account at the Temple in Paris twice a year.[10]

Henry III also stayed in the Temple when he came to Paris in 1254. He may have just wanted to be close to his money, but he seems to have been on good terms with the Templars, as well. In 1247, the Grand Master, William of Sonnac, sent the king "a crystal vase allegedly containing a portion of the blood of Christ."[11]

As the government of the kings of France became more complex, a special section was created called the Chamber of Accounts. "This body met three times a year at the Temple in Paris to act on agenda prepared by a sub-committee which met at the *Chambre des Deniers* in the Louvre."[12] The members were not Templars; they just used the house for their meetings.

The Paris Temple was the heart of the financial connection between the Latin kingdoms and the West. When the patriarch of Jerusalem (in exile in Acre) needed to arrange for money and weapons to defend the city, he wrote to Amaury de la Roche, commander of the Temple in Paris. The patriarch needed funds sent to Acre to pay cross-bowmen, knights, and soldiers.[13] He expected Amaury to be able to make the arrangements for the loans and the transfer of the money.

In 1306, just a year before the **arrest** of the Templars, King **Philip the Fair** felt sure enough of the loyalty of the Templars to seek refuge in the Paris Temple during the riots caused when he devalued the money.[14] By then the Templar compound was surrounded by thick walls and included several buildings as well as the church and living quarters for the brothers. In that year, Philip issued charters that were made "at the Temple."[15]

It was rumored that Philip even spent the night of October 13, 1307, at the Temple so that he could be the first to start counting the loot after the arrests.[16] It's a nice image but there is no evidence.

After the fall of the Templars, the Templar enclosure was taken over by the crown for a time before it was finally turned over to the **Hospitallers**. The surviving daughter-in-law of Philip the Fair, Clemence, seems to have lived there starting in 1317 until her death in 1328.

In a piece of poetic justice, one of the architects of the downfall of the Templars, Enguerrand de Marigny, was briefly imprisoned at the Temple by King Louis X.[17] Enguerrand had been accused of taking bribes and falsifying accounts. When he was proved innocent of those charges, he was then accused of sorcery and hanged.

Even though the Temple in Paris was in the hands of the Hospitallers until the French Revolution, it continued to be called the Temple. It was used as a prison off and on, the most famous prisoners being King Louis XVI and his wife, Marie Antoinette. They were imprisoned in the tower of the Temple and it was from there that they were taken to the guillotine.[18]

The church of the Temple has also vanished but an eighteenth-

From Henri de Curzon, *La Maison du Temple de Paris*, 1888.

century sketch remains. The church was much like the one at the **Temple in London**, with a round nave and a long choir. Parts of it may have been added to in the mid thirteenth century so we can't know what it looked like originally.

Apart from the buildings used exclusively by the Templars, there was an entire village within the walls made up of the people who worked for or were dependent on the Templars and then after the order was dissolved, the Hospitallers. It was made up of kitchen gardens, sheds, storehouses, small shops, and houses. The Templars may have lived in their own world within Paris, but it was a busy one. With all the comings and goings of the wealthy, the nobles, and all of the rest of society that took care of them, it would have been difficult for the Templars to keep many secrets.

Oh yes, when the Metro system was dug for the Temple station, no treasure was found.

---

1 Henri de Curzon, *La Maison du Temple de Paris* (Paris, 1888) p. 1.

2 *Cartulaire Général de Paris, Tome Premier*, ed. Robert de Lasteyrie (Paris, 1887) p. 265, charter no. 270.

3 Ibid., p. 297, charter no. 321. This was made in the presence of **Bernard of Clairvaux** and witnessed by other men from Notre Dame and officials of the king, but no Templars are named.

4 Ibid., p. 288, charter no. 303.

5 Ibid., p. 299, charter no. 324. "Actum Parisius in Temple, presente magistro et conventu militum."

6 Ibid., p. 307, charter no. 334, "alba clamide indutis."

7 Ibid., pp. 422–23, charter no. 507.

8 John Baldwin, *The Government of Philip Augustus* (California University Press, 1986) p. 165. Also, please see chapter 24, **Templars and Money**.

9 Curzon, p. 240.

10 G. P. Cuttino, *English Medieval Diplomacy* (Indiana University Press, 1985) pp. 9–12.

11 Thomas W. Parker, *The Knights Templars in England* (University of Arizona Press, 1983) p. 48.

12 John L. Lamonte, *The World of the Middle Ages: A Reorientation of Medieval History* (New York, 1949) p. 468. For more on the Templar and French finances please see chapter 24.

13 Malcolm Barber, *The New Knighthood* (Cambridge, 1994) pp. 266–67.

14 Curzon, p. 241.

15 Ibid., p. 240.

16 Ibid., p. 242. He cites this story but doesn't seem to believe it.

17 Ibid., p. 259.

18 Saul K. Padover, *The Life and Death of Louis XVI (New York: Appleton, 1939)* pp. 285–91.

❧

CHAPTER TWENTY-SIX

The Temple in London

Tucked away into a courtyard in Temple Bar on the banks of the Thames is one of the oldest churches in London, Temple Church.

The round church was once the center of Templar activities in England, surrounded by living quarters, stables, meeting rooms, and storage facilities. Today one has to follow a pathway between law offices until one finds a small sign pointing to the church.

This is actually known as the "New Temple." The first was built around 1128, soon after **Hugh de Payns** visited on his grand tour to drum up interest in the order. The old Temple was in Holborn in London, then a rural area. When the foundations were uncovered in 1595, it was found that this church was round, made from stone from Caen, in northern France.[1] Many of the Templar churches were round, in imitation of the Church of the Holy Sepulcher in Jerusalem built in the time of Constantine.[2] Round churches were also built for the same reason by the **Hospitallers**.

The Templars moved to the present site, between Fleet Street and the Thames River, in 1161 and began to build the New Temple Church. The church was consecrated on February 10, 1185, by Heraclius, patriarch of Jerusalem and dedicated to the Virgin Mary.[3] In time a "hall of priests" was built and connected to the church by a cloister and, a bit farther from the church, there was a "hall of knights" to house the Templar brothers.[4] In 1240 the rectangular choir was added (see photo

Temple Church nave. *(Sharan Newman)*

above) as well as a chapel dedicated to Saint Anne, the Virgin's mother.[5]

This would have been a busy place, with a bakehouse, smithy, stables, and other domestic buildings. The knights would have taken care of repairs to their armor and other equipment in the Temple area. For serious training, they had a field of about fifteen acres on the other side of the Thames, known as Fickettscroft.[6]

During the **trials** of the Templars in England, one accusation made against them was that they had murdered an Irish Templar by putting him in the "penitential cell" in the northwest corner of the choir. The cell is four and a half feet long and two feet, nine inches wide. There are two window slits that would have allowed the prisoner to see the round part of the church and the altar.[7]

At the dissolution of the Templars in 1313, all their goods were to be turned over to the Hospitaller Knights. However, Edward II of

England instead gave the Temple property in London to his cousin Thomas, earl of Lancaster. Thomas, however, lost his head (literally) as a result of a rebellion against the king. Edward then gave the property to the earl of Pembroke, Aylmer de Valence.[8] It passed through several other hands before the Hospitallers finally received the property. Since they already had a headquarters in London, the Hospitallers leased the Inner and Middle Temple to a group of lawyers.[9]

The former servants of the Templars stayed on during the transition, Edward II paying their wages and pensions.[10]

Over the years, through changes in kings and governments the lawyers held on to the Temple.[11] In 1677 they were finally rewarded for their tenacity by being allowed to buy the property from King Charles II.[12] During the sixteenth century, the church was used in between services for lawyer-client conferences, which took place while walking about between the knightly effigies on the floor.[13]

During the Reformation the church was whitewashed over, then the floor was covered with "hundred of cartloads of earth and rubbish."[14] A restoration was made in 1840, including clearing the floor and reconstructing the shattered effigies.

The effigies in the church are of nine knights and a bishop. Unfortunately, it is not certain which sculpture is which knight. They have been moved around so much over the centuries that the identifications have been scrambled. They have also been "restored" several times. The originals date from the twelfth and thirteenth centuries. We know that one of them is Sir Geoffrey de Magnaville, earl of Essex, who died in 1144 and was first buried in the Old Temple and moved to the New. Others are of William Marshal, the first earl of Pembroke, who was admitted to the society of the Templars on his deathbed, and two of his sons. Marshall is considered the prototype of the perfect knight, loyal, brave, and valiant. He was the subject of stories and songs even in his lifetime. The Templars must have been pleased to have his patronage.

Most of the other effigies are just known as "knight" or "crusader knight."[15]

The effigies represent not Templars but their *confrators*, or "associates," nobles who wished to support the order without actually joining.

A straight-legged knight at the Temple Church. *(Sharan Newman)*

Temple Church in 1837, before bombs and restorations. (*Art Resource, NY*)

The men were buried in Templar cemeteries and commemorated in stone in the church. The cross-legged knights are those who have either gone on a crusade or at least taken a vow to do so.

The church survived intact until 1941, when it was bombed by the Germans. The vault survived but the columns cracked in the heat and had to be replaced. Much of what we see today is restoration and re-creation.

It's difficult these days to imagine the Temple church in its proper setting. Brick buildings crowd around it now. Originally, it would have had a grassy courtyard between all of the buildings of the Templars. Inside the church, Templar knights would have recited the Hours by daylight and candlelight. The wind might have blown in from the river or from the direction of the stables, a scent the knights would have preferred. The greatest lords and the richest merchants would have come to deposit their treasure for safekeeping or to beg a loan.

There would have been noise and color and excitement. But now all that remains is a small and lonely church.

---

1 George Worley, *The Church of the Knights Templars in London: A Description of the Fabric and Its Contents, with a Short History of the Order* (London, 1907) p. 14.
2 Malcom Barber, *The New Knighthood* (Cambridge, 1994) p. 195.
3 Worley, p. 15. "Dedicate hec ecclesia in honore Beate Marie." The inscription was destroyed during repairs in 1695 and rewritten on an inside wall.
4 Thomas W. Parker, *The Knights Templars in England* (University of Arizona Press, 1963) p. 24.
5 Worley, p. 15.
6 Parker, p. 24.
7 Worley, pp. 49–50. This doesn't mean that the Templars were all four feet tall, but that the cell was intended to be horribly uncomfortable.
8 Worley, p. 16.
9 Ibid.
10 C. G. Addison, *The Temple Church* (London, 1843; reprint) p. 11.
11 Addison, pp. 3–4.
12 Worley, p. 16.
13 Ibid., p. 21.
14 Ibid., p. 43.
15 Ibid., pp. 30–37.

CHAPTER TWENTY-SEVEN

The Last Stands;
The Fall of Acre and
Loss of the Holy Land

By the end of the thirteenth century the principalities established by the first crusaders were reduced to a few small settlements clinging to the Mediterranean coast and the cities of Tripoli and Acre. The title of king of Jerusalem was almost an afterthought, tacked on as an honorific to more substantial ones, such as king of Cyprus or emperor of Germany. There were still some trade routes that brought in enough revenue to make the land worth putting up a fight for, but not much more.[1]

Of course, there was always the possibility that the lost territory could be recovered. Jerusalem had been lost and regained before as had Acre. So there was still interest in the title. In 1277 one of the people claiming the right to the throne of Jerusalem was Maria of Antioch. She was convinced to sell it to the younger brother of Saint Louis, Charles of Anjou.[2] After his death the title reverted to the Lusignan family, descendants of Baldwin II. They continued to call themselves kings of Jerusalem, but they and many of the noble families of the Latin kingdoms had by then established themselves on Cyprus.[3]

In 1289 the city of Tripoli fell to the Mamluk sultan Malik al-Mansour. The Templar commander of the city, Peter of Moncada, was killed along with other Templars and Hospitallers.⁴ The king of Jerusalem at the time, Henry II, arrived in Acre from his home in Cyprus. He didn't come at the head of an army to take back Tripoli but to arrange a truce with the sultan.⁵ This truce was signed by Odo, the bailiff of Acre; William of Beaujeu, Grand Master of the Templars; Nicholas Lorgne, Grand Master of the **Hospitallers**; and Conrad, the representative of the Grand Master of the Teutonic Knights.⁶

We have an eyewitness account of what happened next made by the secretary of Templar Grand Master William of Beaujeu. The writer is known as the Templar of Tyre although he wasn't a Templar and he probably wasn't from Tyre, but Cyprus. But once a name is attached to someone, it's hard to change it without confusion. So, here is the story according to the secretary of William of Beaujeu, who wasn't from Tyre:

> It happened that, because of the fall of Tripoli, the pope sent twenty galleys to the aid of the city of Acre. These galleys were armed in Venice; their captain was a great nobleman of Venice named Jacopo Tiepole. . . . A great number of common people of Italy also took the cross and came to Acre.
>
> When these people came to Acre, the truce which the king had made with the sultan was well-maintained between the two parties. Poor Saracen peasants came into Acre carrying goods to sell, as they were accustomed to do. It happened one day, . . . that the crusaders, who had come to do good and to arm themselves for the succor of the city of Acre, brought about its destruction, for one day they rushed through Acre, putting all the poor peasants who had brought goods to sell in Acre to the sword. They also slew a number of bearded Syrians who were of the law of Greece. (They killed them because of their beards, mistaking them for Saracens.)
>
> This was ill-done indeed, for Acre was taken by the Saracens because of it, as you shall hear.⁷

Word of this outrage was sent at once to the sultan in Cairo, who demanded retribution. William of Beaujeu suggested a pragmatic solution for this. Rather than turn over the misguided crusaders to the sultan, he suggested that the citizens of Acre send condemned men from the local prisons, since they were to die anyway.[8]

However, William was overruled and the sultan was told the truth, adding that, since the perpetrators of the atrocity were Italians, they weren't subject to the laws of Acre so they couldn't be prosecuted.

In hindsight, honesty may not have been the best choice.

"The Sultan took this answer badly, and gathered his forces and his siege engines, and also collected his host of armed men."[9] He took his time preparing a massive expedition in order to drive the Franks out of Acre forever.

The Templar of Tyre and the various Arabic Chronicles agree on the basics of the siege and taking of the city. The sultan of Egypt arrived at Acre on the fifth of April, 1291, with a large army and many siege engines.[10]

By the beginning of May, the sultan had managed to undermine and destroy one of the major towers of the city. Some negotiating went on, but no agreement was made, and so "the two sides began again their labors, firing mangonels at one another, and doing the things that are usually done between enemies."[11]

A major assault was made on the city and the master of the Temple, William, took his men and went to the gate that was being attacked. The master of the Hospital and his men joined them.[12]

They were overwhelmed by the number of soldiers and by the Greek fire that was being thrown at them. The Templar of Tyre must have seen this happen for he gives a gruesome picture of the burning to death of an Englishman who was unlucky enough to be caught in the flames.[13]

The fate of William of Beaujeu was not so dramatic but equally fatal. He was struck by a javelin and "the shaft sank into his body a palm's-length; it came through the gap where the plates of the armor were not joined."[14]

The master must have stayed upright enough to appear unharmed, for when he turned his horse to go, some of the other defenders panicked and begged him not to leave. He answered, "'My lords, I can do no more for I am killed, see the wound here!' . . . and as he spoke he dropped the spear on the ground and his head slumped to one side."[15] Before he could fall from his horse, his men caught him and carried him to the Templar fortress. He lingered for the rest of the day, dying in the evening. "And God has his soul—but what great harm was caused by his death!"[16]

It seemed that the city was about to fall, so the king and his men went to their boats and left. The remaining people in the city rushed to the Templar fortress, the strongest in Acre. They held out for ten days but were finally forced to ask for terms of surrender, including safe passage for the women and children inside. However, when the Moslem soldiers came in, they began molesting the women and young boys. At this the Templars went after the soldiers and killed or drove them out of the fortress. They then decided to fight to the end.[17]

All the defenders of the Temple fortress were killed. The remaining noncombatants were taken prisoner. Abu al-Mahasin notes that the city fell on the same day and hour exactly one hundred years after **Richard the Lionheart** had first captured Acre. He adds that it was a just revenge for Richard's slaughter of his prisoners at that time.[18]

The property of the Templars, Hospitallers, and Teutonic Knights was taken as booty. There is no indication that any treasure was on the ships that left before the city fell. A few Templars, including the next Grand Master, Thibaud Gaudin, managed to escape by boat. They went to the fortress of Sidon and then to Cyprus. But the idea, often stated as fact by pseudohistorians, that they could have brought a hoard of treasure with them is highly unlikely. The entire coastline was full of the sultan's soldiers and archers. Men burdened with anything more than their clothes and swords would not have been able to get through.[19]

A unique view of Acre just before the fall comes from an Italian Dominican priest, Ricoldo de Monte Croce. Born near in Florence around 1240, he joined the Dominicans at the age of twenty-five and spent the next few years in study. At sometime around 1288, he decided to embark on a mission of conversion to the East. We find him first in Acre.[20]

In many ways Ricoldo represents the change in the approach to the non-Christian world that had occurred since the foundation of the

William of Beaujeu defending Acre, as depicted by Dominique Louis Papéty in 1845. William is wearing the red tunic and white cross of a Hospitaller and he's standing when he was actually on horseback. Hollywood isn't the only place where history is adapted to make a better picture. (*Art Resource, NY*)

Templars. The Dominicans were founded by Dominic of Castile and the order was given papal approval in 1216. The plan of the Dominicans was to take the word of Christianity to people all over the world. To this end, the Dominican monks were among the best educated of the clergy in languages. They dreamed of bringing Christianity to the masses through persuasion, passion, and logic. In this they were the exact opposite of the Templars.

Under the direction of the popes, the Dominicans also became the chief inquisitors in Europe, but this was not the first desire of many of the priests of the order and Ricoldo seems to have preferred converting the heathen to prosecuting heretics.

Ricoldo stayed at the Dominican house in Acre and also befriended the patriarch of Jerusalem, Nicholas, another Dominican. Then he set out into Moslem territory, where his preaching was largely ignored. He was in Baghdad in 1291 when word came of the fall of the city. So his information was gained through Moslem accounts.

His letter about the fall of the city is addressed to the patriarch, who was killed in the taking of the city, and "to all the brothers who died in the capture of Acre."[21] His shock and grief come through in every sentence. This outpouring of emotion reminds the reader of the human face of war. More than once he anguishes over the fate of the nuns who had now become slaves of Moslem men, of children who had been torn from their mothers and sold to be raised as Moslems.

Particularly chilling is Ricoldo's experience with the sellers of spoils from the city. From a Saracen peddler, he bought a tunic that had been pierced "by a sword or a lance that was partly stained with blood."[22] He wondered if it had belonged to someone he knew. The letter alternates between Ricoldo's attempts to rejoice that his friends are now martyred and in heaven and his intense misery. "Where is Tripoli?" he cries. "Where is Acre, where are the churches of the Christians that once were here? . . . Where are the multitudes of Christians? . . . I have heard that on the sixth day, in the third hour, you were slaughtered."[23] The words tumble over each other in his deep and personal agony.

In the midst of Ricoldo's lamentation, he notes that the master of the Temple was pierced in the stomach and lungs, "as was Ahab, king of Israel," and died around vespers, as is also related by the Templar of Tyre. The next day the city was taken.[24] One scholar feels that this allusion to King Ahab, who wasn't one of the better kings of Israel, is a comment on the weakness of the Templars.[25] This is not impossible, but I think it more likely that it was because Ahab was shot with an arrow in a battle with the Syrians and died in the evening, as did William of Beaujeu.[26]

However, throughout Ricoldo's letter there are the repeated questions: Why did this happen? Why did the bulwark fail? Why did God allow this? Ricoldo assumes that it must be because of the sins of the people. One of these passages is just before the reference to the death of the Grand Master.

This undercurrent of feeling—that *someone* must be to blame for the fall of Acre—seems to have been shared by many people in both the East and West. The Templars were seen as the invincible warriors, the protectors of the Holy Land. The loss of Acre damaged them more than any of the other military orders.

After the loss of Acre and the death of William of Beaujeu, the heart seemed to go out of the Templars. Some of them tried to hold on to Sidon, but they learned that the Templars on Cyprus considered them a lost cause and so Sidon was abandoned by night. Shortly thereafter, Chateau Pelerin was also abandoned. That was the last of the Templar holdings in what had once been the Latin kingdoms.

The Templars made one more attempt to regain the mainland, at the time of the last Grand Master, **Jacques de Molay**. They built a stockade on the tiny island of Ruad, not far from the town of Tortosa. From there, they planned on invading the town, but they were completely overrun by the Mamluk Sayf al-Din Ensendemür in 1302. The surviving Templars were taken to Egypt and sold into slavery.[27]

It was with this background of failure that the Templars had to face the increasing belief in Europe that they were at best useless and at worst traitors to the Christian cause.

1 Jonathan Riley-Smith, *The Crusades* (New Haven: Yale University Press, 2005) p. 231.

2 Ibid., p. 203. For more on Charles please see **The Templars and the Saint.**

3 Hans Eberhard Mayer, *The Crusades* (Oxford University Press, 1972) p. 243.

4 *The Templar of Tyre*, tr. Paul Crawford (Ashgate, Aldershot, 2003) p. 101, section 477.

5 *The Templar of Tyre*, p. 101, section 479.

6 Ibn Abd Az-Azhir, "The Treaty with Acre," in *Arab Historians of the Crusades* tr. Francesco Gabrieli (New York: Dorset, 1989) p. 326. The chronicler was mistaken in the name of the Hospitaller master. He was John of Villiers. Conrad was Conrad of Feuchtwangen (*The Templar of Tyre*, p. 104, note 3).

7 *The Templar of Tyre*, pp. 101–2, section 480.

8 *The Templar of Tyre*, p. 102, section 481.

9 Ibid.

10 *The Templar of Tyre*, p. 105, section 489; Abu al-Fida in Gabrieli, p. 344; Abu al-Mahasin in Gabrieli, p. 349.

11 *The Templar of Tyre*, p. 109, section 493.

12 *The Templar of Tyre*, p. 110–11, section 498.

13 Ibid. If you feel the need to know exactly what happened, get a copy of the book.

14 Ibid., p. 112.

15 Ibid.

16 *The Templar of Tyre*, p. 113.

17 This is recounted in both Abu al-Mahasin in Gabrieli, p. 348, and the *Templar of Tyre*, p. 117, section 507, as well as other chronicles.

18 Gabrieli, p. 149.

19 All accounts mention the difficulty of getting away by sea and stress the number of people who died trying to get to boats.

20 Cecilia Manetti, "'Come Achab al Calar del Sole' un Domenicano Giudica I Templari La Caduta d'Acri nella Testimonianza di Fra Riccoldo da Monte Cruce," *Acri 1291: La fine della presenze degli ordini militari in Terra Santa e i nuovi orientamenti nel XIV secolo* (Quattroemme, Perugis, 1996) pp. 171–72.

21 Ricoldo de Monte-Cruce, "Lettres de Ricoldo de Monte-Cruce," *Archives de l'Orient Latin* Tome II (Paris, 1884; rpt. Brussels, 1964) Letter IV p. 289, "et aliis fratribus qui motui sunt in captione Accon." Ricoldo doesn't mention, and might not have known, that the patriarch drowned while trying to escape (*The Templar of Tyre*, p. 115, note 7).

22 Ibid., p. 289. "Gladio vel lancea perforatuam, que etiam modico sanguine rosea erat."

23 Ibid., p. 291. "Ubi est Tempolis, ubi est Accon, ubi sunt ecclesie christianorum, que ibi erant . . . Ubi est multitudo populi chriniani, qui ibi erant? . . . Audivi enim, quod feria exta, hora tertia, occisi fuistis."

24 Ibid., p. 292. "Percussit magistrum Templi inter stomachum et pulmonen quasi alterum Achab regem Israel, wt mortuus est eaodem sero vesperi . . . et statim sequenti mane capta est civitas subiter."

25 Manetti, p. 174ff.

26 1 Kings 22, 34–35.

27 *The Templar of Tyre*, pp. 160–61, sections 635–38.

PART THREE

The End of the Order
of the Poor Knights

CHAPTER TWENTY-EIGHT

Jacques de Molay: The Last Grand Master 1292–1313

Jacques de Molay, the final Grand Master of the Templars, has become a figure of legend. To some he was a martyr, to others a heretic. He was either the victim of a plot or justly punished for the crimes of the order. Plays have been written about him. A Masonic youth group is named after him. Was he the last master of a secret society? Was he a heretic who denied the divinity of Christ? Or was he just a devout soldier caught up in the snares of the king of France, a relic of a dying world?

Who was this man who presided over the Templars in their last days?

In many ways, the last Grand Master of the Temple is also the least well known. Almost all the personal information on him comes from his own depositions, which were made after he was arrested in 1307.

In the first record that we have, made on October 24, 1307, eleven days after the arrest, Jacques states that he has been a Templar for forty-two years. He was received into the order in the town of Beaune, in the diocese of Autun, by Humbert de Pairaud and Amaury de la

Roche.[1] If he had been around seventeen when he became a Templar, that would put his age at around sixty at the time of the arrests, but he could have been slightly younger or much older.

The place of his birth is not certain, either. He seems to have been from a village in Burgundy, but there are several there named Molay. His biographer, Alain Demurger, has narrowed it down to two towns.[2] But one can't be certain about even that.

If he was born in Burgundy, then he was not under the jurisdiction of the king of France, for Burgundy was then part of the Holy Roman Empire. But it is likely that Jacques considered himself French.

Jacques' family and early life are a complete mystery. We don't know why he decided to join the Templars. There isn't a mention of him in any surviving Templar documents that might tell us what he did before he was elected Grand Master. It seems ironic that the most famous of the Templar Grand Masters is also the one we have the least information on. It's very likely that there was much more about his early years in the documents lost when the isle of Cyprus was conquered by the Turks in 1571. But knowing *where* the information was doesn't help us to know *what* it was.

Jacques de Molay became Grand Master at a critical time for the Templars and the crusader kingdoms. He must have been in the East at the time of the **Fall of Acre** in 1291. He may have even been one of the few who escaped from the city, although it was never mentioned. It's more likely that he was stationed at one of the outposts, such as Sidon or Cyprus.

After the death of William of Beaujeu, who fell defending Acre, the commander in the East at the time, Thibaud Gaudin, became master. He was probably elected because he was the highest-ranking member surviving after the slaughter.[3] Only a few letters survive from Gaudin's short tenure in office. He apparently died sometime before April 1292, for at that time Jacques de Molay sent a letter to Spain authorizing the sale of some property in Aragon. He signed it as master of the Temple.[4]

But what was there left for him to be master of?

Although the Templars had fought bravely at Acre, when the city fell they seem to have taken most of the blame for it, at least in the eyes of the West.[5] Therefore, Jacques' first order of business was to regain as much of the old Latin kingdoms as he could. To do this, he had to ensure the survival of the last of the Eastern Christian kingdoms, that of **Armenia**, now the southeastern part of Turkey.

Early in 1292, Pope Nicholas IV had written to the Templars and Hospitallers ordering that "They must come to the aid and defense of the Kingdom of Armenia with the galleys which, by the command and ruling of the apostolic see, they hold to counter the enemies of the cross."[6] Unfortunately Armenia had been weakened by power struggles within its ruling family and the loss of support from the Latin kingdoms. The attempts to aid the Armenians were also hampered by a war going on between the Venetians and the Genoese.[7] These two merchant powers controlled a great deal of the shipping of men and supplies. Their private war hampered all sea travel in the eastern Mediterranean.

For a time the Templars still held the island of Ruad, just across from the town of Tortosa. From here, Jacques de Molay hoped to prepare an invasion force to begin the reconquest. Ruad was never intended to be anything more than a jumping-off place for a garrison. It is a small, rocky island, with no fresh water.[8] In 1300 the island was a staging ground for a proposed invasion in which the crusader forces would attack from the west and the Mongol army would come in from the east. For a variety of reasons, including weather and problems among the Mongol leaders, the invasion never occurred. The Templars and their allies did capture the city of Tortosa but, without help, they couldn't hold it. They had to retreat to Ruad again.

The Templars managed to hold Ruad until 1302, when the island was invaded by an Egyptian fleet. It was headed by an emir, Sayf al-Din Esendemür, who was "born of a Christian man and woman in a land called Georgia."[9] That is, he came from slavic lands and had been captured as a slave to the Egyptians. The Templars had no ships large enough to fight at sea or to escape in. After a short battle, the Templars and their dependents were forced into surrender. They were promised safe passage but "the Saracens had the heads of all the Syrian foot soldiers cut off, because they had put up such a stiff defense and had done great damage to the Saracens and the brethren of the Temple were dishonourably conducted to Babylon."[10] This is the chronicler's metaphor to tell the reader that, like the Jews who were stolen from Israel, the Templars were also sold into slavery. In this case, they were probably taken to the slave markets in Egypt.

Jacques wasn't on Tortosa when it was taken. He was in Cyprus trying to arrange for ships to be sent to relieve the garrison. But he might have wished that he had been. The loss of Ruad and the capture of the Templars were to be used against the order at the **trials**.[11]

In the face of disaster and chaos in the East and a lack of funds or reinforcements coming from the West, Jacques de Molay felt it was necessary to do some personal recruiting for the order. He left the new Templar headquarters in Cyprus in 1293 to see if he could spark some enthusiasm among the heads of Europe for retaking Jerusalem. He also needed to oversee some disputes about various properties held by the Templars. Finally, he intended to hold a general meeting of the commanders and other officials in Europe.[12]

The next two years were spent in a tireless crisscross of the countries in which the Templars were most invested: France, Provence, Burgundy, Spain, Italy, and England. In August 1293, he held the general meeting of the order in Montpellier. In June 1295, he held another general chapter meeting in Paris.[13] Since it was traditional that these meetings be held in secret, we don't know what was discussed at them.

We do know that Jacques was in Naples for the coronation of Pope Boniface VIII and that he seems to have had a good working relationship with the pope. This would not have endeared him to the pope's mortal enemy, **King Philip IV**, but the friendship doesn't seem enough to explain why the Templars and Jacques were singled out for the king's vendetta.

However, there is a possibility in something that happened around 1297 to make the king think that Jacques had to go. A short time before, King Philip had borrowed 2,500 livres from the Temple. That was a usual amount for the French kings. But, according to a Cypriot chronicler, the treasurer of the Templars also gave Philip a loan of 200,000 florins. When Jacques found out about this enormous loan, he expelled the treasurer. Even the pleas of the king could not change his mind.[14]

The trouble with accounts like this is that we don't know if they are true or something the chronicler made up. The records were lost long ago. However, if it is true, it would mean that Jacques knew that King Philip was a bad credit risk. For Philip, it would be a reason to have the Templar records conveniently misplaced. It would also indicate that there was bad blood between the king and the order before the arrests.

Jacques returned to Cyprus in late 1296 and stayed in the East for the next ten years. He conducted naval raids on Egypt and participated in another ill-fated expedition to Armenia around 1299, in which the last Templar holding in that kingdom was lost.

By early 1306, Jacques was aware of the effect that all these losses were having on public opinion in the West. He was also embroiled in the politics of the kingdom of Cyprus, just as his predecessors had let themselves become involved in the feuds among the lords of the Latin kingdoms. When the letter came from the new pope, **Clement V**, telling him to come up with a plan for merging the Templars and the Hospitallers, his heart must have sunk. The idea of combining the military orders into one had been around at least since the Second Council of Lyons in 1274,[15] but Jacques may have feared that this time there would be no reprieve for the Knights of the Temple.

If he couldn't convince the pope that there was a reason for the Templars to continue, he knew they would be swallowed up by the Hospitallers, their old rivals. If so, he could see no place for himself in the new order.

When Pope Clement V ordered Jacques to come to the papal court at Poitiers to discuss the matter, Jacques wrote a letter explaining his position on the subject.[16] His arguments against the union must have seemed thin even to him. He tells the pope that it's not right to ask a man who has joined one order to suddenly become part of another and that there would be bickering and nastiness between the members of the two orders if they had to live together. The famous (or infamous) rivalry between the two orders would be lost, and with it healthy competition for each to be braver, more honorable, and more charitable than the other. "For, when the Hospitallers made an armed sortie against the Saracens, the Templars would stop at nothing until they made a better one, and likewise for the Hospitallers."[17]

Jacques does admit that it might be cheaper to have one order, but he feels that the resultant squabbling wouldn't be worth it. All in all, it wasn't the most forceful defense he could have made. But, while he was extremely concerned about the proposal, I believe that his main goal in returning to Europe was still to raise enough men to put Jerusalem back in Christian hands.

An interesting point in the opening to Jacques' letter is something that casts doubt on the reliability of his memory, even when he was not subjected to imprisonment and the threat of torture. He mentions that in 1274 he had attended the papal council at Lyon with William of Beaujeu, who had recently become Grand Master.

Now the inquisitors might have done well to study this letter before they began questioning Jacques, for he tells Pope Clement that he remembers seeing King Louis IX (Saint Louis) at the council.[18] Louis died in 1270, four years before the council was held. If this had been pointed out at the trial, it might have put an entirely different spin on the case. A man who has a vision of a dead saint isn't likely to be a heretic. On the other hand, a man who remembers an event that incorrectly might not be very reliable on other matters.

It wasn't until Jacques reached the port of Marseille in late summer of 1307 that he heard about the rumors that were being spread about the Templars. Up until then, he had assumed that any complaints were just the old ones: Templars were proud; they were greedy; they didn't give enough to charity; they wouldn't tell anyone about what happened in their chapter meetings, etc., etc. Imagine his horror at being told that they were being accused of denying Christ, spitting on the cross, and gross obscenity.[19]

How these stories began is impossible to say, which doesn't mean that scholars haven't tried. Some say that a brother with a nagging conscience confessed to a friend about what he had been required to do upon joining the Temple. Others, that men who had been expelled from the order made up the stories to get even.[20]

Some sort of tale about irregularities in the Templar initiation seems to have been circulating by early in 1307. But Jacques de Molay acted as if he were no more than mildly concerned. He told Pope Clement that he wanted a papal commission set up to investigate and disprove the slanders.[21] He then went on about his business. This was as late as August of that year.

The secret order for the arrest of the Templars was sent out a month later.

All of the contemporary chroniclers state that the Templars, Jacques de Molay in particular, had no idea that they were about to be taken by the king's men. There was no warning. There was no time to prepare, to flee, to hide any important documents or treasure. On Thursday the twelfth of October, Jacques went to sleep as the head of a prestigious religious order. On Friday the thirteenth, he was in prison being interrogated for infamous crimes against Christ.

What must he have felt when **Guillaume de Nogaret** and the soldiers started beating down the doors at the Paris Temple? Did he think it was a fire, an invasion, news of some disaster in Cyprus? When the soldiers burst into his sleeping quarters and dragged him out into the streets, did he understand what was happening?

The report of his first interrogation was made on October 24. It is a stark legal document, a confession that when he was received into the Templars, forty-two years before, he had been told to deny Christ and "he, although unwillingly, did it."[22] When asked if he then spit on the cross he answered, no, he had spit on the ground.[23]

Jacques admitted to these things but denied that he had been told he could "join carnally with the brothers and he insisted under oath that he had never done such a thing."[24]

That was all. But it was enough for his adversaries. The next day they had Jacques repeat his confession before the masters of the University of Paris. They also made him write an open letter to the other Templars, stating that he had admitted his guilt and repented. He begged them to do the same. Some of them did, but by no means all.[25]

Why did Jacques confess? He later said that he had been starved and threatened with torture.[26] I suspect that in those first days, he was simply in a state of shock.

At some point he must have realized that the king of France had no legal power over him or the order. In all later interrogations, he refused to answer any of the questions, insisting that he be taken to the pope, who alone could judge him.[27]

For the next six years, Jacques de Molay stuck to that position. The trials and defense of the Templars continued without him as he remained silent in prison.

There is no doubt that his "confession," such as it was, damaged the defense of the order. I think that if he and the other officers of the order had held fast, it would have been much harder to convince the general public of the Templars' guilt. Many people were doubtful that they were as evil as Philip and his councilors insisted and the knowledge that the master of the order refused to admit to the truth of the accusations might have kept the pope from issuing the command for the arrest of Templars outside France. Sadly, we'll never know what might have happened.

Jacques gave no leadership to the more than six hundred Templars who soon came forward to defend themselves and the order. On October 25, 1307, he did recant his confession in the presence of two cardinals sent by Pope Clement. However, in August 1308, the cardinals questioned him again at Chinon, where he was now imprisoned. At this time, he admitted to the same errors as before.[28]

Had he been tortured in the meantime? Was prison wearing him down? It is intriguing that he never admitted to more than the irregularity of his reception into the order. He spat next to the cross and denied Christ and then got on with the job as a good Christian knight.

At the interrogation of 1309, he again insisted that he be judged only by the pope. When reminded of his confession, "he seemed to be stupefied by this."[29] The image is of a man emotionally and mentally broken.

It's hard not to be critical of Jacques de Molay, sitting silent in his cell while so many others risked, and lost, their lives defending the Templars.[30] He seems to have placed his entire defense on the belief that only the pope could judge him. He did at one point defend the order as a whole, saying that the priests were orthodox, that he knew of no other religious order that gave so much to charity and that he knew of no other order, nor people, who were willing to put their lives on the line defending the faith against infidels.[31] But he retreated back into horrified silence as the accusations became more numerous and more bizarre: that the Templars worshipped a black cat; that they worshipped an idol that they believed could make them rich as well as cause crops to flourish; that every Good Friday they urinated on a crucifix.[32]

After being questioned by the papal commission, Jacques was imprisoned for the next four years at the royal chateau at Gisors. Along with him were Raimbaud de Caron, the grand commander; Geoffrey of Charney, the commander of Normandy; Geoffroy de Gonneville, commander of Aquitaine-Poitou; and Hugh de Pairaud, Templar Visitor of France. These were the highest-ranking Templars in custody and Pope Clement had insisted on judging them himself.[33]

The pope took his time about it.

There is no information about Jacques and his colleagues during the time that the pope was deciding how to handle the matter. Finally, in December 1313, a year after the Order of the Temple had been officially disbanded, Clement decided to delegate the problem of Jacques and the others to three of his cardinals. They gathered in Paris in March 1314.

Before a group of church dignitaries, including the archbishop of Sens, who had allowed fifty-four Templars to be sent to the stake in 1310, Jacques and the others confessed to everything. "On the Monday after the feast of St. Gregory [March 18] in the public place before the cathedral of Notre Dame, they were condemned to perpetual imprisonment. But, just when the cardinals thought the whole affair was finished, all at once, two of the Templars, the Grand Master and the Master of Normandy, defended themselves tenaciously against the cardinal who pronounced the sentence and against the archbishop of

Sens. And without any respect, they denied everything they had previously sworn, which caused many people to be greatly surprised."[34]

King Philip was at his palace nearby and was immediately informed of the stand taken by Jacques and Geoffrey of Charney. The king had had enough. The chronicler, Guillaume de Nangis, says, "Without telling the clergy, by a prudent decision, that evening, he [the king] delivered the two Templars to the flames on a little island in the Seine, between the royal garden and the church of the Hermit brothers."[35]

Guillaume continues by saying that "they endured the suffering with such an air of indifference and calm that . . . to all the witnesses it was a matter of admiration and astonishment."[36]

One of the witnesses was Geoffrey of Paris, a cleric in the employ of King Philip. He included the episode in his verse account:

> *The Master, who saw the fire near*
> *Removed his clothing without fear*
> *And then, as I saw with my own eyes*
> *He went, naked in his shirt*
> *Freely and with a brave face;*
> *Never did he tremble,*
> *Even when they shoved him this way and that*
> *As they took him and tied him to the stake.*
> *He let them bind him without fear.*
> *They tied his hands with a rope*
> *But he said to them, "Lords at least*
> *Let me join my hands a little*
> *To make a prayer to God*
> *For it is now the season*
> *Here I see my judgment.*
> *And death suits me well.*
> *God knows who is wrong and who has sinned*
> *The time will come soon for evil*
> *To those who have wrongly condemned us*
> *God will avenge our deaths . . .*

And he went so softly to his death
That everyone there marveled at it.[37]

Jacques de Molay made a good death. Whether he actually gave a speech on the pyre, I don't know. Geoffrey of Paris is the only witness who mentions it and he was a poet and therefore inclined to license. But it is agreed that the manner of his death caused many to question his guilt and that of the order.

After reading the few records that are left—the letters he wrote, his statements during interrogations, the accounts of his travels—I get the impression that Jacques de Molay was a man of average intelligence and courage. He was reasonably pious and genuinely devoted to the Templars and the goal of recapturing Jerusalem for Christianity. He knew that the order needed reform, but not because of heretical rites. He seems to have had in mind making the Rule clearer to the many Templars who were not educated and may have misunderstood things.

At no time did he give the impression that he had a secret agenda. On the contrary, Jacques appeared stunned by the charges against the Templars. This may have been because he was not the kind of man who was good at intrigue. His misfortune was to come up against a king who was a master at it.

---

1 Georges Lizerand, *Le Dossier de L'Affaire de Templiers* (Paris, 1923) p. 34.

2 Alain Demurger, *Jacques de Molay: Le crepuscule des templiers* (Paris: Biographie Payot, 2002) pp. 1–5.

3 Ibid., p. 94. For more on Gaudin, please see chapter 22, **Grand Masters 1191–1192/93**.

4 Ibid., pp. 96–97.

5 Malcolm Barber, *The Trial of the Templars* (Cambridge University Press, 1978; rev. ed. Canto 2006) p. 233.

6 Reg. Nicholas IV t. II, p. 913, n. 6834–35, quoted in Demurger, p. 114, translation mine.

7 *The Templar of Tyre*, tr. Paul Crawford (Ashgate, 2002) p. 130ff. The Templar was neither a Templar nor from Tyre but someone in the nineteenth century called him that and the name stuck. He was in Acre and Cyprus during the time of the events he chronicles.

8 Paul Crawford, private correspondence, Aug. 26, 2006.

9 *The Templar of Tyre*, pp. 160–61.

10 Ibid., p. 161. The Templars were not actually taken to the city of Babylon. This is a biblical reference meaning that they were sold into slavery. They were probably taken to Egypt.

11 J. Michelet ed., *Le Procès des Templiers* (Paris, 1841) pp. 36–39.

12 Demurger, p. 118.

13 Ibid., p. 364.

14 Henri de Curzon, *La Maison du Temple de Paris* (Paris, 1888) p. 257.

15 Hefele and Leclerq.

16 Text in Lizerand, pp. 1–15.

17 Lizerand, p. 8, "quia si Hospitalarii faciebant aliquod bonum exercitium armorum contra Saracenos, Templari numquam cessabant nisi fecissent tantumdem vrl plus et e converso."

18 Lizerand, P. "Certe recolo quod papa Gregorius, dum esset in concilio Lugdunensi et sanctus Ludovicus cum eo."—"I definitely remember that Pope Gregory was at the council with Saint Louis and others."

19 Whether you believe the Templars were guilty of these things or not, it still must have been a shock.

20 Demurger, pp. 214–19. Demurger seems to feel that the allegations were true but that the entry ritual was just a test of the recruit's obedience, a sort of fraternity prank. I disagree. I give my reasons in chapter 30, **The Arrest and Trials of the Templars**.

21 Ibid., p. 230.

22 Ibid., p. 34, "qui, licet invictus, fecit."

23 Ibid., "sed spuit ad terram."

24 Ibid., p. 36. "Interrogatus . . . si sibi fuit aliquid dictum quod commiceret se carnalier cum fratribus, dixit per juramentum suum quod non nec umquam fecit."

25 Guillaume de Nangis, *Chroniques capétiennes: Tome II* (Paris: Paleo, 2002) pp. 93–94.

26 Lizerand.

27 Jules Michelet, *Le Procès des Templiers* (Paris, 1841; rpt. Paris: Éditions du C.T.H.S., 1987) pp. 32, 42, and 87 for three different interrogations.

28 Demurger, pp. 246–49.

29 Michelet, p. 34, "videbatur se esse valde stupefactum de hiis."

30 Please see chapter 30.

31 Michelet, p. 45.

32 Malcolm Barber, *The Trial of the Templars* (Cambridge University Press, 1978; rev. ed. Canto, 2006) pp. 248–52.

33 Demurger, p. 265.

34 Guillaume de Nangis, p.128.

35 Ibid.

36 Ibid., pp. 128–29.

37 Quoted in Demurger, pp. 268–69 (my translation).

CHAPTER TWENTY-NINE

Philip the Fair

Philip IV of France was known as *le Bel* or "the Fair," not for his sense of justice, as will be seen, but for his light coloring and good looks. He was the grandson of Louis IX, who died while on crusade, and much of Philip's reign was directed at seeing that Louis was recognized as a saint.[1]

Philip was born around 1267. His mother, Isabella, died in 1270, while returning from the crusade. Philip's stepmother, Marie de Brabant, was apparently not sympathetic to the children of her husband's first marriage.[2] She seems to have resented her husband's sons because of the fact that hers would not inherit the throne.

Philip became king of France in 1284, shortly after his marriage to Jeanne, heiress of Navarre and Champagne. Philip's bride brought with her a territory nearly the size of her husband's, which she managed in her own right. More importantly, she seems to have loved him and he her. Unfortunately this seems to have happened too late in his life to make Philip a nicer person. By all accounts he was withdrawn and uncomfortable in public. Not the best personality traits for a ruler. He acquired a reputation for being aloof and perhaps not very bright. But he was at least ornamental. Several people commented on his good looks.

Philip and Jeanne had three sons and one daughter. From his later actions, it doesn't seem that Philip cared much for his sons, but he

Philip's happy family. *(Art Resource, NY)*

may have just had strange ways of showing it. Isabella was in every sense daddy's little princess. Even after she married Edward II of England, he kept in close touch with her and often gave presents to her husband at her request.[3]

In October 1285, when Philip was eighteen, his father died, leaving him the kingdom, a disastrous war in Aragon, and a mountain of debt.[4] So, besides being obsessed with the canonization of this grandfather, Philip was also driven to find new ways to get cash. The major conflicts of his reign are all tied to these two goals.

PHILIP THE FAIR AND POPE BONIFACE VIII

Money was at the heart of Philip's conflict with the Pope Boniface. To support his war against Edward I of England, Philip had levied a tax on lands owned by the Church. This was not unknown and usually the Church allowed taxes "for the defense of the realm," although previous kings and clerics had always pretended that it wasn't a tax but a voluntary contribution.[5]

Philip got carried away with the percentage of their income that he charged the Churches of France and King Edward, seeing that no one was complaining too much, decided to do the same in England. At this point Boniface stepped in and, in 1296, issued a bull, *Clericos Laicos*, forbidding the clergy to pay or agree to any "aids or subsidies" to any lord without the permission of the Holy See.[6]

Since the church owned a large share of the land in both France and England, Philip and Edward weren't happy with this. But it was Philip who went ballistic. He organized a media campaign against the pope. Pamphlets began to appear castigating Boniface and the clergy. Since the authors were government employees, they didn't have to worry about libel laws.

This tactic worked so well that Philip would use it again when he decided to go after the Templars.

At first Boniface backed down, but then decided to fight back. As is the case with many major events, the spark was something minor. A bishop in the Languedoc, Bernard Saisset, was in the habit of getting a bit tipsy and running down the king. This was a common a pastime then as it is today. But Languedoc was the home of the **Cathar** heresy and it had also only recently been added to the French possessions. This made Philip more sensitive to criticism coming from that region. One comment that Saisset made became famous throughout Europe: "Our king resembles an owl, the fairest of birds, but worthless. He is the handsomest man in the world, but he only knows how to look at people unblinkingly, without speaking."[7]

This and other pithy remarks caused the bishop to be charged with treason. Now, it had been the rule for centuries that clerics charged of crimes could only be tried in Church courts. If they were guilty of major crimes, like murder, they might be turned over to civil authorities for punishment, but the decision to do so was made by other clerics. However, instead of finding some bishops willing to try Saisset in their courts, Philip had the bishop arrested and brought to Senlis for trial.[8]

Boniface had had enough. He issued one bull after another

declaring that the papacy was above any monarch and that Philip had better turn Saisset over to him or else. This declaration of papal supremacy was an old issue. The popes kept insisting that they were the leaders of Christendom and that kings were merely their lieutenants. This never went over well with the kings, who thought the popes were meddlers. Soon this led to an all-out war between Boniface and Philip. It was clear to most people that the pope would lose. The wisest course would be to come to some sort of compromise, but Boniface refused. He met Philip head-on.

Why did Boniface set himself on a suicide course? One historian suggests that "he had gallstones and that soured his character."[9]

The battle did not confine itself to words. Philip, through his adviser **Guillaume de Nogaret**, accused Boniface of heresy, sodomy, and other unclerical behavior.[10] They also implied that he wasn't really a lawful pope, having driven his predecessor, Celestine V, out of office.[11] There was enough truth in their accusations to put Boniface on shaky ground. He was one of the many popes who had been elected as part of a power struggle between the great families of Rome. When Philip needed help to condemn the pope, Boniface's enemies, the Colonna family, were happy to oblige.

Nogaret then went to Italy and led a band that arrested and imprisoned Boniface at his home town of Anagni. However, after a short time, the citizens of Anagni became nervous about locking up a pope. Public sympathy outside France was changing in support of Boniface, if not his policies. But we'll never know who would have won. Boniface was released and went back to Rome an aged and broken man. He died a month later on October 11, 1303.[12]

This is a quick summary of a very complex issue, but the arrest of Boniface is important to understanding what happened to the Templars because there is a pattern being established here. Philip's battle with Boniface began with the king's need for money to support his various wars. The need came first. The moral and legal justifications followed. These were backed up by accusations of wrongdoing, some provable, some clearly made up, like heresy and sexual misconduct. From Philip's point of view, everything was justified.

PHILIP AND THE JEWS

Money still being a problem, Philip's next target was the Jewish population. The situation of the Jews in France was always unstable. As non-Christians, they were already set apart from the rest of the population and could be more easily targeted. They were not numerous and concentrated mostly in the major cities, living in their own enclaves and following their own customs. Jews were also considered a separate society, with their own courts. In most places they were under the direct protection of the king or bishop, to whom they paid huge taxes for the privilege.

Although there had been sporadic accusations of ritual murder, the worst being in Blois in 1171,[13] there had been no mass persecutions in France. Philip II had expelled the Jews from his territory in 1180 but invited them back by 1198.[14] Since then, the Jews were generally left in peace in France.

Even in the thirteenth-century determination to stamp out heretics, Jews were left relatively alone. Never having been Christian, they couldn't be heretics. But, by the end of the century, there was once again a general feeling that they shouldn't be allowed to live in Christian lands. Edward I expelled them from England in 1290 and many went to France.

By 1306, Philip IV had lost the county of Gascony to Edward and the county of Flanders to Countess Margarite along with the revenue from those lands. He began looking around for a new source of cash. In the Jews he suddenly noticed a section of the population that had a good deal of disposable income and who wouldn't be missed at all.

Philip felt that this was a chance to kill two birds with one stone. Along with his constant need for money, his approval rating in the eyes of the French people was at an all-time low. Not long before, he had debased the coinage, causing rampant inflation. We all know how popular that makes politicians. In Paris this caused "fatal sedition." "The inhabitants of that town were forced to rent their houses and receive the rental payments in the new coin, according to royal decree. Most of the common people found this very onerous for it tripled the usual price."[15]

Philip made a plan to expel the Jews and take their property. His excuse was that they were known to be usurers who gouged honest Christians with exorbitant interest. Actually, the rates the Jews charged were often lower than those of the Christian lenders but that made the general anger worse since that meant they were taking business from Christians.[16]

Philip and his advisers decided that it was better to keep the matter quiet until the day of the arrests. They didn't want nobles protesting, Jews fleeing with their valuables, or local mobs getting into the spirit of things and looting Jewish property before the king's men arrived.[17]

The lightning arrests didn't go as smoothly as planned. Some Jews got away with their goods. Some lords tried to protect them. But Philip got enough out of the episode to make it worth his while. For good measure, he also expelled the Lombards, another group of foreigners associated with banking.[18]

Still Philip needed more. He cast about for another group that was perceived as wealthy and wasn't all that popular. He settled on the Templars. His attack on them used all the tools he had perfected in his earlier vendetta.[19] Evidence that the Templars weren't expecting to be put among the outsiders was the fact that they bought the synagogue complex in Belvèze either from the fleeing Jews or from the king. The complex was walled and had a moat, perfect to the needs of the Templars.[20] They only had a few months to redecorate before their turn came.

LAST YEARS

Historians have disagreed as to how much Philip was the instigator of the deeds attributed to him. Bernard Saisset wasn't the only contemporary who had a low opinion of the king. Another contemporary said, "Our king is an apathetic man, a falcon. While the Flemings acted, he passed his time in hunting. . . . He is a child; he does not see that he is being duped and taken advantage of by his entourage."[21]

Was he? I can't be sure. His close adviser **Guillaume de Nogaret** has been blamed for every evil thing Philip did, especially regarding

Pope Boniface and the Temple. It's possible that Philip was easily duped. It's also possible that Philip, like many people, preferred to make a good impression on the public and let underlings take the heat. He might have been a Teflon king. From looking at the records, I'm inclined to think he was smarter than people thought and not just a puppet.[22] I'm sure the matter will continue to be debated for years.

After the execution of the Templars, Philip had one more major scandal. In November 1314, all three of his daughters-in-law were accused of adultery and arrested. It appears that two of them were guilty, although I wouldn't swear to that, either. The third managed to prove her innocence. The men involved were executed. The two women who were convicted were imprisoned and died soon after.[23]

This whole situation is extremely odd. One wonders just what was wrong with Philip's sons. I've never found a reference to them either condemning or defending their wives. Everything was done by the king. It's another indication that Philip always called the shots.

While the three sons each became king in his turn, none of them produced an heir. In an ironic twist, Philip's only descendant would be the son of his daughter, Isabella, whose marriage to Edward II of England produced King Edward III. That led to what is called the Hundred Years' War between the two countries. If her actions in England are any indication, Isabella was a chip off the royal block.[24]

Another of the significant changes in King Philip's reign is his reliance on lawyers to maintain the workings of the state. Unlike his ancestors', Philip's advisers were not relatives or knights who owed him military service, but legal administrators. "The strongest, most highly developed . . . branch of the government was the judicial system."[25] Philip was a master at using this system to give a legal justification for all his actions, including annexing the land of other countries, bringing down a pope, expelling the Jews, and, of course, destroying the Templars.

His legacy is still being disputed. In many ways he strengthened the French government. He proved that a king in his own country can be more powerful than a pope in Rome. He established a weblike bureaucracy that, as far as I can tell, still thrives. He certainly made the law a very lucrative profession in France. But even his greatest supporters admit that a chilly, arrogant personality coupled with rampant overspending made him one of the most disliked kings France ever had. His treatment of the Templars is only one of many misdeeds Philip committed in his single-minded quest for financial security.

Philip's passion for hunting was legendary and it surprised no one when he died in a hunting accident, November 29, 1314.

1 He was, of course, or there would be no St. Louis, Missouri.

2 Joseph Strayer, *The Reign of Philip the Fair* (Princeton: Princeton University Press, 1980) p. 6.

3 Ibid., p. 19.

4 Ibid., p.11.

5 Robert Fawtier, *The Capetian Kings of France* (London: Macmillan, 1965) pp. 90–91.

6 Ibid.

7 Bishop Bernard Saisset, quoted in Charles-Victor Langlois, "Philip the Fair: The Unknown King" in *Philip the Fair and Boniface VIII*, ed. and tr. Charles T. Wood (New York: Holt Rinehart Winston, 1967) p.85.

8 Strayer, pp. 262–68.

9 Jean Favier, *Philippe le Bel* (Paris: Fayard, 1978) p. 268 (my translation).

10 Strayer, pp. 275–77.

11 Ibid., p. 287.

12 T. S. R. Boase, *Boniface VIII* (London: Constable and Co., 1933) pp. 341–51.

13 Robert Chazan, *Medieval Jewry in Northern France*, (Jolins Hopkins University Press, Baltimore, 1973) p. 37.

14 Ibid. p. 74.

15 Continuator of Guillaume de Nangis, *Chroniques Capétiennes.Tome II*, tr. François Guizot (Paris: Paleo, 2002) p. 88.

16 William Chester Jordan, *The French Monarchy and the Jews* (Philadelphia: University of Pennsylvania Press, 1989).

17 Jordan, pp. 202–3.

18 Favier, p. 205.

19 See chapter 30, **The Arrest and trials of the Templars**.

20 Cyril P. Hershon, *Faith and Controversy: The Jews of Mediaeval Languedoc* (University of Birmingham, UK, 1999) p. 102.

21 Favier, p. 86.

22 Strayer leans to this opinion and makes a very good case for it.

23 Guillaume de Nangis, pp. 129–30.

24 Isabella's life is another interesting story. Just don't believe anything you saw about her in *Braveheart*. She was only five years old when William Wallace died.

25 Strayer, p. 33.

CHAPTER THIRTY

Friday the Thirteenth;
the Arrest and Trials
of the Templars

A t the beginning of October 1307 **Jacques de Molay** was mainly concerned with fending off the proposed union of the Templars and the **Hospitallers** and with getting together the men and materials necessary to retake the Holy Land. He seems to have had no idea that **Philip the Fair** was already preparing the mass arrest of every Templar in France.

De Molay may have even felt that he had a real chance of success. The new pope, Clement V, had proclaimed from the beginning of his pontificate that the recovery of the Holy Land was one of his main goals.[1] King Philip also seemed disposed to leading a crusade, although the terms under which he would do so weren't what the master of the Temple had in mind. Philip wanted the Templars disbanded and a new order created, possibly under the leadership of his younger brother, Charles de Valois.[2] Charles had married Catherine de Courtenay, granddaughter of the last Western emperor of Constantinople, and he had dreams of one day retaking the city from the Greeks and ruling it himself.[3]

Therefore, De Molay seems to have been oblivious to the coming storm. When he came to Paris in October 1307, he had no idea that Philip had already sent out the order for the arrest of every Templar in France.

Why did Philip decide that the Templars would be his next target? It's not really clear, even with the mass of material his counselors wrote to justify his actions. If we take these documents at face value, the pious king had recently been horrified to learn that the Templars were not as they seemed. Instead of being the pillars of Christendom, a bulwark against the heathen, they had really renounced Christ and were working actively against Him and, by extension, against the most Christian king of France and, oh yes, the papacy.

One month before the arrest, on September 14, 1307, Philip sent secret orders to his officials throughout the land. His words leave no doubt of his shock and horror at what he was asking them to do: "A bitter thing, a doleful thing, a thing horrible to contemplate, terrible to hear, a detestable crime, an execrable pollution, an abominable act, a shocking infamy, something completely inhuman, even more, outside of all humanity."!!!![4]

The men who received this must have been quaking in their boots as they read, not knowing what monster was about to be unleashed. Philip's orders continue in this way for a full page before he lets on that the perpetrators of this evil are, gasp, the Templars! "Wolves in sheep's clothing, under the habit of their order, they insult the faith. Our Lord Jesus Christ, crucified for the salvation of mankind, is crucified again in our time."[5]

He then reveals the blasphemies that they are guilty of. These would become familiar to everyone soon, but one has to wonder what the bailiffs and seneschals felt when they heard them for the first time.

In their initiation ceremonies, Philip states, the Templars ritually deny the faith three times. Then they spit three times on the face of the cross. Finally, the new recruit strips naked and kisses the Templar who has recruited him, first at the base of the spine, then on the navel, and then on the mouth, "as is the profane rite of their order."[6]

As if that isn't enough, then the new recruit to the Templars is told that he must now give himself to the other brothers, not refusing anything they ask, lying together in "this horrible and dreadful vice."[7] And, by the way, they also worship idols.

Philip winds up by telling his officials that he is only taking this drastic step at the request of the Inquisitor General of Paris, and with the permission of the pope, because the Templars pose a clear and present danger to all the people of Christendom. Therefore, he commands his men to arrest all the Templars in their jurisdiction and hold them. The officials are also to seize all their goods, both buildings and property, and hold them for the king (*ad manum nostrum*—"for our hand"), without using or destroying anything. Because, of course, if it should turn out that the Templars were innocent, everything ought to be returned to them just as they left it.[8]

Guillaume de Paris, the Inquisitor, was also Philip's private confessor. Of course that didn't affect his loyalty to the Faith or to the pope, not at all.

Everything was in place.

On Thursday, October 12, 1307, Jacques de Molay attended the funeral of Catherine de Courtenay, the wife of Charles de Valois. He was given a place of honor and even held one of the cords of the pall.[9] That night, he must have gone to bed feeling fairly sure of his place in court society.

I have often heard that our superstition about Friday the thirteenth being an unlucky day stems from the arrest of the Templars. It's very difficult to trace the origin of a folk belief. It does seem that thirteen was an unlucky number long before the Templars, and there are traditions that Friday is an unlucky day, perhaps stemming from Friday being the day of Jesus' crucifixion. I haven't been able to discover when the two beliefs were joined. It was certainly unlucky for Jacques and the rest of the Templars. In fact, Jacques' world was shattered in the predawn hours of the next morning, Friday, October 13, when the **Temple in Paris** was invaded by agents of the king. "All the Templars that could be found in the kingdom of France were, all at once, in the same moment, seized and locked up in different prisons, after an order and decree of the king."[10]

It's not clear if they knew at first what they were charged with. Jacques de Molay had apparently heard the rumors of improprieties in the order and had asked Pope Clement to look into them.[11] Clement promised to do so but put the matter off because of his chronic illness. Neither man seemed to feel it was anything urgent.

By October 24, Jacques de Molay had confessed to every misdeed his accusers suggested. He did this, the records state, not because of torture or fear of torture or because he'd been thrown into prison but "on the contrary, he spoke the pure truth for the good of his soul."[12]

Almost all of the Templars arrested that night produced almost identical confessions within the next few weeks. Either they were obviously guilty or the inquisitors had all been working from the same script.

People who heard of this tended to one side or the other depending on their experience with the Templars and their distance from the court of Philip the Fair. James II, king of Aragon, wrote to Philip that he was astonished by the accusations, as the Templars had "lived as religious men in these parts in a laudable manner according to popular opinion."[13] Edward II of England, Philip's son-in-law, told him that he and his council found the whole matter "more than is possible to believe."[14]

The person who was most amazed, apart from the imprisoned Templars, was Pope Clement. As one of the exempt orders, the Templars were answerable only to the pope. Not even the local bishops could prosecute them. This had been a source of friction ever since the military orders had been founded. Therefore, for the king of France—who was, when all is said and done, only a layman—to arrest and question the Templars without even telling the pope first, that was just too much.

Clement let Philip know that he wasn't happy. He immediately wrote to the king, "You . . . have in our absence, violated every rule and laid hands on the persons and property of the Templars. You have also imprisoned them and, what pains us even more, you have not treated them with due leniency [that means "you tortured them"] . . .

Your hasty act is seen by all, and rightly so, as an act of contempt towards ourselves and the Roman Church."[15]

Clement was right to be alarmed. He remembered only too well what had happened to Boniface VIII in his hometown in Italy, when he had made an enemy of Philip. How much more dangerous was it for a pope to challenge Philip the Fair in his own kingdom? Clement had been driven out of Rome and was at that time in Poitiers. Still, he had to say something. Philip seemed to be usurping the role of leader of the faithful. Clement probably knew that he was already widely regarded as nothing more than Philip's puppet. But this was going too far. The pope knew that he had never agreed to let Philip's men arrest the Templars, but Philip had told everyone that he had blessed the deed.

Clement had to find a way to get control of the situation.

Philip argued in return that, since the Templars were so dangerous and the threat so imminent, as a good Christian and crowned defender of the faith, he had no choice but to act, since the pope wouldn't. Clement didn't agree with that, nor did the masters at the University of Paris when Philip put the matter to them.[16]

Actually, Philip never said just what threat the Templars posed. There was a veiled insinuation that they might be luring more men into the pernicious heresy of the order, but there was no mention of an upcoming plot to destroy the kingdom or assassinate the pope. As a matter of fact, until Jacques de Molay confessed, none of the charges were anything but rumors. But after Jacques and other leaders of the Templars admitted their guilt, the fate of the Templars was sealed.

Still, it would be another five years before the order was officially dissolved. The story of these years reflects the politics and emotional climate of the time as much as the guilt or innocence of the Templars.

They were, to some extent, pawns in the struggle of Pope Clement to escape the control of the king of France. They also suffered from the resentment of local bishops and priests against the exempt orders along with a popular feeling that the Templars had grown too arrogant and powerful. Added to that was a growing unease in Europe about heresy and the beginning of a belief that it was somehow connected to sorcery and magic.[17] This was to culminate in the seventeenth century, during the "Enlightenment," with the witch trials.

At first, Clement simply tried to make the best of a bad situation. In order to appear that he was in charge, on November 22, 1307, he ordered that all Templars in all countries be arrested. He also sent emissaries to try to find out what was going on.

While the pope dithered, the king's men continued to question the Templars energetically. It was said that at least thirty-six of them died as a result.[18]

WHERE DID THE CHARGES COME FROM?

Most of **the charges** against the Templars are so commonplace that for a long time people assumed that Philip and his counselors had made them up. Accusations of defacing holy objects, idolatry, sexual deviation, and wild orgies have been staples of condemnations of outsiders since long before the Christian era.[19] As a matter of fact, the accusation of heresy without orgies seems to be almost unheard of, even against groups that preach celibacy.

In any case, it turns out that at least one person was spreading salacious stories about the Templars in the months before the arrests. A man from Gascony, Esquin de Floyran, had been trying to get the kings of Europe to pay attention to him for some time. He had first gone to King James II of Aragon with the information, but James had told him that his stories were nonsense.[20]

Undaunted, Floyran took his information to Philip the Fair, who was much more receptive and sent spies into the Templar commanderies to find out if the charges were true. The spies reported back that they were.[21] It's not clear exactly how the spies found that out. They don't seem to have actually joined the Templars themselves. Perhaps they hung about in local taverns asking servants and others. That's what investigators do on television.

The Templars were aware of Floyran's accusations, but don't seem to have been that worried about him. For an experienced leader, Jacques de Molay acted in a manner that was most unworldly.

In January 1308, Floyran wrote a letter to King James II to say "I told you so." In it he specifies that he told James that the Templars denied Christ and spit on the cross, that they were encouraged to have sex with each other, and that the reception ceremony included kissing on various parts of the body. He reminds James that "you were the first prince in the whole world to whom I exposed their actions. . . . In this you were unwilling, lord, to give full credence to my words."[22] He then goes on to give the main reason for his letter: "My Lord, remember that you promised me . . . that if the activities of the Templars were found to be proved, you would give me 1,000 livres in rents and 3,000 livres in money from their goods."[23]

There is no record of James paying.

I haven't found anything that indicates where Esquin de Floyran found the information about the Templars in the first place. Was he a good citizen reporting a crime or a greedy bastard with an ax to grind? As with so many things, we may never know.

IF THE TEMPLARS WERE INNOCENT, WHY DID THEY CONFESS?

For several centuries, people have debated this question. Some people have said that they must have been guilty. If they weren't doing something bad, why were their reception ceremonies secret? Others have assumed that there was something in the charges but the actions weren't signs of heresy. The spitting on the cross and denying of Christ were just tests to judge the obedience of the new recruit. The kisses were just medieval boyish high spirits, to show humility. The ceremony was nothing more serious than a fraternity initiation.[24]

Some people have taken the confessions more seriously. They have assumed that at least parts of the confessions reflected real events and used them to assert that the Templars were really a secret mystical and/or pagan society.[25] While they were accused of blasphemy and denial of the divinity of Jesus, none of the accusations imply that the Templars had a coherent secret agenda.

I believe that many of those searching for explanations have ignored the situation that the Templars found themselves in as well as the beliefs of the world in which they lived.

First of all, most of the men arrested were not knights, but "serving brothers" or even servants. The average age of those questioned in Paris was 41.46 years.[26] Jacques de Molay was at least in his early sixties. Others were still in their teens and had only recently joined the order. This was natural, as all men of fighting age were sent to the East as soon as possible, so the ones left in France would have been either too old and infirm to fight or not yet trained. But it meant that the weakest of the brothers were the ones who fell into Philip's trap.

In order to make sense of the accusations against the Templars and their confessions, one needs to understand how heresy was viewed at this time. It was not enough simply to believe something that went counter to Church teaching. One had to hold to a contrary belief even after the accepted doctrine was explained. Also, the heresy usually was ignored unless the believer tried to convert others.

An established group of heretics who didn't answer to Church or civil authority could lead to a breakdown of society. This was one reason why kings and other rulers were eager to stamp it out. This danger had been made all too clear fifty years before the Templar trial when whole counties had refused to obey local religious leaders, preferring the teaching of the **Cathars**.

However, in theory, the Church did not want to punish sinners, but save them. Therefore, if a heretic confessed, showed contrition, and was prepared to do penance, he or she would be forgiven and brought back into the fold. In the case of the Templars, when they were arrested, they were presumed to be guilty. A chronicler reports, "Some of them confessed, sobbing, to most or all of these crimes.

These were allowed, it seems, to repent. Some others were questioned with various tortures, or frightened by the threat or sight of the torture instruments. Still others were led or coerced by inviting promises. Many were tormented and forced by starvation in the prison to swear to the truth of the accusations."[27]

After days or weeks of imprisonment and torture, it may well have seemed to the Templars that it would make more sense just to confess, do the penance, and get on with their lives. Seen in this light, the mass confessions make some sense.

What is amazing is that the confessions were retracted. The chronicler is also amazed. "But a great number of them denied absolutely everything, and more, who had at first confessed, later recanted and persisted in their denials right up to the end. Some among them died while being tortured."[28]

Finally, Pope Clement became fed up with Philip's determination to continue the unauthorized interrogation of the Templars. Since the king insisted that he was only acting on behalf of Guillaume de Paris, the papal inquisitor, Clement was able to find a loophole. In February 1308, he suspended the Inquisition in France, "thereby bringing the trial of the Templars to a dead-end."[29]

But it was too late to go back. Templars all over Christendom were in prison or on the run. Their goods had been confiscated. And the Grand Master had confessed to horrible crimes that, by extension, made every Templar suspect of the same.

Clement may have been hoping to make the investigation of the Templars purely an internal matter, but Philip was having none of that. He stepped up his media campaign against the Templars. One of his clerks, Pierre Dubois, wrote a "people's proclamation," supposedly a reflection of popular French opinion. It was written in French and widely distributed throughout the kingdom. In it, the "people" profess themselves to be horrified by the "buggery of the Templars."[30] They are also upset about the confessions of blasphemy and can only imagine that the Templars have bribed the pope to stop the proceedings.[31]

Instead of attacking the Templars, the proclamation goes for Pope

Clement, who is really an easier target. It accuses him not only of taking bribes but of putting many of his relatives in important positions in the Church. Both of these things were true. His nephew Bernard de Fargues had been made archbishop of Rouen. Another nephew, Arnaud de Cantiloup, became archbishop of Bordeaux.[32] Yet another, Gaillard de Preissac, was given the bishopric of Toulouse.[33] The pope was very much a family man.

Clement had reason to be nervous, as the letter continued to hint that a pope who didn't act in the interests of the faith might not be around long.

This was followed by a second proclamation, in Latin, that focused more on the sins of the Templars but still begged the king to see that the pope take action at once. "The people of the Kingdom of France urgently and devotedly ask Your Majesty that however . . . the discord between you and the pope over the punishment of the Templars, he swore to uphold the Catholic faith."[34] Again it urges the king to help the pope see his duty and condemn the Templars.

The king then called together a group of representatives from the kingdom, consisting of minor local officials and bourgeoisie. He put the matter to them as spokesmen for the people of France and they came through by agreeing that something should be done.[35]

Clement got the message. Even so, he refused to allow the king to judge the order. In early 1309, he set up a papal commission to interview the Templars in custody and gather evidence for a decision on the order as a whole. He had already announced that there would be a general council of the Church that would meet in October 1310.[36]

THE PAPAL INVESTIGATION

Pope Clement's commission, headed by Gilles Aycelin, archbishop of Narbonne, didn't meet until August 9, 1309. The bishops issued a proclamation that all who wished to defend the Templars should come to meet with them at the monastery of St. Genevieve, in Paris.

The first day they met no one came.

The second day no one came.

The third day no one came, even though the porter, John, had shouted the invitation all over the city.

The same thing happened for the following five days. Finally, the commission was about to adjourn and try again in November. After all, everyone knows August is when the French all leave Paris for someplace cooler.

However, they made one last attempt. They sent a letter to the bishop of Paris asking if he could hurry things up a bit. The bishop decided to go to see the Templars for himself and found that some did want to testify. It's hard to get away to attend a meeting when you're shackled to a wall.

The next day seven Templars appeared, including the Visitor, Hugh de Pairaud. However, each one told the commission that they were "simple knights, without horse, arms or land and had no idea how to defend the order."[37] When Hugh was led in, he said only that the Templars were an honorable order and only the pope should judge them.[38]

This wasn't the defense the commission had in mind.

A few men did straggle in later. One, Peter of Sorayo, had left the Templars some time before and had come to Paris looking for work. No, he didn't know anything bad about the order, but could the commission give him a handout? Another couple of men had been sent by Templars in Hainault in the north, to find out what was going on.[39] They didn't know what they were supposed to defend.

The commission adjourned until November.

THE INTERVIEWS

When the cardinals returned in November, they found an entirely different situation, although the first witness didn't give any indication of that. It was Jacques de Molay.

The Grand Master of the Templars insisted that he thought it unlikely that the pope would want to destroy an order that had done so much for the faith. He added that he couldn't afford counsel, for he had only four denarii to his name. The commission had his previous confession read to him. Upon hearing it, "he made the sign of the cross twice over his face and moved his hands in other signs, seeming to be stupefied by this."[40]

Either Jacques was a great actor or his two years in prison had rattled his brains.

Undaunted, the commission continued to interview Templars. Some repeated their confessions but, day by day, they seemed to gain courage. Ponsard of Gizy, preceptor of the first commandery at Payns, admitted that he had previously confessed to all the charges. Then he told the cardinals that he and the others had only done so through force and fear because they had been tortured, and all information gathered that way was false.

Ponsard then told the commission whom he thought might have had a grudge against the order. One of the four men he listed was Esquin de Floyran.[41]

Other Templars began to come forward. Some recanted their confessions. Others, who had never confessed, told of the torture they had endured, designed to get them to admit wrongdoing. Some had had their hands tied behind their backs and then were pulled up by their wrists until their arms were dislocated.[42] One man told the commission that weights had been hung from his genitals and other parts of his body during the questioning.[43] Another had had grease rubbed over his feet and then held to a fire until the skin was burned away.[44] Many had been starved and confined in spaces too small to rest in comfort. Even the ones who hadn't been tortured knew that it was happening. Several men admitted that the threat of torture had been enough to make them give in.

Eventually nearly seven hundred Templars came forward. Most of them felt that they were too ignorant to present a solid legal defense but finally one of the priests of the order, Peter of Bologna, was convinced to speak for all. Peter had been trained as a lawyer and had been the Templar representative to the papal court in Rome.[45] His rhetoric was a match for that of the king's counselors.

On April 23, 1310, Peter and three other defenders came before the commission and declared that the actions of King Philip had been outside of law and reason. "The proceedings against the Order had been 'rapid, unlooked for, hostile and unjust, altogether without justice, but containing complete injury, most grave violence and intolerable error,' for no attempt had been made to keep to proper procedures." He added that as a result of this sudden and horrible arrest, imprisonment, and torture, the Templars had been deprived of "freedom of mind, which is what every good man ought to have. Once a man is deprived of his free will, he is deprived of all good things, knowledge, memory and understanding."[46]

This passionate speech was followed by a demand for all the documentation heretofore gathered in the case, along with the names of all witnesses called and to be called. The defenders also demanded that witnesses not be allowed to talk with each other and that the testimony be kept secret until it was sent to the pope.[47]

The commission agreed. Suddenly, there seemed to be a hope that the Templars would be declared innocent and at last, after two long years, set free.

PHILIP'S END RUN AROUND
THE PAPAL COMMISSION

It was now May of 1310, almost three years after the arrests. The Templars had not yet been judged as an order. Most were still imprisoned at various places in France. Philip the Fair still did not have legal access to their property. It was beginning to look as though he might have to give it all back. Philip needed to take decisive action.

By an odd coincidence, the new archbishop of Sens, Philip de Marigny, was the brother of King Philip's new favorite counselor, Engerrand de Marigny. Now, at that time, Paris was under the jurisdiction of the archbishop of Sens. It also happened that, while the commission had been set up to try the Templars as an order, the local bishops had the right to try and sentence individual Templars. The archbishop decided to do just that. He announced that the Templars imprisoned in Paris would be tried in the archiepiscopal court.

This sent the defenders into a panic. Peter of Bologna and the others hunted down the commission even though it was a Sunday. Peter begged them to prevent the archbishop from taking them, especially those who had confessed under torture and then recanted. The level of terror is clear even in the notorial records, which repeat the plea verbatim.

"It would be against God and justice and completely overturn this investigation. . . . We call upon the Pope and the Apostolic See both out loud and in writing . . . that all the brothers who have offered or will offer a defense be taken under the protection of the Apostolic See. We beg the pope, again we beg, and we beg with the greatest urgency!"[48]

The image of these brave men standing in the chapel of St. Eligius at the monastery of St. Genevieve, in the Sunday calm, pleading for their lives, is a haunting one. We don't know how it affected the commissioners. Gilles Aycelin, who was also a counselor of the king, excused himself from making a decision. The other commissioners asked the Templars to return at vespers that afternoon, to hear their answer.

This is one of those times when it's hard for me to keep a scholarly objective.

The commissioners William Durant, bishop of Mende; Reginald of La Porte, bishop of Limoges; Matthew of Naples; and John of Mantua, archdeacon of Trent, joined by John of Montlaur, archdeacon of Maguelonne, returned to face Peter and his comrades.

They told the Templars that there was nothing they could do. The law was clear on this and they couldn't poach on the territory of the archbishop of Sens. They were very sorry, but that was that.[49]

Were these men sticklers for the law? Were they cowards, afraid of Philip the Fair? Did they believe that the Templars were guilty and deserved whatever they got? They definitely knew that they were putting all the Templars in grave danger.

Two days later, the archbishop of Sens ordered the burning of fifty-four Templars. They "were burned outside of Paris in a field not far from the convent of the nuns of Saint Anthony."[50] The victims seem to have been picked at random from those who had not yet been reconciled with the Church. Only a few of them had said they would defend the order.[51]

And yet, they all died proclaiming their innocence. "All of them, not one excepted, refused to admit to the crimes of which they were accused and persisted firmly and consistently in general denial, not ceasing to declare that it was without cause and unjust that they were sentenced to death. A great number of people saw this with great astonishment and excessive shock."[52]

The shock rippled back to the Templars still in prison. Now no one was eager to defend the order. The pope either wouldn't or couldn't protect them. The pillar they had trusted to support them had crumbled.

The next witness brought before the commission, Aimery of

Philip the Fair watches as Templars burn. *(The British Library)*

Villiers-le-Duc, was so terrified that he told the commission he would confess anything as long as it would keep him from the flames. Trying to distance himself from the order as much as possible, Aimery appeared with his beard shaved and without his Templar mantle. He was clearly upset. "And when the commissioners saw that the witness was at the edge of a precipice," they told him to go home and not to reveal anything of what he had said.[53]

Things were looking bad for the Templars, but they were about to get worse. The next time that the commissioners asked to see Peter of Bologna, the best trained of the defenders, they were told that he had vanished. When they asked for more information, they were told that he had suddenly returned to his former confession, then broken out of jail and fled.[54]

Right.

There weren't many Templars who had the legal training to argue their case, and his loss was a severe blow.

PETER of Bologna was never seen or heard from again. You can draw your own conclusions.

One scholar has suggested that the increased interest in education shown by the Hospitallers in the fourteenth century might be due to "how much the illiteracy and legal incompetence of the Templars had contributed to their downfall."[55] The effect of the loss of their main advocate seems to support this theory.

The commission continued off and on until June 1311 but the heart had gone out of it. Most of the Templars who came forward did not attempt to defend the order but rather to confess their crimes. They seemed eager to outdo each other in the details of their blasphemous reception into the order. They minutely described the crosses they had spat on or next to. The heads they were supposed to have adored were gold or copper or flesh. They looked like a woman, a monster, or a man with a long gray beard.[56] Everyone seems to have had their own personal idol.[57]

In the end the commissioners closed the proceedings and had all the information sent to Pope Clement at Avignon. They made no recommendation as to the fate of the Templars.

That was now up to Pope Clement and the **Council of Vienne**.

---

1 Sophia Menache, *Clement V* (Cambridge University Press, 1998) p. 17. Catherine's death just before the arrest of the Templars (see below) may have forced Charles to revise his plans for conquest.

2 Jean Favier, *Phillippe le Bel* (Paris: Fayard, 1978) p. 315.

3 Ibid., p. 309.

4 Georges Lizerand, *Le Dossier de L'Affaire des Templiers* (Paris, 1923) p. 16. "Res amara, res flebilies, res quidam cogitatu horribilis, auditu terribilis, detestabilis crimine, execrabilis scelere, abhominabilis opers, detestanda flagicio, res penitus inhumana, immo ab omni humanitate seposita."

5 Lizerand, p. 18, "gerenets sub specie agni lupum et sub religionis habitu notre religioni fidei nequiter insultantes, dominum nostrum Jhesum Christum, novissimis temporibus, pro humani generic redemtione crucifixum."

6 Ibid., "juxta prophanus ordinis sui ritum."

7 Ibid., "professionis sue voto se obligant quod alter alterius illius horribilis et tremendi concubitus vicio."

8 If you believe this, I have some land in Atlantis I'd like to sell you.

9 Malcolm Barber, *The Trial of the Templars* (Cambridge University Press, 1978; new edition forthcoming) p. 47.

10 Continuator of Guillaume de Nangis, *Chroniques capétiennes Tome II 1270–1328* (Paris: Paleo, 2002) p. 92. Guillaume was attached to the court of Philip and his chronicle follows the information given in the public announcements.

11 Barber, p. 48.

12 Lizerand, p. 37, "immo dixit puram veritatem propter salutem anime sue."

13 Quoted in Alan Forey, *The Fall of the Templars in the Crown of Aragon* (Ashgate, Aldershot, 2001) p. 3.

14 Barber, p. 69.

15 Quoted in Menache, p. 207.

16 Barber, p. 80. And darned brave it was of them, too.

17 Norman Cohn, *Europe's Inner Demons*.

18 Jules Michelet, *Le Procès des Templiers* (Paris, 1841–51; rpt. Paris: CNRS, 1987) Vol. I p. 36.

19 There are a number of books that address this. For medieval attitudes: Jeffrey Richards, *Sex, Dissidence, and Damnation: Minority Groups in the Middle Ages* (Routledge University Press, 1991), and Norman Cohn, *Europe's Inner Demons* (St. Albans, 1976). Also anything by Jeffrey Burton Russell.

20 Alan Forey, *The Fall of the Templars in the Crown of Aragon* (Ashgate, Aldershot, 2001) p. 2.

21 Barber, p. 66.

22 Translated in Malcolm Barber and Keith Bate, *The Templars: Selected Sources Translated and Annotated* (Manchester University Press, 2002) p. 256.

23 Barber and Bate, p. 257.

24 Alain Demurger, *Jacques de Molay: Le Crepuscule des Templiers* (Paris: Payot, 2002) p. 294. Demurger leans to this belief. He feels that the reception ceremony existed but was a sort of hazing.

25 This is the premise in, Maichael Baigent, Richard Leigh and Henry Lincoln, *The Holy Blood and the Holy Grail* (London: Jonathan Cape, 1982). I do *not*, under any circumstances, recommend this book.

26 Barber, p. 54.
27 Guillaume de Nangis, p. 94.
28 Ibid.
29 Menache, p. 218.
30 Lizerand, p. 84, "la bougrerie du Templiers." My modern dictionary says it means "idiocy." Maybe it does today but, trust me, that's not what it meant in the fourteenth century. Actually, the word only came into use in the thirteenth century, and was applied to the **Cathars** and so carried with it a sense of heresy as well as homosexual practice.
31 Lizerand, p. 86.
32 Menache, p. 48.
33 Lizerand, p. 87, note 4.
34 Lizerand, p. 96. "Cum instancia devote supplicat populus regni Francie quatinus advertat regia majestas quod quelibet . . . pro domino popa allegate (sunt) super dsicordia punitionis Templariorum inter vos commota, fidem catholice profitbatur se tenere et tenebat."
35 Michelet.
36 Barber, p. 126.
37 Michelet, vol. I, p. 28, "quod simplex miles, sine equis, armis et terra, erat, et non posset nec sciret ipsum ordinem defendere."
38 Ibid., vol. I, p. 29.
39 Ibid., vol I. pp. 32–33.
40 Ibid., vol. I, p. 34, "bis signum cruciscoram facie sua et in aliis signis pretendere, videbatur se esse valde stupefactum de hiis."
41 Ibid., vol. I, p. 36. While most of the report is in Latin and only gives the gist of what each man said, this part, in Middle French, seems to be a direct quote.
42 Ibid.
43 Ibid., Vol. I, p. 218, "fuit questionatus ponderibus apensis in genetalibus suis et in aliis menbris quasi usque ad exeminacionam."
44 Ibid.
45 Barber, p. 244.
46 Quoted and summarized in Barber, pp. 168–69. Where is Peter of Bologna when we need him?
47 Barber, pp. 169–70.
48 Michelet, pp. 264–65.
49 Michelet, p. 265; Barber, p. 177.
50 Continuator of Guillaume de Nangis, vol. II, p. 279.
51 Barber, *Trial,* p. 179
52 Continuator of Guillaume de Nangis., p. 283.
53 Michelet, vol. I, p. 276.
54 Barber, pp. 181–82.
55 Anthony Luttrell, "The Hospitallers of Rhodes and the Mausoleum at Halicarnassus," in *The Meeting of Two Worlds: Cultural Exchange between East and West during the Period of the Crusades* ed. Bladimir P. Goss (Kalamazoo, MI: Medieval Institute, 1986) p. 161.
56 Barber, p. 185.
57 For more on this, please see chapter 40, **Baphomet.**

CHAPTER THIRTY-ONE

The Charges Against
the Templars

When **Jacques de Molay** was first questioned, on October 24, 1307, about the sins of the Templars, the only accusations were about his entry into the order. Did he deny Christ and spit on a crucifix? Was he told that he could have sex with the other brothers?[1] These seem to have been the only things that the accusers of the Templars had come up with at the time.

In the next few months, the list of accusations grew to 127. Many of these, however, are almost identical. For instance, there are five that deal with spitting, trampling, or urinating on a cross. Then there are two more that say they did this "in contempt of Christ and the Orthodox faith," and that the men who received them into the order made them do this.[2] Templars confessed to just about everything suggested to them.

One can imagine a Templar sergeant or knight brought in after several months of imprisonment and torture:

"Good day," the inquisitor begins. *"We're here from the church and the king and we only want the truth for the good of your soul."*

The Templar is distracted by the smell of roast venison, which reminds him that he's starving and also that his fate will be similar to the deer's if he doesn't get the answers right.

"Now, when you joined the Templars, were you told to spit on a cross?"

"Yes, sir, but I cleverly spat next to it and no one noticed."

"Were you ordered to stomp on the cross?"

"I sort of remember something like that."

"Did you stomp on the cross?"

"No, I didn't."

"Did you stomp and urinate on the cross on Good Friday? Was that the ritual for the day Our Lord died for your sins, you heretic scum?"

"No, my lord, it wasn't."

"Ah, then you must have stomped and urinated on another day. What day was it, Holy Thursday? Just when did you desecrate the cross? We know you did. All the other Templars have confessed. Are you saying that you were the only one who didn't do this?"

And so on. Eventually, the Templar is so cowed and confused that he's happy to confess to anything and go back to his quiet cell.

Although this scene is the product of my imagination, I have heard that this technique of interrogation—asking the same question several times in various ways—is still being used. Fortunately, I don't have firsthand knowledge.

Since so many of the charges are almost the same, we can group the 127 charges into more manageable groups:[3]

A Summary of the Charges

1. That the Templars denied Christ in their reception ceremony or soon after. They also spat and trampled on a cross.

2. That they exchanged kisses on various parts of the body, the navel and base of the spine being favorites.

3. That at the reception they were told they could have sex with other Templars. They were made to swear that they would never leave the order. Also, the receptions were held in secret.

4. That they were not allowed to reveal what happened in the reception to anyone.

5. That they did not believe in the Mass or in other sacraments. Their priests did not say the words of consecration over the Host.

6. That they were told that the masters could absolve their sins, implying that they had no need of a priest.

7. That they venerated an idol, as their God and savior. Well, some of them did. That is, most of them in the chapters did.[4] Each province had one, it was said, sometimes with three faces, sometimes one. Sometimes it was a human skull. Anyway, they believed that it could make them rich and also make the flowers bloom and the land be fertile. Each of them wore a cord around their waist that had touched the idol and they even slept in it.

8. That they were only allowed to confess their sins to a priest of the order.

9. That they didn't give charity as they ought and they believed that it was not a sin to make money and that they were authorized to do so by any means possible, legal or illegal.[5]

10. That they met at night and in secret.

11. That everyone, well, almost everyone, in the order knew about these things and did nothing to correct them.

12. That many brothers left the order because of the "filth and errors."[6] (But see number 3.)

13. That the whole matter has caused public gossip and scandal throughout Christendom.

14. That the Grand Master and other officials of the order have confessed.

As the reader will notice, even broken down like this, some of the charges aren't charges at all but statements. Others are qualified so many times that it seems as if the inquisitors were trying to make various individual confessions make sense.

I address the first five charges in the chapter on the **Secret Rite of Initiation**. The sixth charge, that they believed the master could absolve their sins, seems to be true. Apparently, some of the brothers were confused between the absolution they received after confession to a priest and the absolution that the master or commander gave them after confessing in the weekly chapter meeting about breaking the rules of the order.

The question of the mysterious Templar idol is covered in my chapter on **Baphomet**. Since to modern readers it seems to be one of the most fascinating of the charges, I don't think it hurts to repeat that no idol of any sort was ever found in any of the commanderies. In Paris a search revealed a silver reliquary containing the skull bones of one of the eleven thousand virgins martyred with Saint Ursula in Cologne in the fourth century.[7] And, even under torture, most of the Templars only appeared confused by the question about an idol.

Templars did have their own priests but many of them were only hired for a certain term. The number of priests of other orders who testified for and against them from information learned in confessions proves that this accusation was false.

On the accusation that the Templars did not give charity, it's hard to say. Answering that would need more records than we have. However, they seem to have given alms at least three times a week and the **Rule** had strict guidelines for giving to the poor. Anything might be given as alms except military equipment.[8] When the Grand Master visited a commandery, five poor people were to be fed the same food as the brothers ate, in his honor.[9] Also, every day one-tenth of the bread prepared should be given to the almoner to give to the poor.[10]

The Templars did not set up hospices as the **Hospitallers** did, but they did spend a great deal to ransom poor prisoners of the Moslems and they had places to give shelter to pilgrims.[11] Did they give enough? I don't know. Do any of us give enough?

The Templars were on thin ice with the charges about money. There are too many cases in charters where they seem to go to great lengths to get all that they legally could and one or two times when they may have taken money that they weren't entitled to. Please see the section on **Templars and Money** for a more complete look at this issue.

On the accusation that the Templars met at night, and in secret, that's one of those no-win accusations. They sometimes met at night in the time after reciting the predawn prayers called matins. According to the Rule, they were first to check up on their horses and gear and then they could go to bed. But this was also a convenient time for holding chapter meetings. The meetings were held in secret in the sense that what happened in them was not to be discussed with outsiders.

The odd thing about the charge is that most religious orders had closed meetings. The purpose of the chapter was to discuss faults and problems. These weren't things they wanted the public at large to know about. I don't know why no Templars bothered to mention this. It's possible that they didn't know much about the practices of other orders.

The real problem was the secret reception. Most orders had public ceremonies for new members. It was a big day and families looked forward to seeing it. It was stupid for the Templars to welcome new recruits privately. But it does seem to be something that select societies like to do.

The accusation that everyone in the order knew these things were going on is classic distortion. It assumes all the other charges to be true.

I love the charge that brothers had left the order because they were disgusted with the heretical behavior. First of all, the inquisitors already accused the Templars of forbidding members to leave. Of course, men could have left without permission and some did. But the number who left legally for various reasons was far too many for the order to have a policy of silencing those who wanted out.

One of the men who testified against the order in Paris was a priest named Jean de Folliaco. He stated that he had been forced to do all the nasty things at his reception and that he had complained to the king's provost in Paris in 1304. He told the pope that he had a letter proving his complaints were true, but it was missing. Eventually, he admitted that his main objection to remaining in the order was that the life was too hard and he was afraid of being sent overseas where the fighting was.[12]

One interesting case, however, concerns a Spanish brother, Pons of Guisans, who became a Templar when he fell ill on his way to the East. He thought he was dying and assumed he'd get a shorter time in purgatory if he died a Templar. But he didn't die. Instead, he became a full member of the order and had a position of responsibility in Jerusalem. Then he met this woman. He left the order to marry her. After her death, he decided that he wanted to come back. He had to do penance for a year for leaving, but they let him back in.[13] Obviously Pons was not put off by "filth and error."

Finally, the last two charges aren't charges at all. They are simply excuses. The final reason for the dissolution of the Templars at the **Council of Vienne** was that the scandal was so great that no one would take the order seriously again. It may seem odd to people today but a fear of creating scandal was something that medieval organizations and individuals dreaded. They knew the power of a well-placed rumor. Even if one were innocent of all charges, the shame of being accused was enough to ruin a person's life, as the Templars found out to their sorrow.

---

1 Georges Lizerand, *Le Dossier de l'Affaire des Templiers* (Paris, 1923) pp. 33–37.

2 Jules Michelet, *Le Procès des Templiers* Vol. I (Paris, rpt. 1987) pp. 90–91. These charges are all translated in Malcolm Barber, *The Trial of the Templars* (Cambridge, 1978) pp. 248–52S.

3 The following is taken from Helen Nicholson, *The Knights Templar* (Sutton, 2001) p. 206. Her organization is slightly different from mine but it was a handy starting point.

4 Michelet, p. 92. "Item, quod aliqui eorum. Item quod major pars illorum qui errant in capitulis." I'm not making this up.

5 Ibid., p. 94, "dicti ordinis quibuscumque modis possent per fas aut nephas procurare."

6 Ibid., p. 96, "multi fraters de dicto ordine propter feditates et errors ejusdem ordinis exierunt." Translation in Barber, p. 251.

7 Paul Guéron, *Vie des Saints* Vol. XII (Paris: Bollandistes, 1880) pp. 496–97.

8 Laurent Dailliez ed., *Règle et Statuts de l'Ordre du Temple* (Paris, 1972) p. 126. Rule no. 82.

9 Ibid., p. 129. Rule no. 92.
10 Ibid., p. 27. Rule no. 27.
11 Desmond Seward, *Knights of the Cloister: Templars and Hospitallers in Central-Southern Occitania c. 1100–300* (Woodbridge: Boydell, 1999) pp. 111–15.
12 Barber, p. 99.
13 Seward, p. 122. The case is from the Barcelona Rule of the Temple.

CHAPTER THIRTY-TWO

Guillaume de Nogaret

O f all the people involved in the **arrest and trials of the Templars**, Guillaume de Nogaret has been considered the most sinister, the man who was the mastermind behind everything that happened. This servant of the king had cut his teeth on the struggle with Pope Boniface VIII in 1303 and was ready once again to prove himself to his master, **King Philip IV,** by destroying the Templars as well. Many have considered him the evil genius behind the trial of the Templars as well as the campaign against Boniface.

Who was this man? Was he pulling the strings to make King Philip dance to his tune or was it Guillaume who was the puppet, taking the fall for the king?

Guillaume de Nogaret was born in the town of Sant-Félix de Caraman in southwestern France. The date isn't certain, perhaps around 1260. Nogaret is not the name of a place but is a variation on the Occitan word *nogarède*, or "walnut grower."[1]

Unlike many of the officers of the government of Philip the Fair, Guillaume was not nobly born. It was said that his grandfather had been burned as a Patarine heretic.[2] It's not clear if this is true or not. However, it was a charge that was thrown back at him more than once over his life, and it must have affected him strongly. Since it was he who wrote most of the broadsides condemning the Templars as heretics, his background in this is important. Did he actually believe that the

Templars were bad Christians or had he simply trained himself to see heresy everywhere he looked, to prove that his religion was orthodox?

Despite their suspect origins, Guillaume's family had enough money to educate him. He may have studied for a time at Toulouse before going to the town of Montpellier to study law. By 1293 he was a "doctor of law."[3]

Sometime around 1296, Nogaret received a call from Paris. He'd made the big time, legal counsel to the king![4] Over the next few years he successfully handled several negotiations for Philip. In 1299, he was rewarded by being promoted to the nobility. After that, he was entitled to call himself "knight."[5] This was another of the innovations of the king. The ennobling of nonmilitary men led to what was called the "noblesse de robe." These nobles were dependent upon the king who created them for their livelihood rather than having inherited lands to fall back on.

Nogaret seems to have been Philip's main counselor during the king's battle with Pope Boniface. The reasons behind the dispute are rooted in the ongoing struggle between the rulers of Europe and the church for power. On one side, the popes felt that kings should not be allowed to appoint their friends and family to bishoprics and other high church offices. On the other side, the kings wanted the clergy of the realm to be subject to the same laws as everyone else.

Throughout the Middle Ages, clerics were tried in a church court. If they were judged guilty, they might either be sentenced to hard time in a strict monastery or, if the crime warranted it, turned over to the state for execution.[6]

In Philip's confrontation with the pope, Nogaret was apparently the guiding hand and also the one who physically led the attack on the pope in his retreat at Anagni in 1303.

Two precedents were set in this episode. The first was that Philip established, in his own mind at least, that if the pope was corrupt, then it was up to secular powers to overthrow him. No one could be above God's law.[7] The second was the use of the media to convict Boniface in public opinion even before he was arrested by Philip's men.

In this, Nogaret was a master. According to Nogaret's defense of the king's actions, Boniface was a heretic, idolater, murderer, and sodomite. He also practiced usury, bribed his way into his position, and made trouble wherever he went.[8] These charges were never proved but they convinced many. They also gave Guillaume de Nogaret good material for his diatribe against the Templars four years later.

After the death of the pope, Nogaret wrote to the College of Cardinals justifying his actions. "If some antichrist were to invade the Holy See, we must oppose him; there is no insult to the Church in such opposition. . . . If, in the cause of right, violence is committed, we are not responsible."[9]

Whether Nogaret was responsible for the violence at Anagni or not, he was seen as being the ringleader. The next pope, Benedict XI, had witnessed the attack on Boniface. When, as part of a deal, he issued absolution for the deed to King Philip and other instigators, Nogaret was not among them. Actually, he was at the top of the naughty list, the head of the "sons of perdition, of the first-born of Satan."[10] Benedict was about to convene a tribunal to excommunicate Nogaret and twelve others when he suddenly died on July 7, 1304.

It was popularly believed that Nogaret had arranged to have him poisoned. There was no proof of this, either, but that didn't stop the rumors.

He had also earned the enmity of a much better writer than he. In the *Divine Comedy* Dante compared Nogaret to Pontius Pilate.[11]

Nogaret not only instigated the arrest of the Templars, he also did his best to guide the interrogations. In 1309, when **Jacques de Molay** was being questioned for the third time, the inquisitors were interrupted by Nogaret, "who arrived unexpectedly." He confronted the master and told him that the chronicles of the abbey of St. Denis said that at the time of **Saladin**, the Templars had paid homage to the sultan and that at that time, Saladin had said publicly that the Templars had done this because they "worked at the vice of sodomy and because of this they had lost all their faith and their law."[12]

The twentieth-century editor of the deposition adds in a footnote, "This accusation . . . is not found in the text of the chronicles of St.

Denis that we have."[13] One wonders how many of the inquisitors or the people of France who heard Nogaret's accusation ever bothered to check the library of St. Denis to find out if it was true.

At the **Council of Vienne**, Nogaret was again eager to prove that all he and Philip had done was for the good of Christendom. To finance a projected crusade to regain the Holy Land, he suggested that they use "not only all the wealth of the Templars but that of the whole ecclesiastical Order: the clergy would, therefore, be left with only those funds necessary for its daily subsistence."[14]

That must have gone over well with the cardinals and bishops.

After the Templars had been arrested, Nogaret should have felt he'd accomplished all his goals. However, one problem remained. He was still excommunicated. Nogaret was terrified that he would die still under sentence from the pope.

One reason that Nogaret fought so hard to have his excommunication lifted was to ensure that his family would be taken care of. He had a wife, Beatrix, and three children, Raymond, Guillaume, and Guillemette.[15] Beatrix seems to have come from a noble family of Languedoc so the new man, born into a family of walnut growers, had come far. But it would be for nothing if his property was confiscated at his death.

Nogaret went to the king's brother, Charles de Valois, to put pressure on Clement V. He even wrote a bull for the pope to sign that explained how he had acted only for the good of the church.[16] It was rumored that money changed hands. Finally in April 1311, Clement signed the decree stating that all those involved in the attack on Boniface VIII were reconciled with the church. A penance was assigned to Guillaume. He had to go on a pilgrimage to Compostela in Spain and then take a party of soldiers to fight in the Holy Land, an ironic twist.[17]

He never did either.

Guilluame de Nogaret died in November 1314. He was probably buried, as he had requested, at the monastery of the Dominicans near Nimes.

Outside of France, where he did his best to see that the history books would justify his actions, Nogaret was totally reviled. Dante

had no doubt who was pulling the strings of King Philip. I don't believe that Nogaret's actions can be justified, but they deserve to be
looked at objectively in the light of the times. There are those who
might say that, by arresting a pope and by destroying the Templars,
neither of whom were all that innocent, Nogaret also struck a blow at
the unfair dominance of the papacy and those it protected.

However, I'm not ready to be that objective.

---

1 Ernest Renan, *Guillaume de Nogaret: Un Minister du Roi Philippe le Bel* (Quebec: Numerus,
2006; rpt. of 1872 ed.) p. 3.

2 Ibid. The Patarines were only one of the many heresies in Europe at the time. They were not
connected with the **Cathars**.

3 Ibid., p. 4.

4 Ibid., p. 5.

5 Ibid., p. 6.

6 For a good overview of this issue, see Ute-Renate Blumenthal, *The Investiture Controversy*
(University of Pennsylvania Press, Philadelphia, 1988.)

7 Except Philip, of course.

8 Renan, p. 49.

9 Quoted in Sophia Menache, *Clement V* (Cambridge University Press, 1998) p. 15.

10 Quoted in Renan, p. 44.

11 Dante, *Purgatorio*, Canto XX, ll. 85–93.

12 Georges Lizerand, *Le Dossier de l'Affaire des Templiers* (Paris, 1923) p. 168. "Verum, cum per
nobilem virum Guillelmum de Nogareto, cacellarium regium, qui supervenerat, . . . fuisset
dictumeidem magistro quod in cronicis que erant apud Sanctum Dionisium, continebantur
quod tempore Saladini, sodani Babilonie, magister ordnis Temple qui tunc erat et alii majores
ipsius ordinis fecerant homagium ipsi Saladino et quod idem Saladinus, auditaadversitate
magna quam dicti Templarii tunc passi fuerant, dixerat in publico predictos Templarios fuisse
dictam adversitatem perpessos, qui vicio sodomitico labarabant et quia fidem suam et legen
prevaricati fuerant."

13 Lizerand, p. 169.

14 Menache, p. 114.

15 Renan, pp. 88–89. I worry about someone who feels the need to name both a son and a daughter
after himself.

16 Ibid., pp. 113–15.

17 Ibid., p. 116.

CHAPTER THIRTY-THREE

The Council of Vienne and the End of the Order

Pope **Clement V** was determined to keep some sort of control over the problem of the Templars, despite the determination of King **Philip the Fair** to dictate their fate. So far the trials had been of individual Templars, not the order as a whole. Legally, the Templars could only be condemned or declared innocent of all charges by the pope.

Clement knew that if he made the decision alone, he would bring down the wrath of one side or the other. He had to make it clear that a pronouncement on the Templars would come from the leaders of the Church acting together. Therefore, he called for a council to meet in the town of Vienne, just south of Lyon. Vienne was not yet part of France but Lyon had recently been taken over by King Philip. Clement knew that anything that he and the council did would be in the shadow of Philip and his army, but at least not under the king's jurisdiction.

The first summons to the council was written on August 12, 1308. In it Clement ordered all the archbishops, bishops, and abbots of Christendom to meet in October 1310. He didn't mention the Templars by name in the summons. Instead he asked the attendees to prepare reports listing areas in which the Church needed reforming.[1]

He also sent invitations to most of the major rulers of Europe. It was understood that the main issues would be the suppression of the Templars, the need to regain the Holy Land, and the reform of the Church as a whole.

It is a tribute to Clement's skill at procrastinating that the council wouldn't actually begin until October 1311. This gave many of those invited (or commanded) to attend time to come up with excuses.

THIS was not a popular council. Over a third of the Church officials didn't show up, even though they had been ordered, not invited, to appear. It's possible that they were worried that they would be asked to provide more money for the support of the papal curia.[2] None of the rulers came, except Philip IV (with his army) and he was only there for the meetings concerning the Templars.[3]

So, instead of creating a show of unity and willingness to support any papal decision, Clement found himself facing a group of largely disgruntled prelates. These men were mostly noblemen, with regional and family connections that meant more to them than punishing the sins of the Templars. Few of them were willing to get on the wrong side of King Philip.

And many of them were not at all sure that the Templars were guilty.

Added to that, the town was crowded, prices had been jacked up to meet demand, and the weather was terrible. On November 9, Raymond Despont, bishop of Valencia, wrote to King James II of Aragon, "It is very tedious here, since the land is cold beyond measure and . . . it is not suited to my age. The place is small with a multitude of people, and therefore crowded. As a result many remain inconvenienced, but it is necessary to endure it with patience."[4]

There were also complaints that the council had been packed with French prelates who were too afraid to vote against the wishes of King Philip.

It seems that Clement had hoped to get a quick vote on the condemnation of the Templars, assign their property to another order, and get on with his dream of a new crusade. He also wanted to keep King Philip from pushing for a denunciation of Pope Boniface VIII. It wasn't a good idea to let kings think they could dispose of popes, even ones that were dead.

Things didn't work out at all according to plan. First of all, to give an appearance of fairness, Clement had invited Templars to come to Vienne and defend the order personally. Remembering the burnings of 1310, Clement apparently assumed that they wouldn't dare show up.

However, on December 4, 1311, seven men did. The next day, two more joined them. They told the council that they were prepared to give a defense and that there were over a thousand others in the area who would also speak on behalf of the Templars.[5]

Clement had them arrested.

He then held a secret meeting of a small group of prelates. Clement's biographer, Ptolomy de Lucca, later reported what happened. "The bishops and the cardinals were called together by the pope to deliberate on the subject of the Templars. . . . The pope interrogated them one at a time. They told him that they were agreed that the Templars should be allowed to present their defense. All the Italian bishops, with one exception, came round to this opinion, along with all the bishops from Spain, Germany, Dacia, England, Scotland, Ireland and France, except the three archbishops of Reims, Sens and Rouen."[6]

The archbishop of Sens was the one who had ordered the conflagration of Templars in 1310 and was also, you may remember, Philip de Marigny, the brother of King Philip's trusted counselor Enguerrand de Marigny. The archbishop of Rheims, Robert de Courtenay, was related to the French royal family through marriage.[7] And Gilles Aycelin, archbishop of Rouen, was also the chancellor of France and nephew of ones of Philip's former advisers, Pierre Flote.[8]

Everyone at the council was very much aware of this.

That's not to say that many people were willing to defend the Templars themselves. There was still the problem that **Jacques de**

Molay and the other officials of the order had confessed, retracted their confessions, and then confessed again. How could they declare someone innocent when they had admitted they were guilty?

But one man, at least, Jacques de Thérines, was willing to defend them at the council. In 1311 he was the abbot of a Cistercian monastery in what is now Belgium. In 1307 he had been one of the masters of the University of Paris who told King Philip that he didn't have a case against the Templars. Then, he had been one voice in a group of fourteen scholars.[9] Now, he stood alone.

In his address to the council, Abbot Jacques stated many of the arguments that have been echoed for the past seven hundred years. Was it logical that the charges against the Templars were true? These were men from widely different backgrounds, who had entered the order at different ages. It seemed incredible to Jacques that "commoners and nobles, men of different speech and lands, raised not as bastards but in stable, god-fearing households, men who had fervently expressed the desire to defend the holy places would all have the appetite to fall to precisely the same temptations."[10]

Jacques concluded, as many have since, that the confessions of the Templars were patently untrue, torn from the men by torture and through terror. The fact that some had been brave enough to recant and face the stake spoke even more for their innocence. The fact that **trials outside of France** had turned up no evidence of guilt was also suspicious. And, in any case, the matter wasn't for the king of France to decide, but the pope.[11]

The ball was back in Clement's court and he wasn't pleased about it. It seemed a good time to call a winter recess.

Clement spent the next three months trying to find a way out before the council convened again in March.

It's hard to say what he really thought of the guilt of the Templars. I believe that if he had been certain of it, he would have condemned the order immediately. As it was, he must have known that they would have to be sacrificed in one way or another. If he saved the Templars, he would still be faced with Philip's determination to have Pope Boniface excommunicated posthumously, which would include digging up his body and burning it for heresy.[12] If the Templars were condemned, then it would only encourage the clerics who were opposed to the exempt orders. Next, it might be the Cistercians or the Franciscans and Dominicans, not to mention the **Hospitallers,** who were attacked. The suppression of a religious order was not new. In 1274, two Provençal orders, the Pied Friars and the Friars of the Sack, had been dissolved. The Templars had benefited from this when they received property that had belonged to these orders.[13]

There seemed no way for Clement to win. No wonder the poor pope's stomach always hurt.

Finally, Clement made up his mind to act. This may have been encouraged by the arrival, on March 20, 1312, of Philip the Fair, accompanied by his three sons, his brothers, and his army. Two weeks earlier, Philip had sent Clement a letter insisting that the Templars be suppressed at once. He says that "burning *with zeal for the orthodox faith* and that such a great injury to Christ not go unpunished, we humbly and devotedly beg Your Holiness that the aforesaid order be suppressed."[14]

Therefore, "On the day of the moon after the Quasimodo [March 22], the second session of the general council was held in the great cathedral."[15] The returning leaders of the Church gathered and prepared to hear Clement's opening sermon.

With the king on one side and his eldest son, the future Louis X, on the other, Clement read out the bull suppressing the order of the Templars.

He first made it clear that he found the things that **Jacques de Molay** and the other Templars had confessed to absolutely disgusting: "it was against the lord Jesus Christ himself that they fell into the sin of impious apostasy, the abominable vice idolatry, the deadly crime of the Sodomites, and various heresies."[16] But, fortunately, "Then came the intervention of our dear son in Christ, Philip, the illustrious king of France. . . . He was not moved by greed. . . . He was on fire with *zeal for the orthodox faith.*"[17]

At this point, can't you just see the pope glancing nervously toward the king?

After outlining the **arrest and trials of the Templars,** and how the information gathered from all the trials in Europe had been studied by a committee of cardinals and bishops, he admitted that 80 percent of the assembly felt that the Templars should be allowed a defense. However, the name of the order had been so soiled that it could never function with any credibility again.[18] "Therefore, with a sad heart . . . we suppress, with the approval of the sacred council, the Order of the Templars, and its rule, habit and name, by an inviolable and perpetual decree, and we entirely forbid anyone from now on to enter the Order, or receive or wear its habit or to presume to behave as a Templar."[19]

It's not certain that the members of the council had agreed to the suppression but it didn't matter since the pope had made the decision and could enforce it without their approval.

He also cautioned that the property that had belonged to the Templars was to be reserved to the papacy, to be used for the retaking of the Holy Land, and no one was to touch it. I imagine that he didn't look at the king while reading this.

Clement also ordered that Templar brothers who had not confessed or who had been judged innocent were to be pensioned off. Those who had confessed and been absolved were to be assigned to various monasteries to perform their penance.

On May 2, the pope announced that all the Templar property was to be given to the Hospitallers, with the exception of that owned by the Templars in Aragon, Castile, Portugal, and Majorca.[20]

This was the end of the Order of the Templars, but their story was far from over. Several thousand men had to be accounted for and goods consisting of "houses, churches, chapels, oratories, cities, castles, towns, lands, granges, places, possessions, jurisdictions, revenues, rights, all the other property, whether immovable, movable or self-moving, and all the members together with their rights and belongings, both beyond and on this side of the sea, in each and every part of the world . . ."[21]

How all that was sorted out is another chapter.

While the affair of the Templars overshadows the whole Council of Vienne, it wasn't the only subject of interest to the Church. Clement's death in 1314 prevented the immediate publication of the decrees of the council but his successor, John XXII, who attended, had them sent out. They included clarifications of articles of faith, such as baptism, and the issue of a heretical sect that had started in the Low Countries, known as the Free Spirits.[22] They set down rules for the mendicant orders, the Franciscans and Dominicans, who wandered about far too much for some people's taste. The universities of Paris, Oxford, Bologna, and Salamanca were told to start teaching Hebrew, Arabic, and Chaldeic "that they might be able to instruct the infidel."[23]

The council finally closed, on May 6, 1313. The last few days were taken up with administrative business. The prelates may have thought they were finally getting away, but they discovered that Philip had one last surprise for them. He agreed to go on crusade in 1319, and asked for a portion of the Church tithes be put aside to pay for his expedition.[24]

Wearily, the council agreed.

Neither Philip nor his sons ever went on crusade.

1 Charles-Juseph Hefele and Dom H. Leclercq, *Histoires des Conciles d'aprés les documents originaux* Vol. VI second part (Paris, 1915) p. 648.

2 Sophia Menache, *Clement V* (Cambridge University Press, 1998) p. 283.

3 Malcolm Barber, *The Trial of the Templars* (Cambridge University Press, 2006; 2nd ed.) p. 259.

4 Heinrich Finke, *Papstum und Untergang des Templerordens* (Münstyer, 1907) Vol. 2, pp. 251–52, quoted in Barber, pp. 259–60.

5 Barber, p. 262.

6 Quoted in Hefele and Leclercq, p. 651.

7 He was the brother of the wife of the king's brother.

8 Jean Favier, *Philippe le Bel* (Paris: Fayard, 1978) pp. 27–29.

9 William Chester Jordan, *Unceasing Strife, Unending Fear: Jacques de Thérines and the Freedom of the Church in the Age of the Last Capetians* (Princeton: Princeton University Press, 2005) p. 31.

10 Ibid., p. 53.

11 Ibid.

12 Hefele and Leclercq, p. 661. Philip's ambassadors really suggested this.

13 Dominic Sellwood, *Knights of the Cloister: Templars and Hospitallers in Central-Southern Occitania c. 1100–1300* (Woodbridge: Boydell, 1999) p. 98. And no, I did not make up those names, but I can't imagine many people would want to admit to being a "pied friar."

14 Georges Lizerand, *Le Dossier de L'Affaire de Templiers* (Paris, 1923) p. 196. "Quare, zelo fidei orthodoxe succensi et ne tanta injuria Christo facta remaneat impunita, vestre sanctitati

affectuose, devote et humiliter supplicamus quatinus tollatis ordinem supradictum." (italics mine)

15 Continuator of Guillaume de Nangis, ed. and tr. M. Guizot (Paris, 1825) p. 289.

16 Malcolm Barber and Keith Bate, eds. *The Templars: Selected Sources Translated and Annotated* (Manchester University Press, 2002) p. 311. From *Decrees of the Ecumenical Councils* ed. N. P. Tanner, vol. 1 (London: Sheed and Ward, 1990) pp. 336–43.

17 Ibid. (italics mine)

18 Ibid., p. 316.

19 Ibid., p. 318.

20 Ibid., p. 318–22. The bull is named *Ad providam*.

21 Ibid., pp. 320–21.

22 See chapter 37, **Marguerite Porete**.

23 Hefele and Leclercq, p. 689, "qui infideles ipsos sciant et valent sacris institutis instruere." Okay, mine is a loose translation.

24 Menache, pp. 112–16.

CHAPTER THIRTY-FOUR

Time Line of the Trials

This is adapted from Malcolm Barber, *The Trial of the Templars*.

1292 Jacques de Molay becomes Grand Master of the Templars

1305 November 14, Bernard de Got becomes Pope Clement V

1306 June, King Philip the Fair forced to restore the old value of coinage

July, Jews expelled from France and their property confiscated

Autumn, Jacques de Molay arrives in the West from Cyprus

1307 September 14, Philip sends secret orders for the arrest of the Templars

September 23, Clement writes Philip saying that he is opening an inquiry into the charges against the Templars

October 13, all Templars in France arrested and imprisoned

October 19, interrogations begin in Paris

October 24, Jacques de Molay confesses to all charges

October 25, Jacques de Molay repeats his confession for the masters of the University of Paris

October 27, Pope Clement writes to King Philip protesting the arrests

November 9, Hugh de Pairaud, Templar Visitor for France, confesses to all charges

November 22, Pope Clement issues a bull calling for the arrest of Templars in all lands

December 24, Jacques de Molay is taken before the pope's representatives and there revokes his confession

1308   February, Pope Clement suspends the Inquisition in France

Later in February, Philip asks the masters of Paris to judge his role in the arrests

March 25, in reply to his questions, the masters of theology at the University of Paris state that King Philip did not have the right to arrest the Templars

May 4–29, Philip calls the Estates-General to Tours to justify his actions, which they do; Pope Clement leaves France and settles in the papal town of Avignon

1309   Local inquiries begin, overseen by the bishops

August 8, in Paris, the papal commission opens inquiry on the order (as opposed to individual Templars)

November 22, the first hearings of the papal commissions begin

November 26, Jacques de Molay appears before the commission

November 28, Jacques de Molay again appears before the commission; the commission goes on Christmas break

1310   February 3, papal commissio n again in session

March 2, Jacques de Molay appears once again; he insists that only the pope can judge him

March 14, 127 accusations read to Templars who wish to defend the order

March 28, nearly six hunderd Templars meet in Paris to defend the order

April 7, Peter of Bologna and Reginald of Provins, as spokesmen, give the defense of the order

May 12, the archbishop of Sens turns over fifty-four Templars to be burned at the stake for retracting their confessions; the defenders scatter

May 28, Peter of Bologna disappears

May 30, the papal commission decides to take an early summer holiday

November 3, papal commission reconvenes

1311   May 26, papal commission hears the final deposition

June 5, papal commission adjourns for the last time

October 11, **Council of Vienne** opens

Late October, seven Templars ask to be allowed to defend the order

1312   March 20, Philip the Fair and his army arrive in Vienne

March 22, Clement V reads out the bull *Vox in excelso*, which dissolves the order; the bull *Ad providam* transfers all of its property to the Hospitallers

1314   March 18, Jacques de Molay and Geoffrey of Charney assert their innocence once again and are immediately sent to burn at the stake in Paris

April 15, Guillaume de Nogaret dies

April 20, Pope Clement V dies

November 29, King Philip IV dies

CHAPTER THIRTY-FIVE

The Trials Outside
of France

While King Philip and his associates were doing their utmost to see that the Templars and the order as a whole were tried and convicted as soon as possible, the rulers of other lands were not so eager to prosecute, or even to arrest the members of the order. The Templars were known for being proud and greedy, but this was a stereotype handy for satire but not used on a daily basis. Most people had good relations with the Templars who lived among them. It was only the order by **Pope Clement V** that convinced them to take any sort of action, with results that varied according to place.

ARRESTS AND TRIALS IN SPAIN

In the early fourteenth century the Iberian Peninsula was made up of several kingdoms: Castile, Leon, Navarre, Portugal, and Aragon, which included Catalonia and Valencia. The southern part of Iberia was Andalusia, still in Moslem hands.

The experience of the Templars in Aragon is the one for which we have the best information. The king, James II (1292–1327), loved to keep records and copies of messages and many of them still exist.[1]

At first there were only rumors about the happenings in France concerning the Templars. Then, late in October 1313, the Spanish Templars learned of the arrest of several of their brethren in the kingdom of Navarre, then ruled by Philip the Fair's son Louis. Three of the Aragonese Templars set out to find out what was going on. As soon as they arrived in Navarre, they were arrested, too.

The Templar master of Aragon, Jimeno de Lenda, immediately wrote to King James. James sent an envoy to Navarre to have the Templars released. The envoy also tried to get information on just exactly what was going on with the Templars in France.

He reported back to King James, telling him of the accusations against the Templars. By the middle of November, James had received a letter from King Philip telling him in strong language that the Templars were horrible heretics and homosexuals and that they must be arrested at once.

James answered him politely, but did nothing. He sent word to the pope that "We can scarcely envisage that they do anything in secret or perpetuate any hidden deed attacking Christ, for whose faith they fight."[2]

But again, it was the news of the confessions of Jacques de Molay and the others that convinced James that he ought to put the Templars under guard. That and the fact that the Templars in his lands had been busy fortifying their castles. They weren't going to be caught unawares.

Since the Templars in Iberia had been fighting against the Moslems in their own land for two hundred years, they had a different status than in other Western countries. Unlike the Templars in the Latin kingdoms, they hadn't lost territory, but helped to regain it. The castles they owned had once been on the borders of Christian lands. Now they were far from the frontier. People living around them knew what the Templars had done and could do.

Another difference was that, unlike the French Templars, many of the knights from Aragon came from the upper nobility. Guillermo de Rocaberti, archbishop of Tarragona, was the brother of a Templar.[3]

These men were less easily intimidated and their families were close enough by to lodge protests if they were badly treated.

In December 1307, James finally gave in to papal pressure and ordered that the Templars be taken into custody. However, he was not as forceful about it as King Philip. There was no sudden mass arrest. Instead, the Aragonese messengers went from one Templar house to another, surprised to find that very few of them were at home. Some had simply fled; others had made their way to one of the Templar castles to wait out the storm. The Templar master of Aragon was one of those who had refused to run. He was taken and imprisoned.

From their strongholds, the Templars sent letters to the king, not of defiance, but pleading with him to be allowed to prove their innocence and return to their commanderies.

James refused to do this. He had received the order from Pope Clement and felt compelled to obey it. He ordered the knights to surrender. The Templars had heard about the torture and starvation of the men in France and decided not to trust in the goodwill and justice of princes. James had to besiege their castles. It was a year and a half before the last one fell.

Once captured, the Templars were placed, for the most part, back in their commanderies, under guard. They were questioned by papal commissions along with the local inquisitor of the diocese.[4] The first interrogations didn't even start until November 7, 1309, two years after the French arrests. In the meantime, the Templars in Aragon had been decently fed, clothed, and housed. They weren't tortured.

During the questioning, although some of the men were unsure about some of the minor offenses, such as thinking that the commander of the house could absolve their sins, not one confessed to spitting or defiling a cross or any of the other more sensational charges.

By 1311, the **Council of Vienne** was scheduled and Clement hadn't received any good confessions from Iberia. He sent a letter to the bishops in charge of the interrogations authorizing them to use torture to get the truth. Eight Templars were tortured, but still none would confess.[5] Finally, on November, 4, 1312, after the order had been dissolved

The Templar fortress of Monzón. *(Photo by Joan Fuguet Sans)*

by the pope, a council in Aragon declared all the Templars in the kingdom innocent.[6]

Since there was no longer an order, something had to be done with their property and also with the men themselves. For King James, his Templar headaches were only beginning. The king spent many years dealing with the needs and demands of the ex-Templars.

ARRESTS AND TRIALS IN ENGLAND

The number of Templars in England in 1307 has been reckoned at a total of 144. Of these, 20 at most were knights, 16 priests, and around 108 sergeants.[7] Their extensive properties in the country were maintained for the most part by servants and tenants.[8]

When **Philip the Fair** arrested the Templars in France, he wrote to Edward II of England, who was engaged to Philip's daughter, Isabella, telling him to arrest the British Templars at once. Edward, despite only having been king for four months, was not inclined to believe his prospective father-in-law. He not only wrote back that he doubted the truth of the charges, but also sent messages to the kings of Portugal, Castile, Aragon, and Naples, supporting the order. Then he wrote to Pope **Clement V**, saying that the Templars in England had been "constant in the purity of their faith."[9]

Edward was inclined to think that the charges were totally false and the product of envy. He knew Philip.

However, the confession of Jacques de Molay and other Templars in France, along with the papal order for arrests everywhere, issued on November 22, 1307, seems to have convinced Edward that he should look into the matter further.[10]

He ordered that the Templars in England be arrested on January 10, 1308. This was done in a rather casual manner. Many of the Templars were put under house arrest in their own commanderies. The master in England, William de la More, was imprisoned at Canterbury but was given a daily allowance and the use of a "bed, robes and various personal possessions."[11] Torture was not used in England; it was illegal.

The Templars waited in relative comfort, supported by the income from their property, until the inquisitors arrived to interrogate them in October 1309.

The inquisitors might have saved themselves the trip. The Templars all gave totally orthodox accounts of their entry into the order. This included the preceptor of Auvergne, Imbart Blanc, who had either been visiting in England at the time of the trials or had escaped there. There are many speculations about why he happened to be in England but no hard facts.

Imbart was questioned on October 29. He had been a member of the order for thirty-six or thirty-seven years and had been received into it by William of Beaujeu, the master who had died defending Acre. He denied all the charges, stating only that he had been kissed on the mouth [as was customary] and that each and every one of the articles were evil lies and had never happened.[12]

One of the Templars, Thomas of Ludham, had entered the order only eleven days before being arrested, three months after the arrests in France.[13] The implication is that the British Templars assumed that the problem was only in the French houses and that they should carry on as usual.

By June of 1310, the inquisitors were completely frustrated by the lack of confessions. Since torture was forbidden under English law, they asked the archbishop of Canterbury if they could take the Templars to Ponthieu, which was one of the king's French holdings. There "torture could be more fully and freely applied."[14] To Edward's credit, he did not allow the English Templars to be taken abroad for torture.

Edward did buckle a bit under pressure from the pope and some of his bishops. He had the Templars put under the authority of the inquisitors in prisons attached to the city gates of London. He said they could do what they wanted to the prisoners, but he was only allowing it out of reverence for the Apostolic See.[15]

It seems that, in London at least, some torture was finally applied but to no avail. The British Templars would not confess. The inquisitors added one more question to the list put to the French Templars. Why were Templars buried in secrecy?

Why they asked this is unknown. They may have been grasping at straws. The answer was that they weren't buried in secrecy, and further investigation proved that this was so. Templar funerals were well attended.

This was becoming extremely embarrassing for the inquisitors.

In desperation, they decided to get evidence from witnesses from outside the order. By now it was 1311. The **Council of Vienne** was about to start and they worried they would be the only inquisitors to show up without some juicy tales of Templar sin.

The outside witnesses were much more fun.

One man, a serving brother from Ireland named Henry, said that he had heard tell that "Hugh the Master of Castle Pilgrim received many men with the denial of Christ as part of the ceremony."[16] He also knew of a Templar on Cyprus who owned a gold head, or maybe it was bronze, that answered any question put to it.

But he didn't think the Templar worshipped it, just used it for general information.[17]

Master John of Warrington, in York, announced that a Templar, William de la Fenne, had given (John's) wife a book that said that Christ was not God and had not been crucified. De La Fenne responded that he had given Master John's wife a book but there was nothing heretical in it, and, by the way, why had he waited six years to mention it?[18]

Several people said that they had heard about secret meetings held at night and, while they didn't know what went on there, it stood to reason that it was something bad. One witness, described as a "loose woman," told of "disgusting abominations concerning a black cat and a stone."[19]

While not at all reliable, the testimony of witnesses, or those who knew someone who was a witness, is much livelier, if less credible.

Finally, a Franciscan witness said that "he had been told by a woman, who had been told by a man, who had been told by someone else, that a servant of the latter's acquaintance had been put to death when caught watching the Templars worship an idol."[20]

At this point even the most die-hard inquisitor would have to have thrown down his quill and quit.

They did manage to get three Templars, or possibly former Templars, to confess to the charges. All three had only recently been arrested and had been hiding out since 1307. It was now the summer of 1311. They seem to have been tortured to confess, but it's not certain.

After these three confessed, they all publicly asked forgiveness. They were given a penance and absolved.[21]

Eventually the rest of the Templars, still in prison, although they hadn't been convicted of anything, decided they might as well confess, too. The ones who were strong enough stood on the steps of St. Paul's Cathedral and announced that they were no longer heretics but orthodox Christians. They were given penances, forgiven, and sent off to various monasteries around the country with a pension of four pence a day from Templar revenues.

Only the Templar master in England, William de la More, and

the French preceptor, Imbart Blanc, refused to ask forgiveness. De la More insisted to the end that "he would not ask for absolution for something he hadn't done."[22]

Both men died in prison.

ARRESTS AND TRIALS IN GERMANY

There were not many Templars in Germany. The **Hospitallers** and the Teutonic Knights were more popular, especially the latter, being the home team, as it were. In all of central Europe, the Templars only had fifty houses at the time of the dissolution.[23] This includes all the various German states and Poland. They did own property throughout the area that was administered for them and the rents collected, but there were few places where Templars actually lived, even in small groups.

After the failure of the crusades of **Saint Louis**, the Templars had established a few new commanderies in Moravia (one named Tempelstein). Toward the end of the thirteenth century, they began to be in control of small territories, although nothing on the scale of the Teutonic Knights, who governed whole countries.[24]

There are no records of the trials in Germany. It's known that in some areas, the Templars were arrested. But this was more complicated than in England or France. For instance, the archbishop of Magdeburg imprisoned a number of Templars, including Frederick of Alvensleben, who was preceptor of Germany. This should have been quite a coup. However, the bishop of Halberstadt took exception to this. The Templars had been poached from his territory. So the bishop excommunicated the archbishop. I'm fairly sure it's against the rules to excommunicate one's superior but the bishop of Halberstadt tried it anyway. Pope Clement had to step in, revoke the excommunication, and remind them that it was the Templars who were on trial.[25]

In Trier on the western edge of Germany, the archbishop tried three Templars. He also listened to some witnesses. The Templars in Trier were acquitted.[26]

Two brothers, Hugh and Frederick of Salm, were commanders of houses in Grumbach and the Rhineland. They were much more forceful in the defense of the order. Hugh burst into the council meeting in Mainz on May 13, 1310. He told the archbishop and the court that he had heard that the council was trying to destroy the order. This was completely "harsh and intolerable." Hugh announced that he wanted to be heard by "a future pope," not Clement V.[27] Smart man.

Hugh also added something that may have been one of the earliest of the legends that grew up after the trials. He said that "those who had constantly denied these enormities had been delivered up to the fire, but that God had shown their innocence by a miracle, for the red cross and white mantle they wore would not burn."[28]

The archbishop saw the logic in Hugh's protest and said he would see what the pope said about it. Hugh and the twenty armed Templars he had brought with him were satisfied with his promise and left.[29]

Frederick of Salm told his inquisitors that he knew Jacques de Molay well and did not believe the charges. He offered to undergo the ordeal of red-hot iron, in which the suspect must hold onto a bar of iron brought straight from the forge. If the burns heal quickly, he is innocent. Frederick's offer was turned down and the trial went on in the usual way, without torture. After hearing the evidence, the archbishop declared the Templars innocent.[30]

In other areas the pope's orders were simply ignored. Otto, the Templar commander of Brunswick, had no intention of stepping down. He eventually became commander of the Hospitaller house at Süpplingenburg, with a yearly pension of one hundred marks. Of course, he was the brother of the duke.[31] But it appears that less important Templars in the German states fared almost as well. Few of them were ever imprisoned and none of them were killed.

ARRESTS AND TRIALS IN CYPRUS

Cyprus was now the seat of the Kingdom of Jerusalem in exile. Both the Templars and the **Hospitallers** were based there. The king of

Cyprus, Amaury of Lusignan, had been supported by the Templars in his takeover of the government from his brother, Henry. At the Templar headquarters on the island of Cyprus, seventy Templars were interrogated.[32] None of them confessed to any of the charges. Outside witnesses were also questioned. Most of them actually defended the Templars.[33]

Unlike the other Templar centers outside of Spain, the knights on Cyprus were the fighting force. The records of their trial finally give us an idea of the makeup of the Templar forces in the East. For the first time, there is a real sense that this was an international order. Brother Nicholas was English and had entered the order at Lidley in Shropshire in 1300.[34] Brother John was also English but had become a Templar in Italy and, although a sergeant, had become the commander of a house.[35] Brother Francis came from Slavonia and had been received into the order by Jacques de Molay himself.[36] Brother Bertrand came from Brindisi and Brother Pierre from Provence.[37]

There were even Templars from Acre: Brother Guy, who had been received in Acre, and Brother Hubald, who came from Acre but had joined in 1299 on Cyprus.[38]

These were the younger, fitter men who had been sent east as soon as possible to be ready to mount an expedition to regain the Holy Land. Most of them had fought and seen their friends die for the cause and they were even more indignant at the charges than the serving brothers in Europe, who may never have been to the East.[39]

In the middle of the trials, King Amaury was murdered, not by a Templar, I hasten to add. His body was found "stuffed beneath the stairs in his house at Nicosia."[40] The most likely suspect was his brother, Henry, who now became king, but I don't believe the matter was looked into very closely.

Since the Templars had helped Amaury take the throne from Henry a few years before when the trial was reopened and new witnesses brought in, they had good reason to expect the worst.

It didn't happen. The new witnesses, important men of the

kingdom, told the inquisitors that the Templars were the most valiant fighting men they knew and all seemed devout. They regularly went to Mass and received the Host. One of the Templars' guards had started out certain that the men were guilty. After two years with them, he not only had changed his mind, he felt that God had performed a miracle in order to prove it to him.[41]

Pope Clement wasn't satisfied with these results and, in 1311, sent a papal legate to Cyprus to reopen the trial and this time to use torture. I'm not sure if he wanted to torture the Templars or the witnesses or both, but there is no record of anything more happening.

ARRESTS AND TRIALS IN ITALY

Italy, of course, is a modern nation. In the fourteenth century, the Italian peninsula was made up of several territories, such as Lombardy and Tuscany, or city-states, such as Venice, Pisa, and Genoa. Scattered among them were the various Papal States (see below). There was also the Kingdom of Naples, ruled by Charles II, uncle of Philip the Fair.[42]

Naples was one place where the Templars were seriously prosecuted. During the course of the trials, Charles died and was succeeded by his son, Robert, who wished to press his claim to the thrones of Jerusalem and Sicily. In the summer of 1309, Robert made a trip to Anjou to see Pope Clement and receive official confirmation of his rights.[43]

Few records remain of the trial in Naples but it appears that the six Templars arrested there were tortured in order to make them confess. The trial was held in April 1310 and the highlight of it was the testimony of one Galcerand de Teus, who regaled the inquisitors with the story of how he had been received in Catalonia and not only told to deny Christ but assured that Jesus, while on the cross, had confessed that he was not divine and had been forgiven. He insisted that all the Catalonian Templars knew this. However, it later came out that Galcerand had become a Templar in Italy and may not have ever been to Catalonia.[44]

In Tuscany only thirteen Templars were taken. Six of them confessed under torture. The other seven didn't.[45] As was usual in other countries outside of France, more attention was paid to occupying and taking inventory of Templar property than in capturing the men themselves.[46]

Again the main thrust of the questioning involved the secret reception of new members of the order. The deposition of Brother Giacomo di Phighazzano sums up the frustration and exasperation the rest of the Templars must have felt:

"The reception of the brothers to the community was done as the Rule commanded," he insisted. "No brother was received who was not received according to the rules handed down by the blessed **Bernard** and by which father James had received him.[Giacomo]"[47]

ARRESTS AND TRIALS IN THE PAPAL STATES

The Papal States were areas of Italy that came under the legal jurisdiction of the popes. They consisted of several towns and regions scattered up and down what is now the country of Italy. The total wasn't a huge area, but it is rather surprising that in all of it, when there were at least thirty commanderies, only seven Templars were arrested. There were six serving brothers, Ceccus Nicolai di Langano, Andreas Armanni de Monte Oderisio, Gerard de Placentia, Petrus Valentini, Vivolus de villa Sancti Iustini, and Gualterius Johannis de Napoli, all Italian. The seventh was a Templar priest, Guillelmo de Verduno.[48] None of them had ever been overseas; they had never even left Italy.[49]

The seven Templars all confessed that they had spit and stamped on the cross, except the priest, who had been allowed to stamp on two pieces of straw. Four of them said they had been asked to worship an idol. Each one described a different idol. Ceccus saw a young boy made of metal; Andreas saw one with three heads; Gerard's idol was made of wood and had one face; Vivolus saw a white head with the face of a man.

None of the Templars appeared to have been tortured. They were all absolved.

There is no record of what happened to the rest of the Templars in the Papal States.

OUTSIDE of France very few Templars confessed, or were judged guilty, of anything. Many never came to trial at all. In spite of Pope Clement's attempts to get the regional church authorities to prosecute the Templars rigorously, using torture if necessary, it doesn't seem to have often happened.

The result of the trials was to put a lot of Templars out of work. The Hospitallers eventually got most of the Templar property but they were saddled with the job of paying pensions to the ex-Templars and their dependents.

The real losers in the whole affair were Clement V and the popes who came after him. Clement was shown to be a weak man and his office as one with very little real power. He could order the arrest of the Templars because they were under his direct authority. But he couldn't make local bishops hunt the Templars down. He had the power to suppress the order but not enough to see that its property was delivered where he wanted it.

And now the whole world knew it.

---

1 In Barcelona at the Archivo de la Corona de Aragón, if you want to check them. Or see Alan Forey, *The Fall of the Templars in the Crown of Aragon* (Ashgate, Aldershot, 2001); he has searched the archives extensively for you and me. I am extremely grateful.

2 This is my summary of Forey, pp. 1–6.

3 Forey, p. 215.

4 Ibid., p. 75.

5 Malcolm Barber, *The Trial of the Templars* (Cambridge, 2006) p. 236.

6 Barber, p. 237.

7 Thomas W. Parker, *The Knights Templars in England* (University of Arizona Press, 1963) p. 17.

8 Evelyn Lord, *The Knights Templar in Britain* (London: Longmand, 2002) pp. 44–137.

9 Barber, p. 218.

10 Anne Gilmour-Bryson, "The London Templar Trial Testimony," in *A World Explored: Essays in Honour of Laurie Gardiner*, ed. Anne Gilmour-Bryson (Melbourne, 1993).

11 Barber, p. 219.

12 Roger Sève and Anne-Marie Chagny-Sève, *Le Procès des Templier d'Auvergne 1309–1311*, p. 253. "dixit quod osculantur se in ore, et omnia alia et singula in predictus articulis contenta sunt fallsa et mala, nec facta fuerunt."

13 Gilmour-Bryson, p. 48.

14 Parker, p. 95.

15 Ibid., p. 96.

16 Gilmour-Bryson, p. 52.

17 Ibid. This was before the Internet, of course, but just imagine what a great science fiction story this would make. Remember, I had it first.

18 Lord, p. 198. It's possible that John couldn't read, but his wife could.

19 Ibid.

20 Parker, p. 97. All of these come from the records of the testimony.

21 Lord, p. 199

22 Ibid., 200.

23 Karl Borchardt, "The Templars in Central Europe," in *The Crusades and the Military Orders: Expanding the Frontiers of Medieval Latin Christianity*, ed. Zsolt Hunyadi and Josef Laszlovszky (Budapest: Central Hungarian University, 2001) p. 233.

24 Please see chapter 39, **Other Regional Military Orders**, for more on the Teutonic knights.

25 Barber, p. 251.

26 Ibid.

27 Ibid.

28 Ibid.

29 Ibid.

30 Ibid., p. 252.

31 Borchardt, p. 239.

32 Peter Edbury, "The Military Orders in Cyprus," in Hunyadi and Laszlovszky, p. 102.

33 Ibid.

34 K. Schottmüller, *Der Untergang des Templer Ordens* (Berlin, 1887) Vol. II, p. 168. Prof. Anne Gilmour-Bryson has translated the records of the trial into English. Unfortunately, I was not able to obtain a copy of her book.

35 Ibid., p. 185.

36 Ibid., p. 191.

37 Ibid., pp. 207–9.

38 Ibid., pp. 188–89 and 217.

39 Barber, pp. 255–56.

40 p. 256.

41 Schottmüller, pp. 157–58.

42 Barber, p. 213.

43 Fulvio Bramato, *Storia dell'Ordine dei Templari in Italia, Vol. II Le Inquisizioni, Li Fonti* (Rome: Atanor, 1994) p. 29.

44 Ibid., pp. 30–31.

45 Barber, p. 215.

46 Bramato, pp. 47–49.

47 Quoted in Bramato, "receptions frutrum cominter predictis modis in ordine sic fiebant, tamen aliqui non sic recipiebantur, sed recipiebantur secumdum regulam eis traditam a beato Benardo secundum quam ipse fr. Jacobus asseruitse receptum."

48 Gilmour-Bryson, pp. 34–35.

49 Ibid., p. 38. The following paragraphs are a summary of Gilmour-Bryson's excellent edition of the transcripts of the trials.

CHAPTER THIRTY-SIX

The Secret Rite
of Initiation

The most serious charges brought against the Templars by King Philip—and the ones that still seem to fascinate people today—all revolved around the secret ceremony of initiation into the order. All of the Templars who were arrested were asked about what they did at their entry. The answers fell into two categories. The first was the normal rite that was spelled out in the **Rule**.

The ceremony of reception is in the Old French version, so it was accessible to anyone who could read or have it read to him. It was a secret ceremony not in the sense that no one could find out what happened, but in that family and friends were not invited.

Here are the main parts of the initiation:

If a man wishes to become a Templar, he is first brought into a room near the chapter hall where the Templars gather for their weekly meetings. There he is asked several questions.

The first questions are about his willingness to join the order: "Brother, do you ask to join the company of the house?"[1]

If he does, then they are to tell him about all the difficulties of the job and the suffering he will endure and ask if he is prepared to be a serf and a slave of the house for always, all the days of his life.[2] This is stressed several times. It is not an unusual request. Anyone joining a religious order is told that they must obey their superiors without question. This was true of the Benedictines, Cistercians, Franciscans, Dominicans, and all other orders.[3] However, it was considered that men who had been trained as knights would have more trouble being subservient than most monks.

If the applicant is not deterred by this information then he is asked questions that concern reasons why he may not become a Templar. Is he married? Is he a member of another order? Does he owe money that he can't repay? Does he have a communicable disease?

If the answers to these are satisfactory, then one of the brothers questioning him goes into the chapter hall and says to the master:

"Lord, we have spoken with this worthy man who is outside and have told him of the hardships of the house as well as we could. And he says that he wishes to become a serf and slave of the house. . . ."[4]

Then the applicant is brought in. He kneels before the master and joins his hands, saying:

"Lord, I have come before God and before you and before the brothers and implore and ask you by God and by Our Lady, that you may welcome me into your company and the benefits of the house as one who desires to be a serf and a slave of the house for all my days."[5]

The master tries again to dissuade the man:

"Good brother," he says. "You ask a very great thing, for of our order you see only the outer appearance. For in appearance you see us having fine horses, and good equipment, and good food and drink, and fine robes, and thus it seems to you that you would be well at ease. But you do not know the harsh commandments which lie beneath: for it is a painful thing for you, who are your own master, to make yourself a serf to others. For it will be difficult for you to do as you wish; for if you wish to be in the land this side of the sea, you will be sent to the other side; or if you wish to be in Acre, you will be sent to the country of Tripoli or Antioch or Armenia. . . . And if you wish to sleep, you will be wakened; and if you sometimes wish to stay awake, you will be ordered to stay in your bed."[6]

If the applicant is not a nobleman, he is reminded that he will be made a sergeant. This means an even harder life, doing work that he may think beneath him. The master doesn't mince words. He lists all the irksome jobs the man might be required to do. Honestly, I would have changed my mind when he got to the part about cleaning out the pigsty and sweeping up after the camels. But many men remained firm in their desire to join.

The applicant is then sent outside to await the decision of the chapter. If they decide to accept him, he is called back in and asked once more if he's willing to endure all that they have told him.

When he agrees, the master rises and asks them all to stand and pray to "Our Lord and Lady Saint Mary that he may do well."[7] They then say the Lord's Prayer and the chaplain gives another prayer to the Holy Spirit. After that the applicant is given the Gospels and, with his hands on them, is asked one final time if there is any reason why he should not become a Templar.

Lastly, the man takes the oath, "Do you promise God and Our Lady that all the days of your life you will be obedient to the master of the Temple and whatever orders that will be [given] you? Again, do you promise to live chastely, without property, that you will live according to the customs of the house? Do you promise to God and Lady Saint Mary that, for all your life, you will aide in conquering the holy land of Jerusalem with the force and power that God has given you? And that you will help to protect and save any Christian who may need it? Do you promise never to leave the order without the permission of the master?"[8]

To all of these, the man answers, "Yes, if it pleases God."[9]

Finally, the master says:

"And we, by God and by Our Lady Saint Mary and by my lord Saint Peter of Rome and by our father the pope, and by all the brothers of the Temple, we welcome you to all the benefits of the house which have been done since the beginning and will be done until the end, and . . . you also welcome us to all the good deeds that you have done and will do. And so we promise you the bread and the water and the poor clothing of the house and more than enough of pain and torment."[10]

At last the new Templar is given his cloak, white for a nobleman or black or brown for a sergeant. The chaplain reads Psalm 133, "Behold how good it is for brothers to live together in unity." The brothers recite the Lord's Prayer again and the master raises the new recruit up and kisses him on the mouth.[11]

A kiss on the mouth was the normal way to seal an oath. This was done both in religious communities and in royal treaties, as well as official greetings. My impression is that it was ceremonial and not sexual. I'm fairly sure no tongues were involved.

At least on paper, this is a sacred and completely orthodox reception. There is nothing in it that needed to be secret. The Templars simply preferred that the ceremony be private.

This desire for privacy was to lead to their downfall. In the minds of some people, things that are secret are automatically suspect. If they weren't doing something bad then why couldn't anyone come and watch? Therefore, there must be something blasphemous about the reception or a second ceremony must also take place.

This theoretical second ceremony was spelled out in the charges: after the usual reception, the new Templar was supposedly taken aside and told to deny Christ and spit on the crucifix. Then he either kissed the master on the base of the spine and the navel or the new Templar was kissed. Reports varied. This ceremony was described mostly by Templars who had either been tortured or expected to be if they didn't give the answers that their inquisitors wanted.[12]

The problem with the reports of the interrogations is that they are all in the third person, not in the exact words of the men. Each Templar was asked if he had participated in the crimes the order was accused of. These were read out one at a time. Then the inquisitor wrote down the gist of the answer.

The first statement of Grand Master **Jacques de Molay** is almost a template for these reports of a secret reception.

On October 24, 1307, nine days after his arrest, Jacques told the inquisitors that, after he received his white cloak, he was shown a cross of bronze on which was the image of Christ and he was told to deny. And he, with much distaste (*licet invictus*), did it.[13] Then he was told to spit on the cross, but he spat on the ground. Finally, he was asked if he had taken a vow of chastity. "Yes," he answered. "But they told me I could unite carnally with the brothers, but I swear on my oath that I never did."[14]

Other confessions would follow this pattern. Brother Peter la Vernha, a sergeant, testified that after he received his cloak he was told to kiss the receptor between the shoulder blades, which he did. Then he was told to deny God, for that was the custom of the reception. He did this "by mouth, not in the heart" (*ore, non corde*).[15]

Brother Steven the Cellerer only had to kiss the receptor on the navel over his clothes. He also denied Christ, also *ore, non corde*, and spat next to, not on, the crucifix.[16]

These two confessions were made in Paris. In the Auvergne, far to the southeast, Brother John Dalmas of Artonne, a knight, said that he had been received into the order in 1299 before the preceptor, Imbart Blanc. Imbart told him that the denial of Christ was part of the regulations of the order. So John did it, again *ore, non corde*, and spat next to the cross.[17]

The early interrogations only mention the denial of Christ, spitting on the cross, and sometimes permission to have sex with the other brothers. As the months passed, the Templar prisoners were asked about idol worship. This accusation is treated elsewhere in this book.[18]

Now, many of the Templars insisted that their reception had been completely orthodox but of the ones who confessed, they all follow a pattern. The first two actions, denying Christ and spitting on the crucifix, are almost identical in each statement. The "obscene kiss" varies as to place, with the navel and the base of the spine being favorites. None of the Templars admits to being enthusiastic about it. In their hearts they all remained believers, or so they said.

So what did the inquisitors think was the purpose of this secret initiation?

Did they really believe that every new Templar was immediately let in on the great surprise that the order wasn't really Christian at all, but denied Christ and defiled the crucifix? It seems odd that a new recruit, ready and eager to give his life fighting for Christ, should be told on the first day that that wasn't the reason for the order's existence. I also find it strange that, after they supposedly denied Christ, they were then told to worship an idol that some called **Baphomet**. It seems a lot to throw at a man on his first day on the job.

Also, according to the testimonies of the Templars at their trials, after this ceremony, nothing more happened. They continued hearing the Divine Office and going to Mass, although some said that the priests omitted the words to consecrate the Host. They also continued shipping out for the Holy Land, where they fought and died.

But for what? If they weren't there to protect pilgrims and fight the infidel in order to gain remission of their sins and have the hope of heaven, what were they doing there? While people have come up with lots of theories, at the time of the trials, none of the men who confessed came out with a set of beliefs to replace the Christian ones.

They didn't say they had become Moslems. They didn't give any of the alternate beliefs of other Christian heretics. They didn't say that they were **Cathars.** They certainly didn't tell the inquisitors that they were atheists, a concept that was barely known at this time. It is unprecedented in the history of heretical movements not to have some sort of set of beliefs. And yet, if the Templars weren't Christian, they didn't confess to being anything else.

I tend to think that this was something that the accusers of the Templars slipped up on. Maybe they counted on the public to fill in the blanks with their most dreaded heresy. But it is another reason to suspect that the heretical reception ceremony existed only in the imagination of the inquisitors.

Alan Demurger thinks that there really was some sort of unorthodox part of the ceremony, put in as an initiation test.[19] I don't think it makes sense to demand that an initiate deny the very reason he wants to join a group, even as a hoax. However, I won't completely discount this, just because of the strange things I've heard of modern male initiations. However, I think that the most probable answer is that there never was such a ceremony. No Templar who testified without the threat of torture confessed to a heretical reception.

One of the most shocking accusations was that at the reception, the Templars denied Christ and spat or even urinated on the cross. Like Demurger, some scholars have assumed that this might have happened and explain it as a test of loyalty or obedience. I think that's nonsense. This was just another of the general beliefs floating around concerning heretics.

The Templars opened themselves up to lurid speculations by keeping the reception secret. Why?

The best answer I have heard is one given by Imbart Blanc, the preceptor of Auvergne, who had been captured and tried in England. Despite the testimony of John Dalmas, related above, Imbart insisted that the accusations were all lies.

The inquisitor then asked him why the Templars kept their reception ceremonies a secret.

His reply: "We were foolish!"

Imbart added that there was nothing in the reception ceremony that "was not fit for the whole world to see."[20]

Rather than confess to something he had never done, Imbart died in prison in England.

It seems to me that the mostly likely explanation is Imbart's. For centuries people have tried to make sense of the "secret rites" of the Templars. As I mention in the section on the **Templars and the Saint**, there is a story told about Louis IX, grandfather of Philip the Fair. While in captivity, Louis was asked to take an oath that, if he failed to deliver his ransom, he would be an apostate who denies Christ and spits on the cross. Also, in the 1147 account of the taking of the city of Lisbon by the crusaders, the Moslem defenders of the city are supposed to have "displayed the symbol of the cross before us with mockery: and spitting upon it and wiping the filth from their posteriors with it, and finally making water upon it."[21]

Many people have imagined a religion to fit the testimony given under torture. Most of these "religions" have little or nothing to do with the statements made in the confessions. There is no place where the Templars give any doctrine of belief that goes with the rituals they are supposed to have practiced. It's a very strange heresy that has no dogma. With the information we have, I am forced to conclude that there was probably no secret reception and that there certainly wasn't a heretical alternate religion practiced by the Templars.

The Templars were established to serve God and protect other Christians and that is what they lived and died believing they were doing.

---

1 Laurent Dailliez, *Régle et Statuts de L'Ordre du Temple* (Paris, 1972) p. 307. "Freres, requerés vos la compaignie de la maison?"

2 Ibid., "et qu'il veaut ester serf et esclafe de la maison a tou jors mais tous les jors de sa vie."

3 One good way to understand this is to read the Benedictine Rule, on which most of the others are based. It has been translated into most languages. One in English is Anthony C. Meisel and M. L. del Mastro, *The Rule of St. Benedict* (Garden City, 1975).

4 Dailliez, p. 307. Rule no. 659. "Sire nos avons parle a cest prodome que est defors et li avons mostré les durtés de la maison si come nos avons peu et seu. Et il dit qu'il veaut estre serf et esclaf de la maison."

5 Ibid., p. 308. Rule no. 660. "Ire, je suis venu devant Dieu et devant vos et devant les freres, et vos prie at vos require por Dieu et por Nostre Dame, que vous m'acueilliés en vestre compaignie et en vos bienfaits de la maison come celui qui to los jors mès veaut ester serf et esclaf de la maison."

6 Ibid., p. 308. Rule no. 661: "Biau frere, vos requires mult grand chose, quar nostre religion vos ne veés que l'escoche qui est par defors. Car lescorches se est que vos nos veé beaus chevaus, et beau hernois, at bien bovre et bien mangier, et beles robes, et ensi vos semble que vos fussiés mult aisé. Mais vos ne sav es pas le fors comandemens qui sont par dedans: quar forte chose siest que vos, qui est sires de vos meismes, que vos vos faites serf d'autrui, Quar a grant poine ferés jamais chose que vos veulles: car si vos veulleés estre en la terre deça mer, l'en vos mondera en la terre de Triple ou d'Antyoche ou d'Ermenie. . . . Et se vos vol es dormir on vos fera veillier: et se vos volés aucunes foi veillier l'envos commandera que vos ailliés en vostre lit."

I have adapted the English quote from the translation made by J. M. Upton-Ward, *The Rule of the Templars* (Boydell, 1992) p. 169. I only found out about this translation toward the end of my work on this book. It is very good, but occasionally her carefully literal translation is a bit hard to follow so I have gone back to the original to clarify.

7 Dailliez, Rule no. 668. "Priés nostre Seignor er madame sainte Marie, que il de doit bien faire."

8 Ibid., Rules no. 675 and 676.

9 "Oil, sire, si Dieu plaist."

10 Dailliez, p. 314. Rule no. 677. "Et nos de par dieu et de par Nostre Dame sainte Marie, et de par mon seignor saint Pierre de Rome, at de par nostre pere l'apostile, et de par tous les freres dou Temple, si vos acuillons a toz les bienfais de la moison qui on esté fais dès le comencement et qui seront fais jusques a la fin, . . . Et vos aussi nos acuilliés en toz les biensfais que vos avés fais et

ferés. Et si vos prometon dou pain et de l'aigue et de la povre robe de la maison et de la poine et dou travail assés."

11 Ibid., p. 315. "et le baiser en la bouche."

12 Please see chapter 31, **The charges Against the Templars**.

13 Georges Lizerand, *Le Dossier de l'Affaire des Templiers* (Paris, 1923) p. 34.

14 Ibid., p. 37. "Interrogatus, quum vovit castitatem, si sibi aliquid dictum quod commisceret se carnaliter cum fratribus, dixt per jarmentum suum quod non nec numquam fecit."

15 Jules Michelet, *Le Procés des Templiers* Vol II (Paris, 1987; rpt. of 1851 ed.) pp. 216–17.

16 Ibid., pp. 241–42.

17 Roger Sève and Anne-Marie Chagny-Sève, *Le Procès des Templiers d'Auvergne 1309–1311* (Paris, 1986) pp. 127–28.

18 See chapter 40, **Baphomet**.

19 Alain Demurger, *Jacques de Molay: Le Crepuscule des Templiers* (Paris: Biographie Payot, 2002) p. 335.

20 Malcom Barber, *The Trial of the Templars* (Cambridge, 2006; 2nd. ed.) pp. 220–21.

21 Charles Wendell David, ed. and tr. *The Conquest of Lisbon* De Expugnatione Lyxbonensi (Columbia University Press, 1936; rpt. 2002) pp. 132–33, "atque in illam expuentes, feditis sue posteriora extergebant ex illa, sique demum micturientes in illam." I am grateful to Malcolm Barber for pointing out this reference to me.

CHAPTER THIRTY-SEVEN

Marguerite Porete

The Belgian mystic Marguerite Porete may seem an odd person to include in a book about the Templars. She never went to the Holy Land. She may never have even met a Templar. But their fate affected hers in the most disastrous manner.

Marguerite was one of a group of laypeople known as the Beguines. The movement was strongest in the Low Countries but reached all through Europe. Beguines lived in towns in communal homes, worked outside or begged for alms, and pooled their possessions for the common good. Their beliefs ranged from a completely orthodox desire to live a religious, semimonastic life to deeply mystical, sometimes heretical revelations. Although the movement was condemned at the **Council of Vienne**,[1] it survived into the twentieth century. Some of their homes, or beguinages, have been turned into museums.

Many Beguine mystics were revered locally and accepted by the hierarchy of the Church. Marguerite wasn't one of these. She wandered about, preaching her belief in the Free Spirit (another heretical movement condemned at the **Council of Vienne**) and explaining to people that the soul can achieve union with God without the guidance of what she called "the little church."[2]

Now, first of all, no one was supposed to preach publicly without permission from the local bishop and women weren't allowed to preach at all, at least not outside the family. Marguerite not only did so, but she also wrote a book about her mystical experiences, *The Mirror of Simple Souls*. The book was condemned and burned by the bishop of Valenciennes in 1306. Undaunted, Marguerite submitted the book to three scholars at the University of Paris, each of whom said that the book contained nothing heretical.[3]

The masters of the university were apparently getting quite a reputation for deciding matters of religion. **Philip the Fair** went to them several times in his attempts to justify the **arrest and trials of the Templars**. So Marguerite must have felt secure in their approval as she carried on with her work.

However, in 1308, Philip's confessor, Guillaume de Paris, who was also the papal inquisitor, happened to get a copy of *The Mirror of Simple Souls*. At this point he was frustrated by **Pope Clement V**'s lack of enthusiasm for condemning the Templars. Unlike the masters of the university, Guillaume found several heretical passages in Marguerite's book. He had her brought to Paris to be questioned.[4]

Marguerite, who had spoken her mind to all and sundry for years, refused to say anything to the inquisitors. After a year and a half in prison without defending herself, she was condemned on June 9, 1310, and burned at the stake the next day.[5]

This was less than a month after the archbishop of Sens had ordered the burning of fifty-four Templars. It has been suggested that "because of his acts of intolerance against the Templars, the king of France had angered the Pope."[6] Philip may have hoped that Clement was ready to follow the king in all things but he may have worried that the burning had pushed the pope too far.

Therefore, Philip and Guillaume needed an example of a true heretic, someone who had openly derided the authority of the Church. Marguerite was a perfect choice. She was a free spirit in many ways, not attached to a convent or to an important family. And her work could be seen as decidedly unorthodox.

But would she have been burned if the case of the Templars hadn't been going so badly? I suspect not. It is more likely that her book would have been burned and she would have been shut up somewhere. On the other hand, Marguerite also represented a growing interest among literate laypeople in understanding the faith on their own. This independence threatened the stability of all of society, not just that of the Church. The various reforms in the Church over the previous two hundred years had emphasized personal devotions. Many people were trying to make sense of the beliefs they had been taught. Marguerite was one of the more vocal but she was not as alone as she may have felt.

Evidence of this is that, although all copies of *The Mirror of Simple Souls* were to be handed in and destroyed, several people kept them. It is a testament to her work that it was translated into English, Italian, and Latin (!). Clearly her mystical experiences touched a wide range of people.[7]

Did Marguerite fall into a trap set for the Templars or were she and the Templars caught up in a general panic on the part of those in power? Were they accused of heresy because of valid evidence or because that was the charge most likely to be taken seriously, given the mood of the times?

I honestly don't know. But it is something to think about.

---

1 Charles-Joseph Hefele and Dom H. Leclercq, *Histoire des Conciles d'après les Documents Originaux* Tome VI deuxième partie (Paris, 1915) p. 681. The fifth canon of the council lumps the Beguins in with the heresy of the Free Spirit and condemns both.

2 Peter Dronke, *Women Writers of the Middle Ages: A Critical Study of Texts from Perpetua (d. 203) to Marguerite Porete (d. 1310)* (Cambridge University Press, 1984) p. 217.

3 Catherine M. Müller, *Marguerite Porete et Marguerite d'Oingt, de l'autre côte du miroir* (New York: Land, 1999) pp. 14–15.

4 Ibid., p. 15.

5 Ibid.

6 Ibid.

7 Dronke, p. 217.

CHAPTER THIRTY-EIGHT

Who Were the Templars?

While there are some notable men who became Templars, and occasionally one of the rank-and-file Templars was singled out for approval by a chronicler for the glory of his death, most of the time the Templars seemed interchangeable. This was intentional. Unlike secular knights, they were not supposed to be interested in personal fame. They were not just soldiers, but monks. Their lives combined the discipline of an army unit in the field with the rigor of the monastic schedule of prayer eight times a day.

The **Rule** tells us what the daily life of the Templar should be. There was of course a big difference between the lives of those who were on duty in the Latin kingdoms and those who never left the West. But the Rule gives us a pattern that every Templar was supposed to follow. It is probable that when not actively in battle, most of them did their best to keep to it.

What did they look like? First of all, unlike the dandyish knights and courtiers of the twelfth century, clean shaven with long curly locks, the Templars wore their hair short and had nicely trimmed beards.[1] The Latin Rule, written by regular cloistered monks, makes it clear that they weren't to dress in the latest styles. The monks particularly despised the fashion for *rostris*, or shoes with long, pointed toes and laces, "which are obviously a heathen fashion."[2] Their clothes should be plain and serviceable, without fur or frills. Like monks, the clothes were not their own, but distributed by the Draper, who was told to make sure that they fit so that no brother looked like a fool in something too long or too short.[3]

Also like other monks, the Templars ate together and in silence. Out of regard for the amount of extra energy they would need, they were allowed meat three days a week, except for some feast days.[4] They might have wine before bed, but in moderation.[5] When they got to bed, there should always be a light burning, "so that the shadowy enemies might not lure them to evil."[6]

Many of the rules were designed to make sure that the brothers had no chance for any sort of sexual contact, with men or women. They were always to go in pairs, or more, but, should they stop at an inn, they were not to go into each other's rooms.[7] This rule puzzles me because most inns did not have private rooms—one might well have been asked to share a bed with a stranger. Either the monks who wrote this rule didn't get out much or the Templar cash was going for the best lodging available.

Their daily lives were based on those of the monastery. They got up in the middle of the night for the prayers of Matins. At dawn they said the prayers of Prime and then heard Mass. They stopped for the other six times of prayer, ending with Compline, after which they were not allowed to speak until the next Matins.

It was understood that few of the brothers would have the Latin to recite the psalms of the Divine Office or even be able to read them in French. So they only needed to listen to the priest recite and to say the Lord's Prayer thirteen times at each of the hours.[8] At the end of each Office, the brothers were given any necessary orders or important announcements.

After Matins, long before dawn, the Templars did not go back to bed until they had checked their horses and equipment, repaired anything that needed it, and conferred with their squires about any other problems.[9] Then they could go back to bed until the sun rose.

Instead of the usual monastic duties, such as copying manuscripts or working in the garden, the Templars in the field spent most of their free time taking care of their armor and their horses. The care of the

A nineteenth-century idealized image of a Templar. *(Art Resource, NY)*

horses was a major concern. The monk Odo of Deuil, who went with Louis VII on the **Second Crusade**, was impressed with the way the Templars kept their horses fed, even though they themselves were starving.[10] The Rule gave guidelines for feeding and exercising the horses and for military training. The **Temple in London** had a field across from the house which was probably used for jousting and other exercises, so not only the brothers serving in the East were expected to stay in training.[11]

As in a monastery or a modern army, a Templar was strictly under the authority of the master. He had to ask permission to do almost anything and was expected to obey an order instantly, saying, *"De par Dieu"*—"For the sake of God."[12]

One concession that the writers of the later sections of the Rule had to make was about gambling. Games of chance were the second most popular recreation for medieval soldiers and, since the Templars had vowed chastity, the first was out of the question. So rule number 317 gave limits on what the Templar may wager. It appears as if the idea was to let them play without risking anything. Because they had taken a vow of poverty, they had no money, so they were forbidden to bet anything valuable, such as a saddle. Instead they could wager with tent pegs or pieces of candle or worn-out cord from a crossbow. They were not to play chess or backgammon at all.[13]

These men had grown up in a society where everyone played games of chance. The fact that the Rule had to bend a bit to accommodate this shows how ingrained the knightly life was in the men who chose to become Templars.

There was a great difference between the lives of the Templars in the East and in the West. With the exception of the Iberian Peninsula, the Templars living in the various commanderies and small houses never saw combat. Their life was much more like that of the monks living in the countryside near them. These men had two main jobs: to recruit knights to send to Jerusalem or Acre and to bring in the money to support them.

In Paris and London, especially, some Templars became financial servants of the kings. But we still have only a few of their names, no sense of who they were. I think that this is because most of the Templars were not on the same social level as the men who hired them. Even the knights who wore the white cloak tended to come from the lower nobility. The sergeants only had to be freeborn to enter the order. When it came down to it, with a few exceptions, the nobility considered the Templars in Paris and London as no more than civil servants.

It is possible to give a picture of a few of the Templars, mostly from charters.

INDIVIDUAL TEMPLARS

One of the unusual things about the Templars is that men could join for a limited amount of time.[14] One of those who did was a knight named Humbert of Beaujeu.[15] Humbert was the son of Guichard, lord of Beaujeu, in Burgundy, and Lucienne of Rochefort. The date of his birth isn't known but it many have been between 1115 and 1120.[16] He signed on with Louis VII for the **Second Crusade**. He was going to travel to the Holy Land with his father-in-law, Amadeus III of Savoy, but one night he had a vision warning him to go on his own.[17] It's not quite clear what disaster the vision expected. Amadeus III, who was also the uncle of Louis VII, was bringing a huge force on the expedition. Amadeus and Louis shared in the disasters of the journey across Anatolia and were among those who went too far ahead, causing the slaughter of Louis' rear guard in Turkey.[18] But Amadeus himself survived the crusade and died on Cyprus of a fever.

When Humbert, traveling on his own, reached Jerusalem, he joined the Templars, although he was married. Either he told them he was single or he offered to sign up for a term and lied about having his wife's permission. He must have served with them only for the duration of the crusade, for he was back in Burgundy by 1150.[19] He may have accompanied the Grand Master, Everard de Barres, who returned to the West at about this time.

Humbert's father, Guichard, had entered the monastery of Cluny, near Macon in Burgundy, in 1137 and Humbert was apparently very active in the area, keeping the peace and getting rid of brigands and thieves. Everard may not have wanted the lord of Beaujeu to leave the Templars. It's always hard to lose an enthusiastic worker. The abbot of the monastery, Peter the Venerable, was all for ridding the Holy Land of the Saracens but the marauders in Burgundy, though Christian in name, were much closer and posed an immediate threat to him and his monks.

Abbot Peter wrote to Everard, begging him to release Humbert from the Templars so that he could continue to protect Cluny and the surrounding region. This is another reason why I think that Humbert was a temporary Templar. The abbot of Cluny would not have suggested making someone revoke a monastic vow. But if Humbert had promised to serve the order for a short time and he had left before the time was up, Peter might have considered his need greater than the Templars'.[20]

He points out to the master that, while all the good men were off fighting, the bad ones stayed behind to prey on the innocent. But Humbert, "who has but lately come back from overseas and returned to our neighborhood to take up the care of the land, to general rejoicing," is now able to protect widows, orphans, and defenseless monks.[21]

So Humbert did not remain in the Templars. He stayed in Beaujeu, where he was active in clearing his land of criminals. He also was known for his battles with his son, Humbert IV, who probably wished the old man had stayed in Jerusalem. Their quarrel was finally settled by the bishop of Lyons, who arbitrated their peace:

> Among all the misfortunes which have struck our region, one must place first that upheaval (*tempestas illa*), that pitiless war which Humbert of Beaujeu and his son waged against each other, and which men almost despaired of ever seeing ended. . . . [At last] The father received his son like his natural heir, and as the legitimate seignor after him of his whole fief and

domain of Beaujeu, and he swore to this before all the witnesses. The son, in his turn, did him homage. And it was in this way that, through our mediation, the young Humbert gave back to his father the greater part of the seignory on which he had laid his hand.[22]

The younger Humbert died on the Third Crusade. His father died around 1192, in his late seventies or early eighties. I hope he was feisty to the end.

Humbert is a good example of how the Templars were not just men who gave up families and the world. I haven't been able to find any indication of him staying in contact with the local Templars after his return, but this may be due to a lack of records. The fact that his son went on the next crusade implies that Humbert believed in the cause, although the younger Humbert did not follow his father's example and join the Templars.

BUT in some cases, the Templars *were* a family affair. One of the most important donors to the Templar commandery at Richendes was the local lord, Hugh of Boubouton. In 1136, he and his nephew, Bertrand, along with many of their friends and neighbors, gave the Templars a fairly large parcel of land. To be certain that no one contested this, they had the bishop of St. Paul Trois Châteaux, Pons de Grillon, witness it.[23] Two years after that Hugh, with his wife, son, and nephew among others, gave the Temple more land. The next day, Hugh became a Templar. He eventually became the commander of Richendes.[24]

Hugh's example seems to have inspired his son, Nicholas. On December 3, 1145, he also became a Templar, in spite of the protests of his mother, who was finally convinced to accept his decision. He must have been an only child, for he gave the remainder of the family property to the order, for, as he quoted, "One may not be My disciple unless one gives up all that one possesses." Enough was left to support his poor mother, Marchesa. One wonders how she spent the rest of her life, for it's clear from the document that Nicholas knew how his decision had hurt her.[25]

In this case we can sense the deep religious dedication of Hugh and his son. They had property and position but they gave it up to fight for God. There is no indication as to what prompted their decisions, but the religious devotion is obvious. It's one of the tantalizing unknowns that makes historical research both exciting and frustrating. I imagine Hugh staying at the commandery while Nicholas went off to Jerusalem, perhaps to die at one of the battles of the Second Crusade or in some unimportant skirmish. Did Hugh regret encouraging his son? Did his wife ever speak to him again? There's no way to know.

Perhaps if we had more of these personal images of the Templars and their families, there wouldn't be so many imaginary tales about their lives.

---

1 Rene Grousset, *Histoire des Croisades et du Royaume Franc de Jérusalem* Vol. I (Paris, 1934) p. 543.

2 Henri de Curzon, *La Règle du Temple* (Paris, 1886) pp. 32–33, "manifestum est esse gentili."

3 Ibid. Rule no. 18.

4 Ibid. Rule no. 26.

5 Ibid. Rule no. 30.

6 Ibid. Rule no. 37. This was customary in both monasteries and convents.

7 Ibid. Rule no. 41.

8 Ibid. Rule no. 282.

9 Ibid. Rule no. 283.

10 Odo of Deuil, *De Profectione Ludovici VII in Orientem*, ed. and tr. Virginia Gignerick Berry (New York: Norton, 1948) p. 134.

11 George Worley, *The Church of the Knights Templars in London: A Description of the Fabric and Its Contents, with a Short History of the Order* (London, 1907) p. 15.

12 Curzon. Rule no. 313.

13 Ibid. Rule no. 317.

14 Ibid., Rules no. 65 and 66.

15 I haven't found a connection between him and Grand Master William of Beaujeu, but one may exist. Families tended to choose a religious order and support it over the generations.

16 Constance Brittain Bouchard, *Sword, Miter, and Cloister: Nobility and the Church in Burgundy, 980–1198* (Ithaca: Cornell University Press, 1987) p. 292.

17 Jonathan Riley-Smith, "Family Traditions and Participation in the Second Crusade," in *The Second Crusade and the Cistercians* (New York: St. Martin's Press, 1992) p. 104.

18 Yves Sassier, *Louis VII* (Paris: Fayard, 1991) p. 178.

19 Giles Constable, *The Letters of Peter the Venerable* Vol. II (Cambridge, MA: Harvard University Press, 1967) p. 214.

20 Constable, p. 212, does mention that Humbert had left without his wife's permission. Humbert wouldn't have been the first man to join up to escape a bad marriage but there is no information on this point.

21 Constable, p. 408, "nuper a partibus transmarinus veniens ad partes nortras rediit, et cum immensa exulatatione."

22 Edward Benjamin Krehbiel and Achille Luchaire, *Social France at the Time of Philip Augustus* (New York: H. Holt, 1912) p. 264.

23 Marquis d'Albon, *Cartulaire Général de l'Ordre du Temple* (Paris, 1912) no. 122, p. 85.

24 Dominic Selwood, *Knights of the Cloister: Templars and Hospitallers in Central-Southern Occitania c.1100–300* (Boydell, Woodbridge, 1999) p. 68.

25 D'Albon, p. 237, no. 381.

CHAPTER THIRTY-NINE

The Other Guys;
Regional Military Orders

THE TEUTONIC KNIGHTS

During the Third Crusade, part of the German army, minus their leaders but with the body of Frederick Barbarossa, arrived at the city of Acre. They were in poor shape and were overjoyed to be greeted by the monks of the German hospital of St. Mary.[1] When the army went home, some of the German soldiers stayed to work at the hospital. In 1198 it was decided that St. Mary's should be divided into a service to care for the poor and the sick among the German pilgrims and also into a military order following the rule of the Templars.[2] They were known as the Teutonic Knights.

The members of the Teutonic Knights mostly came from the group known as the *ministeriales*.[3] This was a class of people who were the serfs of the kings of the German states. They were ministers of finance and handled much of the bureaucratic work. While many of the families became rich and influential, they were not considered free and not allowed to marry into the nobility.[4] Men of this class who had military training might well have seen the Teutonic Order as an opportunity for the knightly activity that their birth denied them.

By the time of the Fifth Crusade, the Teutonic Knights were part of the armies supplied by the military orders. They fought alongside the **Hospitallers** and the Templars during the failed campaign in 1218–1221 to conquer Egypt. They also helped the Templars to rebuild their fortress of Chateau Pelerin, now known as Atlit.[5]

But the Teutonic Knights soon realized that their sphere of activity was not the reconquest of Jerusalem.[6] They were convinced that it was just as important to expand the faith by bringing Christianity to the pagan Prussians, Livonians, and Estonians.

They started their pursuit of this in Hungary in 1211, when King Andrew II gave them some land north of the Transylvanian Alps. A short time later he could write, "They have been placed like a new foundation on that frontier, and in withstanding the constant onslaughts of the Cumans [a pagan group] and in providing a strong defense for the kingdom they do not fear to expose themselves to death every day."[7]

However, within a few years, Andrew had gone off the Teutonic brothers. It's not certain why. But one record states, "They are to the king like a fire in the breast, a mouse in the wallet and a viper in the bosom, which repay their hosts badly."[8] So it seems they outstayed their welcome. They were expelled from Hungary in 1225.

They had better luck with Emperor Frederick II, who was discovering that it's not easy to rule a territory that reaches from the Mediterranean to the Baltic. So he was happy to give the Teutonic Knights the district of Culmerland plus anything they could take over in Prussia.[9]

They didn't have to be asked twice.

This does not mean that the Teutonic Knights weren't serious about religion. Their order was as strict as any other. Knights took vows of celibacy, personal poverty, and obedience. When they were on campaign, the master's tent served as a church. Where the Templars were allowed low-stakes gambling, the Teutonic Knights could only do wood carving for recreation. Military discipline was severe.[10]

By 1230, the Teutonic Order had a monopoly on the military orders in eastern Europe. A small house of the Calatravan Order (see below) vanished. Two other German orders, the Swordbrethren and the Order of Dobrin, were absorbed.[11] They steadily took over large parts of Prussia. They were able to bring German peasants into the area to colonize it under their authority, which gave them a better base than the Templars had, even better than the Hospitallers, who didn't have many colonists even when they settled on Malta.

Two years before the Templars were arrested, the Teutonic Knights in Livonia were put on trial. The charges against them were "the imprisonment of the bishop of Riga, infringement of ecclesiastical privileges, preventing missionary work, corruption of the Order's ranks and the sale of castles and weapons to the Lithuanians."[12] They were actually guilty of quite a few of these things, but they had no one like Philip IV against them and they had their own country to fight from so they emerged unscathed.

In the mid fifteenth century a Carthusian monk wrote a history of the various orders in the form of a dialogue between a mother and son. When she arrives at the Teutonic Order, the mother describes how they began, although stating that they followed the Rule of the Hospitallers, not the Templars. They started out noble defenders of the faith, she says, "But, [now] alas! Deceived by wealth they try to overthrow almost every order and wickedly destroy every single state!"[13]

In 1525 the Teutonic kingdom of Prussia was made into a Protestant duchy. There were not many knights left by then. Some of the younger ones left the order and married. The elder knights mostly preferred to stay true to their monastic vows and found religious houses to take them in.[14] In Germany the order reorganized to fight the Turks in the Balkans. Eventually the headquarters moved to Vienna and became "a military and chivalric extension of the House of Hapsburg."[15]

THE CALATRAVANS

This group of knightly monks took their name from the fortress of Calatrava in Spain. They were formed in 1158 after the Templars had abandoned the fortress for reasons still unclear.[16] At that time there was great fear of an attack by the Moors from Granada. King Sancho III of Castile sent a frantic letter to Raymondo, the abbot of the Cistercian monastery of Fitero, in Navarre, asking for his help. This isn't the first place I would have looked for military aid, but the abbot came through, offering his support and taking the new order under the protection of the Cistercians.[17] This was the first of the Spanish orders.

Although the Templars were very active in the *reconquista* in Spain and Portugal, they also sent a portion of everything they took in to support the work in the crusader kingdoms.[18] Since the kings of these countries felt that there was enough work to do at home, they encouraged the native order of warrior-monks, whose loyalty was strictly to their own country.

King Sancho started the Calatravans off well, giving them not only the town and fortress of Calatrava but also another village in a more secure area.[19] They were also promised the revenue from specific towns, if they could conquer them.[20] That, along with the promise of a portion of booty from other conquests, encouraged the Calatravans in their efforts.

The Calatravans must have been appreciated by the local population, for there are numerous records of donations to them of estates and rights. They also benefited by their connection to the Cistercians, who, like the Templars, were responsible to the pope and not local bishops. This, as usual, created friction with the Spanish clergy but it also brought in a sizeable income.[21]

The knights of Calatrava were active, along with the other military orders, in most of the battles in the Iberian Peninsula throughout the twelfth and thirteenth centuries. Although they lost the town of Calatrava in 1195, they continued to operate from the town of Salvatierra until forced to surrender that.[22] Undaunted, they continued fighting and regained Calatrava in July 1212.[23]

The orders in Spain provided medical treatment for those wounded in battle. Calatrava had at least six hospitals. The commander of one of them, Santa Olalla, traveled with royal armies "to provide for knights and footsoldiers, both the wounded and the poor, the ill and the sick, and to take a chaplain with him to offer *viaticum* [last rites] to the wounded, if necessary, and a master of surgery to give medicine to the wounded."[24] In this they seem to have combined the duties of the Templars and the Hospitallers.

The Calatravans attracted the formation of smaller orders in León, the Order of St. Julián del Pereiro, and in Portugal, the Order of Avis.[25] Castile-León was also home to the Orders of Santiago and Alcántara. While the Templars also had commanderies in this area, by and large the Castilian kings preferred native orders.[26]

They seem to have been correct in this judgment. The military orders of the Iberian Peninsula did not have to rely on donations from other lands and only had to deal with the squabbles of their own rulers. It's possible that, since they didn't have to operate on an international scale, they could put more time and energy into their main goal, the expulsion of the Moors from Spain. This was finally accomplished in 1492.

THE ORDER OF ST. LAZARUS

One of the most intriguing of the military orders was known as the Order of St. Lazarus. At least at the beginning, it was composed entirely of lepers.

As early as 1130, a man of Burgundy named Wido Cornelly, "judged to have contracted leprosy," volunteered to go to Jerusalem and serve as a knight of the Templars to the end of his life. Judging from the list of names witnessing his vow, Wido was a nobleman. He arranged for the care of his wife and children before he left.[27] He definitely joined the Templars first, not St. Lazarus. However, if he did indeed have leprosy, the Templars would have had to find a way to care for him once his illness became debilitating.

There was already a hospital for lepers in Jerusalem. Like most such hospitals, it was dedicated to Saint Lazarus. There were two men by that name in the Gospels. The first was a beggar, covered with sores, who lay, ignored, at the gate of a rich man until he died. He was then taken to heaven while the rich man was sent to hell.[28] This Lazarus might well have been considered a leper and the parable illustrates the punishment for not sharing what one has with those less fortunate. The other, better known, Lazarus was Lazarus of Bethany, brother of Mary and Martha, whom Jesus raised from the dead. To many people lepers were the living dead. So which one was it? The answer is probably both. Like Mary Magdalene, the saint venerated in the Middle Ages as Lazarus was likely a blending of two men with the same name.[29]

The hospital was in existence at the time that Wido made his vow to join the Templars. It wasn't exactly in Jerusalem, more up against an outer wall. While people did not yet believe that leprosy was a punishment for one's sins, they didn't know how one got it and so most houses for lepers were not in densely populated parts of the city.

The royal family of Jerusalem, starting with **Fulk** and **Melisande**, gave generously to the "church and convent of the infirm" of St. Lazarus.[30] Most of the other nobility of the Latin kingdoms did as well. Often there are Templars who witness these charters. Some of them are even contracted at the Temple of Solomon.[31] That might appear as if the Templars and the lepers had an early arrangement for the care of leprous knights—that is, until we remember that the Temple had become a general meeting place for people in Jerusalem to transact business.[32] After all, people might want to give to the poor lepers but not have to actually visit them. So we can't be certain that the Templars were connected to the Hospital of St. Lazarus yet.

Sometime around 1153, the hospital seems to have developed a second function as a home for leperous knights who were still well enough to fight. The first known master of St. Lazarus was a certain Bartholomew. He carried water for the use of the lepers and took care of them.[33] In 1155, Almaric, the son of Fulk and Melisande, gave a villa to the "brothers of St. Lazarus of Jerusalem and to Hugh of Saint Paul, who is now master of this place and of all the lepers."[34]

It's not clear when St. Lazarus started sending knights into combat. Some of the charters are to the brothers and others to the lepers. Is it simply a matter of the term the scribe felt like using that day or did it make a difference? My feeling is that the military order evolved slowly as men in the early stages of leprosy came to the hospital but were still able to bear arms. There were never enough fighting men in Jerusalem. Also, several skin conditions were misdiagnosed as leprosy, especially at the beginning. These men would have been well enough to fight for quite a while.

It wasn't until the fall of Jerusalem in 1187 that the Order of St. Lazarus received papal privileges similar to those of the other orders.[35] At this point we can say that it was official. The first time the knights are mentioned as having participated in a battle is that of La Forbie in 1244, where they were all killed.[36] That didn't stop Stephen of Salerno from donating ten sous four years later, on condition that they accept his "most blessed and beloved" son, Astorge, as a brother.[37]

These men had all seen what kind of death they would face from leprosy. The agony of dying in battle must have seemed pleasant by comparison.

The Templars must have agreed. Sometime in the early thirteenth century they added to their **Rule,** "If, by the will of God, it happens that a brother seems to have leprosy and the thing is proven, the brothers of the house should advise him and beg that he ask to take leave of the house and go to Saint Lazarus and take the habit of a brother of Saint Lazarus."[38]

The Order of St. Lazarus moved to Acre along with the Templars and **Hospitallers.** They had a house there, a hospital, and a convent for sisters of the order.[39] Again, when the Mamluks took the city, all the knights of St. Lazarus were killed.

One would think that a military order like this would have ended with the fall of Acre. But they seem to have established themselves for a while on Cyprus. Eventually, however, they were left with only their properties in Europe, principally in England and France.[40]

By this time, there were no more lepers among the Knights of St. Lazarus. This had happened gradually but by the end of the thirteenth century the knights were all men in reasonably good health. Sometime before 1307, they decided to move their headquarters to their French holding in Boigny. Then things got really weird.

In 1308, **Philip the Fair** took the Knights of St. Lazarus under his personal protection.[41] Considering what was happening to the Templars at the time, they might have wondered if this was a great idea. But they also may have thought it a safe port in a nasty storm.

The Knights of St. Lazarus continued to exist in England until Henry VIII discontinued monasticism there. But they didn't have much to do with hospitals anymore and they didn't go on crusades so their purpose was nonexistent. In France, they had ups and downs. Under Louis XIV, they became a military order again, fighting against the heathen British. In a fitting end to what had become an increasingly bizarre story, the last French Grand Master of the Knights of St. Lazarus of Jerusalem was Louis XVI. The order ended with him at the guillotine in 1792.[42]

But, like the Lazarus of the Bible, the order was resurrected in 1910. It is now a worldwide Christian relief agency with branches in Europe and North America.[43] Like the Templars, the Knights of St. Lazarus were too intriguing to let die.

THE ORDER OF ST. THOMAS AT ACRE

According to the English pilgrim and chronicler Ralph of Diceto, the Order of St. Thomas at Acre began with a vow made by a terrified and seasick priest named William. He promised that, if he ever managed to set foot on dry land again, he "would build the most elegant chapel possible and staff it and consecrate a cemetery in honor of St. Thomas the Martyr. And it was done."[44]

However, later chroniclers state that a crusader named Hubert Walter founded the order, and Matthew Paris, writing in the mid thirteenth century, decided that the man who made the shipboard vow was none other than **Richard the Lionheart**. Of course, it was Richard who got the ultimate credit for it.[45] Not only was he the king, he was also the son of the man who had supposedly ordered the murder of Saint Thomas. That makes a much better story.

Whoever made the original foundation, the Order of St. Thomas of Acre was most likely founded during or after the Third Crusade, after the loss of Jerusalem in 1187 and the removal of the seat of the kingdom to Acre.

The original purpose of the order was to care for the poor and to bury the dead. The priests at the church of St. Thomas paid particular attention to English pilgrims who did not speak French, the language of the Latin kingdoms.

The order doesn't seem to have been flashy enough to attract many donations. They scrimped along until about 1228, when the bishop of Winchester, Peter des Roches, paid them a visit. He decided that the church was too poor to survive, and the priests had become "dissolute."[46] The priests seem to have been canons rather than monks. That meant that each had his own home, rather than living together. In other places this had sometimes led to the canons ignoring the vows of chastity and poverty. One of the great reforms of the twelfth century had been to replace many of the cathedral canons with monks who were under the close supervision of an abbot.

Bishop Peter was having no truck with concubines and gluttony or any other form of dissolution. He was in the Holy Land with a party of crusading knights and was not above leading a battle charge personally.[47] He got rid of the canons (without bloodshed) and turned St. Thomas of Acre into a military order. The Rule it was to follow was not that of the Templars but of the Teutonic Knights. That meant that the order still had some obligation to care for the poor and sick, although the members' fighting ability was the most important aspect of their job.[48]

How much fighting they did is hard to say. They are not mentioned by the chroniclers as having been in any of the major battles. But, by 1256, they managed to get the same papal privileges as the Templars and **Hospitallers** had.[49]

They did receive donations of property, mainly in England, but also some on the continent. Peter des Roches had been a strong supporter of King John, Richard's baby brother, and also guardian of John's son, Henry III. So his patronage allowed the order to receive some royal gifts. But it never really thrived. In 1279, the church in Acre was still unfinished, due to lack of funds.[50] In the late thirteenth century, there was even a move to have the Order of St. Thomas be absorbed into the Templars. The Templars already owned the building they lived in at Acre. Although an agreement of some sort was made, enough of the members must have protested, for the union never came about.[51]

The remnants of the order in the East went to Cyprus with what was left of the Templars and Hospitallers after the fall of Acre in 1291. But they really had little purpose there and in the early fourteenth century the headquarters of the order was finally moved to London, although there seems to have been a small outpost on Cyprus for some time.[52]

After the settlement in London, the Order of St. Thomas seems to have decided that the Teutonic Rule didn't suit anymore. It changed to the rule of St. Augustine, which means that the men must have returned to being monastic canons rather than knights.

In its later days, the order mainly gave noble patrons a place to stay when they visited London. It also started a grammar school in London that lasted until the time of King Henry VIII. By the time the king closed all the monasteries, the patrons of St. Thomas were no longer the nobility but the merchants of London. The property of the Order of St. Thomas was bought by the Mercers Guild.[53]

The Order of St. Thomas of Acre is one of many quasi-military orders that were founded in the wake of the Templars. They may have wished at times that they were as influential and well funded as the two important orders. But when the soldiers came for the Templars in 1307, there must have been many who gave prayers of thanksgiving that the plans to make the Knights of St. Thomas part of the Templars had failed to occur.

---

1 Annales aevi Suevici (MGH SS XVI. Hannover, 1879) p. 153. "Imperator Fridericus, pacato imperio, cum filio suo Friderico duce Suevorum et mango pocerum et aliorum comitatu Terram Sanctam visitavit. Sed cum quadam die lavaretur in flumine, periit et dictus filius eius exercitum strennue rexit; sed et ipse in brevi obit in ecclesia sancta Marie hospitalis Theutonicorum, quam pater et ipse inchoaverant, sepultus fuit."

2 Alan Forey, *The Military Orders from the Twelfth to the Early Fourteenth Centuries* (London: MacMillan, 1992) p. 20.

3 William Urban, "The Teutonic Knights and Baltic Chivalry," in *The Historian* Vol. 57, No. 4, 1995, p. 520.

4 John B. Freed, *Noble Bondsmen: Ministerial Marriages in the Archdiocese of Salzburg, 1100–1343* (Ithaca: Cornell University Press, 1995) provides a good explanation of the minsteriales.

5 Oliver of Paderborn, *The Capture of Damietta*, tr. John J. Gavigan (University of Pennsylvania Press, 1948) chapter 5, p. 18.

6 Blonds sunburn so easily.

7 Forey, p. 34.

8 Ibid., p. 35.

9 Ibid.

10 Eric Christiansen, *The Northern Crusades* (London: Penguin, 1997) pp. 86–87.

11 Forey, p. 36.

12 Sophia Menache, *Clement V* (Cambridge University Press, 1998) p. 215.

13 Anonymous, "De Religionum Origine," in *Veterum Scriptorum et Monumentorum, Historicorum, Dogmaticorum, Moralium, Amplissima Collectio* Vol. VI (Paris, 1724) col. 62. "Sed, heu! Fallaces divitiae omnem pene ordinem nitutur evertere, omnem statum prorsus moliuntur depravate." (My thanks to Jeffrey Russell for correcting my initial translation of this.)

14 Urban, p. 523.

15 Ibid., p. 524.

16 Joseph F. O'Callaghan, *Reconquest and Crusade in Medieval Spain* (University of Pennsylvania Press, 2003) p. 52.

17 Clara Estow, "The Economic Development of the Order of Calatrava 1158–1366," in *Speculum* Vol. 57, No. 2, April 1982, p. 267.

18 O'Callaghan, p. 52.

19 Estow, p. 271.

20 Ibid., p. 272.

21 Ibid., pp 274–75.

22 O'Callaghan, p. 67.

23 Ibid., p. 71.

24 Quoted in O'Callaghan, p. 147.

25 O'Callaghan, p. 52.

26 Malcolm Barber, *The New Knighthood* (Cambridge, 1996) p. 246.

27 Marquis d'Albon, *Cartulaire General de l'Ordre du Temple 1119?–1150: Recueil des chartes et des bulle relatives* à l'ordre *du Temple* (Paris, 1913) p. 19, charter 27.

28 Luke 16:19–31.

29 David Marcombe, *Leper Knights: The Order of St. Lazarus of Jerusalem in England 1150–1544* (Boydell, Woodbridge, 2003) p. 5.

30 Comte de Marsy, "Fragment d'une Cartulaire de S. Lazare," in *Archives de l'Orient Latin* Vol. II, p.124.

31 Ibid., pp. 126–27. An 1148 charter of Barisan d'Ibelin that is not only enacted at the Temple but confirmed with the seal of the Temple. Maybe Barisan left his at home that day.

32 Barber, p. 93.

33 Marcombe, p. 8.

34 Marsy, p. 114. "Santo Lazaro de Jerusalem fratri videliciet Hugoni de Sancto Paulo, qui nunc est magister loci illius et toti leprosorum."

35 Marcombe, p. 15.

36 Ibid., p. 14.

37 Marsy, p. 157.

38 Laurent Dailliez, *Règle et Status de l'Ordre du Temple* (Paris, 1972) p. 238, rule 443. "Quant il avient a aucun frere que par la volenté de nostre Seignor il chiet en meselerie et la chose est

provée, li prodome frere de la maison le doivent amonester et proer que il demande congié de la maison et que il se rendre a saint Ladre, et que il preigne l'abit de frere de saint Ladre." I find it interesting that the Old French word used for leprosy, "meselerie," actually means "spoiled" or "led astray." Perhaps the seeds of intolerence were already there in the thirteenth century. It has nothing to do with the topic, but if you're obsessive enough to read the footnotes, it might interest you, too.

39 Marcombe, p. 12.

40 Ibid., p. 20.

41 Ibid., p. 21.

42 Ibid., p. xx.

43 http://www.st-lazarus.net/world/menu.htm

44 Ralph of Diceto, *Opera historia* ed. W. Stubbs (Rolls Series, ii, London, 1876) pp. 80–81. "Sancto Thomae martyri sumptibus suis juxta facultum possibiliatem capellam consturueret, et procruraret ibidem ad honerem martyris cimiterium consecrati. Quod et factum est." St. Thomas the Martyr is Thomas Becket, killed in Canterbury Cathedral Dec. 29, 1170, by henchmen of King Henry II of England.

45 A. J. Forey, "The Military Order of St. Thomas of Acre," in *The English Historical Review* No. 364, July 1977, p. 482.

46 Ibid., p. 487.

47 Ibid., p. 487.

48 Forey, "St. Thomas," p. 487.

49 Ibid., p. 491.

50 Ibid., p. 492.

51 Ibid., p. 493.

52 Ibid., p. 497.

53 Ibid., pp. 502–3.

✣

CHAPTER FORTY

Baphomet

During the trial of the Templars, one of the **charges** against them was that they worshipped an idol, sometimes called "Baphomet." The inquisitors may have accepted this as plausible because they had heard the name before. In the Middle Ages most Europeans knew little about the beliefs of Islam. The Koran had been translated into Latin in the 1140s at the request of Peter the Venerable, abbot of Cluny.[1] However, most people received their knowledge of the faith through fiction.

The French *chansons de geste*, tales of the deeds of great warriors, were full of battles against "Saracens," their term for Moslems. In these stories, the Saracens were pagans who worshipped many gods, among them Apollo and "Baphomet."

Under various forms, Baphomet appears often in the *chansons de geste*, always associated with Islam. For instance, in the twelfth-century epic *Aymeri de Narbonne*, Baphomet is one of the Saracen kings of Narbonne whom Aymeri must fight.

> *Rois Baufumez . . .*
> *avec aus .xx. paien armé*
> *Qui Deu ne croient le roi de majesté*
> *Ne sa mere hautisme.*

> King Baphomet . . .
> with twenty pagan warriors
> Who don't believe in God, the king of majesty
> Nor in his mother most high.
>
> ll 302–306[2]

This late-twelfth- or early-thirteenth-century crusade poem has a character called Bausumés or Baufremé, who is the uncle of a Saracen warrior.[3] The *Enfances Guillaume* of the thirteenth century also has a Moslem character named Balfumés.[4]

It is generally agreed that "Baphomet" is a corruption of the name "Mohammed," and linguistically, this is probable. There is a quote from the mid 1200s from a Templar poet, Ricaut Bonomel, lamenting the number of recent losses of Christian forces. "In truth, whoever wishes to see, realizes that God upholds them [the infidel]. For God sleeps when He should be awake, and *Bafomet* works with all his power to aid the Melicadeser [Baibars, the Mamluk ruler of Egypt at that time]."[5]

There is no information that indicates that Baphomet was the name of an ancient god. It is only in a few cases that the so-called idol of the Templars was even given a name at all.

During the trials most Templars said they didn't know anything about an idol. One sergeant, Peter d'Auerac, admitted to denying Christ in the reception ceremony, but he "neither knew nor had heard it said that there was an idol in the form of a head."[6] The same is true for Elias de Jotro, a servant, and for Peter de Charute.[7] As a matter of fact most of the Templars, even the ones who had been tortured, claimed to have no idea what the inquisitors were talking about.

However, the ones who did tell of an idol all described it differently. One said it was the head of a bearded man, "which was the figure of Baphomet." Another said it was a figure called Yalla (a Saracen word [possibly Allah]). Others called it "a black and white idol and a wooden idol."[8]

One Templar, the knight William of Arreblay, stated that he did see a head venerated in Paris. "He frequently saw a certain silver head upon the altar that he saw adored by most of those at Chapter, and he heard it said that it was the head of one of the eleven thousand virgins."[9] Saint Ursula and her eleven thousand virgins were popular among the Templars as saints who were steadfast in their faith even in the face of death. If mere women could do so much, the Templars could do no less.[10] After a little more coaching, William realized that "it seemed to him that the head really had two faces, a terrible aspect and a silver beard."[11]

A servant was sent to go through the possessions of the Temple of Paris to look for any heads, either of metal or of wood. After some searching, he came back with the head of a woman, gilded in silver. Inside were bones from a skull, wrapped in a linen bag. There was a tag on the bag that said that this was head number fifty-eight of eleven thousand.[12] No other head was found.

The historian is left with two choices. The first is that somehow the Templars managed to find out that the inquisitors were coming and hid the idol they normally worshipped. The second is that William made up the description of the two-faced idol under duress and that the only head owned by the Templars was the reliquary of Virgin Number 58. I think number two is the most likely.

There was also supposed to be another head belonging to the Templars, that of Saint Euphemia of Chalcedon, an early Greek martyr. This was kept in the Templar headquarters in Cyprus. It was among the property that was given to the **Hospitallers** after the dissolution of the order. They took it with them to Malta, where it was probably captured by Napoleon in 1798. If this is so, then Saint Euphemia went down with Napoleon's ship, *l'Orient,* off the coast of Egypt.[13]

Even though we don't have the head of Saint Euphemia that the Templars owned, it was likely much like the one of Virgin Number 58. If there had been anything odd or sacrilegious about it, the Hospitallers or a later scholar would have said something.

And, for those who are sorry that part of a saint has gone missing, don't worry. Euphemia's entire body is still kept at the Church of St. George in Istanbul.[14] As with those who bought slivers of the True Cross or the foreskin of John the Baptist, it appears that the Templars were taken in by a shady relic salesman.

As for Baphomet the idol, he belongs firmly in the realm of fiction.

1 Charles Bishko, *Peter the Venerable and Islam*.
2 *Aymeri de Narbonne*, ed. Louis Demaison (Paris: Société des Anciens Textes Français, 1887) pp. 13–14.
3 *La Chanson de Jérusalem*, ed. Nigel R. Thorp (Alabama University Press, 1992) p. 236, line 9019.
4 *Les Enfances Guillaume* (Paris: Société des Anciens Textes Français, 1935) p. 117, line 2755.
5 Alain Demurger, *Jacques de Molay: Le Crepuscule des Templiers* (Paris: Biographie Payot, 2002) p. 63.
6 Roger Séve and Anne-Marie Chagny Séve, *Le Procès des Templiers d'Auvergne 1309–1311* (Paris, 1986) p. 142. "Nescit nec audivit dici quod illud ydolum sue capud."
7 Jules Michelet, *Le Procès des Templiers* Tome I (Paris, 1987; rpt. of 1851 ed.) pp. 531–33.
8 Malcom Barber, *The Trial of the Templars* (Cambridge University Press, 1978) p. 62.
9 Michelet, vol. I, p. 502. "Vidit super altare frequenter quoddom capud argenteum, quod vidit adorari a majoribus qui temebant capitulum, et audivit dici quod erat caup unius ex undecim milibus virginum."
10 Helen J. Nicholson, "The Head of St. Euphemia: Templar Devotion to Female Saints," in Susan B. Edgington and Sarah Lambert, *Gendering the Crusades* (Cardiff, 2002) pp. 112–14.
11 Michelet, vol. I, p. 502, "quia videtur sibi quod haberet duas facies, et quod esset terribilis aspectu, et quod haberet barbam argenteam."
12 Ibid., vol. III, p. 218. That must have been a gold mine for the relic sellers. As a matter of fact, in 1156, some new holes were dug near Cologne that turned up some extra virgins to distribute. In Paul Guéron, *Vie des Saints* Vol. XII (Paris: Bollandistes, 1880) p. 497.
13 Nicholson, p. 111.
14 Ibid., p. 110.

CHAPTER FORTY-ONE

The Cathars

The Cathars have several things in common with the Templars. They were celibate, they were accused of heresy, they were supposed to have a hidden treasure, and they were wiped out. And one thing more: they are pulled into all sorts of interesting speculations on subjects that they had nothing to do with, such as the **Grail**.

Who were the Cathars?

The religion contained beliefs that had been floating around for centuries, perhaps millennia. Looking at the cruelty and essential unfairness of life, some people have decided that a good god could not be responsible for such a mess. Instead of assuming that God was testing people or punishing them for their sins, these people came to the conclusion that God was not all-powerful. Some forms of this belief assumed that there must be two gods, one good and one evil, in constant battle over humanity. In religions that assumed one all-powerful god, this evil force, or the devil, was still under the control of heaven. The Cathars were among those who gave the devil a more dominant role in human fate.

The belief that the world is evil led to the belief that the evil god is responsible not just for the bad things in the world but also for the world itself. The good god rules in heaven and wishes to have human souls go (or return) there. In that case, everything that has to do with property or procreation is detestable because it just lengthens the time spent away from heaven. This means that truly devout dualists eat nothing that has been produced through sex, not meat, eggs, or milk products. At least one heretic hunter said that one way to spot them was because they were so pale.[1]

There were many varieties of this two-god belief. Some scholars have tried to trace the Cathars back to the early Gnostic Christians or the Manichians, a late Roman religion that fascinated Saint Augustine for a time.[2] But, while some of the beliefs are similar, it's likely that they were not directly connected.

The religion that became Catharism apparently developed in what is now Bosnia in the mid tenth century and established itself in Bulgaria. The first known preacher of a coherent theology was a Bulgarian priest who named himself Bogomil, which means "worthy of the pity of God."[3] From a sermon we have that was written against them by Cosmos, a tenth-century priest, it seems the Bogomils were one of many groups that wanted to reform the Christian church rather than secede from it. They did not venerate the cross, for why glorify a murder weapon? They pointed out the hypocrisy of many of the church authorities, something that Cosmos was forced to agree with. But he was shocked that they rejected the whole Old Testament and allowed only part of the New Testament.[4]

Cosmos complained that the Bogomils were falsely religious, that they were humble and fasted just for effect. They carried the Gospels with them but misinterpreted it. One of the worst of these mistakes was that "everything exists by the will of the devil: the sky, sun, stars, air, earth, man, churches, crosses: everything which emanates from God, they ascribe to the devil."[5] Finally, these heretics saw no need for priests, confessing instead to each other and forgiving each other.

These two beliefs were what set the dualists apart from other Christians and it was a difference that could not be bridged.

In the mid twelfth century, there were many reform movements. Some were sanctioned by the Church and resulted in new monastic orders, such as the Cistercians and the Franciscans. Some were deemed heretical and forbidden, like the Waldensians and the Cathars. There were many in that time who were dissatisfied with what was happening in their lives and in the world. They were open to alternate beliefs, especially if these were preached using the stories about Jesus that they already knew and if they railed against the corruption of the church administration.

The religion of the Bogomils slowly worked its way into western Europe, following the trade routes through Italy, the Rhineland, and southern France, where it was only one of many that people were being presented with.

For example, in the early twelfth century a preacher named Henry came to the town of Le Mans and asked the bishop, Hildebert, for a license to preach. Hildebert granted it then left for a trip to Rome. When the bishop returned, he discovered that the people had decided to reject the clergy. He was not allowed back into his own town. Eventually, Hildebert regained control. Henry recanted his heresies and went into a monastery. But he was soon out again and off preaching somewhere else.[6] Apart from a strong dislike of the clergy, it's not certain what Henry believed, but that may have been enough to make him popular.

Another man who preached for nearly twenty years (c. 1116–1136) was Peter of Bruys. He spent most of his time in the Rhone Valley, in the southeastern part of France. Some of Peter's "heresies" resurfaced as doctrine in later Protestant churches. His main points were that infant baptism is pointless, for one must be at the age of reason to accept religion; that churches are unnecessary, "since God hears as well when invoked in a tavern as in a church", that the cross, as an instrument of torture, should not be adored; that the Mass is not a sacrament; and that prayers and offerings for the dead are useless, for the dead are beyond human help.[7]

Henry never was punished. Peter tried to burn a cross in the town of St. Gilles and was instead tossed on the fire by the enraged citizens.

Peter and Henry were only two of many wandering preachers. Some of them attracted followers and formed communities. Most of them didn't. Few ever got as far as writing down their doctrines. They were not just in the south of France but all over Europe.

The first hint that the Cathar sect of the Bogomils had come west was in the early 1140s, when the prior of a monastery near Cologne, Germany, wrote to **Bernard of Clairvaux**, asking him to preach against a group of heretics in the area. These had some of the practices of the Cathars, especially that of baptism of adults by the laying on of hands, rather than with water, but we don't know enough about them to be sure.[8]

In 1145, Bernard went south to preach against heretics. At the time, he was concerned with the followers of Peter and Henry but he also ran across some people that his companion and biographer, Geoffrey of Auxerre, called "Arians." He didn't elaborate on them but the implication is that they had a belief about the nature of Christ that differed from the Church's. He thought they were mostly cloth workers and that there "were many who followed this heresy, mostly in this city" [Toulouse].[9] But, as yet, the Cathars were too small a group to attract much attention.

Over the next forty years, however, the Cathar movement exploded throughout Occitania. The reasons for this have been puzzled over for centuries, for in other places they did die out after having some initial success. It seems to have been a combination of a lack of leadership in the local church, the appeal of the doctrine, the commendable behavior of the believers, and an acceptance of women on an equal footing with men. I don't think it's a coincidence that women were in the majority among the Cathars. They were allowed to become priests, and I'm sure that many thought it high time.

Unlike most of the heretical sects, the Cathars were well organized. By the 1160s they had their own priests and bishops.[10] This made them far more visible and far more threatening than other heretical groups. It also meant that members were not supporting their local priests, either morally or financially.

The Cathars were divided into two groups. The majority of them were known as *credentes*, or believers. They tried to live a good life according to the faith, but did not practice the extreme renunciation of the flesh that the second group, the *perfecti*, did. As the name implies, the *perfecti* held themselves to a much higher standard of behavior. Their time was spent in fasting, prayer, and preaching. They were celibate and ate no meat, eggs, or cheese.

At first various orders sent preachers to the Cathars to try to convince them of their errors. Much of the information we have about them comes from arguments written by these preachers, but it is possible to figure out many of the Cathar beliefs from the rebuttals that were made. For instance, "they [the *perfecti*] falsely claimed that they kept themselves chaste, they sought to give the impression of never telling a lie, when they lied constantly, especially concerning God; and they held that one should never for any reason take an oath. . . . They felt, in truth, more secure and unbridled in their sinning because they believed that they would be saved, without restitution of ill-gotten gains, without confession and penance, so long as they were able in the last throes of death to repeat the Lord's Prayer and receive the imposition of hands by their officials."[11]

From this we can assume that they were chaste, tried not to lie, didn't take oaths, and didn't believe in the intercession of priests. They also had a kind of baptism, called the *consolamentum*, that one could take only once. As with baptism in the early days of Christianity, many believers waited until their deathbeds to take this. How many people can be certain that they won't backslide? That's why those who accepted the *consolamentum* early were so honored as perfect ones.

Finally, it was considered by the pope, Innocent III, and many others that the situation was out of control. Even the count of Toulouse, Raymond VI, was considered to be, if not a Cathar, at least a sympathizer.[12] In 1208, Pope Innocent excommunicated Raymond VI and called for a crusade against the Cathars.[13]

The resulting war was long and terrible. At the end, the Cathars were decimated and most of Occitania was under the control of the king of France.

The last stand of the Cathars took place at the fortress of Montségur on top of a rugged mountain in southern France. A group of several hundred had held out against the French army for nearly two years. Finally they realized they would have to surrender. On March 14, 1244, the defenders of the fortress came down the steep path and calmly walked to the pyre that had been prepared for them. Over two hundred men, women, and children died in the flames, including the most important leaders of the church.

A persistent and unsupported legend holds that on the night before the Cathars surrendered and were taken to the pyre, a treasure was lowered down the cliff upon which the Cathar castle of Montségur was perched. Since it is supposed to be a secret treasure important enough to die for, with no evidence that it ever existed, of course some versions of the legend say that it was eventually given to the Templars.

Looking at the fortress of Montségur, I find it hard to imagine how large treasure chests could have been lowered down, by night, with an enemy army all around. I do find it easy to understand how the Cathers and their supporters could have held out there for so long.

So what was the relationship of the Templars to the Cathars?

The fortress of Montségur. *(Sharan Newman)*

A popular but deeply flawed book posited that some of the Cathars were secret Templars and that one of the **Grand Masters**, Bertrand of Blancfort (or Blanchefort), was a Cathar, from a Cathar family, and that the Templars provided a refuge for the Cathars.[14] This is footnoted(!), so I went to see the proofs the authors gave.

The first, that Bertrand was a Cathar, is based on two Templar charters from the 1130s, ten years before there is any mention of Cathars in Occitania.[15] Well, I thought, trying to keep an open mind, maybe the family converted early. However, when I went to look at the charters, I discovered that Bertrand of Blancfort was not in them. It was Bernard de Blanchefort, an entirely different person. They may have been related, but there is no indication of that. Also, the book that the authors used is a compilation of Templar charters from many archives. These particular ones come from the Cartulaires de Douzens, one of the earliest of the Templar commanderies in Occitania.[16] So I went to check that.

The commandery at Douzens has several more charters from Bernard de Blanchefort. All of them are group donations, in which Bernard is giving property along with several of his neighbors. Still, it is established that in the 1130s the family were donating to the Temple. As a matter of fact, in 1147, Bernard's niece gave land to Douzens.[17] Does that mean that the family were Templar supporters? Probably; of course, they may have just been going with the group. Does that mean that Grand Master Bertrand of Blancfort was a member of that family? No. There are a number of Blancfort/Blancheforts in France. We need more evidence.

We also need more evidence for the statement that the family was Cathar, whether or not Bertrand was a member of it. Most of the people in Occitania were not active members of the Cathar church.

What about the charge that the Templars offered shelter to Cathars? The footnote for that is "A document found in the archives of the Bruyères and Mauléon family records how the Templars of Compagne and Albedune (le Bézu) established a house of refuge for Cathar 'bonhommes.' *This document and others disappeared during the war, sometime in November, 1942*" (emphasis mine).[18]

Well, darn!

Apart from lost documents that were apparently never copied, there is no evidence that the Templars had anything to do with the Cathars. They refused to fight against the heretics for the same reason that they refused to join the crusade against Constantinople or get involved in the wars of the popes. Their job was to fight Saracens and regain land for Christianity.

William of Puylaurens, a chronicler of the crusades against the Cathars, rarely mentions the Templars, but when he does, it's always on the side of the Roman Church. When Cathar sympathizer Count Raymond of Toulouse ordered that his brother, Baldwin, be hanged, "The brothers Templar asked for and were granted possession of his body, which they took down from the gallows-tree and buried in the cloister at Lavilledieu near to the church."[19]

It's popular now to think of the crusade against the Cathars as something done by outside forces, the pope and the king of France. But it was also a civil war. Baldwin had taken the side of the Church against his brother. The Templars were on his side.

The same group of Templars also gave shelter to the bishop of Toulouse, who could not get into the city while the Cathars held it.[20]

It's certain that the Templars in Occitania knew Cathars and were even related to some. Everyone was. The schism divided many families.[21] One scholar who has tried to find contacts between the Templars and the Cathars only came up with the names of three men who were tried for heresy, all after their deaths. Each had donated or sold land to the Templars of Mas Deu. Two were found innocent.[22] The third man, Pierre de Fenouillet, had received the last rites and been buried at Mas Deu in 1242. At the trial, twenty years later, it was said that he was a practicing Cathar and that the Templars had allowed the *perfecti* to come to the commandery and give Pierre the *consolamentum*. Pierre was convicted; his bones were dug up and burned.[23]

Did this really happen? I don't know. The Inquisition doesn't have a great record for accuracy, but it's possible. If it is true, does it mean that the Templars of Mas Deu were heretics? No. There are lots of other reasons why they might have allowed Pierre to be buried in their cemetery. If Pierre had been a rich patron or just a good friend, they might have looked the other way. It's hard to refuse the wish of a dying man, especially if he's someone you know and like.

A few years before the death of Pierre de Fenouillet, the commander of Mas Deu had been a witness for the prosecution at the trial of the Cathars.[24]

There is absolutely no evidence that the Templars were Cathars or Cathar sympathizers. The Hospitallers, on the other hand, are known to have taken in and protected Count Raymond VI while he was under excommunication for heresy.[25]

So why weren't the Hospitallers the ones who were supposed to have helped the Cathars save their treasure? It couldn't be because the Templars had been accused of heresy and suppressed and therefore couldn't be questioned about it. Of course not. It is true that the **charges against the Templars** were written with the intention of reminding people of the Cathars, who really had been outside of orthodox belief. But there are no similarities between real belief of the Cathars and those of the Templars. Both groups were accused of worshipping a black cat. Both were accused of homosexuality, the Cathars because they preached against procreation and the Templars because they were a bunch of young fighting men who had taken vows of chastity and we all know what that leads to, don't we?

No serious scholar has ever found a connection between them.

---

1 Cosmos, "Sermon against Bogomilism, 970," in *Heresy and Authority in Medieval Europe*, ed. Edward Peters (University of Pennsylvania Press, 1980) p. 109.

2 Steven Runciman, *The Medieval Manichee: A Study of the Christian Dualist Heresy* (Cambridge University Press, 1947).

3 Peters, "Introduction to the Cathars," in *Heresy and Authority*, p. 104.

4 Cosmos, pp. 112–13.

5 Ibid., pp. 113–14.

6 Walter L. Wakefield and Austin P. Evans ed. and tr., *Heresies of the High Middle Ages* (Columbia University Press, 1969) pp. 107–15.

7 Peter the Venerable, abbot of Cluny, "Against the Petrobrusians," in Wakefield and Evans, pp. 120–21.

8 Beverly Mayne Kienzle, *Cistercians, Heresy and Crusade in Occitania 1145–1229* (York Medieval Press, Boydell, Woodbridge, 2001) pp. 82–84.

9 Geoffrey of Auxerre, "Vita Bernardi," "ex his vero qui favebant haeresi illi plurimi erant et maximi civitatis illius." Bernard of Clairvaux, *Omni Opera*, Vol IV p. 227.

10 Élie Griffe, *L'Aventure Cathare 1140–1190* (Paris, 1966) p. 39.

11 Peter of Vaux-de Cernay, "A Description of Cathazrs and Waldenses," in Wakefield and Evans, p. 239.

12 Joseph Strayer, *The Albigensian Crusades* (Michigan University Press, 1992; rpt. of 1971 ed.) p. 59.

13 Michael Costen, *The Cathars and the Albigensian Crusades* (Manchester University Press, 1997) p. 120.

14 Michael Baigent, Richard Leigh, and Henry Lincoln, *The Holy Blood and the Holy Grail* (New York: Random House, 1982) p. 70. This book needs an entire team of scholars to explain all the mistakes in it. I would be happy to volunteer to be one of them.

15 Marquis d'Albon, *Cartulaire Général de l'Ordre du Temple 1119?–1150* (Paris, 1913) p. 41, charter no. 41, and p. 112, charter no. 160.

16 Ibid., and *Cartulaires des Templier de Douzens* ed. Pierre Gérard and Élisabeth Magnou (Paris, 1965) p. 49, charter no. A 38, and p. 164, charter no. A 185.

17 *Douzens*, pp. 180–81, charter A 207.

18 Baigent et al., p. 515. That's why footnotes are so important.

19 W. A. Sibly and M. D. Sibly tr., *The Chronicle of William of Puylaurens* (Boydell, Woodbridge, 2003) p. 50.

20 Ibid., p. 77.

21 For a start on learning about Cathars, see Malcolm Barber, *The Cathars: Dualist Heretics in Languedoc in the High Middle Ages* (London: Longman, 2000); also Griffe, Strayer, Wakefield and Evans, and Peters, cited above.

22 Robert Vinas, *L'Ordre du Temple en Roussillon* (Trabucaire, Carnet, 2001) p. 113.

23 Ibid., pp. 113–14.

24 Ibid., p. 114.

25 Dominic Sellwood, *Knights of the Cloister: Templars and Hospitallers in Central-Southern Occitania 1100–1300* (Boydell, Woodbridge, 1999) p. 110.

PART FOUR

The Beginning of the Legends

CHAPTER FORTY-TWO

Templars in Fiction

Considering the amount of popular fiction about them today, it may seem odd that Templars appeared very rarely in the epic and romance literature of the Middle Ages and never as the main characters.

The earliest reference to them is in the dark epic *Raoul de Cambrai*. The story, written in the last quarter of the twelfth century, is set in what is today northern France, supposedly in the tenth century. It is a tale of betrayal, honor, murder, and redemption. The Templars only figure in the last of these. At the very end of the story the antihero, Bernier, faced with execution for killing his mother's murderer, volunteers instead to go to Acre and become a Templar as his penance.[1]

The Temple is used as a place of penance in other epics, such as *La Chevalerie d'Ogier de Danemarche* and *Renaut de Montauban*. In *Ogier* the knight is willing to serve in the "Hospital or the Temple" as his penance.[2] This is an early indication that the order of the **Hospitallers** and the Templars were interchangeable in the minds of many people. Like Raoul, the knight in Ogier, named Charlot, is joining the Temple (or Hospital) as penance for the murder of another knight. It is pointed out, by the way, that Charlot is deeply sorry for this and he leaves all his property to Ogier, father of the murdered knight.[3] It was well understood that penance without repentance was useless.

Joining the Templars with the wrong attitude earned no points in heaven.

These popular medieval works of fiction underlined the purpose of the military orders as religious houses. They were seen by the authors as places where a well-born fighting man could atone for his sins of violence by using that violence against the enemies of Christ. This is the aspect of the Templars that was stressed in **Bernard of Clairvaux**'s exhortation to the knights. So in this case, the fictional knights are mirroring the actions of contemporaries and, perhaps, encouraging others to follow their example.

It is surprising that in the many works which make up the epic stories of the crusades, the Templars only appear in a supporting role. In the *Chanson des Chétifs* ("the song of the miserable prisoners," sometimes translated as "the song of the bastards"). The character Harpin is based on a real person who was in captivity during the First Crusade.[4] While in prison the real Harpin made a vow that, if he were ever freed, he would end his life as a monk. He joined the monastery of Cluny in 1109. However, that didn't make good drama, so the author of *Chétifs* has him join the Templars instead.[5]

Again, in the story the Templars exist, but we never see them fighting or taking an active part.

One role that the Templars often played in medieval fiction was as protectors of lovers. In the thirteenth century a number of romances featured lovers who went to the Templars seeking refuge. In *Sone de Nancy*, the Templars help the lovers escape from a queen wishing to have Sone for herself.[6] I wonder if they weren't assigned this role in literature because in reality they and the Hospitallers so often made up the escorts for royal brides on their way to their new homes.

In some epics Templars also are those who arrange for the burial of doomed lovers.[7] Neither of these roles is that important and, for the most part, the Templars are generic examples of kind, pious, and chivalrous men.

The fact is, the Templars were not that important in medieval literature. Unlike **Richard the Lionheart** or **Saladin**, there are no rousing poems extolling their exploits. Why not? I think it's because the

Templars were seen as background. They were a fine group of men doing an important job but not the real players. They were often mentioned in passing as examples of selfless knights, generally to chastise those who neglected their duty. An example is the crusader poet Marcabru, who wrote, "In Spain and here, the Marquis and those of the Temple of Solomon suffer the weight and the burden of pagan pride."[8] Marcabru thinks someone should help.

In modern fiction the Templars are associated with Arthur and the Knights of the Round Table but in medieval lore their only connection with Arthurian literature is as the guardians of the **Grail** in Wolfram von Eschenbach's *Parzival*. The Templars are knights who "dwell with the Grail at Munsalvaesche. Always when they ride out, as they often do, it is to seek adventure. They do so for their sins, these *Tempeleisen*, whether their reward is defeat or victory."[9] The Templars in *Parzival* are a small part of the story, more background than anything else, and they have several characteristics that the real Templars didn't share. For instance, in Wolfram's story there were female *Tempeleisen*.

Apart from a few authors who drew on Wolfram's work, the Templars are not seen in association with the Grail or with the very popular tales of King Arthur and his court. In the world of medieval fantasy, the Templars had no place. By the end of the thirteenth century they were considered more symbols of debauchery than guardians of secret wisdom. The phrase "drunk as a Templar" became commonplace in France. In the sixteenth century, Rabelais uses it in his work. "Once he got together three or four good country fellows and set them to drinking like Templars the whole night long."[10] In Germany, "going to the Temple" was a popular euphemism for visiting a brothel.[11]

For over six hundred years, popular writers didn't consider the Templars worth their time. This changed at the beginning of the nineteenth century, with Sir Walter Scott's two novels *The Talisman* and *Ivanhoe*. Set in the time of the crusades, these works, a blend of history, legend, and imagination, reintroduced the Templars to a world that, outside of **Freemasonry**, had forgotten them.

Scott's villain is Brian de Bois-Guilbert, a Templar who embodies the medieval complaints of pride and greed. Added to these character flaws, Bois-Guilbert also plots against the true king and lusts after the Jewish woman Rebecca. He is the consummate evil adversary in the neomedieval revival that began in Britain in the early nineteenth century.

Ivanhoe was first published in 1820. It has been filmed many times and the book is still in print. Generations have received their first, sometimes their only, impression of the Templars from Scott's rousing fiction.

It is only at the beginning of the twenty-first century that the Templars seem to have come into their own in fiction. The last part of the twentieth century saw an explosion of myths and theories about the Templars, most of which can be categorized with Bigfoot and UFOs. These unhistorical theories yielded a gold mine of plot ideas that are still being refined into fun and exciting stories.

Most recently there have been at least three novels about the Templars. Two, *The Last Templar* by Raymond Khoury and *The Templar Legacy* by Steve Berry, are set in the modern world. They both show how the legend of the Templars can be relevant to concerns that we have today. The third, *The Knights of the Black and White* by Jack White, is a historical novel that uses some of the recent legends, placing them in the time of the real Templars.

It seems a shame that the Templars had to wait seven hundred years to finally be given a starring role in fiction.

---

1 Helen Nicholson, *Love, War and the Grail: Templars, Hospitallers, and Teutonic Knights in Medieval Epic and Romance 1150–1500* (Boston: Brill, 2004) p. 35.

2 Ibid., p. 38.

3 Jean-Charles Payen, *La Motif du Repentir de la Littérature Française Médiévale* (Geneva: Droz, 1968) pp. 212–13.

4 I know that the Templars weren't around then. That didn't bother medieval writers of fiction any more than it does modern ones.

5 Suzanne Duparc-Quioc, *Le Cycle de la Croisade* (Paris, 1955) p. 85. "Au Temple pourservir s'est Harpins adonés."

6 Nicholson, p. 53.

7 Ibid., p. 54.

8 Marcabru, "Pax in Nomine Domini," ll. 55–58 in *Marcabru: A Critical Edition* ed. Simon Gaunt, Ruth Harvey, and Linda Paterson (Cambridge, MA: D. S. Brewer, 2000) p. 440. "En Espaign' e sai lo Marques et cill del temple Salamo soffron lopes e'l fais del orgoill painaor."

9 Wolfrom von Eschenbach, *Parzival*, tr. Helen M. Mustard and Charles E. Passage (New York: Vintage Books, 1961) book 9, paragraph 469, p. 251.

10 François Rabelais, *Gargantua and Pantagruel*, tr. Burton Raffel (Norton, 1990) p. 184.

11 Jean Favier, *Philippe le Bel* (Paris: Fayard, 1998) p. 332.

CHAPTER FORTY-THREE

What Happened to the Templars?

The story of the Templars only begins with their dissolution. Their fate was so dramatic and sad that some people still don't want to let them go. So especially over the past one hundred years the Templars have been woven into all kinds of theories that allow a large number of them to escape, almost always with a treasure.

A lot of people think they know what happened to the Templars after the end of the order. My favorite scenario is that they all either went cheerfully into monasteries and lived long dull lives of prayer and garden duty or they wandered around for a while, met the right girl, and settled down to live long, chaotic, but happy lives.

Unfortunately, there isn't more than a shred of proof for either of these, especially the cheerful and happy parts.

In France we know that fifty-six Templars were burned at the stake. Many more died in prison between 1307 and 1312, as a result of torture, deprivation, and, possibly, outright murder.[1] The remaining French Templars were either sent to monasteries or prisons and swallowed up, as far as history is concerned.

In Britain only two Templars died in prison, William de la More, the master in Britain, and Imbart Blanc, the preceptor from

Auvergne who happened to be in London at the time of the arrests.[2] The rest of them confessed in order to be absolved and were sent off to monasteries, where the Hospitallers paid four pence a day for their upkeep.[3]

In Provence, which was not yet part of France, twenty-one Templars were arrested. The arrests took place on January 24, 1308, two months after **Pope Clement V** issued the order. All twenty-one were eventually imprisoned in Aix. There is no record of a trial ever taking place.[4] In other places outside the control of **Philip IV** the Templars simply did as they did in England: confessed to whatever, were absolved, and retired to a monastic life. But we don't know if that is what happened to those twenty-one men.

This worried historian Joseph-Antoine Durbec, as it would anyone who had studied the Templars long enough to know them. One day, in a list of members of the Hospitallers in Nice in the year 1338, he found two familiar names from the Templars of Provence: Guillaume Bérenger and Rostand Castel. One was from the house of Grasse and the other either from Ruou or Nice. What are the odds, Durbec considered, that two Templars with these names would be the same men as two Hospitallers with the same names thirty years later? He admits that it could be just a coincidence. There is no solid proof. But he wants to believe that two Templars survived.[5] Because if two did, then maybe others did, as well.

Historians have to be hardheaded when they do research, but not hard-hearted.

In Aragon the trials of the Templars didn't take place until after the dissolution of the order. On November 4, 1312, the Templars were all judged to be innocent.[6] That was great for them, of course, but it still left them out of work.

While they had been kept under arrest, their upkeep had been provided for from Templar property. Now the same property was used to pension them off. Unlike the fate of Templars in other countries, most of the brothers in Aragon were not sent to various monasteries, but back to the ones they had come from. Sometimes other people had taken over the house, but the Templars were still assigned rooms in it.

They were also given money for their support according to their status in the order.[7]

These terms were good enough that some Templars who had escaped, returned. One, Bernardo de Fuentes, had become head of the Christian militia in Tunis and returned to Spain on a diplomatic mission. He arranged for his absolution and pension and then returned to Tunis to complete the treaty he had been assigned to arrange.[8]

The king of Aragon, James II, also worked for the release of Templars who had been taken prisoner in Egypt. What they must have felt when they discovered what had gone on since their capture is hard to imagine.

In theory, the ex-Templars were supposed to stay in their assigned houses and live off their pensions, which didn't always arrive on time. In practice, many of the brothers, still in their twenties and thirties, weren't ready for retirement.

They were only trained for one thing, fighting. So quite a few of them signed up as mercenaries in various sorties against the Moors in Spain or even in Africa. Some ignored the old vow not to fight against Christians and enlisted to fight for Aragonese noblemen. One, Jaime de Mas, turned pirate and seems to have made a good living at it.[9]

Pope John XXII heard about the unclerical lives many of the ex-Templars were leading and sent a letter telling them to stop living like laymen: to get rid of their concubines, behave more like monks, and stop wearing striped clothing.[10]

This letter and others were largely ignored and the Templars in Aragon continued to live in a variety of ways, according to age and taste. The Hospitallers, once they had managed to get the Templar property, were stuck paying their pensions. The last year one was recorded was to Berenguer de Coll. It was 1350, thirty-eight years after the Templars had officially ceased to exist.[11]

In Portugal a new order was created from the Templar property, called the Order of Montesa.[12] Some former Templars joined this.

In the Germanic countries, the Templars had also all been acquitted, so the Hospitallers had to pay pensions to them as well. Because many of them came from influential local families, their fate was much milder than in other areas. Otto of Brunswick both took the pension and took over the Hospitaller commandery at Süpplingenberg. He was commander there until 1357 and, after he died, the Hospitallers had to pay nine hundred marks to get the commandery back.[13]

In Mainz, the Templar property was kept by the family of two of the Templars. The Hospitallers had to buy it back from them.[14]

So in many cases, the Templars in Germany just went on being Templars. Others probably followed like patterns. Some entered other military or monastic orders. Others may have felt that, without an order, their vows were no longer valid. So they found work, got married, and settled down.

The truth is, there isn't much information on what happened to many of the Templars after the order ended. Most of them were not noblemen and so not likely to show up on donation charters or in chronicles. The ones we do know about were those who did something unusual, like turn pirate. Others got into less dramatic trouble with the law. But, other than that, they just drifted back into private life.

MANY feel that is just too dull an ending for the Templars. Therefore, a number of books, articles, television programs, and films have been based on the idea that the Templars got away. One of the most popular theories is that they went to America, sometimes via Scotland, sometimes Portugal. And they took their "treasure" with them.

Well, someone had to pave all the streets with gold, right?

Obviously, fiction is fiction, and novels, television shows, and movies can rewrite history as much as they would like. The confusion, however, in separating fact from fiction arises when this fiction is based on faulty theories put forth in books published as nonfiction. I've read these books and found reading them tough going. The "facts" they give remind me of why I am inflicting so many footnotes on my patient readers. I want you to know what sources my conclusions are based on. Many times I would find that the information I found least believable in these books had no footnotes. Other times there were footnotes but only to other books that give unsubstantiated opinions.

I'll try to summarize what I think the main erroneous Templar theories are. It's not easy. To do this properly one must be like the White Queen in *Through the Looking-Glass*, who could believe six impossible things before breakfast.

1. The Templars had some secret knowledge. They may have dug it up under the **Temple in Jerusalem** or learned it from the Arabs or maybe aliens. It varies.

2. They knew in advance that they were going to be arrested and had time to get their treasure out from under the nose of **Philip the Fair** and to their fleet in La Rochelle in Normandy. The number of ships ranges from four to eighteen. That's a lot of treasure to take along French backroads. They couldn't have taken it down the river because there were tolls collected all along the rivers and someone would have noticed. And, of course, no one has proved there was a treasure in the first place. Nevertheless, we should forge on.

3. The Templars made it to Scotland, where they were greeted by the Sinclair family, who are descended from Vikings and Jesus. The knights fought with Robert the Bruce at Bannockburn. That's actually not impossible. Fighting is what they were trained for, after all. But in Scotland, the ex-Templars are also said to have gotten into building and navigation, because they were training to be **Freemasons**. Part of this conclusion seems to be based on the idea that Templars built churches.[15] Now, most of us when we say we're building a house don't mean we're pouring cement and hanging drywall, although I have friends who can and do. The Templars didn't. They hired people to build their churches, farm their lands, wash their clothes, and pick their grapes. They had to spend half the day at prayers and much of the rest of it taking care of their horses and gear and practicing how to kill Saracens without getting killed. There wasn't time left over to learn another trade.

There is nothing in the **Rule** about taking an hour to lay bricks or study Euclidian geometry.

4. Henry Sinclair, prince of Orkney, was not only of the "Holy Bloodline," supposed descendants of Jesus, but a secret Templar, and he or one of his family took a band of Templar knights to America, along with the treasure. This treasure is now hidden on an island off Novia Scotia.[16]

5. While in America they wandered as far as Minnesota and also built a tower in Rhode Island. I don't know who built this tower or when, but one explanation says that it is Romanesque and based on the round churches that the Templars introduced to Europe and they were helped by a party of Cistercian monks, who were well known for their engineering skills, which allowed them to control commerce. Wow. Romanesque churches are not round and the style began over a hundred years before the Templar order was founded. They did not introduce round churches to Europe. Cistercians did invent some practical machinery and were good at diverting water for irrigation and waterwheels. They didn't build cathedrals any more than I built my own house. And I can't see them traveling to America with a bunch of Templars. The Cistercians frown on gadabout monks.

And that's just from two paragraphs in one book. Not daunted, I shall conclude with . . .

6. The Templar treasure was then buried under New York City and the Templars battened down to wait for the founding of the United States so that their beliefs could live again.

I didn't make any of this up.

There are no footnotes in the last half of this chapter because none of the books I consulted used any. Their authors want the reader to believe all of this on their word alone.

In the Middle Ages, belief without proof was called Religion.

1 Please see chapter 30, **The Arrest and Trials of the Templars.**
2 Evelyn Lord, *The Knights Templar in Britain* (London: Longman, 2002) p. 200.
3 Ibid., p. 200.
4 Joseph-Antoine Durbec, *Templiers et Hospitalliers en Provence et dans les Alpes-Maritimes* (Grenoble, 2001) p. 268.
5 Ibid., p. 269.
6 Alan Forey, *The Fall of the Templars in the Crown of Aragon* (Ashgate, Aldershot, 2001) p. 210.
7 Ibid., p. 213.
8 Ibid., p. 216.
9 Ibid., p. 222.
10 Ibid., p. 226.
11 Ibid., p. 240.
12 Malcom Barber, *The Trial of the Templars* (Cambridge University Press, 2006) p. 275.
13 Karl Borchardt, "The Templars in Central Europe," *The Crusades and the Military Orders: Expanding the Frontiers of Medieval Latin Christianity* ed. Zsolt Hunyadi and Josef Laszlovszky (Budapest: Central Hungarian University, 2001) p. 239.
14 Ibid.
15 Lynn Picknett and Clive Prince. *The Templar Revelation.* (NY: Simon and Schuster, 1998) pp. 110–13.
16 Steven Sora. *The Lost Treasure of the Knights Templar* (Rochester VT: Destiny Books, 1999) p. 177ff.

✣

CHAPTER FORTY-FOUR

The Holy Grail

I n any discussion of the Holy Grail, one thing must be clearly understood:

THE GRAIL IS FICTION. IT DOESN'T EXIST AND NEVER DID.

I know that recently some imaginative writers have decided that "Holy Grail"—*San Greal*—is simply a misprint for *Sang Real*, "Royal Blood," and that medieval writers were using it as a code for a hidden secret. This is cute but there are a number of problems in the theory, the most important being that this only works in modern Spanish. Old French, the language of the first Grail poems, would write it *Saint Graal, Grel*, or even *Gresal*.[1] Spelling was an art form in the Middle Ages. The Old French word *grail* meant "grill," as in "barbeque." Malory, in the fifteenth century, called it the *Sankgreall*. "Thys ys he by whom the Sankgreall shall be encheved."[2] The German, used by Wolfram von Eschenbach, is *Helligen Grâl*.[3] The Basque is *azken afarian Kristiok erabili*," or "Christ's last meal stirred liquid."[4] (All right, my Basque is minimal.)

At any rate, in no other language of the Middle Ages can "Holy Grail" be twisted to mean "Holy Blood."

Are we all convinced?

Now we can look at the history of the tale of the Grail and its connection to the Templars.

Detail of Holy Grail, "Roman de Tristan," second half of the fifteenth century.
(Giraudon/Art Resource, NY)

The first story mentioning the Grail was written by the poet Chrétien de Troyes at the end of the twelfth century. It concerns a young knight, Perceval, who stops for the night at a castle. There he discovers a lord who is bedridden. The lord greets Perceval and invites him to stay the night. As they are eating dinner, a strange procession passes through the room. First comes a man carrying a lance. At the tip of it is one drop of blood, which slides down the lance until it reaches the hand of the man carrying it. He is followed by two other servants, each with a tray of candles. After them is a beautiful girl who holds in both hands a "graal," or vessel of gold covered in precious gems. She is followed by another girl carrying a silver platter.

Perceval is very curious about this but has been told that it's rude to ask questions, so he says nothing. The next day he leaves the castle. Some distance away he finds a young woman sitting under an oak tree, sobbing because her lover has just had his head chopped off. She stops her lamentation long enough to tell Perceval that he has been at the castle of the Fisher King, who has been crippled in battle. She can't believe that he didn't ask why the lance bled or where the girl was going with the graal. If he had, the king would have been cured. Perceval grieves that he has missed the opportunity to heal the king. Then he continues on with other adventures. The story moves to Gawain and never returns to Perceval or the Grail.

We don't know where Chrétien got the material for the tale of Perceval. It was composed for Philip of Alsace, the count of Flanders, who was the cousin of Henry II of England. Henry and his wife, Eleanor of Aquitaine, were fond of the Arthurian legends. Eleanor was even at Glastonbury when the supposed bodies of Arthur and Guinevere were disinterred in 1191. Philip was also the grandson of **Fulk of Anjou**, king of Jerusalem. Both his parents had been to Jerusalem several times and his mother, Sybilla, had joined a convent there, where she died.

The idea for the Grail may have come from a Breton story or even Welsh, since Perceval is said by Chrétien to be from Wales. In the Welsh saga, *The Mabinogian*, the story of Culhwch and Olwen has a passage in it where the hero must find the cup of Llwyr, "for there is no vessel in the world which can hold that strong drink, save it."[5] Next he must get the "food bag of Gwyddneu Long-Shank: if the whole world should come around it . . . the meat that everyone wished for he would find therein."[6] These tasks are part of a long series of seemingly impossible feats that must be done if Culhwch is to win the hand of Olwen. The magic cup and food bag are in the same tradition as the horn of plenty. It isn't likely that Chrétien read Welsh, but various scholars have suggested that the theme for Perceval came from a tradition that would have been familiar to his listeners.[7]

While not everyone agrees with the theory that the story grew from Celtic myth, I tend to think that parts of his Grail legend are an attempt by Chrétien to make sense of a myth that he doesn't really understand. One example of this is when the woman under the tree explains to Perceval that the lord is called the Fisher King because he likes to go fishing.[8] But this may have just been Chrétien's sense of humor.

Perhaps if Chrétien had told the reader what he had in mind for the Grail, it would not have become such an object of mystery and speculation. But the story caught the imagination of many and over the next fifty years a number of Grail stories were written, usually as part of the Arthurian legends.

The word "graal" was in common use in France then. It meant a vessel or a goblet.[9] However, in the grail stories, it soon came to mean a chalice. It was in the thirteenth-century work by Robert de Baron that the word "holy" began to be used with it, as the Grail became identified with the story of Joseph of Arimathea, who provided the tomb for Jesus.[10] In Christian apocrypha Joseph was also supposed to have used a dish to catch the blood of Jesus as he was dying on the cross.[11] A much later legend had Joseph, like Mary Magdalene and James, the patriarch of Jerusalem, finding refuge in Europe, in this case, England.

As legends tend to run together, it was a short step from this to making the Grail the cup that caught the blood and Joseph a part of the Arthurian body of tales.

A thirteenth-century version of the Perceval story gives Joseph of Arimathea a nephew, also named Joseph, who is a "good knight, chaste and a virgin in his body, strong and generous of heart."[12] This is the man who becomes the Fisher King and guards "the lance with which Jesus was wounded and the cup with which those who believed in Him . . . collected the blood that flowed from his wounds while he was being crucified."[13] But many other authors gave other names to the king and other explanations for the Grail. Since the story had no basis in fact, writers were free to imagine anything they liked.

In the later medieval French romances the Grail was clearly seen as a Christian relic, something associated with the act of transubstantiation in the Mass. In several of them, the vision of the Grail includes that of a child or of Jesus on the cross.[14]

It is only in Wolfram von Eschenbach's German version that the Templars are connected with the Grail. Wolfram makes the Grail a stone, fallen from the sky. It has magical powers that give health and eternal youth. The power of the stone, however, comes from a "small white wafer" brought by a dove every year on Good Friday. "And from that the stone derives whatever good fragrances of drink and food there are on earth, like to the perfection of Paradise. . . . Thus, to the knightly brotherhood, does the power of the Grail give sustenance!"[15] The knightly brotherhood is, of course, the *Tempeleisen*, the guardians of the Grail. This was based loosely on the Templars. However, unlike the Templars, there are women in the *Tempeleisen*.[16]

Even though there might be a folkloric base for some of the plot, there is no doubt in any of the Grail stories that the author is a Christian. I see no problem with Wolfram making the Templars guardians of the Grail. When he was writing in the early thirteenth century, the Templars were still seen as those who protected the way for pilgrims to Jerusalem. They might well have been added to the story to make it more immediate, as thriller writers put known organizations in their books to place them firmly in the current time. However, Wolfram and those who drew their stories from his were the only ones who used the Templars in the Grail story. It was not part of the core tradition.

In an interesting study, an art historian has pointed out images of the Virgin Mary in several twelfth-century churches in the north of Spain in which she is holding a dish from which rays of light radiate. He thinks that this might represent the gifts of the Holy Spirit and could be a basis for the Grail story.[17] This is intriguing and needs to be followed up by scholars in other areas of Medieval Studies. The main problem is in connecting the authors of the first Grail stories to northern Spain. There is no evidence to support this. A link in other art or literature would be very exciting.

Unfortunately, information like this is too often taken up by people without historical training. They look at the image and fit it into their own pet theories without doing the background research, as we saw with the term *San Greal* earlier.

Although there is a certain common thread, all the medieval stories about the Grail have a different emphasis. That's because they are fiction and not intended to be historical accounts. Like the rest of the Arthurian stories, those about the Grail reflect the outlook of the authors and the times in which they lived. At the end of the fifteenth century, when Thomas Malory made his English version of the legend of Arthur, the Grail stories were about the adventures and duties of a Christian knight. Most listeners understood that the magical quests were fantasy and they enjoyed them as many people do science fiction today.

However, the stories about King Arthur and the Grail lost popularity soon after Malory wrote. The message of the Grail was too full of imagery from the Mass to be acceptable to the newly formed Protestant denominations. Along with this, taste in literature changed. "The coming of the Reformation was the moment at which the Grail vanished from poetic imagination."[18]

But two centuries later, it appeared again, in an entirely new form. In the eighteenth century the fashion arose for secret societies. Perhaps it was in reaction to the egalitarian beliefs that would produce the American and French revolutions. Perhaps all that rational thought and enlightenment was unfulfilling. I don't really know. But groups such as the Rosicrucians and **Freemasons** borrowed freely from arcane texts and mystical treatises of the medieval and ancient world, taking symbols from them and creating new meanings. The Grail was one of these symbols.

The connection between the Templars and the Grail seems to have been reestablished through the efforts of an Austrian named Joseph von Hammer-Purgstall. In 1818 he wrote a book that condemned the Masons as a group of heretics directly connected to the Templars and Gnostics. "The conclusion of his work is that a pagan religion survived alongside Catholicism into the Middle Ages, and in the guise of Freemasonry, remained a threat to the Church even in the early nineteenth century."[19]

At the same time that the mystical aspects of the Grail were mutating, nineteenth-century-romantic writers and artists were creating their own versions of the stories. Tennyson's *Idylls of the King* was arguably the most popular of these in English. In Germany, Wagner's operas *Parsival* and *Lohengrin* combined the renewed interest in national origins with his own image of Christianity.

It was the twentieth century that took the Grail to unexplored territory. For the most part, it was still entwined with the story of Arthur, Guinevere, Lancelot, Perceval, and Galahad. But these familiar characters appeared in totally different forms. The Grail could be a pagan vessel, as in Marian Zimmer Bradley's *The Mists of Avalon* or a made-up excuse to get out of the house, as in Mark Twain's *A Connecticut Yankee in King Arthur's Court*. In the film *Monty Python and the Holy Grail* it was a pointless quest. None of these modern stories mention the Templars in connection to the Grail.

A whole generation has the Grail and the Templars forever combined thanks to Steven Spielberg and Indiana Jones. However, the knight in the film is never called a Templar. He is only the most worthy of three brothers who found the Grail. In this version, the cup never came to Europe but stayed in a hidden place that looks remarkably like the ancient city of Petra.

Today the Grail is still as much a mysterious symbol to us as it was to medieval listeners. As was true then, the Grail is something different for each person. No two people have ever completely agreed on what the Grail looks like, never mind what it represents. But in current usage today the Holy Grail is everywhere. Awards are "the Holy Grail of Beach Volleyball" for instance. The Holy Grail of a collector is that one rare piece that has been rumored to exist but never seen. It's the goal just out of reach.

Dan Brown put it very well at the end of *The Da Vinci Code*: "the Holy Grail is simply a grand idea . . . a glorious unattainable treasure that somehow, even in today's world of chaos, inspires us."[20]

At the end of his excellent study of the Grail legend, Richard Barber gives a listing of the number of times the term "the Holy Grail" has been used in major Western newspapers from 1978 to 2002. In 1978 there were sixteen uses (fifteen in the *Washington Post*). In 2002 alone, there were 1,082.[21]

The fact that recent fiction has attached the Grail to the Templars says more about how we see the Templars now than what they were in reality. Perhaps it says that we prefer our Templars to be fictional.

---

1 Larousse, *Dictionnaire de l'Ancien Francais* (Paris, 1992) p. 296. Also, Fredéric Godefroye, *Lexique de l'Ancien Français* (Paris, 1990) p. 261. Both dictionaries give the first meaning as "cup" or "vase."

2 Thomas Malory, *Works* ed. Eugéne Vinaver (London, 1971) p. 519.

3 Matthias Lexer, *Mittel-hochdeutsches Taschen-wörterbuch* p. 75.

4 Gorka Aulesti and Linda White, *Basque-English, English-Basque Dictionary* (Reno: University of Nevada Press, 1992) p. 516.

5 *Mabinogian*, ed. and tr. Gwyn Jones and Thomas Jones (Everyman's Library, 1949) p. 82.

6 Ibid.

7 Richard Barber, *The Holy Grail, Imagination and Belief* (London: Putnam, 2004) pp. 240–43.

8 "Perceval le Gallois ou le Conte du Graal," tr. Lucien Foulet, in Danielle Régnier-Bohler, ed., *La Légende Arthurienne, le Graal et la Table Ronde* (Paris: Robert Laffont, 1989) p. 47.

9 Frédéric Godefroy, *Lexique de l'Ancien Français* (Paris: Champion, 1990) p. 261.

10 Matthew 27:57–60.

11 Gospel of Nicodemus.

12 Christiane Marchello-Nizia, "Perlesvaus, le Haut Livre du Graal," in Régnier-Bohler, p. 121. (English translation mine)

13 Ibid., p. 124. (English translation mine)

14 Barber, p. 112. I find it interesting that these legends were at their most popular in the first half of the thirteenth century, when the crusade against the Cathars was at its height (Barber mentions this) and when anti-Semitism was on the rise, along with the beginning of the libel that Jews stole and desecrated the Host. But that is another subject altogether and I'll refrain from following it here.

15 Wolfram von Eschenbach, *Parzival* tr. Helen M. Mustard and Charles E. Passage (New York: Vintage Books, 1961) book 9, paragraph 470, p. 252.

16 Ibid., book 9, paragraph 471.

17 Joseph Goering, *The Virgin and the Grail: Origins of a Legend* (New Haven: Yale University Press, 2005).

18 Ibid., p. 223.

19 Ibid., pp. 308–9.

20 Richard Barber, p. 444.

21 Ibid., p. 380. I hope I added it correctly, but that's the rough amount.

※

CHAPTER FORTY-FIVE

Templars in Denmark:
Bornholm Island

There are no records of any Templar activity in Denmark.[1]
I realize that recently a book, *The Templars' Secret Island*,[2] has made a case for the Templars living in round churches on the Danish island of Bornhom, just off the south coast of Sweden. The authors of this book, Elring Haagensen and Henry Lincoln, further state that the Templars used this island for mystical astronomical study. Part of this book contains geometric studies of possible results the Templars might have come up with on Bornholm. But first they give historical background to prove that the scholars are completely wrong in their belief that the Templars never settled in the area. The trouble is the history is based on a few pieces of data and several assumptions that rely on inaccurate information.

First, let's look at the "historical" narrative as given in this book and how it doesn't match known information.

I have already given a short essay on **Bernard of Clairvaux** and his connection to the Templars. The story of his life in *The Templars' Secret Island*, doesn't exactly agree with the information I found. In fact, it sometimes directly contradicts it.

The biography begins with the standard information about Bernard's birth and entry into the monastery of Citeaux.[3] The footnote for this is the *Catholic Encyclopedia*, 1913. This is the same version that is in the online *Catholic Encyclopedia* of 1917, which is online because it has been replaced in print by an updated version.[4] But it's essentially the same information concerning Bernard. So far, so good.

The authors continue to say, as is also well established, that Eudes I, the duke of Burgundy, had donated the funds to keep the monastery going in the early days. The next lines are: "The Burgundian nobility seemed unquestionably to be deeply involved in the Order's creation. The Abbot of Citeaux was *ex officio* Prime Counsellor of the Burgundian Parliament with the right to sit at the assembly of the States General of the Kingdom, as well as the Province of Burgundy."[5]

There is no footnote for this piece of news and I am very disappointed because, as far as we know, there was no Burgundian Parliament in 1113. The first one was in 1349 at Beaune.[6] The Estates-General of France began as a mandatory meeting attended by members of the nobility, bourgeois, and clergy at the order of the king. This happened now and then in the thirteenth century, but didn't get going again until the fourteenth century.[7] And, of course the Burgundian Parliament, even if it had existed, wouldn't have mattered to the Estates-General because Burgundy didn't become a part of France until 1316. Before that it was part of the Holy Roman Empire.[8]

I think that if the authors have really discovered that these institutions existed two hundred years before any records have been found for them, they should share their sources. Graduate students the world over are hungry for thesis topics.

Now, having established in the mind of the reader that the Cistercians were movers and shakers at the court of Burgundy, the authors then go over the history of the foundation of the Templars and Bernard's part in it (a subject I discussed in the section on Bernard). Then they take the connection another step further, linking Bernard and the Cistercians to the establishment of the crusader kingdoms.

One statement they make is that "Godfrey of Bouillon and Baudwin [Baldwin, first Latin king of Jerusalem] were of the nobility of Lower Lorraine, the dukedom adjacent to Burgundy and of course, Clairvaux [the monastery founded by Bernard]."[9] The authors apparently never bothered to look at a map, odd since so much of the book is based on geographic connections. In the eleventh century, Lorraine was just north of Champagne and affiliated with the county of Flanders. While borders have changed, the land hasn't moved. Burgundy is, and was, much farther south. Clairvaux, just north of Dijon, was not in existence when the First Crusade took place.[10]

From this and other equally inaccurate or unconnected statements, the authors come to the conclusion that Bernard of Clairvaux was "the real—if covert—Grand Master of the Templars."[11] It's true that Bernard was an early and enthusiastic supporter of the Templars but I'd need more proof to believe that he directed their actions, especially based on an inaccurate assumption of the secular power of the Cistercians along with a conclusion that relies on mistakes in chronology and geography.

Let's move on to the Danish connection.

Eskil, archbishop of Lund (in Sweden) from 1137 to 1177, was a big fan of Bernard of Clairvaux. Eskil was a progressive bishop in many ways. He has been called "the first European from the North."[12] He came from a rich family in what is now Sweden and was educated in the cathedral schools of Germany.[13] His uncle Asser was archbishop of Lund and it is reasonable to think that the family expected Eskil to follow him. Eskil was determined to drag Denmark into the modern world of the twelfth century. This was shown by his enthusiasm for the new religious orders. In the first half of the twelfth century, the Cistercians were the latest thing. Bernard of Clairvaux was arguably the most famous monk in Europe at that time. In 1144, Eskil asked to have a group of Cistercian monks come to Denmark to establish a monastery there and to show Danish monks the customs of the order.[14]

Just the year before, at the request of the king and queen of Sweden, the Cistercians had sent monks to start two monasteries in that country.[15] They were happy to send monks from Citeaux to Denmark to start the monastery of Herrisvad, as well.

Eskil's main goal for his archbishopric was to make it truly Scandinavian, free of its dependence on the archbishopric of Hamburg-Bremen.[16] Eskil's uncle Asser had convinced the papal legate under Pope Paschal II (1099–1118) to create the archbishopric of Lund—in Sweden, but Hamburg continued to lobby for its return to German dominance.[17] This struggle for primacy was very important to the bishops and archbishops of Europe. A great number of the church councils of the twelfth century spent a large part of their time in the very bitter wrangling over who answered to whom.[18]

Eskil was also hampered by the problems within the Danish royal succession. This, in turn, was tied to the struggle for the control of the Scandinavian church. In the late 1150s Eskil supported Knut Magnussen for the throne. Knut's rival was Swein, who was supported by the German emperor, Frederick Barbarossa. Frederick's relative by marriage was Hartwig, archbishop of Bremen, who wanted to return the archbishopric of Lund to submission to Hamberg-Bremen. Now, Pope Hadrian IV (1154–1159) was in conflict with Emperor Frederick about a number of other things. So Eskil was a strong supporter of Pope Hadrian, who returned the support by making Eskil a papal legate.[19]

(If you want to take out a notebook and start making diagrams of the connections, I wouldn't blame you. Use different colored pens; it helps.)

Eskil had met the pope when he was still called Nicholas Breakspear. The future Hadrian IV was leader of the delegation sent by Pope Eugenius III to set about dividing the Scandinavian archbishopric into two new ones, Sweden and Norway. The pope also wanted to see that the custom of collecting "Peter's pence," a tax to support the papacy, was established in the north.[20] When the delegation arrived in 1152, Eskil was at Clairvaux, meeting with Bernard and collecting more monks for a new Danish monastery.[21] He returned in time to convince Nicholas not to divide his archbishopric at this time.

Nicholas was elected pope shortly after his return to Rome in 1154. In 1156 or 1157 Eskil made the journey to Rome, at which time he was made permanent papal legate in Scandinavia.[22] However, on the way home, while going through Burgundy (a part of the Holy Roman

Empire, see above) he was kidnapped, perhaps by supporters of Emperor Frederick. Pope Hadrian wrote a letter of rebuke to the emperor that was read at an imperial diet held at Besançon in October 1157. Due to a mistranslation of the letter from Latin into German, the emperor took offense and, in the ensuing fuss, Eskil seems to have been forgotten.[23] He was released at some point before Hadrian's death on September 1, 1159.

The dispute that followed Eskil's imprisonment, which had little to do with him, escalated after the death of Hadrian. The struggle, which lasted for centuries between the papacy and the Holy Roman Emperors, caused two popes to be elected at the same time. The first, supported by Eskil, was Alexander III. The other, supported by the emperor and Denmark's new king, Valdemar, was named Victor IV. Eskil didn't want to have to choose between King Valdemar and the popes, and so he kept away from Denmark. He wandered about Europe and made a pilgrimage to Jerusalem at some point between 1161 and 1167. There he could have met the Grand Master of the Templars, Bertrand of Blancfort, but we have no record of such a meeting. It's quite possible that Bertrand was not even in Jerusalem at the time of Eskil's visit.[24]

In 1177, Eskil resigned his bishopric and retired to become a monk at Clairvaux.[25] He spent his last four years as a simple monk and often regaled the younger brothers with stories of his friendship with their founder, Bernard.[26] He died there in 1181.

While he admired Bernard greatly and chose to end his life at the monastery he founded, Eskil was friends with other monastic leaders, notably Peter, abbot of Celle in Champagne.[27] He wrote to both of the abbots in friendship, asking for advice and sharing his problems and frustrations. They wrote him letters of support.

So what has this to do with proving that there were Templars in Denmark? Nothing that I can see. Because Eskil and Bernard were friends, and Bernard was a supporter of the Templars, there was no reason for Eskil to establish the Templars in Denmark. Nor is there any indication that he did so.

As I have already said, there is no sign at all of the Templars ever having had a commandery in Denmark. The Hospitallers had a

Scandinavian province that was made up of Denmark and Norway but that order seems to have concentrated its efforts in the region on the hospital side rather than the military.[28]

Well, it may have been that there were Templars in Denmark but that all the documents have been lost. So, let's look at the physical evidence as presented by the believers.

The churches on the island of Bornholm are indeed round. That is indisputable. We can see them, touch them, and walk around them. However, one can't assume that because a church is round, it was built by Templars. For a time after the First Crusade there was a vogue for them all over Europe.

The idea of building a church in the form of the Church of the Holy Sepulcher in Jerusalem wasn't new. A hundred years before the Templar order was founded, the Benedictine church at Saint-Benigne at Dijon was built with a round nave in imitation of the Holy Sepulcher, as were the churches at Lanleff, Saint-Bonnet-la-Rivière, Rieux-Minervois, and Montmorillon, all in different parts of France.[29] In most of these churches, there are four or eight columns inside. However, "the churches on Bornholm have one central column. They are simply a different type."[30]

Even the Hospitallers built round churches.[31] If the churches on Bornholm are connected to any military order, it would make more sense that it would be the Hospitallers, whom we know were in Denmark, or even the Teutonic Knights. But that would ruin the hypothesis. For some reason, it has to be Templars or nothing.

One shouldn't try to build a very complicated theory based on the idea that Templars were in Denmark, because the basic premise is too shaky to support much of anything. It is based on a lack of understanding of historical data and many leaps in which the logic is not supported. I wouldn't want to risk standing on it.

One positive thing that has come out of this imaginative and unhistorical theory of Templars in Denmark is that it has made serious historians stop and say, "We know there is no evidence for Templars here, but why weren't they in Denmark? What was different about Denmark (and all of Scandinavia) that this didn't happen?" Since it takes much more time to do serious research than to build a castle in the air, few papers have come out on the subject yet, but I look forward to them.

I wish I could believe that my explanations would clear up the confusion surrounding these very badly researched ideas about the Templars. But I don't hold out much hope. What chance do plodding historians have against Mr. Haagensen and Mr. Lincoln, a filmmaker and a journalist, neither of whom seem to feel compelled to waste their time combing through dusty archives for proof?

---

1 Vivian Etting, "Crusade and Pilgrimage: Different Ways to the City of God," in *Medieval History Writing and Crusading Ideology*, ed. Tuomas M. S. Lehtonen and Kurt Villads Jensen (Helsinki: Finnish Literary Society, 2005) p. 187. "However the [Hospitaller] Order had no military functions in Denmark and the competing Order of the Knights Templars [*sic*] was never established in Scandinavia."

2 Elring Haagensen and Henry Lincoln, *The Templars' Secret Island* (Barnes and Noble, 2002).

3 Ibid., p. 29.

4 http://www.newadvent.org/cathen/02498d.htm

5 Haagensen and Lincoln, p. 29.

6 Ferdinand Lot and Robert Fawtier, *Histoire de Institutions Françaises au Moyen Age, Tome II, Institutions Royales* (Paris: Presses Universitaires de France, 1958) p. 486.

7 Achille Luchaire, *Institutions Française* (Paris, 1892) pp. 201–2.

8 Georges Duby, *France in the Middle Ages 987–1460*, tr. Juliet Vale (Oxford: Blackwell, 1991) p. 285.

9 Haagensen and Lincoln, p.153. At least Mr. Lincoln now knows that Godfrey of Bouillon was not king of France, as was stated in one of his earlier books (*The Holy Blood and the Holy Grail*). Bravo!

10 Clairvaux was founded in 1115. See Louis J. Lekai, *The Cistercians: Ideas and Reality* (Kent State University Press, 1977) p. 19.

11 Haagensen and Lincoln, p. 30.

12 Brian Patrick McGuire, *The Difficult Saint* (Kalamazoo, MI: Cistercian Publications, 1991) p. 126, quoting Lauritz Weibull.

13 Ibid., p. 109. For more on the cathedral schools, see C. Stephen Jaeger, *The Envy of Angels: Cathedral Schools and Social Ideals in Medieval Europe 950–1200* (University of Pennsylvania Press, 1994).

14 Ibid., p. 110.

15 Brian Patrick McGuire, *The Cistercians in Denmark* (Kalamazoo, MI: Cistercian Publications, 1982) p. 40.

16 McGuire, *Saint*, p. 110.

17 Anders Bergquist, "The Papal Legate: Nicholas Breakspear's Scandinavian Mission," in *Adrian IV: The English Pope (1154–1159)*, ed. Brenda Bolton and Anne J. Duggan (Ashgate, Aldershot, 2003) p. 41.

18 There are many examples, but the one I know best is the 1148 Council of Rheims, during which the archbishop of Tours demanded primacy over the bishopric of Dol. But that's a subject for

another book and probably not one that would interest anyone but die-hard students of ecclesiastical government.

19 I. S. Robinson, *The Papacy 1073–1198* (Cambridge University Press, 1990) p. 467.

20 Bergquist, p. 42.

21 McGuire, *Saint*, p. 110.

22 Johanis Mabillon ed., *Sancti Bernardi Opera Omnia* Vol. I (Paris, 1889) col. 948. "Eskilum non-modo archiepiscopum Lundensem in Danis, sed et primatem Succiae et decretoAdriani IV papae fuisse lego."

23 Robinson, pp. 466–70; Bergquist, p. 47.

24 Please see chapter 15, **Grand Masters 1136–1189**, for more about Bertrand.

25 McGuire, *Saint*, p. 111.

26 Geoffrey of Auxerre, "Bernardi Abbatis Vita I," in Mabillon, Vol. IV, cols. 2229–30.

27 Mabillon, Vol. 1, col. 948.

28 Helen Nicholson, *The Knights Hospitaller* (Woodbridge, UK: Boydell and Brewer, 2001).

29 Henry de Curzon, *La Maison du Temple de Paris* (Paris, 1888) p. 87.

30 Prof. Kurt Villads Jensen, private correspondence, October 10, 2006.

31 Nicholson, p. 7.

CHAPTER FORTY-SIX

The Templars and the Shroud of Turin

As far as I can tell, the Templars became attached to the story of the Shroud of Turin through a coincidence. Since the shroud has become part of the lore of the Templars we'll need to go over the history of it, as far as is known. I have no intention of exploring what the shroud is or how, when, and where it was made, only the way the Templars were brought into its orbit.

In the thirteenth century, the Church of St. Marie de Blakerne in Constantinople claimed to have the burial shroud of Jesus. I haven't been able to find out how they got it or when but it was there in 1204 when the Fourth Crusade decided to bypass the Holy Land and conquer Constantinople instead. According to Robert de Clari, a chronicler and participant in the crusade, "There is another church that is called Madam Saint Mary of Blakerne, where the *sydoine* which Our Lord was wrapped in was. Every Friday it would raise itself upright so that one could see well the figure of Our Lord; but there is no one, not Greek or French, who knows where the *sydoine* went when the city was taken."[1]

I must admit that this is the sort of information that makes a novelist's eyes light up. A missing relic, stolen in the midst of war: where could it have gone? The possibilities are endless.

Robert de Clari also mentions the veil of Veronica, on which Jesus is supposed to have wiped his face on the way to Calvary, and a holy loincloth that a tilemaker loaned to Jesus for the same purpose. The image on the loincloth had miraculously transferred itself to one of the tiles, which was also kept. Along with these relics from Constantiople were the head of John the Baptist, some pieces of the True Cross, the Crown of Thorns, the tunic Jesus wore while carrying the cross, two of the nails, and a vial of his blood.[2] Some of these would later appear in France in the possession of King Louis IX. He built the Church of Ste. Chapelle to house them. But the holy shroud and the holy loincloth and tile seem to have vanished.

There doesn't seem to be any mention of the shroud again until the middle of the fourteenth century, when a knight named Geoffrey de Charny may have owned it. He was an important figure in the early battles of what would turn out to be the Hundred Years' War.[3] He also joined a crusade to Smyrna in Turkey in 1345, an experience he did not enjoy.[4] Later he became a charter member of the short-lived Company of the Star, a group of knights close to the king of France, John II.[5] Charny was killed at the Battle of Poitiers on September 19, 1356.[6] In between his military exploits, he managed to write three treatises on chivalry. He also had a chapel built on his land at Lirey for the purpose of celebrating masses for the souls of his family and as a family cemetery.[7]

Now, in all his petitions to have his church built and in his own writings, Geoffrey de Charny never mentioned that he had a holy shroud. But, as soon as he had died, his son, also named Geoffrey, began to show the shroud to friends, neighbors, and paying guests as an object of veneration, always taking care not to say that it was the actual burial cloth of Jesus. The local bishop tried to get him to stop doing this, certain that the shroud was a fake. Eventually, he succeeded.

No one mentioned the Templars. There was no reason to. The Templars did not take part in the Fourth Crusade. They did not believe in fighting other Christians—at least, that was what they told the organizers of the crusade, and I think they probably meant it. They were far too busy at the time fighting the heirs of **Saladin** and must have been irked that the crusaders were looting the Greek Empire instead of helping them.

It's possible that Geoffrey de Charny bought the shroud as a souvenir when he was in Turkey, not believing that it was genuine, but rather a full-body icon. Whether his son knew this or not is impossible to say.

So why are the Templars connected to the shroud? It all has to do with the coincidence that the Templar Visitor of Normandy, Geoffrey of Charney, who was burned at the stake just after **Jacques de Molay**, has the same name as the first owner of the shroud. The two Geoffreys may have been related but there is no evidence for this.

That didn't stop a twentieth-century author, Ian Wilson, from deciding that, not only were the two men connected but that the shroud also originally belonged to the Templars.[8] This is an example of taking one fact, that the two men have the same name, and then creating an entire scenario based on no evidence whatsoever.

There are several problems with Wilson's theory.

I've already pointed out that the Templars weren't in on the looting of Constantinople. That's the first problem. However, if somehow they did get something that they thought was the *sydoine* there is no way they would have kept it a secret. As I have pointed out, the Templars were constantly short of cash and relics were big business. The relics they did have were displayed, such as the head of Virgin Number 58 at the Paris commandery or the cross made from a tub that Jesus had once bathed in.[9]

Wilson says that the shroud and the veil of Veronica were confused and they were the same thing.[10] Then he says that the shroud, or maybe images of it, were what the Templars were accused of worshipping at their trial.[11] Considering the number of imaginative descriptions made by the Templars of the head they were supposed to worship, that doesn't work. But also, if they had a genuine relic of the Resurrection, doesn't it stand to reason that they would say so? The idea that this would be a secret makes no sense in the framework of the medieval world, or the modern one for that matter.

One of the more surprising theories that has grown out of connecting the shroud to the Templars suggests that the image on the cloth is actually **Jacques de Molay**.[12] This was made, not surprisingly, by two Masons, neither of whom is a historian.

They base this conclusion on a series of suppositions.

The first assumption is that Jacques was tortured by the inquisitors in an imitation of Christ's passion. Afterward, the bleeding Grand Master was placed on a shroud because, "like the Jerusalem Church before them and Freemasonry after them, the Templars kept a linen shroud to wrap the candidates for senior membership."[13]

They did? I can't find anything about this in the **Rule** or in the various records of the interrogations. I'd love to know where it says this but, unfortunately, the authors don't cite their source.

The book presents a gruesome scenario, complete with illustrations, on how Molay must have been tortured. Oddly, this imagined torture corresponds exactly to the wounds on the image on the shroud. However, there is a problem with this, too. (Actually, there are a lot of problems but I'll go with the most obvious.) First of all, there is no record anywhere of a person being tortured by the Inquisition in imitation of Christ. This would not only be blasphemy but it would also elevate the status of the accused, making his suffering seem equal to that of Jesus. More importantly, the authors state that Jacques de Molay showed the marks of torture when he came before the masters of the University of Paris. Jacques de Molay did not take off his shirt to show how he had been tortured, as the book says, nor did he make the speech the authors quote.[14] They quote it, by the way, not from the records of the trial, but from a translation made in a book called *Secret Societies of the Middle Ages*. The author is that well-known figure Anonymous.

According to the records, Jacques never said that he was tortured. He said he had been starved and threatened with torture. When he rolled up his sleeve before the masters of Paris, it was to show them how thin he had become.[15]

That leads me to the most compelling reason to think that, whatever the shroud is, it's not a portrait of Jacques de Molay. The image on the Shroud of Turin is of a tall and fairly robust young man with long hair and a beard. Now, after some time in prison, Jacques could have let himself go a bit, not trimming his beard or cutting his hair. But Jacques de Molay was in his late sixties, if not older.[16] He had been starved. Looking at the image on the shroud, even with the best intentions, I can't see that the man there is an emaciated seventy-year-old.

Finally, another theory on the Shroud of Turin that has received some notice is that of Lynn Picknett and Clive Prince. At first it seems safely free of the Templars. They think that the shroud was painted by Leonardo da Vinci.[17]

But you know, they just couldn't keep the Templars out of it, even though Leonardo lived over a century after the dissolution of the order. They base the Templar connection not on primary research but on another popular book, *The Holy Blood and The Holy Grail*. This book is based on, among other things, a hoax and forged documents. I have seen these documents and they are riddled with inaccuracies and mistakes.[18]

Again the authors add the Templars to the mix by continuing the assumption that the Geoffreys of Charney and Charny are connected and adding them to the family tree of the rulers of the Latin kingdoms and thence to the Templars again. There is no documentation for this and it doesn't agree with known genealogies of the families.

I don't really care what the Shroud of Turin is. I just think that it's time we left the Templars out of the arguments. The poor guys have had enough.

---

1 Robert de Clari, "La Conquêt de Constantinople," in *Historiens et Chroniquers du Moyen Age* ed. Albert Pauphilet (Paris: Gallimard, 1952) p. 78, "un autre des moustiers, que on apeloit madame Sainte Marie de Blakerne, où li sydoines là où Nostre Sire fu envelopés, y estoit, qui chascun vendredi se dressoit tous drois, si que on y povoit bien voir las figure Nostre Seigneur; ne ne seut on onques, ne Grieu ne François, que cist sydoines devint quant la ville fu prise."

2 Ibid., p. 67.

3 Richard W. Kaeuper and Elspeth Kennedy, *The Book of Chivalry of Geoffroi de Charney: Text, Context and Translation* (University of Pennsylvania Press, 1996) p. 5.

4 Ibid., p. 7.

5 Ibid., pp. 14–15.

6 Ibid., p. 17.

7 Ibid., p. 38.

8 Ian Wilson, *The Shroud of Turin* (New York: Doubleday, 1966).

9 Malcolm Barber, "The Templars and the Turin Shroud."

10 Wilson, pp. 81–98.

11 Ibid., pp. 154–66.

12 Christopher Knight and Robert Lomas, *The Second Messiah* (Boston: Element Books, 1997) pp. 162–96.

13 Ibid., p. 165.

14 Ibid., p. 171.

15 Michelet

16 Alain Demurger, *Jacques de Molay: Le Crepuscule des Templiers* (Paris: Payot, 2002).

17 Lynn Picknett and Clive Prince, *The Turin Shroud: In Whose Image? The Truth Behind the Centuries-Long Conspiracy of Silence* (New York: Harper Collins, 1994).

18 For a more complete discussion of the theories in this book, please see my previous book, *The Real History Behind the Da Vinci Code* (New York: Berkley, 2005).

※

CHAPTER FORTY-SEVEN

Templars in Scotland:
Rosslyn Chapel

Rosslyn Chapel, more properly called Rosslyn Collegiate Church, lies in Lothian by the river Esk, eight miles south of Edinburgh on the edge of the village of Roslin.

The name "Rosslyn" is from the Gaelic *ross*, meaning a rocky promontory, and *lynn*, meaning a waterfall.[1] The church is built on such a point, with a good view of Rosslyn Glen below.

The church was begun about 1450 by William Sinclair, earl of Orkney. It was apparently intended to be much larger but only what would have been the choir was finished. While the church is similar to other collegiate churches being built at the time, the degree of ornamentation is extremely unusual. My first impression on entering was that it was based on Spanish churches I had been in, but apparently art historians don't think this is the case.[2] The nature of the designs has not been commented on by art historians so much as the abundance of them. The effect of the myriad carvings is stunning and whimsical, rather like meeting someone who has decided to wear all her jewelry at once. "The arcade arches, capitals, string courses and window rear-arches are all decorated with foliage carving, and there are corbels and canopies for images between the windows."[3] Elsewhere, the same author comments, "as so often at Roslin, [sic] the desire for richness of

Pillar at Roslin, showing ornamentation and Green Man.

(Sharan Newman, with thanks to the Rosslyn Church Trust)

effect has perhaps been taken further than might have been expected."[4]

The plans for Rosslyn, written on wooden boards, were lost during the Reformation. There are no documents at all to explain why Earl William decided to cover almost every inch of his church with ornamentation. The only remnant of a planning design is on the wall of the crypt, probably the first section built. One can still see scratchings on the wall of an arch, a pentacle, a part of the vaulting for the ceiling, and two circles.[5] It's likely that these survived because they were plastered over shortly after the church was built.

Now, a lack of documentation is a disaster for historians, but great for novelists, who are then free to make up whatever they like. I suppose that's one reason I'm both. I can speculate in fiction in a way that would be inappropriate in academic work. The highly wrought carvings at Rosslyn have inspired a number of legends. Before I discuss them, let's look first at what is known about William Sinclair, to see if it gives any clues as to why he ordered the church built and why it was never completed.

William was the fourth Sinclair to be earl of Orkney. At the time these islands, north of Britain, belonged to the kings of Denmark. As the Orkney earls also were lords of Roslin and owned other lands in Scotland, this divided allegiance made politics difficult for the Sinclairs. However, the revenues from Orkney were substantial and made it worth the trouble.[6]

At this time it was unusual for the nobility of Scotland to die a natural death, or to keep hold of their lands for more than a generation. The first Stewart king of Scotland, James, had been murdered in 1437, leaving his six-year-old son, James II, at the mercy of the various factions vying for power.[7] The Douglas family was the most formidable enemy of the king and William Sinclair had married Elizabeth Douglas. However, Elizabeth died just before James II came of age in 1451 and William decided to cast his lot with the king.[8] It was about this time that he began work on the church.

It seems to have been a status symbol among the Scottish earls to have one's own collegiate church—a church that was administered by priests, called canons, whose sole job was to say masses, presumably for the souls of the nobles and their families. Collegiate churches were built by Lord Dunbar in 1444 and Lord Crichton in 1449.[9] Neither is as elaborate as Rosslyn.

For a while William's alliance with King James II appeared to bring him even more wealth and power. He became chancellor of Scotland from 1454 to 1456 and was able to regain the earldom of Caithness, lost to his family a hundred years before.

However, the king of Scotland had his eye on the profitable earldom of Orkney. James entered into negotiations with King Christian of Denmark to gain Orkney for himself. This would have left William Sinclair out an important source of income and there were rumors that he tried to sabotage the meeting. Certainly, he fell out of favor with the king. "William . . . must have heaved a sigh of relief when he heard of the sudden demise of the young king at Roxburgh while these negotiations were under way."[10]

But the next king, James III, continued his father's quest for Orkney and in 1470, William was forced to give up his rights in favor of the Scottish crown.

This may be the reason why Rosslyn Church was never completed. Not only was William's income reduced but his eldest son, William "the Waster," was so irresponsible that the earl disinherited him, leaving Rosslyn to his second son, Oliver. It was Oliver who seems to have brought the building to a close.[11]

This is what we know about William Sinclair, fourth and last earl of Orkney. The original charters for the church were lost; the plans destroyed. Only the fantastic building remains, the choir with a truncated wall of the proposed nave jutting out on either side.

THE LEGENDS BEGIN

The fate of the chapel of Rosslyn was tied to the Sinclair family and they had a bad spell of close to two hundred years. The Sinclairs chose the losing side in the power struggles in Scotland and then remained Catholic when the country became Protestant. The chapel was first neglected and then, after long resistance from the lord, another William Sinclair, the altars were demolished.[12]

The connection of the Sinclair family to the guild of masons and then to the order of **Freemasons** began in the early seventeenth century. The guild of masons was under the direction of a "master of works," who was usually from a good family rather than a working mason. In 1583 the title went to William Schaw, from the family of the lairds of Sauchie. The Schaw family was Catholic in Protestant Scotland but that didn't stop William from making a good career for himself at court. He was a diplomat and served the crown overseas, despite being listed as "a possible Jesuit" by the Scottish equivalent of the secret police.[13]

When he became master, Schaw set about organizing the guild of masons, setting up statutes for them.[14] In about 1600, he decided that the masons needed a lord-protector. It is not known why the current William Sinclair, lord of Rosslyn, was chosen. Perhaps because he was also Catholic; perhaps because of Sinclair's attempt to preserve the "images and uther monuments of idolatrie" of the chapel.[15] As a patron, Sinclair was not an obvious choice. He had been hauled up before the local magistrates on charges of fornication and eventually moved to Ireland with his mistress, a miller's daughter, leaving the lordship to his son, also named William Sinclair.[16]

The next William was a model citizen and, although Schaw had died in the interim, a charter was drawn up making Sinclair an official patron of the masons. A copy of this is on display in the museum above the gift shop at Rosslyn.

This had nothing to do with what would later become Freemasonry. It was an agreement between the lord of Rosslyn and the guild of masons.

Nevertheless, the lords of Rosslyn were among the first of the Scottish Freemasons and in 1697 were "obliged to receive the Mason Word."[17]

It is from about this time that the legends surrounding Rosslyn began to grow.

The story of the two pillars, the "master" and "apprentice," is one that can be found in other churches in Scotland. There is a like pair of

Apprentice pillar (*Sharan Newman, with thanks to the Rosslyn Church Trust*)

Master pillar *(Sharan Newman, with thanks to the Rosslyn Church Trust)*

pillars at twelfth-century Dunfermline Abbey, although the more elaborate of the two is considered the work of the master.[18]

The story of the pillars is that the master mason finished the first pillar and then went on a journey. When he returned, he discovered that his apprentice had carved a second pillar that far surpassed his. In a rage, the master killed the apprentice. At Rosslyn, the faces of the master and the apprentice are supposed to be among the heads carved into the corners of the ceiling in the chapel. However, there are six heads, not two. One is female and another a demon of some sort.[19] This story of the homicidal master mason is first recorded in 1677, by an English tourist, Thomas Kirk.[20]

The association of the Templars with Rosslyn may have started with Sir Walter Scott, who mentions the lords of Rosslyn in *The Lay of the Last Minstral*.[21] Scott is best known for his novel *Ivanhoe*, which features a Templar as the villain.

The stories about Templars in Scotland, and specifically at Rosslyn, seem to have started at the same time as the society of Freemasons did. The story in its most recent form is that a group of Templars fleeing the Inquisition arrived in Scotland and were given refuge by the Sinclair family at Rosslyn Castle. Over the years the Templars in Scotland are said to have fought for Robert the Bruce, gone to America with the Vikings, and kept a guard on their treasure and/or the Holy Grail.

At the time of the suppression of the order, some Templars may have found refuge in Scotland, but again, there is no record of this and certainly no reference to Rosslyn. I have found no Templar or Grail references in connection to Rosslyn that are earlier than the nineteenth century. None of these stories ever bothers to say how the Templars kept their numbers up over the centuries. Did they marry and raise little Templars? Did they recruit subversively in the neighborhood? Enquiring minds want to know. And that, I suppose, is why we have to invent answers.

How do legends begin? With a chance meeting, a visit to a remarkable chapel, the notice of an odd carving that reminds the viewer of another that is connected to yet another by the imagination. The art of Rosslyn Chapel is an enigma. Why the first William Sinclair had it built and what the designs meant to him will probably never be known. They are fantastic, opulent, and evocative. It's no wonder that the chapel was brought in to share in the preeminent myths of Western civilization.

1 The Earl of Rosslyn, *Rosslyn Chapel* (Roslyn Chapel Trust, 1997) p. 34.

2 Barbara E. Crawford, "Lord William Sinclair and the Building of Roslin Collegiate Church," in John Higgitt, *Medieval Art and Architecture in the Diocese of St Andrews* (British Archaeological Association, 1994) p. 99.

3 Richard Fawcett, *Scottish Medieval Churches* (Gloucestershire: Tempus, 2002) p. 163.

4 Ibid., p. 140.

5 R. Anderson, "Notice of working drawings scratched on the walls of the crypt at Roslin Chapel," in *Proceedings of the Society of Antiquities of Scotland* Vol. 10, 1872–74, pp. 63–64.

6 Crawford, p. 100.

7 Stewart Ross, *Monarchs of Scotland* (New York: Facts on File, 1990) pp. 85–91.

8 Crawford, p. 101.

9 Fawcett, p. 89.

10 Crawford, p. 104.

11 Ibid., p. 106.

12 Rosslyn, p. 239

13 David Stevenson, *The Origins of Freemasonry: Scotland's Century 1590–1710* (Cambridge University Press, 1988) pp. 26–32.

14 See chapter 48, **The Freemasons**.

15 Stevenson, p. 55.

16 Ibid., p. 56.

17 Ibid., p. 60.

18 Fawcett, p. 165.

19 I checked this out carefully when I visited Rosslyn.

20 Karen Ralls, *The Templars and the Grail* (Wheaton, IL: Quest Books, 2003) p. 184.

21 Ibid., p. 193.

❧

CHAPTER FORTY-EIGHT

The Freemasons and the Templars

Today there are thousands of Freemason lodges all over the world. Each country has its own customs and rituals and within them are variations and rites particular to each lodge. There are many stories about the beginnings of the society of Freemasons and its place in history. One reason for this is the myth the eighteenth-century masons created concerning the antiquity of their group and its traditions. Most of these are now considered to be nothing but invention.

The reason for both the myths the Masons created for themselves and the stories told about them is the same: it is a group that jealously guards its secrets, especially those of initiation. A nineteenth-century Mason wrote of this, "Among secret societies . . . a particular knowledge has been supposed always to be communicated to the initiate. . . . The place of Masonry among secret associations is notable in comparison with these exotics of hidden life and activity."[1]

The connection between the Freemasons of today and the ancient trade of stonemasons is still not well understood. The custom of workers in a particular craft forming groups for mutual benefit existed as far back as the late Roman Empire. These groups had different names, but the most common was *collegium*.[2] These *collegia* had both social and economic functions. The merchant's college negotiated monopolies with the government, for instance. Colleges of trades vital to the state, such as wheat merchants, were given exemptions from some taxes and duties.[3] The colleges also held group feasts on the days that honored their patron deity.

These colleges had members who were not workers but important citizens, patrons of the trade "who lent their influence in the state to the colleges in exchange for the social prestige of the title of patron."[4] This may give a clue as to the later development of Masonic lodges in which no one was a working mason.

By the time of Constantine the Great membership in many of the colleges, particularly that of the bakers, was hereditary and mandatory. They were no longer independent corporations but controlled by the state. Any benefits they might have received were canceled out by the services they had to supply to the government.

There is very little information as to whether the Roman colleges survived the time of the invasions by the Gothic and Germanic tribes. Most of the major cities of the empire were depopulated from the sixth through the ninth centuries and there were probably not enough workers in any community to form a trade organization. By the time they resurfaced, these groups now were called by a Germanic name, *guild*, probably from the same root as *gelt*, meaning money.[5]

In the Middle Ages, guilds were started by workers in the same occupation originally as burial societies. Weavers, coopers, leatherworkers, even prostitutes wanted to assure that they not only received a Christian burial, but that prayers and Masses would be offered for the good of their souls. They grew into societies that also regulated the initiation into the craft. Stages of competence—apprentice, journeyman, and master—were created.

Each guild had its own patron saint and held a banquet on that saint's feast day. The patron of the masons was Saint John the Evangelist, whose feast is December 27.[6]

Upon entry into a guild, the new apprentice swore an oath to guard the secrets of the craft. The masons may have added some form of secret code so that members of the guild could be known to each

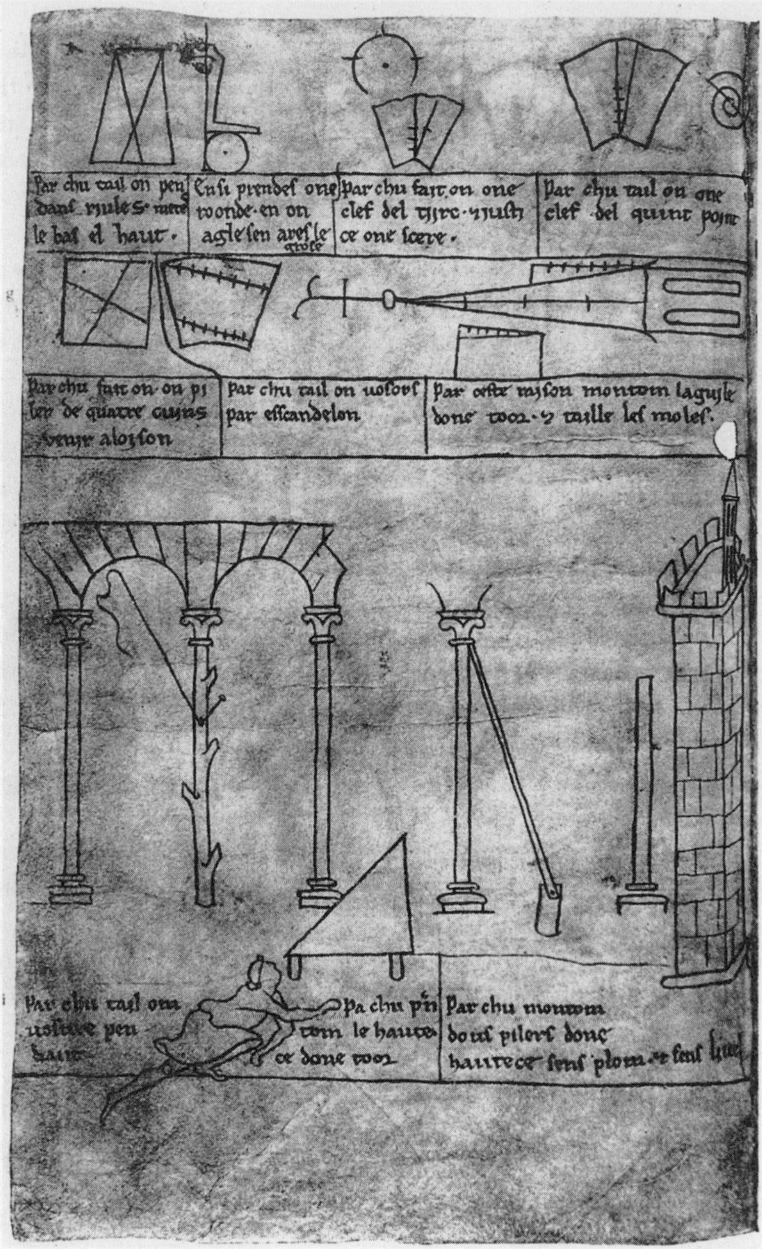

Mason's geometry, Villeard de Honnecourt (c. 1225–1250).

(Foto Marburg/Art Resource, NY)

other. This is because the masons moved from place to place, working on the great cathedrals and castles. The master of works for each project didn't want to hire someone not trained in the craft. A secret password could prevent that.[7] While there is no record of this happening before the late sixteenth century, it seems probable that the password was created long before.

THE BEGINNING OF MODERN FREEMASONRY: HIGHLY "SPECULATIVE"

Modern Freemasonry seems to have borrowed a great deal from the rituals of the Scottish guilds of masons. They, like other masons, had formed groups in the towns but they also formed a tight unit in the temporary homes or "lodges" that were built for them to inhabit while they worked on a project. These lodges may have encouraged a closer bond than in other guilds in which the members spent only part of their time with fellow workers and the rest with family and friends from other occupations.[8]

During the Middle Ages the noble families of Europe constructed mythical genealogies for themselves. They traced their beginnings to Troy, or King Arthur, a patron saint, or even a demon. The guild of masons in Scotland seems to have done the same. They called this story the "Old Charges," a history of the craft built from tales in the Bible, apocryphal books, and folk legend.

According to a Scottish version of the Old Charges, masonry, which goes hand in hand with geometry, was founded by the sons of Lamech, who wrote their craft secrets on stone pillars. After the flood of Noah one of his great-grandsons, Hermarius, found the secrets of masonry/geometry and the other sciences on the pillars. He taught it to the builders of the tower of Babel. Then Abraham, living in Egypt, taught the geometry to a student named Euclid, who presumably took the knowledge to Greece. Eventually, the masons came to Jerusalem, where they built Solomon's Temple. After that was finished, the masons scattered to the nations of the world. One came to France, where he was hired by Charles Martel, the grandfather of Charlemagne. Another, Saint Alban, brought the craft to Britain. Eventually the masons were sponsored by a Prince Edwin, the otherwise unknown son of the Anglo-Saxon king, Athelstan. Edwin was so enamored of the craft that he was made a Mason. It was also Edwin who caused the Old Charges to be written down.[9]

A Masonic legend about the builders of Solomon's Temple is that of Hiram of Tyre, master builder. According to the apocryphal book *The Wisdom of Solomon*, Hiram supervised the construction of the Temple and personally made two brass pillars, called Jachim and Boaz.[10] Hiram was supposedly murdered by other masons who wanted him to reveal the secrets of the Mason Word. As late as 1851, a manual for Freemasons states that both Solomon and Hiram, now a "King of Tyre," were the originators of the society.[11]

These legends were all part of what is called "operative" masonry, that is, guilds of those who actually had the skill to work in stone. Many of these legends became part of the traditions and symbols of "speculative" masonry, or lodges made up of people from other walks of life.[12]

But how did it happen that a traditional trade guild became the base for an organization that has included many artists, composers, noblemen, heads of corporations, and heads of state?

SCOTLAND, WILLIAM SCHAW, AND THE LORDS OF ROSLIN

Late-sixteenth-century Scotland was ruled by James VI, the son of Mary, Queen of Scots, who would soon become James I of England. One of the posts in his government was that of master of works, held by a well-born man who oversaw the finances and administration of all building projects. In 1583 the post went to one William Schaw.[13]

Schaw was a Catholic in a newly Protestant country but he seems to have been able to keep his beliefs from threatening anyone at court. It was Schaw who, in 1598, first wrote down a set of statutes to be followed by "all master masons of the realm."[14] These statutes, mostly regarding admission of apprentices and the chain of authority within the lodges, were agreed to by the master masons. Some of the individual mason marks were recorded and the first mention is made of the Mason Word, the system by which one mason might recognize another.

The following year Schaw expanded the statutes to include the duties of the master masons in training apprentices not only in the craft but in the "art of memory and the science thereof."[15] This indicates not only a rote lesson to be learned but a system of remembering to master.

The reason for Schaw's insistence on these uniform statutes is not clear. He seems to have felt strongly that the independent lodges needed organization. He also felt that they needed a patron, much as the Roman guilds had had.[16] For this position, he selected William Sinclair, the lord of Roslin. Again, this is puzzling. William was descended from the earl who had built **Rosslyn Chapel** and there might have been a residual fondness for the man who had given the masons such an elaborate commission. But this William was a dissolute Catholic who couldn't tell the local Protestant authorities if his latest bastard had been baptized but had had at least one christened a Catholic. He also staunchly resisted attempts by the local authorities to destroy the artwork in the chapel. While he had employed masons to build his home, he doesn't seem a good advocate for the lodges at court. However, in 1601, a charter was drawn up making William Sinclair patron of the masons.

A copy of this charter is preserved at Rosslyn Chapel, which is where I read it. It is clear that the masons are not following an established tradition of patronage from Rosslyn but asking for a totally new arrangement. There is no implication in the document that it is anything other than a normal request for a nobleman to advocate for a group that doesn't have much political power.

It doesn't appear that this William Sinclair was of much use to the masons. However, his son, also named William, took the charge more seriously. He issued another charter, giving himself legal jurisdiction over the masons. By 1697, the lords of Roslin were allowed to be taught the Mason Word.[17]

There is still a leap that must be made from lodges of operative masons to ritualized meetings of Enlightenment intellectuals.

The creation of Freemasonry from guilds of masons seems to have come about through a number of social and political forces that happened to converge. In Scotland throughout the seventeenth century upper-class men had been asking to join the mason lodges and been accepted. Perhaps they were allowed in because they could afford a good initiation banquet or because some of the masons were pleased to be able to rub shoulders with the nobility.

It seems to have been a fad for a time, but most of these men soon dropped out. Historian David Stevenson suggests that they might have joined thinking that they were going to learn some esoteric, magical lore and were disappointed.[18]

There have always been those who were obsessed with the uncovering of ancient secrets. It is a thread that runs through all societies. But the period from about 1580 to 1750 seems to have had a larger number of seekers than usual. It was a time of intellectual inquiry both in the matter of religious truth and about the natural world. The Reformation and Counter-Reformation had left many people in doubt about the truth of any one religion. The increased belief in the malevolence of witchcraft had a flip side in those who wished to seek enlightenment from divine sources, not necessarily Christian. If one could obtain power from Satan then there must be other ways to reveal the mysteries of the universe without going so far as to sell one's soul.

This was also the time that the Rosicrucian books were circulating and people like Isaac Newton and Robert Boyle were experimenting with both chemistry and alchemy and making little distinction between the two. Even the Royal Society in England began with a group of friends meeting for clandestine discussions on alchemical subjects.[19]

It was in this atmosphere that the first English lodges arose at the beginning of the eighteenth century. While using many of the symbols and the basic myth of the origin of the masons guild, the English soon added rituals based on their research into alchemy, Neoplatonism, and Hermetic teaching. By 1720 Freemasonry had spread to France and then to Germany and the rest of Europe. "Rather than saying that Freemasonry was born out of the Guild of Masons, it might be more helpful to say that learned men who wished to work together and exchange ideas adopted the symbolism and structures used by working masons."[20]

ENTER THE TEMPLARS

The reader may have noticed that I haven't yet made a connection between the Masons and the Templars. I'm tempted to say that it's because there isn't any but that wouldn't be fair. Actually, the use of the Templars as an example for the Masons can only be traced back to 1750, when Baron Karl von Hund invented the "Templar Strict Observance." In order to legitimize his creation, he claimed that it was "by way of uninterrupted transmission, the successor of the Knight Templars [*sic*], whose existence had been carried on secretly up to that date."[21]

Von Hund derived his ideas from the Scottish connection, although it's not known where he got his information. "It is claimed that before his execution, the last Grand Master of the Templars, **Jacques de Molay,** assigned Hugo von Salm, a canon, the mission of smuggling important Templar documents into Scotland."[22] Now, Hugo von Salm seems to have been a knight who came to the defense of the Templars in Poland.[23] There is no indication that he was ever in France and certainly not at the time of the dissolution because he was defending Templars in Poland then. There is even less evidence that he ever went to Scotland.

Now the Templars were regaining popularity in newly Protestant eighteenth-century Europe. Instead of being seen as greedy bastards who may or may not have been heretics but good riddance all the same, they were seen as the persecuted keepers of lost esoteric information. After all, if the pope hated them, they must be okay. The idea caught on.

My feeling is that the image of the Knights of the Temple fit in well with the mystical secret societies that developed during the (self-named) Enlightenment. The best part of it was that so many of the Templar records had been lost or destroyed that there wasn't any problem with hard facts getting in the way of the myth. It was rather like the secret societies that based their philosophy on their interpretation of hieroglyphics. When the Rosetta stone was discovered in Egypt and the hieroglyphics finally deciphered, it was a terrible setback for them.

Today no reputable historian of the Freemasons believes that the group was founded by Templars or by Solomon's master mason. Furthermore, most Masonic lodges encourage serious inquiry into Masonic history. "The results may upset some masons, but it would be unthinkable for a Mason to be suspended or dropped from membership for investigating Masonic degrees and believing that they had relatively modern origins."[24]

The problem is that there a large number of non-Masons who don't know this. And they are busy writing **pseudohistory**.

MASONIC SYMBOLS

The most universal symbol of the Freemasons is the compass and square, used by operative masons everywhere. Another, found in every lodge of Speculative Masons, is the pillars of the Temple. The names given to these two pillars are Boaz and Jachim, thought to have been the original Mason's Word.[25] In the American York Rite these pillars are thought to be hollow to hide archives and other documents.

Another symbol that seems to be common to all Speculative Masonic lodges is three pillars, signifying wisdom, strength, and beauty. The mason's apron and gloves are also universal.

Many plants have symbolic meaning in Masonic lore, the acacia, rose, lily, and olive tree among them.[26] The star and the pentangle are both used frequently. Indeed, it would be hard to find anything that couldn't be read as a symbol by Masons. "The first degree initiation ritual, that of Entered Apprentice, states: 'Here, all is symbol.'"[27]

On the other hand, the Templars had few symbols. The only one I am certain of is the image of two riders on one horse. Some of the Templars' seals showed the dome of the Holy Sepulcher. Even the order's banner was simply one white and one black square. They really weren't symbol-minded. They just got on with their work.

MODERN MASONRY

Today Masons can be of almost any religion, including Catholic, despite the Catholic Church's eighteenth-century ban on joining, or no religion at all. There are lodges that include both men and women and some that are single sex. The French, by the way, were the first to admit women into an auxiliary organization, called adoptive masonry, around 1740.[28]

Listing famous Masons would be a book in itself. It would include most American presidents; kings of England, Sweden, and other countries; and Winston Churchill, Tomás Garrigue Masaryk, Voltaire, Goethe, Kipling, Mark Twain, Davy Crockett, Duke Ellington, and Houdini, to name a few.[29] Mozart's opera *The Magic Flute* is full of Masonic references.

Like the Templars, the Freemasons have been accused of subversive activities, including trying to control elections and exerting pressure to ruin personal enemies. In some times and places this may have been true. In Oregon in 1922, the Scottish Rite Masons joined in with the Ku Klux Klan to sponsor a bill to abolish private schools and insist that all children attend public schools.[30] The target of the bill was the Catholic school system, where many immigrant children from Catholic countries were being educated. The governor, Walter Pierce, had agreed to support the bill in return for the support of the Masons and the Klan, who had many members in common.[31]

The law passed, but was challenged and went to the Supreme Court, where it was ruled unconstitutional.

In this case Masons who were also Klansmen spoke for the entire group and did indeed influence an election. Today, most Masons would be horrified at the association with the KKK. They would point out that this was not typical Masonic behavior. They might even deny that such a thing ever happened.

It's difficult to confirm or deny such allegations because of the nature of the organization. Groups with private initiation rites and a cultivated aura of secrecy seem to bring out the worst suspicions in outsiders. The Freemasons are entitled to have secret ritual and rites, but instead of maintaining that they come from ancient Templar knowledge, they might pay more attention to what the Templars' secrecy about their initiation ceremonies led to.

---

1 Arthur Edward Waite, *A New Encyclopedia of Freemasonry* (New York: Wings Books, 1996) p. 53.

2 Steven A. Epstein, *Wage Labor and Guilds in Medieval Europe* (Chapel Hill: University of North Carolina Press, 1991) p. 11.

3 Ibid., p. 17.

4 Ibid., p. 18.

5 Ibid., p. 35.

6 David Stevenson, *The Origins of Freemasonry: Scotland's Century 1590–1710.* (Cambridge University Press, 1988) p. 43.

7 Ibid., p. 9.

8 Loc. cit.

9 Ibid., pp. 19–21.

10 Waite, p. 367.

11 K. J. Stewart, *Freemason's Manual* (Philadelphia: E. H. Butler, A.L. 5851 A.D. 1851) p. 15.

12 Waite, p. 141.

13 Stevenson, p. 26. Unless otherwise stated, the following is a summery of Stevenson's work.

14 Ibid., p. 34.

15 Ibid., p. 45.

16 Although it's doubtful that Schaw was aware of the Roman custom.

17 Ibid., p. 60.

18 Ibid., pp. 77–85.

19 Newton.

20 Daniel Béresniak, *Symbols of Freemasonry*, tr. Ian Monk (Barnes & Noble, 2003) p. 16.

21 Antoine Faivre, "The Notions of Concealment and Secrecy in Modern Esoteric Currents since the Renaissance (A Methodological Approach)," in *Rending the Veil: Concealment and Secrecy in the History of Religion*, ed. Elliot R. Wolfson (New York: Seven Bridges Press, 1999) p. 162.

22 Glenn Alexander Magee, *Hegel and the Hermetic Tradition* (Ithaca: Cornell University Press, 2001) p. 54.

23 http://www.templariusze.org/artykuly.php?id=27 "Moguncji zrobił to osobiście preceptor z Grumbach, Hugo von Salm wraz z dwudziestoma uzbrojonymi rycerzami." Okay, my Polish is

rough. He might have been the preceptor of Grumbach, but I think it says that Moguncji was preceptor. For more see chapter 35, **The Trials outside of France**.

24 Paul Rich and David Merchant, "Religion, Policy and Secrecy: The Latter-Day Saints and Masons," in *Policy Studies Journal* Vol. 31, No. 4 (2003).

25 Stevenson, p. 143.

26 Robert Macoy, *A Dictionary of Freemasonry* (New York: Gramercy Books,) pp. 403, 579, 604–5; Waite, for Rose, pp. 369–71; Béresniak, pp. 75, 78–80.

27 Béresniak, p. 8.

28 Waite, p. 97.

29 Béresniak, p. 114.

30 Paula Abrahams, "The Little Red Schoolhouse: Pierce, State Monopoly of Education and the Politics of Intolerance," in *Constitutional Commentary* Vol. 20, No. 1 (2003) p. 617.

31 Abrahams, p. 624. She adds, "Many Masons actually ended up opposing the bill."

Epilogue

O ne of the many things I learned about the Templars as I researched this book is that, far from being separate from the
world they lived in, they were more than part of it. The Templars and
Hospitallers were the bridge between western Europe and the City of
God. Unlike many other monks, they spent their early lives in the
midst of the constant warfare that existed among the lords of Europe.
Whatever their reasons for joining the military orders they became
examples to the rest of their class. They believed in the use of might
for right's sake. Even though they still fought and killed, it was not for
personal gain but to protect the weak and preserve the earthly kingdom of God.

This was the ideal. If they didn't always measure up to it, they still
came close. Those who fought finally had a way to use their skills in
battle and still achieve salvation.

Over the two hundred years of the Templars' existence, Europe
changed dramatically. In the early twelfth century, society was governed by families and family connections. The advisers and supporters
of a ruler were his cousins and in-laws and brothers. His enemies were
sometimes the same, but it was still all a matter of relations. A marriage, a birth, or a death could change the borders of a country. By the
beginning of the fourteenth century, governments, especially in northern Europe, were becoming more centralized and bureaucratized. The

king's counselors were more likely to be non-noblemen who owed their positions to their usefulness rather than family ties.

The Templars and their fellow knights of the military orders were part of a frontier society. There were like the cavalry, coming to save the day, or the small band of rangers who protected American pioneer settlers from Indians and evil land barons. Eventually, the West was settled, the Indians were defeated; the land barons became state governors. The same sort of thing happened in Europe, only the frontier was lost and its defenders left without a purpose.

Even though in 1307 no one knew that the Holy Land was lost to the crusaders forever, there was still a feeling that the day of the Templars was ending. The small band of brave knights would be replaced by paid armies. Chivalry would become a social game rather than a way of life.

The Knights Templar were not mystics or magicians. They were not a secret society, nor did they have arcane wisdom dug up from hidden treasures. Those who say that they were are denying the real story of these men. They weren't superhumans but pious, hardworking, flawed human beings who, in their own way, were trying to make the world better and save their own souls.

The thirteenth-century Arab chronicler Ibn Wasil may have written the tribute that the Knights Templar would have liked most. In the fighting against the French army of Louis IX, the Mamluks of al-Malik al-Salih were the bravest, fiercest warriors. "They fought furiously," he writes. "It was they who flung themselves into the pursuit of the enemy: they were Islam's Templars!"[1]

---

1 Ibo Wasil, in *The Arab Historians of the Crusades*, ed. and tr. Francesco Gabrieli (Dorset: New York, 1957) p. 294."

How to Tell if You Are Reading Pseudohistory

In the past few years many books have been published about the Templars. The order has been the basis for entertaining works of fiction, from *Ivanhoe* through various works about the crusades to the thrillers of the present that are based on Templar legends and myths. Like the medieval romances, these are not meant to be taken as real history.

But there are also a number of books that are meant to be nonfiction. Some of them are serious studies by trained scholars who have spent years studying the original documents. Others contain theories that may seem fascinating and also well researched, but are actually based on little primary research and a lot of illogical conclusions. I call these books "pseudohistories."

In this book I have tried to give the history of the Templars as it is known by historians who have learned dead languages and worn out their eyes reading handwritten manuscripts in order to find out what really happened. I have also tried to address some of the most popular of the myths written about the order. This has been difficult. Every time I think I've heard them all, new Templar stories pop up like dandelions on a lawn.

Many of the pseudohistories are very well written and sound authoritative. So how can the reader tell if the book can be trusted? Here goes.

1. Is the book published by a university press? If yes, then it's been checked by other historians and, while there may still be errors, it's likely to be as accurate as possible.
If no, then . . .

2. Do most of the footnotes list primary sources that any scholar can find? If yes, then you may be okay, and, if you doubt something, you can go look it up.
One mark of pseudohistory is that most of the footnotes list other pseudohistories or "secret" books (see number 4) and it's impossible to trace down the original information to check it.
If no, then . . .

3. Does the author use phases like "everybody knows" and "historians agree"? If yes, then don't bother reading further. There is nothing that "everybody" knows. That's just a quick way of saying, "I haven't done my research and want to make you feel too ignorant to call me on it."
Historians do agree on things like, "There was a Battle of Hastings and William of Normandy won," or "Machu Picchu is an amazing feat of engineering." Beyond that, everyone has a different way of evaluating the available data. One other thing historians agree on is that a person who presents work that's not based on information that others can check isn't going to last long in the rough-and-tumble academic world.

4. Does the author insist that the theory can't be proved with available data because there was an immense cover-up or that the knowledge is guarded by a select secret society? If yes, then how did the author find the information? How was it authenticated?
An alternate to this is that the author has a "secret" source, a lost book or a document that reveals all. This was used often in the Middle

Ages. The most famous is from Geoffrey of Monmouth, who wrote some of the earliest King Arthur stories. He found the information in a book "in the British tongue"—that is, Breton or Welsh. Since no one else had the book and Geoffrey wouldn't show it to anyone, only he could transmit the truth. I must admit, he did well with it.

Finally . . .

5. Does the author pile one supposition upon another, assuming they are all true? For instance, a book may begin with a known fact, such as "The Templars had their headquarters at the al-Aqsa mosque," and then continue with something like, "As is well-known, the area in front of the mosque is large enough to land a helicopter in."* Then the author might continue by wondering why the space was there before helicopters had been invented. Perhaps he has found, by chance, a manuscript illustration that resembles a helicopter about to land. Even though the manuscript was made in, say, Ireland, the author of a pseudohistory will imagine a previously unknown Irish monk coming to Jerusalem in time to see the Templars' secret helicopter landings. "Everybody knows" the Irish were great pilgrims.

From this, the author will claim to have established that there were helicopters flown by Templars and that it is proved by the picture made by the phantom pilgrim monk. Of course, the only way this could be is if the Templars were really time-traveling soldiers of fortune determined to grab all the artifacts they could, including mystical talking heads (really a twenty-fourth-century communication device) that would give them the secret of the universe. This makes perfect sense because "everyone knows" that this is the site of Solomon's Temple and Solomon, as you must have heard, was a great magician who hid advanced technology in the basement of the Temple to keep

---

* Another interesting trait of pseudohistorians is that the author won't have bothered to find out that the Templars filled in the courtyard with buildings, including a large church, and that it was only when Saladin took the city of Jerusalem and cleared them out that there was room to land a helicopter.

ignorant and superstitious people from gaining knowledge that their primitive minds couldn't handle.

The author is sure that now is the time when all should be revealed.

You heard it here first.

Templar Time Line

1153: The Latin kingdoms conquer the city of Ascalon

1154: Zengi's son, Nur ad-Din, takes Damascus

1169: Saladin becomes vizier of Egypt

1173: An Assassin envoy is murdered by some Templars. King Almaric imprisons the murderer and Grand Master Odo of St. Amand protests that only the pope can judge a Templar.

1174: Nur ad-Din dies; Saladin takes over Damascus

1187: Battle of Hattin—Saladin takes Jerusalem

1189–1192: Third Crusade, led by Richard the Lionheart, king of England, and Philip Augustus, king of France

1191: Templars and Hospitallers set up headquarters at Acre

1191–1192: Templars occupy Cyprus, which Richard had conquered

1197–1198: German Crusade fails to take Jerusalem, but wins back some towns

1201–1204: Fourth Crusade—the crusaders are persuaded to conquer Constantinople instead of Jerusalem. The Templars have little to do with this, as they didn't believe in invading Christian lands

1217–1221: Building of Atlit (Castle Pilgrim)

1218–1221: Fifth Crusade—a group of noblemen take and then lose the Egyptian town of Damietta

1228–1229: Crusade of the Holy Roman Emperor, Frederick II— Jerusalem is regained through negotiation. This is hard on the pope, for Frederick is excommunicated at the time

1239–1240: Crusade of Thibaud of Champagne and Navarre; Templars are criticized

1240–1241: Crusade of Richard of Cornwall; more land gained through negotiation

1244: Battle of La Forbie—Jerusalem lost permanently to Moslems

1248–1254: First Crusade of Louis IX—the Templars fight with him and hundreds are killed

1250: Battle of Mansourah—Louis is captured along with his brothers and most of his army. He is ransomed for 400,000 livres, some of which is taken from the Templars

1260: Grand Master Thomas Bérard sends an urgent message to the rulers of Europe for help against the invading Mongols. Lord Julian of Sidon sells part of the town to the Templars

1266: The Mamluks, under Baibars, take the Templar fortress of Safad

1268: Calalan Rule of the Templars is written; Baibars takes Templar Beaufort

1270: Second Crusade of Louis IX and his death in Tunis

1271–1272: Crusade of Edward I of England; Baibars takes Templar Safita

1274: Council of Lyon—the merging of Templars and Hospitallers is discussed

1277: On the advice of the Templars, Maria of Antioch sells her claim to the Kingdom of Jerusalem to Charles of Anjou and Sicily

1285: Philip IV becomes king of France

1291: Acre is taken by the Mamluk al-Ashraf Khalil, sultan of Egypt. Grand Master William of Beaujeu dies defending the city. Templars leave Atlit and Tortosa for Ruad and Cyprus

1297: King Louis IX is canonized by Pope Boniface VIII

1302: Templars lose Ruad. Most are killed

1303: September, Guillaume de Nogaret, adviser to Philip the Fair, and the Colonna brothers attack Pope Boniface VIII at Anagni

October 11, Boniface VIII dies

1305: November 14, coronation of Pope Clement V

1306: June–September, the devalued money in France is returned to "good money"

July, Jews expelled from France, their property seized

1307: September 14, Philip IV sends secret messages to his officials telling them to arrest the Templars

Friday, October 13, arrest of Templars in France

1308: Clement V settles into the papal city of Avignon, just outside the southern border of France

1310: Fifty-four Templars are burned as "relapsed heretics"

1311–1312: Council of Vienne

1312: Papal bull *Vox in excelso* dissolves the order. The bull *Ad providam* transfers all of its property to the Hospitallers. It will take many years for the Hospitallers to receive a portion of the property

1314: Jacques de Molay and Geoffrey of Charney burned

April 15, Guillaume de Nogaret dies

April 20, Pope Clement V dies

November 29, King Philip IV dies

1574: The Templar records in Cyprus are destroyed by the Ottoman Turks in their conquest of the island

1798: Napoleon takes the island of Rhodes from the Hospitallers. He puts Templar artifacts on his ship, which sinks off the coast of Egypt. This allows for more than two hundred years of speculation on what might have been lost in the shipment, and what it might have meant

Recommended Reading

ON THE TEMPLARS

Barber, Malcolm. *The New Knighthood: A History of the Order of the Temple*. Cambridge, Eng.: Cambridge University Press, 1994. The most accurate and comprehensive of the histories.

Bramato, Fulvio. *Storia dell'Ordine dei Templari in Italia* (2 volumes). Rome: Atanò, 1994.

Nicholson, Helen. *The Knights Templar: A New History*. Sutton, 2001. Full of fascinating information and beautifully illustrated.

Partner, Peter. *The Knights Templar and Their Myth*. Rochester VT: Destiny Books, 1990.

ON THE TRIALS

Barber, Malcolm. *The Trial of the Templars*. Cambridge, Eng.: Cambridge University Press, 2006.

Riley-Smith, Jonathan. "Were the Templars Guilty?" *The Medieval Crusade*. Susan J. Ridyard, ed. Woodbridge: Boydell. 2004. See especially pp. 107–24.

ON THE CRUSADES

Edbury, Peter, and Jonathan Philips, eds. *The Experience of Crusading: 2: Defining the Crusader Kingdom.* Cambridge, Eng.: Cambridge University Press, 2003.
Mayer, Hans Eberhard. *The Crusades.* Oxford University Press, 1972.
Riley-Smith, Jonathan. *The Crusades.* New Haven: Yale University Press, 2005.

ORIGINAL SOURCES

Recently there has been a serious attempt to have many of the most important chronicles of the crusades translated into modern languages. I have been happy to use these very good translations and am grateful to have them. But in some cases, I can only suggest that the reader consult the originals.

Archives de l'Orient Latin, (2 volumes). Paris, 1884.
The Chronicle of the Third Crusade: The Itinerarium Peregrinorum et Gesta Regis Ricardi. Helen Nicholson, tr. Aldershot: Ashgate, 1997.
The Conquest of Jerusalem and the Third Crusade. Peter Edbury, tr. Aldershot: Ashgate, 1996.
Crusader Syria in the Thirteenth Century: The Rothelin Continuation of the History of William of Tyre, with part of the Eracles or Acre Text. Janet Shirley, tr. Aldershot: Ashgate, 1999.
The History of the Holy War: Ambroise's Estoire de la Guerre Sainte (2 volumes). Marianne Ailes, tr., and Malcolm Barber, notes. Woodbridge: Boydell, 2003. Old French text and English translation.
Joinville, Jean de. *Vie de Saint Louis.* There are a number of translations for this.
Oliver of Paderborn. *The Capture of Damietta.* John J. Gavigan, tr. University of Pennsylvania Press, 1948.
The Rare and Excellent History of Saladin or al-Nawadir as-Sultaniyya we'l-Mahasin al-Yusufiyya, by Baha' al-Din ibn Shaddad. D. S. Richards, tr. Aldershot: Ashgate, 2002.
The Templar of Tyre. Paul Crawford, tr. Aldershot: Ashgate, 2003.
The Templars: Selected Sources. Manchester University Press, 2002. Malcolm Barber and Keith Bate, eds. and tr. A good selection of material covering the entire existence of the order.
Vitry, Jacques de. *Histoire Orientale.* Marie-Geneviève Grossel, tr. and notes. Paris: Honoré Champion, Paris 2005.

TEMPLAR CHARTERS

Marquis d'Albon, Cartulaire Général de l'Ordre du Temple 1119?–1150. Paris, 1913.

Cartulaires des Templiers de Douzens. Pierre Gérard and Élisabeth Magnou, eds. Paris, 1965.

Le Cartulaire de La Selve: La Terre, Les Hommes et le Pouvoir en Rouergue au IIXe siècle. Paul Ourliac and Anne-Marie Magnou, eds. Paris: CNRS, 1985.

Index